Reform and Transformation in Communist Systems:

Comparative Perspectives

Edited by Ilpyong J. Kim
and Jane Shapiro Zacek

A Washington Institute Press Book

Paragon House • New York

Published in the United States by
Paragon House Publishers
90 Fifth Avenue
New York, New York 10011

ISBN 0-88702-059-3

A Washington Institute Press Book

First Printing, June, 1991

Library of Congress Catalog Number: 91-61757

Printed in the United States of America
Cover design by Foundation Typography, New York

To Irene and Katherine Kim,
Leslie and Peter Shapiro

CONTENTS

PREFACE

The editors of this volume have had a long-standing interest in teaching, conducting research, and publishing research findings on the communist-ruled states ever since they took a graduate seminar in comparative communist systems at Columbia University jointly offered by the Russian Institute and the East Asian Institute in 1961–1962. In 1988 the editors met to discuss the possibility of convening a conference and publishing papers from such a conference. In the spring of 1989, we proposed the idea to Neil Albert Salonen, executive director of the Washington Institute for Values in Public Policy, and it was accepted.

We are grateful to Neil Salonen and to Richard Rubenstein, president of the Washington Institute, for their generous support in convening the conference, "Reform in Communist Systems," on October 27–29, 1989, in Washington, D.C. The thirteen papers collected in this volume were commissioned in May 1989 and were presented and critiqued at the conference in October. They were subsequently revised and updated in the early months of 1990 and have come off the press against the background of continuing rapid political change, economic reform, and social transformation, particularly in the communist systems of central and eastern Europe. We are grateful to the paper writers for their willingness to make original contributions to this volume and to meet the deadline.

Robert Sullivan, deputy director of the Washington Institute, worked tirelessly in communicating, facilitating, and following up on the conference and the post-conference details with the participants. His logistical support was superb. The views expressed in this book are those of the authors and do not necessarily reflect the views of the Washington Institute for Values in Public Policy.

1. INTRODUCTION

Ilpyong J. Kim
and
Jane Shapiro Zacek

Planning for this volume began in 1988, with the idea of looking at change and reform in communist-ruled states. Little did we expect that events would move so quickly, making it difficult to step back and assess their probable impact on real reform. National and international news coverage of some events has been unprecedented, encouraged in part by the openness of the regimes and made possible by telecommunications technology. By the fall of 1989 it was clear that events, particularly in Eastern Europe, had moved beyond mere reform of the communist-ruled systems. What we were witnessing was the collapse of communist domination and the first stage of transformation to a post-communist political, social, and economic system. In preparing this volume, we tried to establish some common criteria for use of the terms "change," "reform," and "transformation." We have used "change" when different policies or procedures have been introduced, adopted, and implemented aimed at producing specific desired results or outcomes. These changes are generally limited in scope, depth, and intensity, as well as in duration, and are efforts to establish improved methods of managing identified problems. They typically do not involve structural alterations or, if they do, only in a minor way that may be quite readily restrained or reversed if sufficient opposition builds to sway policy direction, or if circumstances arise that render these changes incompatible with newly determined needs.

"Reform" implies an ongoing process. It encompasses movement from one mode of operation to another. It is composed of a variety and number of substantial change elements and includes policies and practices designed to bring about very different consequences than if reforms had not been adopted and implemented. Procedurally, the development, adoption, and implementation of reforms necessitates a broader base of support among policy makers and implementors (or, in the absence of support, sufficient coercion, or a mixture of coercion, pressure, suasion, and incentives to reach sufficient consensus on what is to be done and how it is to be achieved). Reform as used here implies substantial structural changes that are adopted to implement new procedures or processes. While the scope and intensity of these structural changes may be difficult to measure or quantify, they must be consequential enough to make a real and sustained difference in outcome and not be readily reversible.

While reform presumes structural changes, the pre-reform structures are still in evidence. "Transformation" implies much greater movement from what existed to what is being created, so that the previous condition is scarcely recognizable in the new one. It involves a much more drastic movement from the old to the new than does reform. Because of its encompassing nature, transformation is much more difficult to put in place and sustain than reform, and a longer observation period is needed to determine its durability and the extent to which it has achieved the goals established for it. Transformation may involve overturning some basic tenets of communist-ruled states, including the role of the party itself. In both cases, there are unintended and unanticipated outcomes along the way of implementation, and continual policy intervention is inevitable.

An examination of the reform efforts of the 1980s, while not isolated from earlier reforms (and indeed generally built upon them) yields several common themes. A first theme is that both internal and external conditions conducive to reform need to be present in order for it to succeed. A second, widely recognized theme is that centrally planned economies do not adapt well to rapid technological change. They are not only inefficient but discourage productivity, hinder necessary retooling, render goods internationally noncompetitive, and altogether are too costly for the state to support. The search for how best to modify central planning and public ownership, with all of their ramifications, has led to the development and implementation of a variety of reform strategies. A third theme is that as economic reform has taken center stage, planners and policy makers have recognized the need for accompanying political reforms, thus making economic and political reform interdependent.

Internal conditions conducive to reform include a political leadership willing and able to recognize and act on the need for different ways of operating. Frequently, this occurs after a major leadership change so that the new leader and his supporters are able to disassociate themselves from the past, including previous unsuccessful policies. Less frequently, leaders are able to separate themselves from policies that they themselves championed and chart a new course (an example is János Kádár and the Hungarian New Economic Mechanism, adopted more than a decade after he was installed in power by Soviet authorities during the 1956 Hungarian revolution). The reform-minded leadership must be able to negotiate with both elites and the population at large in order to build sufficient support for the idea of reform. The leaders must also build support for the development and implementation of reform strategies designed to bring about identified desired results, and the leadership must be flexible enough to discard what does not work and to continually search for more effective ways of determining and implementing the reform process. Externally, relaxation of international tensions and curtailment of potential military threats are required so that military preparedness issues do not interfere unduly with reform of the economy. In some instances, the attitude of the Soviet Union toward a country's reform proposals may be crucial; in others, reactions or encouragement from the People's Republic of China may be essential for reform to get under way. As will be demonstrated, Soviet attitudes and assessments of events and Soviet restraint from direct interference constituted the most influential external factors in facilitating the rapid expansion of the reform process in both Hungary and Poland prior to the fall of 1989. Soviet acquiescence, even encouragement, of reform was a most important contributing factor to the tumultuous events of 1989, but it is unlikely that the Kremlin anticipated the rapid collapse of communist rule in Eastern Europe. Finally, attitudes of non-allies (for example, the United States attitude toward reform efforts in Cuba) may also assist the reform process by lessening threats of hostility that, unattended, might accelerate into national security issues.

The need for economic reform has been almost universally recognized within the communist-ruled world. For most policy makers, the issue is not why or whether, but rather how to do it. Are reform strategies compatible with the ideological underpinnings of building and maintaining a socialist society, Marxist-Leninist style? If not, what should yield? And according to which criteria? As a number of chapters in this volume relate, economic reforms are not easily put in place and, once established, may well turn out not to be long lasting.

Economic reform strategies represent special challenges to conceive, build support for, and successfully implement. The extent to which bold restructuring has been called for in diverse settings indicates the imperative of moving along a path of reform in order to reach desired goals and objectives. Some strategies have focused on agricultural reform, others on urban-industrial issues. If strategies do not seem to work, or fail to work well enough, they may be discarded at some point in the review process in favor of more effective alternatives. What will work and what will not is difficult to determine in advance, or even in the early stages of implementation. Leaders may seek modest results rather than attempt the glorious successes with the risk of inglorious failures.

Finally, in the rush to promote economic reform, proper attention to political structures and a political atmosphere that will accommodate and facilitate the reform process frequently has been lacking. Careful planners and policy makers came to recognize that political reform could not be overlooked or sidelined. Essential to economic success are such elements as administrative decentralization and restructuring, allocation of greater authority to intermediate and local state organizations, restraints on the party's direct role in economic decisionmaking at all levels, and opening up of public discussion on economic reform strategies to researchers, managers, and other practitioners in order to develop the most useful ways of tackling the problems, given the stated objectives. As a number of essays in this volume will attest, failure (or inability) to attend to relevant political reforms places a heavy burden on economic reform efforts. In fact, some observers have suggested that political reforms ought properly to precede economic reforms to assist the latter's implementation.

This volume looks in some depth at change and reform in the Soviet Union and the People's Republic of China (PRC). It then considers those East European states that are currently undergoing the most far-reaching reforms and appear headed for real transformation of their systems. Finally, we look at several selected cases of states where some changes and even reform efforts have been introduced but where the systems have not yet been substantially altered or modified.

Rolf H.W. Theen looks at political reform in the Soviet Union and Mikhail Gorbachev's initial position as a rather conservative new leader when he was named general secretary of the Communist Party of the Soviet Union (CPSU) Central Committee in 1985 and espoused greater efficiency, responsibility, and better use of resources within the existing economic and political structures. Within the year, however, Gorbachev was publicly calling for radical reform of the economic system, and soon thereafter he was advocating social, political, and cultural reform as well. Gorbachev, writes Theen, represents a rare example of the politician who has been radicalized while in office. His reform proposals have become increasingly bold in the years since 1986, particularly in the political sphere.

With the continual emphasis on *perestroika* and *glasnost,* Gorbachev has promoted a variety of changes that have led to reform, including a realignment between party and state powers (with much greater attention to the latter), greater decision-making authority for the republics, vastly reduced censorship, and new attention to the rule of law. The general secretary and his supporters have been able to effect a great turnover in personnel within the party as well as in the state administrative structures, not only at the highest levels (Central Committee and above) but on the *oblast* and *krai* levels as well. In part, this has been the consequence of a determined effort to retire the Brezhnev era holdovers and others who opposed the "new thinking." In part, too, it reflects the determination to install a new generation of officials who will not be permanently ensconced as were their predecessors. Finally, it is clear that Gorbachev, while stressing the critical necessity for economic reform, has been much more successful thus far in promoting political reform. Many observers agree that economic restructuring without substantial accompanying political reforms will be limited. The record to date, however, suggests that Gorbachev feels more comfortable and confident in introducing and managing political reforms than he does economic reforms.

Susan J. Linz considers some of the changes introduced into the economic system by the Gorbachev leadership. Does Gorbachev's reform effort address at least some of the basic problems of the Soviet economy, including issues of continued low growth rate, investment strategies, labor availability, export earnings, technical backwardness, consumer goods shortages, and continued poor agricultural performance? The role of central planning, administrative organizational structures, pricing, attention to market forces, enterprise decisionmaking, managerial accountability, and criteria that measure performance are fundamental issues as well.

Gorbachev's reforms have focused on streamlining the bureaucracy, reducing the central planning functions, and permitting greater flexibility in decisionmaking on regional and local levels. Industrial production targets remain centrally planned, and fulfillment of mandatory state orders continues to constitute at least 80 percent of total industrial production output (higher in some sectors). These levels are supposed to decline drastically within the next several years, and enterprises will have much greater leeway in determining their own sales patterns. There is renewed emphasis on self-financing, economic accountability, enhanced labor productivity, and performance-based pay as means to improve operational efficiency and utilize resources more effectively.

Price reforms, which would more accurately reflect scarcity, supply, and demand — but would also engender inflation — have been postponed. Substantial efforts to encourage foreign investment, including joint ventures, have been instituted, the establishment of free economic zones has been proposed, and some enterprises are permitted to engage directly in foreign trade without needing to work through the appropriate ministries. But few of these proposals are new: the Soviet Union is trailing many communist-ruled states that encouraged such trade and investment schemes years ago.

Finally, state ownership in the industrial sector is likely to be replaced by a variety of ownership patterns, including private ownership, cooperatives, leasing arrangements, and employee ownership. Overall, the issue remains very much open of how satisfactorily the reform proposals will be implemented and whether they can adequately respond to identified needs within an established time frame.

Turning to agricultural and rural reform, Don Van Atta emphasizes the current state of flux and the flurry of reform proposals, few of which have actually been adopted and implemented thus far. What is clear is that the traditional structure of agricultural production — state and collective farms, with strong central planning directives for production and sales — will be changed in an effort to improve output and availability of goods. Family farming under long-term leases with cooperatives may become a prominent feature of agricultural reorganization.

At present, return to private property ownership seems unlikely. Reorganization of central agricultural production-related ministries and committees remains an element of reform proposals, though this has not worked well in the past. In spring 1989, Gorbachev called for reorganization of the agricultural management, supply, and procurement systems by turning to "voluntary" cooperatives rather than state-run agencies to manage these critical aspects of the agricultural economy. It remains to be seen whether such issues as reduction of costly food subsidies, establishment of market pricing, and narrowing the standard-of-living gap between urban and rural families will be resolved. In general, though, in agricultural as in political and other areas of reform strategies, Gorbachev has indicated a willingness to consider and promote more substantial reform possibilities as time has passed.

How have Chinese leaders viewed the need for political, economic, and agricultural/rural reform, and what policies have they devised and implemented to respond to these needs?

With regard to political reforms, Parris Chang reviews the leadership changes that occurred after Mao's death and the routing of the Gang of Four (1976–78), details Deng Xiaoping's return to preeminent power, and describes the maneuvering for political authority within the party's top organs, some of which were reestablished after the Mao era.

Political reforms have included the determination to ensure turnover of cadres and promotion of technically and professionally competent personnel. Reform proposals have focused on such elements as separating party and state functions, streamlining the administrative structure, and decentralizing decisionmaking, especially in the economic realm. Of them all, decentralization of decisionmaking seems to have had the best implementation record. In fact, this emphasizes one of Chang's main themes: that the Chinese leadership does not seek political reform as a necessity in itself but only to assist economic reform and enhance economic productivity.

Joseph Fewsmith looks broadly at economic reform efforts in both the industrial and agricultural sectors since 1979. He suggests that there does not seem to have been an overall strategy but rather continuous development as events demanded, and in response to the necessity of negotiating with competing interests in order to have reforms adopted and implemented. Economic reforms have permitted market forces to play an increasingly important role, which has engendered inflation, slowed the pace of reform, and brought about a growing disparity in income distribution based on corruption and efforts to "outwit the system." Much of the problem stems, Fewsmith believes, from the regime's inability to institute reforms in such a way as to reduce and ultimately eliminate the central planning and rigid control functions of the state bureaucracy, the restrictions on labor mobility, the full employment guarantee that inhibits entrepreneurial motivation by both management and workers, and continued operation of inefficient, unprofitable enterprises.

Among the important reform measures adopted have been greater autonomy for enterprises in investment, operation, and output; greater economic authority granted to local governments; and a closer working relationship between the two, especially vis-à-vis the central ministries. Though enterprises and local officials have control over more production revenue, they do not seem to have made the most sound investment decisions. Demand for consumer goods has risen sharply, and in response basic industry sectors of the economy have been neglected in favor of consumer goods production, particularly for such items as color TV sets, refrigerators, and washing machines. In some cases supply has outpaced demand. Enterprises are operating at a loss, but they have not been closed down, and they continue to receive state subsidies.

Reform efforts have not faced issues of structural imbalances. Wise investment decisions are needed to alleviate shortages, control inflation, and confront widescale corruption in the economic realm. Finally, writes Fewsmith, interest in basic economic reform among top-level leaders in Beijing seems to have declined, and the momentum for sustained reform has lost steam. Despite important gains achieved during the early and mid-1980s, the economy continues to present important and growing challenges in its drive for efficiency and enhanced productivity.

Thomas Bernstein looks at the rural economy in China and presents an initially optimistic picture of economic reform in the countryside, based on contracted family farming within continued formal collective ownership of land itself. Reforms were undertaken to rebuild support for the regime; modernize the countryside; improve output, productivity (and availability of goods for urban areas), and farm family income; and achieve self-sustained growth. The restoration of family-based farming does not seem to have been part of the reform planning, but rather emerged as the most satisfactory way to improve agricultural output. The success of family farming has not only substantially improved the rural standard of living but has also permitted a reduction of state investment in agriculture and the utilization of investment funds elsewhere. The expectation that peasant investment would make up for state funding reductions has not been borne out, however, especially in the past several years. Earlier successes have been curtailed in the late 1980s.

On the other hand, peasants have been encouraged to invest in related economic activities, and even to run their own businesses. This frequently has led to tax evasion and corruption, which has not been reined in. Marketization of rural production (excluding subsidized commodities) has been introduced but is limited by the old structures of cooperatively owned land, limited labor mobility, and limits on capital for investment. Further, there are technological limitations to improving agricultural production that, in order to be raised, will need substantial state investment. Persistent inflation has reduced peasants' incentive to produce, especially those commodities that continue to be sold at state-established prices. The government's response has been to tie needed production goods (fertilizer, diesel fuel) at costs lower than market prices to grain contracts in order to enhance production.

Bernstein also looks at the structural reforms implemented to consolidate family farm contracting as well as the ideological implications. Despite claims to the contrary, local party organizations still appear to have real control over local governments and local economic organizations.

Turning to Eastern Europe, Alexander Pacek and Roger Kanet provide an overview of the perceived need for reform in a number of states in the region and the conditions that created an environment conducive to change and reform. Clearly the most important external element has been the Soviet Union's formal repudiation of the Brezhnev Doctrine and concomitant determination of the limits of acceptable behavior in Eastern Europe. Indeed, recent events suggest that the Soviet leadership has encouraged change and reform in the region. Further, the official recognition that centrally planned economies do not adapt well to rapid technological change, which has produced continued stagnation and a decline in economic growth, has been an important impetus to change, perhaps the major one. Internal political pressures for change have mounted, and by 1989 the legitimacy of one-party (communist) control had severely eroded in much of the area. The authors look at some of the roots of reform and how these relate to actual political developments and the reform efforts in the recent period. They also provide an incisive survey of the spectacular events of 1989–90 throughout the region.

Paul Marer takes a much closer look at reform in Hungary, particularly at the "remarkable" reforms adopted and implemented under General Secretary János Kádár's New Economic Mechanism (NEM). Much of the underlying structure and belief system did not change, including the Communist party's monopoly on power and ultimate decisionmaking authority. State ownership of property continued to be espoused as the ideal, although cooperatives and small-scale private ownership were permitted (and even encouraged) to enhance production. Emphasis on forced economic growth at the expense of smart investment decisions and on full employment despite inefficiencies and resultant labor immobility were other features that remained largely unchanged under the NEM as it developed during the 1970s and 1980s. On the other hand, a hallmark of the Kádár strategy was a steady improvement in living standards (based in part on establishment of economic regulators instead of a rigid central plan and in part on foreign borrowing to stimulate production). While enterprises were permitted some decision autonomy, central planners still had ultimate authority, particularly in investment decisions. State subsidies continued, regardless of profit considerations, and debt service for foreign loans was an added burden on the state budget. Partial operation of the market mechanism was permitted but was limited by the regime's belief in the need to respond to consumption demands. In 1979, this was curtailed by the leadership's decision not to reschedule the foreign debt and the accompanying necessity for domestic belt-tightening. At the same time, small-scale private entrepreneurship in the "second economy," especially for services, flourished and contributed directly to inflationary pressures.

In short, the NEM encompassed a variety of contradictions that led to its virtual demise in 1988–89 and the genuine search for alternative models that are likely to transform the Hungarian economic and political systems. The Hungarian leadership is faced with determining not only the most satisfactory reform design, but also how to manage and implement it. And all this at a time of rapid political transformation, including the decline of the Communist party (renamed the Socialist party) and a newly reorganized party that calls itself communist, together with the reemergence of multipartyism, free elections for the national parliament, lifting of censorship, and other measures. To say that Hungary is in the throes of very rapid and largely unguided change is to understate the current situation.

Much of the same may be said for Poland, the first communist-ruled state to establish a noncommunist-dominated government. Political reforms in Poland, according to Andrzej Korbonski, have been taking place as part of the process of democratization. They have occurred because of a serious deterioration in economic conditions coupled with popular dissatisfaction that the leadership is unable or unwilling (or both) to repress as in earlier postwar periods. Korbonski considers the basic issue with respect to Poland to be how a communist-ruled state can transform itself into a democratized one and how that transformation can be institutionalized. He identifies a number of important variables that need to be considered and need to develop in parallel fashion in order to assist the transition (or at least not impede it). The development of an alternative political force, Solidarity, with which the Communist party leadership ultimately had to come to terms and legalize, is unique to the Polish situation. In an effort to restore a semblance of political stability in order to confront and manage growing economic instability, the party leadership agreed to enhanced authority for the national parliament and curtailment of its own political role.

Reform strategies in Yugoslavia have been considered, adopted, discarded, and repudiated with great regularity since the 1950s. Indeed, as Lenard Cohen writes, the Yugoslavs consider their model of socialist development a continuing and dynamic reform of Soviet-type socialism. The continuing "experiment" with collective leadership since Josip Broz Tito's death in 1980 and the federal government's inability to respond to sustained economic crises now characterized by high inflation, high unemployment, huge foreign debt, serious food shortages, and a sharp decline in the standard of living — all are features of the current situation. These conditions, coupled with intensified ethnic hostilities, greater unwillingness of the wealthier republics to subsidize poorer ones, and a serious erosion of support for the federal government and the ruling Communist party (Yugoslav League of Communists, YCL), have led to the articulation of a number of strategies designed to ameliorate the situation, none of which is likely to be satisfactory to enough disparate groups to be adopted and implemented. Cohen describes in detail three of these strategies.

First, the Serbian one, espoused by Serb leader Slobodan Milošević, builds on Serbian ethnic interests and influence within the federal system and emphasizes giving much more attention to market forces and less to the government's regulatory role in the economic sphere. Private property needs to remain secondary to public ownership, and the thrust of reform must be concentrated on the public sector. Second, the Slovene strategy calls for greater autonomy in economic and cultural development with equal authority for all republics in federal government decisionmaking and within the YCL. Slovenes have declared their right to secede from the national party organization, and they promote the general concept of political pluralism, including the establishment of competing political parties.

Finally, the Yugoslav federal government's strategy focuses currently on economic reform and an open market economy, as well as developing a "streamlined" administrative structure. Reform proposals skirt the issue of "how to harmonize political developments," because Serbian interests (representing the most populous republic) and Slovene concerns for continued equality of representation in decisionmaking are unlikely to be reconciled. Cohen concludes that the lack of cooperation among the political elites, with their separate regional loyalties, hinders adoption of difficult economic, let alone political, decisions. The absence of a centrally respected political figure whom enough of the various elites can trust and who would be willing to propose bold reform measures and have them adopted, is especially significant. Whether it will be possible to further postpone both economic and political reform remains an open question.

Ilpyong Kim looks at prospects for reform in North Korea and suggests that real reform is unlikely under the leadership of the aging first generation revolutionary leader, Kim Il Sung. While some changes have been introduced, especially in the economic sphere (including an effort to attract foreign investment to assist in economic renewal and growth), even they have undergone shifts and reversals in the past several years. A new emphasis on the need for technological advances suggested revised strategies for ending the country's isolation and "self-reliance" policies of earlier times. But in fact no structural reforms have been adopted and implemented, and economic advances have been tied almost exclusively to efforts to attract external assistance. When ideological considerations once again took precedence over economic ones, emphasis on the need for continued economic assistance declined. Despite some turnover within the party's ruling Politburo, no substantial political reforms seem to have been considered, let alone adopted and implemented.

Kim sees little likelihood for real systemic reform while Kim Il Sung remains at the helm. The latter's son and established heir, Kim Jong Il, may be able to promote internal reform, though it is by no means clear what the real nature of the reform proposals might be (other than a renewed emphasis on technology, technological competence of political and economic decisionmakers, and a reduced role for ideological considerations). Indeed, there is no guarantee that Kim Jong Il will turn out to be more than a transitional figure. North Korea serves as a prime example of the need for substantial leadership change before meaningful structural reforms can be considered, adopted, and implemented.

Although the overall circumstances are different, the reform situation in Vietnam is similar to that in North Korea in terms of results. Douglas Pike believes that the current Hanoi leadership, long used to working together through war, national consolidation, and constant external challenges, is not equal to the tasks of reform. The leaders are ill equipped to focus on alternative economic reform strategies, in part because of a lack of available expertise and in part because of a failure to understand the essential need for both economic and political reform.

Politically, the fifteen-member Politburo has too complete a monopoly on decisionmaking authority. State institutions are weak and cannot serve as an alternative locus of authority. Devolution of authority, reduction of centralized controls, and many of the other reform measures considered and adopted to some extent in other communist-ruled states have hardly entered the discussion stage in Vietnam and probably have little relevance to the country's current needs. Reform, Vietnamese style, is likely to center on the issues of development and modernization strategies and the costs involved in moving the system from an overwhelmingly agricultural to an industrial-based one. Even on these issues, the leadership demonstrates a real lack of flexibility in considering new approaches to more efficient development. A wholesale generational transfer of power is needed, but even this is unlikely unless a strong younger leader emerges who is capable of retiring many of the top leaders and those on middle levels as well.

Both North Korean and Vietnamese internal policies have been heavily affected by external events and foreign affairs strategies, and by a "siege mentality." North Korea has oscillated between closer relations with the Soviet Union and with the PRC, interspersed with periods of emphasis on self-reliance. For Vietnam, relations with both the USSR and the PRC (especially the latter) have been and remain critical, too. The wartime experience with the United States has shaped the outlook of the present leadership. The impact of external threats on internal developments also deeply affects Cuba, as that country continues to build its own form of socialism ninety miles from the United States. Andrew Zimbalist and Wayne Smith argue, in assessing the current reform efforts in Cuba, that Cuban–United States relations weigh heavily on the island's internal developments.

Cuba has experimented with change to enhance economic performance, although structural reforms have been limited. Never as highly centralized in planning and procurement policies as many Soviet-type economies, Cuba promoted decentralized policies in recent years until it became apparent that state needs for scarce foreign currency to complete important investment projects necessitated tighter controls. The capability of reining in decentralization efforts suggests that the reforms were less entrenched than it had seemed earlier. Market-oriented decentralization efforts have been halted for the time being, and the perceived "excesses" of both urban and rural private-sector activities have been reduced. Still, the authors contend, there is continued recognition of the value of decentralization to promote greater economic efficiency, and the current retrenchment may be only a pause for reassessment with a measure of ideological concern for a growing "bourgeois" mentality within the population, especially among the youth.

Political reforms, especially structural changes (except for administrative decentralization), did not accompany or parallel earlier economic reform efforts in Cuba. Relaxation of some internal restrictions, such as improvements in prison conditions and reduction in the numbers of those detained, or improved dialogue with the Catholic church, have occurred. Cuba has largely curbed its foreign policy adventurism, especially in Latin America. Whether these changes will contribute directly to internal change and reform remains to be seen.

In the concluding chapter, Jane Shapiro Zacek reviews some of the broad concerns that reforms were designed to address and stresses the limits on carefully planned reform strategies and the need for flexibility and constant readjustment as plans are (or are not) translated into reality. It is important to bear in mind, she notes, that some changes are planned, but a great many are not. Frequently, changes occur spontaneously, having grown out of planned change, and alter the direction or rate of change. Both planned and spontaneous developments are likely to have some unanticipated outcomes, to which policy makers on all levels must respond in appropriate fashion. Firmly held beliefs as to what constitutes appropriate socialist development inhibits some strategies, and resistance to change restricts others. The particular mix of political leaders matters, as does their ability to promote some policies successfully at the expense of others. And, as recent events suggest, once the reform momentum accelerates in some states, others in the region are unlikely to be able to withstand pressures for change, reform, and transformation, especially popular pressures from below.

What do these changes, reform strategies, and in some cases systemic transformations within the communist-ruled world suggest for American policy makers? Zacek identifies a number of ways in which American interests would be served by current and likely trends as the post-World War II world, characterized by superpower adversarial roles and opposing military and economic blocs in Europe (and to a lesser extent in Asia), gives way to revised configurations.

The rapidity of change throughout much of the communist-ruled world during the past year has been breathtaking, and no slowdown is in sight. This volume is particularly timely, although both editors and chapter writers have been acutely aware of later developments overtaking earlier ones, sometimes making meaningful analysis difficult and accurate forecasting almost impossible.

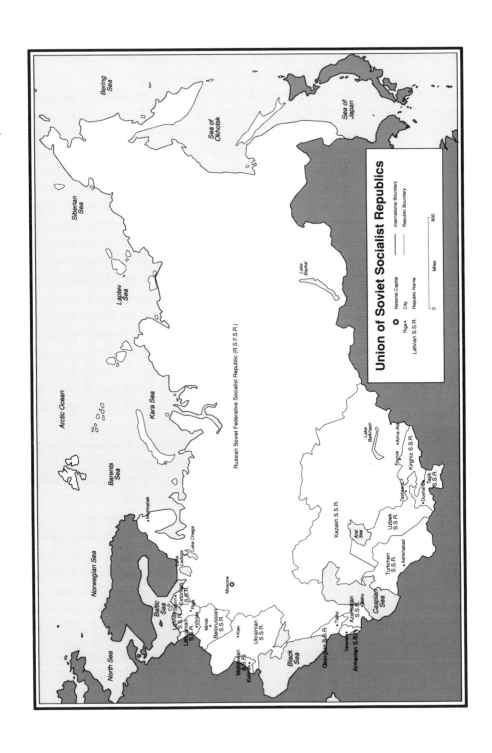

Union of Soviet Socialist Republics

National Capital
Riga • City
Latvian S.S.R. Republic Name

International Boundary
Republic Boundary

0   800
Miles

Bering Sea

Sea of Okhotsk

Sea of Japan

Siberian Sea

Laptev Sea

Arctic Ocean

Kara Sea

Barents Sea

Norwegian Sea

North Sea

Baltic Sea

Lake Baykal

Russian Soviet Federative Socialist Republic (R.S.F.S.R.)

Murmansk

Lake Onega

Lake Ladoga

Minsk

Moscow

Lake Balkhash

Alma Ata

Frunze

Kirghiz S.S.R.

Tashkent

Tajik S.S.R.

Dushanbe

Kazakh S.S.R.

Aral Sea

Uzbek S.S.R.

Ashkhabad

Turkmen S.S.R.

Caspian Sea

Estonian S.S.R.

Latvian S.S.R.

Riga

Vilna

Lithuanian S.S.R.

Belorussian S.S.R.

Kiev

Ukrainian S.S.R.

Moldavian S.S.R.

Kishinev

Black Sea

Georgian S.S.R.

Tiflis

Yerevan

Armenian S.S.R.

Azerbaijan S.S.R.

Baku

2. POLITICAL REFORM IN THE SOVIET UNION

Rolf H. W. Theen

The party strives to direct the work of the soviets, not to replace them.
— *Resolution of the Eighth Party Congress, March 1919*

It is necessary to delimit much more precisely the functions of the party (and of its Central Committee) from those of the Soviet government; to increase the responsibility and independence of Soviet officials and Soviet government institutions, leaving to the party the general guidance of the activities of all state organs, without the present, too frequent, irregular and often petty interference.
—*Vladimir Ilyich Lenin, Letter to V. M. Molotov (1922)*

The Leningrad Manifesto and *Perestroika*

In the summer of 1986, a remarkable political document reached the West from the Soviet Union. Apparently written by a group of high-level party and government officials in the Gorbachev administration, it was distributed to Soviet newspapers, circulated as an unauthorized publication through samizdat channels in 1985 and 1986, and ultimately—perhaps out of sheer despair at the lack of any response—leaked to Martin Walker, correspondent for the *Guardian* in Moscow.[1] Addressed "To the Citizens of the Soviet Union!" and dated November 21, 1985, the "Leningrad

15

Manifesto," as this document came to be called, announced the establishment of a "Movement for Socialist Renewal" (*Dvizhenie sotsialisticheskogo obnovleniia*)—a movement dedicated to the realization of political and economic reforms, as well as freedoms, going far beyond the startling changes already instituted by Gorbachev at that time.

Painting an almost desperately bleak picture of the "state of the union" and the prospects for the socialist world, the Manifesto argued that, without the swift enactment of far-reaching and radical reforms, the Soviet Union was well on its way to becoming "a second-rate power" and "one of the underdeveloped nations."[2] In terms of indebtedness to the financial institutions of the capitalist countries, the Manifesto pointed out that the USSR, with debts of approximately $30 billion, ranks in third place, behind Brazil and Mexico. Extrapolating from current plan figures, the Manifesto projected a 600 percent growth of the Soviet Union's foreign debt by the year 2000 and estimated that by the year 2005, 75 percent of the country's export earnings would have to be spent on servicing the debt.[3] According to the Manifesto, the Soviet Union's standard of living is one of the lowest in the industrialized world, including the CMEA member states. The living conditions of the rural population, especially of the people not living on the central collective and state farms, "are reminiscent of the life of the Russian peasant at the beginning of the 20th century." The constant shortages of consumer goods condemn the people to "an eternal hunt for the most basic necessities," leaving no time or energy for the satisfaction of their cultural and spiritual needs and "killing their human dignity."[4]

Aside from its lucid language and clear argumentation, the Manifesto stands out because of its general sophistication, suggesting high-level access to privileged data and sources. Its significance lies in its insistence on the necessity of radical political change as a prerequisite for economic reform and in its categorical argument that the time for an evolutionary solution of the existing crisis has passed. "The constantly-deepening political crisis," the Manifesto argues, "affects the very foundations of the socialist state, not merely separate aspects of its activity; it touches the foundation of the building of socialism, not just its extensions [*pristroiki*] or stories [*etazha*] of one sort or another."[5]

To deal with the crisis, the Manifesto outlined the following necessary political measures:

1. The establishment of freedom of the press
2. An end to the persecution of people for their political and religious beliefs, as well as the guarantee of freedom of speech
3. The provision of constitutional conditions for the creation of alternative political organizations in the country

Referring to the role of the press in the Watergate scandal in the United States, the Spiegel affair in West Germany, the Rainbow Warrior affair in France, and the Lockheed scandal in Japan, the Manifesto argued that a free and independent press can play an important role in the struggle against corruption and violations of the law by officials in high places. The existing apparatus of repression, according to the Manifesto, has cultivated hypocrisy, bigotry, unprincipled behavior, and servility; it has forced people to live by a double moral standard—one for their family and friends, another for official situations and public meetings. Freedom of speech and of the press would produce a healthier political climate and strengthen the morale and unity of the Soviet people. Freedom of speech and the press, moreover, are necessary for proper public scrutiny. The authors of the Manifesto quoted Lenin to the effect that "without publicity, it is ridiculous to talk of democracy." Finally, and most important, the Manifesto made a strong case against the continuation of the one-party system, arguing for competition in politics and, again quoting Lenin, for the right of every citizen to have an opportunity to participate in public affairs. The natural consequences of a party permanently in power, according to the Manifesto, are inertia and conservatism, bureaucracy, irresponsibility, lack of accountability, and abuse of power.[6]

The Manifesto also proposed the following economic measures:

1. Observance of the objectively functioning economic laws—laws that were disregarded when the Leninist policy of state capitalism (the NEP) was abandoned and when collectivization was adopted

2. Expansion of the rights of enterprises on the basis of full cost accounting

3. Creation of opportunities for the development of private initiative in the sphere of services and the production of consumer goods

4. Granting to Soviet citizens the right to rent state land and farm machinery, allowing and encouraging them to cultivate the land, to pay the state with a part of their crops, and to keep the surplus (This system of leasing land and equipment, according to the argument of the Manifesto, will increase crop capacity and productivity, reduce labor, and ultimately supply the country with needed agricultural produce. The Manifesto pointedly observed that "Russia was once a grain exporter.")

5. Development of private holdings on collective farms, market-gardening, and dacha cooperatives, as well as the sale of unused peasant houses to town-dwellers, in order to take advantage of the greater productivity of privately farmed land

6. Creation of conditions for the development of private trade (Here,

too, the authors of the Manifesto enlisted Lenin's help to state the
case for "the development of small trading enterprises, which is economically unavoidable for the function of the economic mechanism
of state capitalism, as set forth by Lenin."[7])

The Manifesto claimed that its program of political and economic
transformation represents "the further creative development of the
Marxist-Leninist teaching on the state, based on the available experience
of socialist construction in the USSR and the other socialist states." More
specifically, it proclaimed that, "in the political sphere, the Program
excludes violations of the Constitution of the USSR by state and party
organs and offers to citizens of the USSR the real guarantee of such constitutional rights as freedom of the press, freedom of speech, political, creative and religious activity, guarantees the independence of the court, and
law enforcement organs controlled by, and accountable to, Soviet power."
Furthermore, "the new political legal order excludes the possibility for
chance people to occupy high posts in the party and the state, as well as
the repetition of such anomalies of socialism as the cult of the personality,
voluntarism, decisions based on power and volition, inertia of thinking
and irresponsibility." Finally, the Manifesto argued that the new political
structure will make it possible "to realize the Leninist demand, fundamental to a socialist state, concerning the necessity . . . to delimit more precisely the functions of the party (and of its Central Committee) from those of
the Soviet government; to increase the responsibility and independence of
Soviet officials and Soviet government institutions."[8]

There is reason to believe that the ideas expressed in the Manifesto
were born in discussion groups and think tanks in whose establishment
Gorbachev himself was instrumental.[9] As a matter of fact, by the summer
of 1986, when the Manifesto reached the West, a good deal of the
Manifesto's argumentation had become mainstream thinking in reformist
circles. When Gorbachev addressed the Twenty-seventh Party Congress in
the spring of 1986, he endorsed many of the economic reform proposals
set forth in the Manifesto. Indeed, his own thinking on economic reform
seems to have taken more or less concrete shape in informal discussions
held in country houses around Moscow beginning in 1980.[10]

Be that as it may, in 1985, when the Manifesto was put together and circulated, a great distance evidently still separated Gorbachev's ideas on
reform from those espoused in the Manifesto. During his first year in
office, the new general secretary, aside from consolidating his power,
seemed narrowly occupied with the economy. His initial slogan of *uskorenie*
(the acceleration of socioeconomic development) suggested a change of
speed but not of direction. He was widely and correctly perceived as "neither a liberal nor a bold reformist," as a politician who "prefers small mod-

ifications, administrative methods and economic adjustments to structural reform,"[11] as a leader who is interested in "moderate" but not in "radical reform,"[12] as a "basically conservative" politician.[13] An early assessment of Gorbachev argued that his reformism "has nothing to do with liberalism," but rather "stresses authoritarian rule, discipline and predictable conformist behavior," and that "cultural experimentation, not to speak of expanded political rights, has no place in his world."[14]

These and other assessments of Gorbachev during his first year in office reflect—correctly, I believe—the initial point of departure of the future architect of *perestroika* upon assuming the reins of power in the Kremlin. Early in the Gorbachev administration, there was talk about "improving (or perfecting) the economic mechanism," but none about "reform"—a concept which communist ideology has traditionally associated with capitalist societies and politics.[15] It was not until the Twenty-seventh Party Congress in February 1986 that Gorbachev legitimized, as it were, the term "reform" when he talked about the necessity of a "radical reform" of the economic mechanism.[16]

During his first year in office, by contrast, Gorbachev voiced essentially conservative themes. In an unpublished speech to the secretaries for economic affairs of the Central Committees of the East European Communist parties, he defended centralized economic control, especially in investment, pricing, resource allocation, and foreign trade. He attacked market-oriented reforms and left no doubt that he regarded Yugoslavia and China as negative examples.[17] Martin Walker may well be right in suggesting that the Leningrad Manifesto was written and circulated by officials who were profoundly disappointed with the draft Party Program and the draft Economic Guidelines (published in October 1985) and because of the widespread perception, during the first year of the Gorbachev regime, that the new man in the Kremlin, like his predecessors in office, was not willing to undertake the necessary radical changes to deal with the country's urgent problems.[18]

The Leningrad Manifesto, inter alia, makes us aware of the enormous change that has taken place in the general secretary's thinking on the subjects of economic and political reform. Although Gorbachev may well have realized the necessity of change long before he came to Moscow,[19] he clearly lacked a blueprint for reform when he became general secretary. As a matter of fact, if Aleksandr N. Yakovlev, Gorbachev's close political ally and high-level adviser, can be believed, the new leadership was unprepared, "both in practical and in theoretical terms," to deal with fundamental questions of policy.[20] In matters of reform, there apparently was no preconceived idea, no consensus on direction, no agreed-on point of departure, and very little, if any, experience to draw on. Consequently,

"Gorbachev's real apprenticeship in reform occurred on the job"[21] and *per-estroika*—far from being the product of an integral reform concept—turned out to be the child of improvisation and experimentation.

Perestroika versus Reform

Gorbachev represents the rare example of a politician who has become radicalized in office.[22] Within a relatively short time, he moved from the narrow pursuit of the acceleration of economic growth to a full-blown and sweeping concept of radical socioeconomic, political, and cultural reform. When he addressed the activists of the party organization of Khabarovsk krai on August 2, 1986, he stated the case for a program of restructuring that would "encompass not only the economy, but all the other aspects of social life: Social relations, the political system, the spiritual-ideological sphere, and the style and methods of the work of the party and of all cadres." It was in this speech that Gorbachev for the first time defined *perestroika* explicitly as a "revolution." "*Perestroika* is a capacious word," he said. "I would put an equals sign between the words *perestroika* and revolution."[23]

Two months later, in a speech to a national conference of social scientists, Gorbachev talked about "new thinking" as a prerequisite for any social and economic progress, about the need for a climate of greater intellectual freedom. "The search for truth," he said, requires "the juxtaposition of different points of view...discussion and debate, and the breaking of former stereotypes."[24]

Finally, in January 1987, less than two years into his administration, Gorbachev crossed the proverbial Rubicon when he addressed the Central Committee on the subject of "Restructuring and the Personnel Policy of the Party" in a speech that rivals Khrushchev's "secret speech" of 1956 in significance. He now developed a very different analysis of the malaise of Soviet society, attributing it to the "legacy from the past," to inherent defects in the Stalinist system, which had been exacerbated during the "era of stagnation" under Brezhnev. He indicted the Communist party, including "the Central Committee and the top leadership of the country," for the failure "to see in time and in full the need for change and the dangerous growth of crisis phenomena in society," for failure "to formulate a clear-cut policy for overcoming them and making better use of the possibilities intrinsic to the socialist system." He placed a great deal of the blame on the party's personnel policy, in particular on the institution of the *nomenklatura,* called for the cooptation and promotion of non-party cadres, the democratization of election procedures within the party at all levels, as well as the democratization of all of Soviet society and the development of meaningful self-government. In recommending electoral and other reforms, he went so far as to argue that the success of *perestroika* ultimately depended on the prior establishment of democracy.[25] Ever since, democratization (*demokratizatsiia*) has occupied a central place in his political rhetoric. As we shall see, it has also become a key element in his political reforms.

By early 1987 it was clear that Gorbachev had been wise in choosing *perestroika* rather than *reforma* (reform) as the umbrella concept for his administration. The changes to which he was by then committed went far beyond anything encompassed by the ordinary meaning of the word reform. Having explicitly refused to deal in an "evolutionary way, by timid, creeping reforms" with his country's "crisis"—a term with ominous implications for a Marxist-Leninist![26]—Gorbachev provided indirect evidence that he had, in fact, chosen the umbrella concept of his administration carefully. In what is perhaps the most graphic description of the nature and scope of *perestroika* by its architect to date, he wrote:

> In accordance with our theory, revolution means construction, but it also always implies demolition. Revolution requires the demolition of all that is obsolete, stagnant and hinders fast progress. Without demolition, you cannot clear the site for new construction. Perestroika also means a resolute and radical elimination of obstacles hindering social and economic development, of outdated methods of managing the economy and of dogmatic stereotype mentality. Perestroika affects the interests of many people, the whole of society. And, of course, demolition provokes conflicts and sometimes fierce clashes between the old and the new. [27]

The Genesis of *Perestroika*

In any assessment of the meaning, significance, and prospects of the political course now being pursued by Gorbachev the question of the genesis of *perestroika* is of major importance. Is *perestroika* a reflection of basic long-term forces at work in Soviet society, or is it primarily a reflection of the impact of Gorbachev? To what extent is Gorbachev's ambitious program of restructuring Soviet society linked to and dependent on his own person and leadership role? Can *perestroika* continue without Gorbachev's leadership? If so, how will it change?

In an interview with the editors of *L'Unita*, Gorbachev, as it were, addressed himself to this question. Rejecting the argument of those who maintain that "the policy aimed at the renewal of socialism is linked personally with the name of Gorbachev" as "contradicting the truth," he suggested that "the formation of the new policy is a reflection of the fact that in Soviet society and in the Soviet people there has existed and exists a broad understanding of the necessity of changes." This realization, he said, was not a matter of insight or sudden illumination, but rather the product of "the understanding of the objective necessity of changes in our society." In short, "if it would not have been Gorbachev, it would have been someone else."[28] According to Aleksandr Yakovlev, who has played a key role in Gorbachev's drive to restructure Soviet society and reportedly was the moving spirit behind the relaxation of cultural controls, on the other hand, "the seed of revolutionary perestroika was dropped into the soil of the people....[at the Central Committee plenum] in April 1985. It germinated through a massive struggle for the realization of the program for the renewal of socialism."[29]

The contradiction between these two perspectives on the genesis of *perestroika* may be more apparent than real if we assume that Gorbachev's reference to *perestroika* was of a more general nature, while that of Yakovlev was more narrow and specific. Leaving open the question of authorship, the Leningrad Manifesto lends credence to the perspective of Gorbachev, suggesting, if nothing else, that highly placed and thoughtful Soviet officials in the mid-1980s had clearly recognized the need for far-reaching and fundamental political reforms.

In assessing the politics of reform in the Soviet Union under Gorbachev today, it is important to recognize that, in the broad sense, the complex and in some ways contradictory process of *perestroika* is the culmination of a long-term trend toward change and reform in Soviet life that began in the Khrushchev period. While Soviet political development since the death of Stalin has by no means moved in a straight line toward what we now know as *perestroika*, it will be argued here that, in a number of important respects, it helped pave the way for change and reform. To be sure, the movement toward reform suffered setbacks even under Khrushchev,[30] and the Brezhnev regime clearly sought to bring stability— and, in particular, job security for the *nomenklatura*—after the turbulence of the Khrushchev years. Nevertheless, it is clear that the ambivalent legacy of Brezhnev also included a "timid reformism."[31] After the long years of leadership paralysis, policy drift, and immobilism of the Brezhnev regime, the pace of change and reform increased perceptibly during the brief tenure of Andropov and slowed down but continued under Chernenko.

Nevertheless, it was precisely during the "era of stagnation" under Brezhnev that important reform impulses manifested themselves. One of these impulses, which has a bearing on our understanding of the nature of *perestroika* under Gorbachev, has to do with the key principle of Soviet politics, namely, the "leading role of the party."[32]

As is well known, this principle was explicitly enshrined in the Constitution of the USSR, that is, the "Brezhnev" Constitution of 1977. What has been largely overlooked is the fact that certain provisions of that constitution clearly contradict the Communist party's claim to total power. Thus, in affirming the principle of socialist legality, Article 4 stipulates that "all state institutions and public organizations and officials are obliged to observe the USSR Constitution and Soviet laws."[33] Since the Communist party is regarded as a public organization in Marxist-Leninist theory, it, too, falls under this provision. When Brezhnev addressed the Presidium of the USSR Supreme Soviet in June 1977, he spoke not only of the "constantly-growing role of the CPSU" in the life of the Soviet state, but also emphasized that the CPSU executes its leadership "within the framework of the Constitution."[34] He made a similar statement before the USSR Supreme Soviet in October 1977.[35] These pronouncements are in line with Article 4 and may be regarded as a point of departure for the legal limitation of the dictatorial power claimed by the party.

The second reform impulse coming from the Khrushchev period has to do with the place of the soviets in the scheme of things. It was in 1957, under Khrushchev, that the Central Committee adopted a resolution "On Improving the Work of the Soviets of Workers' Deputies and Strengthening Their Ties with the Masses," launching a policy that has continued to this day.[36] During the Stalin era, the development of these potentially democratic representative institutions was arrested: the soviets became part of the facade of Stalin's dictatorial regime, the main act in the "shadow dance of democracy." Under Khrushchev, however, they received a new lease on life. In the aftermath of the 1957 resolution, Soviet social scientists carried out an enormous amount of research on the soviets in an attempt to determine their problems and weaknesses and to make concrete recommendations for improvement.[37] Although these efforts did not lead to the hoped-for change in the status of the soviets, it is important to recognize that they nevertheless continued, even under Brezhnev. Writing in 1987, Gorbachev acknowledged these past attempts to remedy the situation, noting that "in the past fifteen years fourteen res-olutions were adopted on improving the activity of the Soviets." If these attempts proved to be of no avail, it was because "the economic, political and ideological environment of the braking mechanism fully resisted a greater role for the Soviets, which were basically the bodies incarnating broad democracy and openness."[38]

A third reform impulse coming from the Khrushchev era has to do with the revolution in Soviet social science that is under way in the Soviet Union. Not only has Gorbachev repeatedly engaged the members of the intelligentsia, journalists, media executives, and social scientists in a dialogue, but he has emphasized the importance of their contribution to the cause of *perestroika* and enlisted their support.[39] The social scientists—economists, legal scholars, sociologists, and scholars who are political scientists in all but in name—in particular have been a most important moving force behind the ferment and agitation for change and reform. Indeed, the development of political science and the other social sciences in the post-Stalin period has been associated with the emergence of the economic reform thinking of the 1960s.[40]

As Ronald J. Hill has pointed out, the antecedents of the ferment in Soviet social science go back to the Khrushchev period.[41] De-Stalinization led to new questions and new perspectives. The "renaissance of economics" in 1957-1958 had a stimulating effect on the other social sciences. By the mid-1960s, a major campaign was under way in the scholarly community for the recognition of an independent discipline of political science.[42] While this campaign on the face of it was not successful, it was an important part of the broader process of intellectual awakening that characterized the post-Stalin period and led to the questioning of many long-standing ideological canons and dogmas.

It was this process that led to the discovery and public exposure of the problems and contradictions in socialist society—and thus to a more realistic understanding of social problems. In the 1970s, a variety of think tanks became increasingly important in providing inputs into policymaking. By the early 1980s, Soviet scholars were openly discussing "bureaucratic perversions" and "socio-political crises" in socialist society and offering recommendations to deal with them.[43] Finally, among the interesting and significant characteristics of the Gorbachev administration is the presence of a relatively large number of scholars in high-level advisory positions, including scholars like Burlatsky and Shakhnazarov, who for more than two decades have been prominent in the struggle for an independent academic discipline of political science.[44] While the personal aides of Gorbachev are not all scholars or social scientists, they have "the track records of...outspoken reformists."[45] They, too, appear to be the product of the intellectual ferment that began in the Khrushchev period.

Perestroika: The Dismantling of the Stalinist System?

The process of "restructuring" and "revolutionary change" known as *perestroika* that has come to be associated with Gorbachev thus is the product of a rather long period of gestation. It is a process that has become increasingly complex and multifaceted as its parameters have expanded from the narrow pursuit of economic reform to the radical change of all spheres of social life. As *perestroika* has unfolded, developing a dynamic of its own, it has grown into a movement for change that far exceeds the bounds of what is ordinarily understood by reform. Gorbachev's program of "restructuring," in short, is much better and more accurately conceptualized as a revolution in the making, whose essence and basic thrust is the dismantling of the Stalinist system. As success has continued to elude Gorbachev on the economic front, restructuring has increasingly come to focus on changes in the political system.

From the standpoint of political reform, *perestroika* has a number of dimensions, including (1) the growing critique of Stalin and the Stalinist system, (2) the new information policy (*glasnost*), (3) legal reform, (4) the attack on the *nomenklatura,* and (5) a radical change in party-state relations. Taken together, these aspects of *perestroika* suggest the determination to perform major surgery on Soviet socialism in an attempt to modernize it and to enable it to survive in a vastly different world from that of Stalin, a world that continues to change rapidly and that threatens to leave the Soviet Union behind. This political stance, needless to say, rings with echoes of the argumentation of the Leningrad Manifesto and reflects its basic premise that fundamental structural change in the political system is a prerequisite for economic reform. Indeed, Gorbachev himself has repeatedly asserted that the future of socialism is on the line and that socialism without *perestroika* is doomed.

The Stalin Issue

Perhaps no aspect of Gorbachev's public political stance has undergone as dramatic a change as has his attitude toward the crucial issue of Stalinism. In May 1985, two months after his election as general secretary, he paid—what was perceived by some as excessive—tribute to Stalin's role in the defeat of Nazi Germany.[46] In an interview with *L'Humanité* in February 1986, he dismissed Stalinism as "a concept thought up by the enemies of communism, which is widely used to slander the Soviet Union and socialism as a whole."[47] When meeting with a group of writers in June 1986, he again pointed to economic recovery as the top priority. To dig up the past, he said, would only "dissipate our energy and set people at odds with one another." He promised that "when the time comes we will deal with the past as well. We will put everything in its place."[48]

The "time to deal with the past," as it turned out, came much sooner than expected. One of the consequences of *glasnost* was a much more realistic and sophisticated understanding of the genesis, the depth, and the multiple dimensions of the crisis confronting the Soviet Union. While Gorbachev's initial analysis of the malaise of Soviet society had focused on the "era of stagnation" under Brezhnev, it soon came to include—and, in fact, to center on—the Stalin period. Although Brezhnev continued to come in for his share of criticism, it was the "cult of the personality," the "command and administrative system of management developed in the 1930's," as well as the "bureaucratic, dogmatic and voluntarist distortions" and the "arbitrariness" of the Stalin era that, according to Gorbachev, had prevented the "full realization of the Leninist principles of the new social order."[49] Increasingly it was the end of the Lenin era, the subsequent "deformations" of and "deviations" from the Leninist model of socialism under Stalin that became the point of departure for Gorbachev's justification of *perestroika* and his rationale for "the continuation of October" and a "second revolution."[50] Reiterating that the *perestroika* now under way in the USSR will determine the fate of socialism, he called once again for "radical changes in the productive forces and productive relations, the revolutionary renewal of social and political structures, and the growth of the spiritual and intellectual potential of society." The whole point of *perestroika*, he said, is

> to resuscitate, in present-day conditions, the Leninist character of the new society, to cleanse it of all the extraneous features and deformations, and to free it from everything that has fettered society and prevented it from fully realizing the potential of socialism. And, what is the main thing, to impart a new quality to socialism, taking into consideration all the realities of present-day life.[51]

Beginning in 1987, Gorbachev increasingly singled out Stalin and the system he created in the 1930s as being chiefly responsible for the malaise of Soviet society. Addressing the Central Committee in January 1987, he characterized the Stalin era in no uncertain terms as a time when "authoritarian evaluations and opinions became unquestionable truths" that were "viewed as immutable and presented as dogmas that left no room for an objective scientific analysis," a time when "Lenin's ideas of socialism were interpreted simplistically and their theoretical depth and significance were frequently emaciated."[52] Indicting both the person and the modus operandi of Stalin, Gorbachev blamed the "dangerous growth of crisis phenomena in society" on the continued adherence to the "command and administrative methods" instituted in the 1930s.

Important as the evolution of Gorbachev's views on the crucial issue of Stalinism in 1987 and 1988 may be, there were also a number of other significant developments. On February 5, 1988, the legal rehabilitation of Bukharin, Rykov, and other victims of Stalin's purges was announced in

Moscow.[53] It was followed by their political rehabilitation and reinstatement in the party on July 10, 1988.[54] On June 17, 1988, Yu. Afanasyev, the director of the Institute of Historical Archives in Moscow, called for the exoneration of Trotsky in the pages of the Soviet press.[55] In August 1989, articles by Trotsky were published in the Soviet Union—for the first time since 1929![56] These are, indeed, developments of momentous significance.

As far as the architect of *perestroika* is concerned, by mid-1987 he was ready to speak out more explicitly on the issue of Stalinism—without, however, acknowledging the full scale of the tragedy under Stalin. Addressing Soviet journalists and media representatives in July 1987, he said: "I think that we will never be able to forgive or justify what happened in 1937-1938, and never should. Never. Those who were in power at that time were responsible for that."[57] Even more important was the dramatic change in his public stance on collectivization—a change that is fully consonant with the evolution of his thinking on Stalinism, his political pragmatism, and his increasing radicalization. Whereas in November 1987 Gorbachev had still rejected the view that Bukharin constituted a viable and desirable alternative to Stalin and had defended both the necessity and desirability of collectivization, by September 1988 he not only condemned the Stalinist legacy of state and collective farms but also set about dismantling it, thus destroying yet another major pillar of the Stalinist system. Collectivization, he said, had destroyed the Russian peasantry, and the root cause of the country's long-festering crisis in agriculture must be sought in its very structure.[58]

Thus, the views of Gorbachev on the subject of Stalin and Stalinism changed significantly during the first three years of his administration. While it is impossible to make a precise assessment of the importance of this evolution, there is little doubt that it has contributed to the radicalization of his policy agenda. What is more, Gorbachev's analysis of the Stalinist order has found reflection in his approach to political reform.

Glasnost

Of the various aspects of *perestroika*, Gorbachev's new information policy—*glasnost*—has arguably been the most dramatic and successful. Once launched, it produced within a relatively short time an almost inconceivable change in the political atmosphere in the largest country on earth, making it possible—for the first time in many years—to address pressing problems and public issues with candor and honesty. One has to go back more than six decades in the history of the Soviet Union—to the beginning of the 1920s, when Lenin had not yet "put the lid on the opposition" and stifled intra-party democracy—to find a period of comparable freedom.

As so often before in the history of Russia and the Soviet Union, it was in the cultural sphere, especially in the cinema, theater, and literature, that the new climate first manifested itself. Works written and produced "for the drawer" many years before, now saw the light of day. Even before Gorbachev reluctantly recognized the need to fill in the "forgotten names and blank spots" in the history of the country in early 1987,[59] the events, as it were, anticipated the future course.

The year 1986 brought the upheaval in the cinematographers' and writers' unions and the release of Tengiz Aguladze's remarkable film "Repentance," a powerful symbolic representation of de-Stalinization, which had an enormous, almost incredible impact on viewers. The year 1987 saw the posthumous reinstatement of Boris Pasternak as a member of the Soviet Union of Writers, as well as the announcement that his novel, *Doctor Zhivago*, would be published in 1988—some thirty years after it had earned him the Nobel Prize! In April 1987, Mikhail Shatrov's play dealing with the Treaty of Brest-Litovsk, written in 1962, was presented in Moscow, a play which portrays Bukharin and other victims of Stalin as honest and competent Bolsheviks. Vladimir Dudintsev's novel *White Robes*, which deals with the persecution of Soviet geneticists in the 1940s, was published in early 1987. Anatoli Rybakov's novel *Children of the Arbat*, a powerful portrayal of life in Moscow during the Great Terror, written in the 1960s, appeared in the spring of 1987. The fall of 1987 brought the posthumous publication of Anna Akhmatova's poem *Requiem*, written in 1940, recounting her vigil "under the stars of death," in front of the prison in Leningrad where her husband was executed.[60]

The fall of 1987 also saw the announcement of plans to publish the late Vasily Grossman's *Life and Fate*, a novel about World War II, which draws explicit parallels between Stalinism and Nazism. In the summer of 1988, finally, *Oktiabr'*, the monthly journal of the RSFSR Writers' Union, announced the publication of Grossman's *Vse techet* (Forever flowing)—a work that argues that Lenin rather than Stalin was responsible for the crimes of the Soviet state.[61] The publication of this powerful indictment of the founder of the Soviet state perhaps is most indicative of the parameters of Gorbachev's *glasnost*, since Lenin is still the object of an intense cult—a cult, moreover, to which Gorbachev has made his share of contributions.[62] Preceded by a lengthy "philosophical-sociological commentary" defending Lenin, the "diabolical pages" of Grossman's novel, which exceed even the "rather broad limits...achieved by the epoch of perestroika," were nevertheless published.[63]

If any other further test of the limits of *glasnost* was needed, it was provided by the rehabilitation of Aleksandr Solzhenitsyn in 1989. The struggle over the reappraisal of the exiled writer constitutes perhaps the most intriguing chapter in Gorbachev's cultural thaw. Initially unable to forgive Solzhenitsyn for his writings on Lenin and completely opposed to the publication of his works, the general secretary, after "several deep discussions" with Sergei Zalygin, the seventy-five-year-old editor of *Novyi mir*, changed his mind—most likely for sound political reasons.[64] In the meantime, Solzhenitsyn's "Nobel Lecture" and the first installment of *The Gulag Archipelago* have been published in the Soviet Union.[65] Vladimir Boldyrev, the chief Soviet censor, has affirmed that all of Solzhenitsyn's works have been released for publication.[66] According to Zalygin, 1990 will be "the year of Solzhenitsyn."[67] And so, thanks to *glasnost*, even this uncompromising critic of communism, who insists that it was Lenin who was ultimately responsible for the terror and the crimes perpetrated under Stalin, is finally able to reach the readers for whom his literature was written. Clearly, after the publication of the works of Grossman and Solzhenitsyn the Lenin cult will never be the same again.

Thus, one important aspect of *glasnost* has been historical revisionism and—in Gorbachev's words—the filling in of "forgotten names and blank spots" of Soviet history. The writers have not been alone in this endeavor. They have been joined by economic journalists like Vasily Selyunin, who in May 1988 published a sensational article examining the authoritarian elements in prerevolutionary Russia that were not overcome by the Bolsheviks and flourished after the October Revolution. According to Selyunin, it was Lenin who, during the period of "war communism," set up the system of forced labor and concentration camps, whereas Stalin "only revived" the practices of "war communism." Furthermore, portraying Russian and Soviet history as a series of episodes in which conservative forces have time and again prevailed over promising shoots of democracy, individual freedom, and private enterprise, he singled out Lenin as one of the historical figures who encouraged conservative and antidemocratic tendencies to flourish.[68]

Indeed, historical revisionism and filling in the "blank spots of history" has become an enterprise conducted at and from the highest level of the party. The revival of the journal *Izvestiia TsK KPSS*, which was closed down in 1929 on the orders of Stalin, has already resulted in the publication of a great deal of new and important information about Lenin, Stalin, the history of the party, and current Soviet politics. Even Khrushchev's famous "secret speech" of 1956 and the stenographic report of the October 1987 Plenum of the Central Committee, which led to the "resignation" of Boris Yeltsin as Moscow party chief, have now been published.[69]

In addition to encouraging historical revisionism, *glasnost* has also had a

profound impact on contemporary issues. It made it possible to, among
other things, raise such environmental issues as the Siberian rivers diversion project, which in spite of widespread opposition had been pursued by
ministerial bureaucrats since the time of Brezhnev and enjoyed the support of Academician Anatoli Aleksandrov, then president of the USSR
Academy of Sciences. The State Planning Commission (Gosplan) and the
Ministry of Land Reclamation and Water Resources (Minvodkhoz) came
under attack by prominent intellectuals such as Sergei Zalygin, the new
noncommunist editor of *Novyi Mir,* who compared the earth to a "commu-
nal apartment with one sewage-pipe for all," and the writer Yuri Bondarev,
who assailed the bureaucratic culture that had continued to flourish since
Stalin's death and the "chinovnik-type careerists" who were more interested in protecting statistics than man and who had transformed science into
a force capable of murdering both nature and mankind.[70]

Glasnost has also significantly increased the importance of the mass
media. In addition to the greatly enhanced role of television, the Soviet
press has staged a dramatic comeback. Gone is the former soporific
monotony and dishwater-like dullness of the official press. Today such previously stodgy publications as *Pravda, Moscow News,* and even *Kommunist,*
the theoretical journal of the Central Committee, make for instructive
and interesting reading. The new (and deserved) popularity of *Izvestiia,*
the government daily, is reflected in the fact that its circulation has more
than doubled since it decreased by 3 million during the Brezhnev era.[71]
Among the most popular publications are the restructured *Ogonek* and the
newcomer *Argumenty i fakty,* the world's largest circulation weekly.

But while *glasnost* has succeeded in reducing political apathy among
important segments of the population and in mobilizing the intelligentsia
in particular, it has also complicated Gorbachev's political agenda. By
exposing the full depth and range of the country's economic and social
problems, *glasnost* has raised expectations among the people that the party
and the government will deal with the disclosures. These expectations,
however, come at the worst possible time for Gorbachev. He is leading a
party that is in the midst of a serious "crisis of confidence" that has been
openly acknowledged in the Soviet press [72]—a crisis fueled at least in part
by the party's lack of performance—and he is identified with a new form
of government, still in its infancy, which can easily become the scapegoat
for policy failures.

In the aftermath of the startling revelations by Yevgeniy Chazov, the former minister of health, about the dismal state of Soviet health care, the
exposure of social problems—from housing, care for the aged, and education to rampant alcoholism, drug addiction, AIDS, and prostitution—in

the Soviet press, the self-image of Soviet society, official and unofficial, has undergone a dramatic transformation. As the revelations by Soviet officials, including members of the top leadership in party and government, journalists, scientists, and other members of the intelligentsia have unfolded, it has become clear that Gorbachev's use of the term "pre-crisis" to describe his country's situation was by no means far-fetched or exaggerated.[73] In the fall of 1987, it was revealed that state subsidies in the economy amounted to 84 billion rubles—an increase of 2300 percent since 1965, when they came to only 3.5 billion rubles—and that, of this total, food subsidies accounted for some 57 billion rubles, nearly 68 percent.[74] In early 1988, Gorbachev himself informed the Central Committee that "for the duration of practically four five-year plans, we did not have an increase in the absolute growth of the national income, and at the beginning of the 1980's it began even to diminish."[75]

In addition to contributing to a more realistic and sophisticated understanding of the problems confronting the Soviet Union and encouraging vigorous public debate, *glasnost* has served a number of political purposes. The exposure of the depth and the parameters of the crisis confronting the Soviet Union has discouraged the conservatives from developing a political platform on which to challenge Gorbachev. It has also been a useful and necessary instrument in revealing corruption and incompetence among Soviet officialdom, thus facilitating Gorbachev's assault on the *nomenklatura*, especially at the local and regional levels. Finally, it has played an important role in helping Gorbachev to build a constituency in support of *perestroika*, especially among the intelligentsia.

Legal Reform

From the outset, Gorbachev's political reforms have involved the question of the role and substance of law and legality in the USSR. The legal reforms that were contemplated once political reform was on the agenda were notable for their extensive design and their substantive deviation from the Soviet tradition. They included the preparation of new civil and criminal codes and a new code of legal procedures. In the candid discussions involving legal experts, prosecutors, judges, public defenders, writers, officials of the Ministry of Justice, and ordinary citizens, many interesting and important ideas were aired: greater independence of the courts; more extensive rights for the accused; separation of the office of the public prosecutor from the courts, which since the judicial reorganization of 1970 have been part of the Ministry of Justice; increasing the rights and independence of the office of the public defender; and the reformulation of existing legal statutes to reflect the actual and proposed changes in the economy, in the cultural sphere, and in communications.[76]

One of the consequences of *glasnost* was the exposure of the hollowness of "socialist legality," the gap between constitutional theory and actual legal practice, the control of the legal system from above, and the widespread practice of "telephone justice," that is, decisions of judges in response to pressures from high officials.[77] Another one of the slogans that was added relatively early to the vocabulary of the Gorbachev administration was "social justice." Like *glasnost*, this slogan, too, led to an exploration of the legal implications of "restructuring."

One Soviet writer made "the strict implementation of the principles of social justice...an important condition for the unity and political stability of society, for its dynamic development."[78] Academician Tatyana Zaslavskaya explored the nexus between "social justice" and "the human factor in economic development," going so far as to link the Chernobyl nuclear disaster to neglect of "the human factor" and "social justice" under Brezhnev.[79] A highly emotional encounter between Moscow writers and bureaucrats of the legal establishment in late 1986 arrived at the consensus that legal reform was as necessary as economic reform.[80] Aleksandr Yakovlev, one of Gorbachev's closest advisers, wrote in the spring of 1987 that "without law, legality, and justice it is impossible to attain social progress, guarantee the normal operation of material production and the institutions of political democracy, set effective government going, and stimulate the development of the individual."[81] He went on to deplore the continuing conception of rights as "a benefaction from above," which "is indicative of the lack of understanding of that real link that exists among us between the individual, society, law and the state" and to lament the continuing reign of the "presumption of guilt" with respect to economic initiative.[82]

At a meeting on October 2, 1986, the Politburo discussed the need for "a consistent restructuring of the work of the prosecutor's office, the police, courts, and other law enforcement agencies." According to Radio Moscow, the Politburo emphasized "the inadmissibility of any attempts by whatever party to interfere in the investigation and trial of specific cases." The Politburo reportedly also stressed the "strict observance of the laws" to "ensure social justice and the inviolability of the constitutional rights of citizens" as a prerequisite for the success of *perestroika*.[83] The discussions concerning legal reform produced a general consensus about the role of law in Soviet society and the importance of the rule of law—a concept which in some ways is similar to the *Rechtsstaat* of the German legal tradition. The *Rechtsstaat*, a creation of nineteeth-century Prussia, assigned important prerogatives to the state and clearly favored the state over the individual. On the other hand, it emphasized the inviolability of legal norms, the predictability of legal procedures, and the limitations on the rights of the state in its relations with individual citizens and legal entities. Although the legal norms and practices derived from the *Rechtsstaat* tradition are far removed from the conception of individual rights and the limitations on the authority of the state found in common-law countries, the establishment of a legal order based on the *Rechtsstaat* notion would constitute a major change and advance for the Soviet Union.

A socialist "rule-of-law" state (*sotsialisticheskoe pravovoe gosudarstvo*)[84] presumably could not go on governing the country on the basis of a multitude of unpublished directives and decrees as had been the case in the past. Not surprisingly, these "sublegal acts" have, indeed, been criticized and condemned in the Soviet press, in particular since in a good many cases they actually contravene existing law. Reportedly, there are more than 10,000 sublegal acts in force in the Soviet Union. According to Ivan Kazmin and Albert Pigolkin, legal experts affiliated with the All-Union Research Institute of Soviet Legislation, it is the unpublished directive, not the published law, that is enforced in the case of a conflict.[85]

In an apparent attempt to bring legislation into conformity with the 1977 constitution, the USSR Supreme Soviet announced a five-year plan for new legislation in the summer of 1986.[86] Since its publication, there has been a flood of new laws—the evident beginning of an attempt to create an elaborate legal foundation and structure for *perestroika*.[87] A law announced in July 1987 gives citizens the right to sue officials for committing illegal acts, thus putting teeth into Article 58 of the 1977 Constitution.[88] The practice of conducting nation-wide debates on proposed legislation, provided for in Article 114 of the 1977 Constitution, was given a stronger legal foundation by another new law announced at the same time. However, the proposed law providing for a nationwide vote (referendum) was dropped from the agenda of the USSR Supreme Soviet without explanation.[89]

On February 2, 1988, the Presidium of the USSR Supreme Soviet, "taking into account the wishes of the working people," decreed that anonymous denunciations would no longer be investigated, thus—at least in terms of the law—putting an end to a long-standing tradition and practice that has ruined the lives of many Soviet citizens [90] but that until 1987 was the only recourse ordinary citizens had in defending their interests against abuse by Soviet bureaucrats.

Legal reform was the subject of a roundtable discussion in the summer of 1988. In particular, the participants debated the legal safeguards necessary to prevent a repetition of Stalinism and the abuse of power. Focusing on the concept of the "socialist rule-of-law state" set forth in the Theses for

the Nineteenth Party Conference, they agreed that this concept called for
the subordination of both the Communist party and the state to the law.
They also emphasized the necessity of the "separation of powers" and
endorsed the establishment of a Constitutional Court and trial by jury.[91]

The resolution on legal reform adopted by the Nineteenth Party
Conference endorsed many of these proposals. It called for the establishment of an institution to monitor observance of the constitution,
improved supervision of the investigation of criminal cases, the protection
of the judiciary against intervention by local party officials, and a form of
trial by jury. While many legal problems were not addressed—the issue of
the equality of all citizens before the law, the human rights obligations of
the Soviet Union under international law, and others—the resolution
makes clear the important role that law is to play in the political reform of
the Gorbachev administration.[92] This should come as no surprise since
"for the first time since Lenin, the Party and the country are headed by a
professional lawyer who appreciates the political and moral significance of
legality."[93]

Assault on the Nomenklatura

There is general consensus in the literature on Soviet politics that socioeconomic and political reform in the Soviet Union requires, at a minimum, a change in the *nomenklatura*, both as a process of leadership selection and as a ruling stratum.[94] Created in the 1920s to facilitate the party's
consolidation and eventual monopoly of political power,[95] the *nomenklatura* system, it can be argued, did serve a certain purpose in the 1930s and
1940s—especially considering the desperate situation of the Bolshevik
regime during the first decades of its existence and its ambitious goals for
the transformation of Russia. Since the completion of the initial industrialization phase and particularly since the end of the postwar reconstruction drive, however, the *nomenklatura* system has proved to be increasingly
dysfunctional—which accounts for the fact that the vexing "cadre question" has become the most permanent item on the Soviet political agenda.

In spite of numerous efforts to improve its performance and transform
it into an effective instrument of party policy, the *nomenklatura* has
become a permanent fixture in the world of Soviet politics and seemingly
impervious to change and reform. When Khrushchev attempted to introduce major changes in the *nomenklatura* system, he was roundly defeated
and his organizational reforms of the apparatus were rescinded. His political career came to an abrupt end. Accused of a variety of "hare-brained
schemes," he ended up in the Orwellian memory hole—courtesy of the
party apparatus he had tried to reform. Thus ended the first round of
post-Stalin reform politics.

The long Brezhnev era (1964-1982) was in many respects the "golden age" of the *nomenklatura*. After the turmoil and high elite turnover under Khrushchev, the accent under the man from Dnepropetrovsk was on "consideration for cadres." As a result, the *nomenklatura*-elite, already well advanced in age, settled in for an unprecedented era of job security. At the Twenty-Fifth Party Congress in 1976 and the Twenty-Sixth Party Congress in 1981, the reelection ratios of surviving full members of the Central Committee reached all-time highs of 89 percent and 87 percent, respectively. At that point in time, it seemed, only the operation of the laws of biology assured that eventually there would be turnover in the Soviet elite.

Beginning with Andropov and greatly intensifying under Gorbachev, the *nomenklatura* has been subjected to an unprecedented degree of criticism and attack. What is more, since November 1982 the Soviet political and administrative elites have suffered the greatest turnover in their ranks since the 1930s. By March 1986, a year after Gorbachev's election as the new general secretary, 9 of 13 deputy chairmen of the USSR Council of Ministers (69 percent), 48 of 82 other members of the USSR Council of Ministers (59 percent), 8 of 14 first secretaries of republic central committees (57 percent), 85 of 150 *obkom* first secretaries (57 percent), 17 of 20 commanders of military districts (85 percent), and 76 of 164 voting members of republic party bureaus (46 percent) had been replaced; and 103 of 164 voting members of republic party bureaus had been removed or changed jobs.[96] By August 1987, less than six months after the Twenty-seventh Party Congress, the replacement rate for these categories of officials had increased as follows:[97]

Deputy chairmen of the USSR Council of Ministers 85%
Other members of the USSR Council of Ministers 83%
First secretaries of republic party central committees 64%
First secretaries of *oblast* party committees 72%
Commanders of military districts and groups 95%
Voting members of republic party bureaus 63%
Voting members of republic party bureaus who were
        removed from office or transferred to other jobs 78%

Turnover at the very apex of the Communist party leadership has been equally extensive. Of the nine men who were full (voting) members of the Politburo at the time of Gorbachev's appointment as general secretary in March 1985, only Vitaliy Vorotnikov, the president of the RSFSR, who was appointed in December 1983 under Andropov, and Gorbachev himself were still members of that body as of September 1989. At the level of the candidate (nonvoting) members of the Politburo, the turnover by October 1988 was 100 percent. And of the eight men who were members of the Central Committee Secretariat when Gorbachev became general secretary, only two (Gorbachev and Yegor Ligachev) still held seats in the ten-member Secretariat in October 1988. At the level of the Central Committee, the number of "dead souls" (old Brezhnevites who had lost the posts that had qualified them for Central Committee membership, but who managed to hold on to their Central Committee seats) was reduced to about 25 percent of the full members by the end of 1988. In April 1989, finally, Gorbachev engineered the mass resignation of 110 members of the Central Committee and the Central Auditing Commission in a shake-up of unprecedented scope in recent Soviet history that eliminated almost all of the "dead souls" and marked an important step in Gorbachev's drive to restructure the Soviet political system.

The turnover in the Soviet elite has not been limited to the top leadership organs of the party and government. According to Georgiy Razumovsky, the chief of the Organizational Party Work Department of the CPSU Central Committee, by May 1987, two years into the Gorbachev administration, "about one-third of the chairmen of the oblast and krai executive committees, the chairmen of the Councils of Ministers of the union and autonomous republics, and more than half of all the union ministers and chairmen of state committees were replaced." Furthermore, he indicated that nearly 50 percent of the party district and city committee secretaries had been newly appointed.[98] Gorbachev himself told a group of media executives and representatives of cultural and ideological institutions and creative unions on May 7, 1988, that "66 percent of all our ministers are new, as are 61 percent of all the first secretaries of oblast party committees and the chairmen of oblast soviet executive committees and 63 percent of all the first secretaries of city and district party committees."[99]

The magnitude of the turnover in the Soviet Union since 1982 not only signifies the end of the "golden age" of the *nomenklatura*, but also reflects the determination and seriousness of the Gorbachev administration in its pursuit of change and reform. Aside from the considerations that would impel any newly elected general secretary to raise the "cadre question" and to wield the "cadre weapon," Gorbachev has had the additional motivation and impetus deriving from his ambitious plans for the thorough and multidimensional restructuring of the Soviet economy and Soviet society.

On numerous occasions, the general secretary has been very explicit about the linkage between *perestroika* and the "cadre question." As a matter of fact, he has emphasized that the success of *perestroika* is dependent on the successful resolution of this problem. The importance assigned to this issue by the Gorbachev administration is evidenced by the fact that in

January 1987 an entire Central Committee plenum was devoted to the question of "cadre policy."[100] Addressing the Central Committee, Gorbachev put the issue as follows:

> The problems which have accumulated in society are connected to a considerable extent with the shortcomings in the activity of the party itself and its personnel policy....What is needed today is a cadre policy that is consonant with the tasks of perestroika and the need to accelerate socio-economic development.[101]

Similarly, Georgiy Razumovsky, the man in charge of the nerve-center of the *nomenklatura* system in Moscow, has described cadres as "the most important and key link of the restructuring now taking place in the country." Addressing his colleagues, the secretaries in charge of the personnel departments of the central committees of the Communist and workers' parties of the socialist countries, he observed that the success of *perestroika* "depends to a decisive degree on how deeply our cadres realize the necessity of changes, how consistently and creatively they will put into effect the party line. This has made it necessary to make significant revisions and radical improvements in all [our] work with cadres."[102]

Indeed, from the very outset, the "restructuring" envisaged by Gorbachev entailed a challenge to the modus operandi of the *nomenklatura* and threatened its privileged position in society, its monopoly of power and its life style—in short, its corporate interests and, indeed, its existence as a "special administrative class."[103] As the revolutionary dimensions of Gorbachev's political program for the socioeconomic, cultural, and political transformation of Soviet society became more and more evident, the very raison d'être of the *nomenklatura* was called into question and its members, individually and collectively, came under attack. The political slogans advanced under the umbrella concept of *perestroika*—acceleration of socioeconomic development, *glasnost,* social justice, new thinking, and democratization—all challenge and threaten to undermine the seemingly secure and impregnable world of the *nomenklatura.* Individually, the new policies mean the destruction of the "collective anonymity" of the *nomenklatura;*[104] the exposure of corruption, incompetence, and abuse of power in its ranks; the introduction of rational, performance-oriented norms and values; the elimination or reduction of special privileges, the triumph of reason, logic, and innovation over dogma, and the end to the monopoly on information and power. Collectively, they constitute an indictment of the *nomenklatura* as a morally bankrupt class and an obsolete institution that—at least in its present, unreformed configuration—has become dysfunctional.

For the most part, Western scholarly attention to the dramatic developments in the Soviet Union under Gorbachev has focused on his struggle to reform the Soviet economy. But relatively early in his administration, Gorbachev also became involved in the struggle with the *nomenklatura*. Virtually on the eve of the Twenty-seventh Party Congress, an unprecedented attack on the special privileges of the Soviet elite was published in *Pravda* under the title "Purification"[105]—a media event that produced extremely varied reactions among the speakers and other delegates.[106] At the congress itself, the party's personnel management was subjected to scathing criticism by Boris Yeltsin, the ill-fated champion of *perestroika*, who, after his ouster by the party "mafia" in Moscow a few months after the congress, would rise like the legendary phoenix from the ashes and become the Soviet Union's first successful maverick politician.[107]

At the Central Committee Plenum in January 1987, Gorbachev was brutally frank in dissecting the malaise of the Soviet system and the failings of the party leadership, including the top echelon of the *nomenklatura*. In its present configuration and with its traditional modus operandi, he clearly suggested, the party had not only failed to find solutions but, on the contrary, was very much part of the problem. Holding the party leadership responsible for the shortcomings and problems in Soviet society, he described the Soviet system as one that encourages corruption and waste, that has become "deaf to social issues" and, therefore, suffers from "social corrosion"—a system, in short, that is not responsive to the problems and needs of ordinary Soviet citizens. In no uncertain terms, the general secretary indicted the CPSU as an institution, from the highest to the lowest level, for its failure to cope with the problems confronting the Soviet Union. Senior party officials had become involved in criminal activities, and many primary party organizations had failed to wage "a resolute struggle against negative phenomena, permissiveness, mutual cover-up, slackening of discipline, and the spread of drunkenness," as well as "departmentalism, regionalism and manifestations of nationalism." The moral atmosphere of Soviet society, the general secretary told the Central Committee, had been poisoned by the widespread "disregard for laws, report-padding, bribe-taking, and the encouragement of servility and adulation."[108]

Along with the reorganization of the Soviet political system, party reform was the most important agenda item at the Nineteenth Party Conference in June 1988. Of the ten theses for the conference, the thesis dealing with the democratization of the party was by far the longest and most detailed. Inter alia, it called for "serious reform of the party's personnel policy," including an end to the "outdated formal-nomenklatura approach to the selection and placement of cadres," as well as the "recommendation of both party members and people not belonging to the party for leading posts"[109]—themes that also found reflection in Gorbachev's opening speech. Again emphasizing the need for a *perestroika* of the party, Gorbachev told the delegates that the party, too, had become afflicted with the "deformations," the bureaucratization, and the moral decay associated with the "cult of the personality." In violation of Leninist norms, he charged, the party apparatus had freed itself of control by the rank-and-file membership, free debate had been banned, and a split had developed in the party membership between "bosses" and "subordinates," that is, the *nomenklatura* and the ordinary members. The party, in short, had become a house divided. The natural process of cadre renewal had been restrained to the point that "whole generations of communists" were deprived of any real opportunity to participate in the life of the party—the result being costly political mistakes, declining moral standards among party leaders, and abuse of power. Without going into specifics, he called for a reduction in the size of the party apparatus and its responsibilities.[110]

When the full text of the conference resolutions was published four days after their adoption, it became evident that the final resolution dealing with the all-important cadre issue represented, once again, a compromise between the "friends and foes of change." Nevertheless, in their totality these resolutions, if implemented, constitute the death warrant for the *nomenklatura* system in its present form. The proposed legal reforms and the creation of a socialist rule-of-law state "assuring the supremacy of law in all spheres of public life," the proposed reduction of the functions and responsibilities of the party, the change in election procedures, the limitations on the terms of elected and appointed officials in the party and government, the subordination of the apparatus to the elected organs of the party, and the explicit authorization of future national party conferences to make changes in the composition of leading party organs, including the Central Committee, if implemented, would mean the curtailment of the prerogatives and powers of the *nomenklatura* as a class and its qualitative transformation as an institution.[111]

As Gorbachev's program for the modernization and restructuring of the Soviet system has unfolded and both his rhetoric and his policy agenda have become progressively more radicalized, it has also become apparent that the opposition to *perestroika* is centered in the party apparatus and the government bureaucracy. The evidence suggests that Gorbachev's drive to restructure the Soviet system has not only forced the party apparatus and the state bureaucracy into an alliance for survival, but at the level of the top leadership it has also pitted the defenders of an essentially unreconstituted party apparatus as the "engine of progress," the "driving force behind 'reform,'" and, most important, as the mechanism for the

control of *perestroika*, against those who have come to regard that apparatus as hopelessly compromised and unredeemable. Most likely it was their
respective attitudes to the apparatus and its role in *perestroika* that put
Yeltsin and Ligachev at loggerheads—a conflict that ended with
Gorbachev's faithful disciple as the proverbial sacrificial lamb on the altar
of *perestroika*, a casualty of the machinations of the party "mafia" in
Moscow, in particular the Moscow party organization, the country's
largest.[112]

The circumstances surrounding the ouster of Yeltsin, the most outspoken champion of *perestroika*, as head of the Moscow party organization
and, subsequently, as candidate member of the Politburo, the publication
and widespread dissemination of the Andreeva letter, the battle over the
election of delegates to the Nineteenth Party Conference, and the successful deflection of the conference as an instrument for engineering further
change in the Soviet elite, especially the Central Committee, attest to the
fact that in 1987 and 1988 the *nomenklatura* rose to the challenge which
Gorbachev's *perestroika* posed to its interests. Generally speaking, however,
things have not gone well for the *nomenklatura*. In September 1988 the
nomenklatura suffered a major defeat when, in the most radical reorganization of the Soviet leadership in the last three decades, Gorbachev virtually
decimated the traditional nerve center of the party apparatus: the
Secretariat of the Central Committee. When the proverbial smoke
cleared, six holdovers from the Brezhnev era on the Politburo—Andrei
Gromyko, Mikhail Solomentsev, Petr Demichev, Vladimir Dolgikh, Ivan
Kapitonov, and Anatoly Dobrynin—had been sent into retirement. Yegor
Ligachev had been removed from his influential post of party second secretary and Vitaliy Vorotnikov had been relieved of his post as chairman of
the RSFSR Council of Ministers (premier of the RSFSR) and appointed
president of the Russian republic. Two of Gorbachev's closest associates,
Vadim Medvedev and Aleksandr Yakovlev, were promoted to supervise ideology and foreign affairs, and Gorbachev himself was elected head of
state. Most important, the powerful Secretariat was completely reorganized. Fifteen former departments were dissolved or reorganized. At least
three new departments were established and six commissions, each super-
vised by a Politburo member, were set up.[113]

The ouster of Yeltsin, moreover, turned out to be a Pyrrhic victory for
the *nomenklatura*. The elections in the spring of 1989, among other things,
enabled him to make a spectacular and unprecedented political come-
back in a competitive contest against a party-backed candidate in Moscow.
Leaving the political "resurrection" of Yeltsin aside, the outcome of the
elections added up to a resounding vote against the party apparatus. To a
far greater extent than anyone could have foreseen, the Soviet voter rose

to the occasion and made use of his newly found power "to throw the rascals out."[114]

If the revamping of the Secretariat in the fall of 1988 left the party apparatus in organizational disarray, the outcome of the elections in the spring of 1989 added psychological disorientation to the problems that *perestroika* has produced for the *nomenklatura*, thus aggravating the already serious "crisis of confidence" in the party.[115] At a Central Committee conference of party leaders in July 1989, finally, the tension and conflict between Gorbachev and the party apparatus came to a head, resulting in an unprecedented confrontation and political showdown. It was the first time since the ouster of Nikita Khrushchev in October 1964 that a general secretary (or first secretary) was openly attacked and challenged by his colleagues in the Politburo.

Although much of the criticism was oblique, it was nevertheless clear that many of the participating party leaders blamed the chaos and confusion in the party, the government, the economy, and society in general on Gorbachev's leadership, in particular his impatience and impulsiveness, and on his misconceived policies. They complained about the lack of guidance from the reorganized party Secretariat; they charged that Gorbachev's "restructuring" of the party had effectively deprived it of its control over policy formation, cadre questions, and ideology, and in so doing had emasculated it to the point where it was no longer capable of maintaining law and order in Soviet society; they attacked the excesses of *glasnost* and the lack of party control over the media, which, as Prime Minister Ryzhkov put it, had resulted in "the increasing de-ideologization of society."[116]

In pointed criticism of Gorbachev, L. F. Bobykin, the local party chief in Sverdlovsk, described the reorganization of the CPSU as "premature" and called for restrictions on Gorbachev's powers as general secretary, including the establishment of the post of a Central Committee second secretary.[117] Demands were voiced urging the Gorbachev leadership to deal more resolutely with extremist groups—"all manner of scum," which "has come to the surface on the wave of the healthy processes in society," as Ryzhkov put it in his speech. Clearly, the majority of the participants felt that it was high time to end the "open season on the party," which had turned it into "an object of total criticism" and given it a public image of "a party of mistakes and crimes." The party chief of Belgorod oblast, A. F. Ponomarev, went so far as to demand sanctions against "certain deputies" in the Congress of People's Deputies for their criticism of the party.[118]

Gorbachev was apparently unruffled by the criticism. Reacting to the despondent mood of the conference, at which only a few party leaders had expressed confidence that the party's authority could be restored, he admonished them not to panic. Responding to their criticism, however, he took a hard line and categorically refused to make any concessions. In his concluding speech, which was almost peremptory in tone, he threw the gauntlet to his critics, threatening a comprehensive party purge. Admitting that "the apparatus is needed," he emphasized that "what we need is a new apparatus."[119]

Party-State Relations

The confrontation between the party apparatus and Gorbachev at the Central Committee conference of party leaders reflected, above all, the recognition that Gorbachev has, in fact, engineered a major, indeed revolutionary, change in party-state relations. After a few hesitant forays in 1988 and in the spring of 1989, the party apparatus and the government bureaucracy, that is, the *nomenklatura*, rose in more or less open rebellion against *perestroika* and its architect. Belatedly the party *apparatchiki* and the government bureaucrats recognized that, if the restructuring of the Soviet economy and Soviet society required far-reaching political reform, including breaking up the *nomenklatura* and removing it from the levers of power, Gorbachev was more than willing to pay the price.

As Leonard Schapiro has emphasized, the relationship between the party, in particular its professional apparatus, and the administrative institutions of the state has always been a key problem in Soviet politics.[120] Deceptively simple in theory, this relationship has undergone important changes during the history of the Soviet regime and, especially in the post-Stalin period, has become a seemingly intractable conundrum in Soviet political life.[121]

Although the ideological maxim of "the leading role of the party" has always been maintained, in actual practice the preeminent role and place of the CPSU in the Soviet political system was increasingly eclipsed by the rising state bureaucracy under Stalin. The political preponderance of the party was restored by Khrushchev but was subsequently undermined and compromised by its growing involvement in the day-to-day decisions of the government and management organs. In short, the CPSU tried not only to rule but also to govern—and ended up doing a poor job of both. This, in a nutshell, is the analysis underlying Gorbachev's political reform. When addressing the Nineteeth Party Conference on the subject of political reform, he emphasized "the fundamental significance" of "the correct distribution of powers between the basic links of the political system and, above all, between the party and the state."[122]

The institutional realignment and the redefinition of political power at the center of the Soviet system clearly constituted the real issue between Gorbachev and the party apparatus at the Central Committee conference in July 1989. Ryzhkov, in particular, emerged as the spokesman for the interests of the party apparatus, claiming that the party "is in fact losing authority in the eyes of the people," is faced with "federative trends" in a number of republics that threaten not only the party but also the integrity of the state, and "is being relegated to a backseat in public life."[123]

Ryzhkov's position, needless to say, is not without foundation. As a result of what Gorbachev called "a very serious regrouping of forces in the party" at the Central Committee Plenum in April 1989, the representation of the party apparatus on the Central Committee declined from 44.5 percent in 1986 to 33.9 percent in 1989.[124] The creation of the new Congress of People's Deputies, the new executive presidency, and a much more powerful USSR Supreme Soviet, the first working parliament in Soviet history, clearly elevated Gorbachev above his colleagues in the Politburo and placed him out of their immediate reach. Operating from his new political base as the duly elected president of the Soviet Union, supported by a more powerful and independent parliament, he was the beneficiary of a degree of invulnerability and independence in dealing with the "revolt in the party apparatus" not enjoyed by any general secretary since Stalin.

When he addressed the Central Committee conference of party leaders in July 1989, Gorbachev reaffirmed his belief in "the leading role of the party" and even stated unequivocally that his program of *perestroika* cannot be realized without the active support and participation of the CPSU. But he also made it clear that it is necessary to rethink the functions and role of the party, to transform it into a democratic institution, and to extricate it from the "state of siege" in which it has found itself as the result of its involvement in the administrative command system. The shift of power from the party to the soviets, he told the conference participants, was nonnegotiable. "The old practice of party *diktat* [dictate] over the soviets at every level," he declared, "is completely obsolete" and "unacceptable." "Certain comrades," he noted, "seem to regard the transfer of power to the soviets as virtually the end of the universe. But if this is the end, comrades, it is only the end of a deformed universe."[125]

The party, Gorbachev told the conference participants, had in essence "towered over everything and controlled all processes in state, economic, and ideological life, supplanting and trampling down all and everything, issuing peremptory directives and edicts to state and economic organs and to social organizations." While in a certain sense "it was easier and simpler to lead in those conditions," he observed, "the most important thing in the party's work was lost—its role as the political vanguard of society and its living link with the masses."[126]

If the party is not to become irrelevant, Gorbachev suggested, it must itself be "an expression of the highest and most consistent form of democratism and set an example of democratic development to the whole society." It must be a party that closely collaborates with various social organizations, that is at the service of the people and under its constant democratic control, that operates within the framework of the law, and that does not have a monopoly on the truth.[127] Such a restructured, democratized, open and responsive party, in Gorbachev's view, is indispensable for the creation of a socialist rule-of-law state and a civil society.[128]

Gorbachev thus insisted on redefining both the nature of political leadership in the Soviet Union and the role and function of the party. Rejecting both the counterposition of the party to the soviets and the staticization of the party, that is, its subjugation to the state, he instead argued for "the Leninist principle of the demarcation of the functions of the party, the soviets, and the management organs." Accordingly, the party, properly restructured and democratized, is to continue as the political vanguard of society, but the exercise of power and administration are to be separated from the party and transferred to the soviets.[129]

During the summer of 1989, a substantial part of the decision-making power of the supreme party organs was apparently transferred to the Supreme Soviet. The "revolt of the party apparatus" in July 1989 was perhaps the most telling evidence that this transfer had, in fact, occurred or was under way. The KGB, the Ministry of Internal Affairs (MVD), and the Ministry of Defense, all headed by Gorbachev appointees, were placed under the control of the Supreme Soviet, chaired by Gorbachev. There is some evidence to suggest that, at least by 1988, the decision-making process may have been increasingly shifted from the party to the government. In a fascinating bit of detective work, John Loewenhardt has shown that the Politburo under Gorbachev meets less regularly and less frequently than it did under Andropov.[130]

The Defense Council, which until Gorbachev's rise to power had functioned as an executive committee of the Politburo, initially was slated to play an important role in this transfer of power from the party to the state—by assuming responsibility not only for "defense" but also for internal "security" matters, becoming transformed into an advisory body modeled after the UN Security Council. In March 1990, however, it was announced that the Defense Council would be abolished. Its past and projected functions evidently will be absorbed by the Presidential Council (*Presidentskiy sovet*)—a new fifteen-member advisory body appointed by Gorbachev as part of the new executive presidency established in 1990.

Along with the spring 1990 abolition of Article 6 of the constitution, guaranteeing the political monopoly of the CPSU, these are, indeed, developments of momentous significance. Given the transitional nature of the Soviet political system today, it is likely that there will be further changes in party-state relations. In spite of the dramatic shift of power from the party to the soviets that Gorbachev has engineered as part of his political reforms, he, like Ligachev and Ryzhkov, one suspects, recognizes that, imperfect as it is, the party is at present the only institution in Soviet society potentially capable of containing the centrifugal forces that threaten to destroy the Soviet federation—assuming they can in fact be contained. The key question is: Can Gorbachev transform the CPSU into an effective instrument of change and reform?

Ideology, Nationality, and Foreign Policy

Three other areas of importance in any consideration of political reform in the Soviet Union are ideology, the nationality problem, and foreign policy. While they cannot be addressed here at any length, they deserve at least to be mentioned in order to round out our discussion of political reform.

While *perestroika* was slow in penetrating the sphere of ideology, there is ample evidence that this bastion of conservatism, too, is now under siege. Long-standing ideological doctrines and tenets central to Marxism-Leninism have not only been attacked by writers, economists, historians, and journalists, but also by members of the top Soviet leadership. Clearly referring to Marx and Lenin, Aleksandr Yakovlev has categorically rejected "the idea of violence as the midwife of history" and "the idea of the power of dictatorship relying directly on violence" as obsolete.[131] Eduard Shevardnadze has stressed that "general human values" are "more important than class interests."[132] The doctrine of the "class struggle" has been quietly abandoned—along with the Brezhnev Doctrine and the principle of agricultural collectivization. Such sacrosanct pillars of Marxism-Leninism as state and public ownership in agriculture and industry, central planning, and even "the leading role of the party" have increasingly come under attack. Gorbachev himself has admitted that entirely new thought categories are necessary for the definition of the concept of "socialism."[133]

Nearly five years into the Gorbachev administration, nationalities policy remains a seemingly insoluble conundrum in Soviet politics. Postponed several times, a special plenum of the CPSU Central Committee at last addressed this most difficult and explosive problem in the fall of 1989.[134] Predictably, this meeting failed to come to grips with the underlying issues, which include the aspirations of the non-Russian and Russian nationalities for sovereignty or greater autonomy; open and violent inter-ethnic conflict; religious and cultural freedom; social, economic, and political equality; the history and nature of the Soviet federation; center-periphery relations; and the future structure of the Soviet state. While the CPSU platform on Soviet nationalities policy referred to the current "forms of national-state structure" as "ossified" and not allowing full "consideration of new needs and exploitation of new possibilities in this important sphere of social life," it also rejected any basic structural change of the Soviet federation. The current formula is a strong center and strong republics. But as Viktor Afanasyev, the former editor of *Pravda*, has pointed out, this formula has yet to be defined and does not begin to solve the thorny problem of the division of power between the center and the periphery.[135] In the meantime, the basic problem remains, namely, to find a policy that effectively addresses the grievances of the non-Russian nationalities and "the Russian question" without weakening the cohesion of the Soviet state and exacerbating inter-ethnic conflict—a policy, moreover, that takes into account the ongoing process of federalization. Such a policy is urgently needed in view of the growing disparity in pace between the disintegration of the old (Stalinist) order and the emergence of a new and restructured Soviet system.

In foreign policy, by contrast, Gorbachev's *perestroika* has resulted in a veritable revolution. The "new thinking" in Moscow has led to a fundamental change and dramatic improvement in East-West relations, the abandonment of the Brezhnev Doctrine and the subsequent disintegration of communist regimes everywhere in Eastern Europe, and a general policy of disengagement by the Soviet Union. Clearly, under Gorbachev there have been many signs that the Soviet Union is retreating from its traditional Marxist-Leninist approach to foreign policy. No longer is foreign policy perceived as class struggle on an international scale, as the exploitation of the differences among capitalist states; it is also seen as a function of growing worldwide interdependence. There has been a notable shift in emphasis from military power to political means as the primary basis of national security. Indeed, Soviet diplomacy under Gorbachev may well represent the most fundamental change in Soviet foreign policy since 1917.

Conclusion

The above analysis suggests that many of the key ideas underlying the reform program of Gorbachev were foreshadowed in the Leningrad Manifesto of 1985 and shows that the architect of *perestroika* is a politician who has become radicalized while in office. It further argues that the radical policy agenda known as *perestroika* is not only the product of the leadership of Gorbachev, but also the result of a number of reform impulses and social forces that have their antecedents in the Khrushchev period.

The analysis presented here also suggests that the main directions and parameters of *perestroika* have not been defined by an integral reform concept or strategy, but are the product of a good deal of improvisation and experimentation in response to the multidimensional crisis of the Soviet Union. The widening critique of Stalin and Stalinism and the cultural thaw (*glasnost*) have played key roles in creating a new and different climate for the discussion of public issues, leading to a more sophisticated analysis of the country's problems and the consideration of a wider range of alternative solutions. Unlike past reformers in Russian and Soviet history, Gorbachev basically assumes that the level of education of the population has not only outpaced the political structures and beliefs of the Stalin era but has rendered them obsolete.

Finally, the above analysis suggests that the centerpiece of Gorbachev's political reform thus far is a dramatic change in party-state relations, involving a basic shift of power from the party to the state, in particular to the Supreme Soviet. Central to Gorbachev's endeavor to bring about socioeconomic, political, and cultural reform has been a massive assault on the *nomenklatura* and an emphasis on the importance of law. While legal reform is still in the beginning stages, it has clearly emerged as an important institutional basis for the multidimensional aspects of *perestroika*.

NOTES

1. Martin Walker, "Kremlin Radicals Seek Reform: Secret Manifesto Calls for Freedom of Speech," *Guardian*, 22 July 1986, pp. 1, 19-20. I am indebted to the National Council for Soviet and East European Research, Washington, D.C., for making the Russian text of the Manifesto (cited subsequently as *AS* No. 5724) available to me.

2. *AS* No. 5724, pp. 1, 2.

3. Ibid., p. 3.

4. Ibid., pp. 3, 4.

5. Ibid., p. 12.

6. Ibid., pp. 14-17.

7. Ibid., pp. 17-20.

8. Ibid., p. 21. The Manifesto here is citing a letter written by Lenin on March 23, 1922, to V. M. Molotov, with instructions for the preparation of the Political Report of the Central Committee to the Eleventh Party Congress. See V. I. Lenin, *Polnoe sobranie sochinenii* (Moscow: Izdatel'stvo politicheskoi literatury, 1975), vol. 45, p. 61.

9. Martin Walker, "The Party Men Who Looked West and Saw the Warning," *Guardian*, 22 July 1986, p. 19.

10. See Philip Taubman's interview with Abel Aganbegyan, "Architect of Soviet Change," *New York Times*, 8 July 1987, p. D1.

11. See Zhores A. Medvedev, *Gorbachev* (New York: W. W. Norton, 1986), p. 244.

12. Timothy J. Colton, *The Dilemma of Reform in the Soviet Union* (New York: Council on Foreign Relations, 1986), p. 132.

13. Martin McCauley, ed., *The Soviet Union under Gorbachev* (New York: St. Martin's Press, 1987), p. 35.

14. Seweryn Bialer and Joan Afferica, "The Genesis of Gorbachev's World," *Foreign Affairs*, vol. 64, no. 3 (1986), p. 620.
15. On this point, see Rolf H. W. Theen, "Reform Conceptions in China and the Soviet Union," *World & I*, vol. 3, no. 7 (July 1988), pp. 570ff.
16. *Pravda*, 26 February 1986, p. 5.
17. Bialer and Afferica, "Genesis of Gorbachev's World," p. 612.
18. Walker, "The Party Men Who Looked West," p. 19.
19. See the account of Gorbachev's interview with the editors of *"L'Unita,"* in *Pravda*, 20 May 1987, p. 1.
20. A. Yakovlev, "Dostizhenie kachestvennogo novogo sostoianiia sovetskogo obshchestva i obshchestvennye nauki," *Kommunist*, no. 8 (May 1987), p. 4.
21. Timothy J. Colton, "Gorbachev and the Politics of System Renewal," in Seweryn Bialer and Michael Mandelbaum, eds., *Gorbachev's Russia and American Foreign Policy* (Boulder, CO: Westview Press, 1988), p. 157.
22. On this point, see Rolf H. W. Theen, "Perestroika vs. Reform: The Radicalization of Gorbachev," *World & I*, vol. 4, no. 3 (March 1989), pp. 511-37.
23. *Pravda*, 2 August 1986, p. 1. The literal meaning of the Russian word *perestroika* (or *perestroyka*) is "restructuring." For a more detailed discussion of this concept, see Theen, "Perestroika vs. Reform," pp. 515ff.
24. *Pravda*, 2 October 1986, p. 1.
25. *Pravda*, 28 January 1987, pp. 1ff. For an English translation of this speech, see Mikhail Gorbachev, *Reorganization and the Party's Personnel Policy* (Moscow: Novosti Press Agency Publishing House, 1987).
26. For an argument that the Soviet Union today meets most, if not all, of the criteria of a "revolutionary situation" set forth by Lenin in 1915, see Theen, "Perestroika vs. Reform," pp. 536-37.
27. Mikhail Gorbachev, *Perestroika: New Thinking for Our Country and the World* (New York: Harper & Row, 1987), pp. 51-52.
28. *Pravda*, 20 May 1987, p. 1.
29. Yakovlev, "Dostizhenie kachestvennogo novogo sostoianiia sovetskogo obshchestva," p.4.
30. On the Khrushchev era, see Carl A. Linden, *Khrushchev and the Soviet Leadership, 1957-1964* (Baltimore, MD: The Johns Hopkins University Press, 1967).
31. Colton, *Dilemma of Reform in the Soviet Union*, rev. and exp. ed., pp. 11ff.
32. This principle goes back to Lenin, who insisted that "not a single important organizational or administrative question is decided by a single state institution in our republic without the guiding directions of the Central Committee of the party." The post-revolutionary dictatorship, he explained, "is exercised by the proletariat organized in the soviets; the proletariat is guided by the Communist Party of Bolsheviks." See Lenin, *Polnoe sobranie sochinenii*, pp. 30-31.
33. Robert Sharlet, *The New Soviet Constitution of 1977* (Brunswick, OH: King's Court Communications, Inc., 1978), pp. 77-78.
34. *Pravda*, 18 June 1977. The preamble of the constitution also observes that "the leading role of the Communist Party—the vanguard of all the people—has grown." (See Sharlet, *New Soviet Constitution of 1977*, p. 74).
35. *Pravda*, 5 October 1977.
36. For the text of the resolution, see Grey Hodnett, ed., *Resolutions and Decisions of the Communist Party of the Soviet Union. Vol. 4: The Khrushchev Years, 1953-1964* (Toronto: University of Toronto Press, 1974), pp. 73-81.
37. See Ronald J. Hill, "Party-State Relations and Soviet Political Development," *British*

Journal of Political Science, April 1980, pp. 150 ff.

38. Gorbachev, *Perestroika*, p. 112.

39. For Gorbachev's speeches, see Mikhail Gorbachev, *Izbrannye rechi i stat'i* (Moscow: Izdatel'stvo politicheskoi literatury, 1987-1988), 5 vols.

40. Moshe Lewin, *Political Undercurrents in Soviet Economic Debates* (London: Pluto Press, 1975), p. 190.

41. Ronald J. Hill, *Soviet Politics, Political Science and Reform* (Oxford and New York: Martin Robertson/M. E. Sharpe, Inc., 1980), p. 7.

42. See Rolf H. W. Theen, "Political Science in the USSR: 'To Be, Or Not to Be.' Some Reflections on the Implications of a Recent Soviet Critique of American Political Science," *World Politics*, vol. 23, no. 4 (July 1971), pp. 684-701, and, by the same author, "Political Science in the USSR," *Problems of Communism*, vol. 21, no. 3 (May-June 1972), pp. 64-70.

43. For a discussion of this literature, see Rolf H. W. Theen, "Current Reform Thinking in the Soviet Union: Official, Academic and Samizdat." Paper presented to the Kennan Institute for Advanced Russian Studies, Woodrow Wilson International Center for Scholars, Washington, D.C., 10 September 1986.

44. For example Academician Abel Aganbegyan, chairman of the Commission for Study of Productive Forces and deputy chairman of the Council of Labor and Social Questions; Leonid Abalkin, director of the Institute of Economics, Department of Economics, USSR Academy of Sciences; Boris Kurashvili, sector head of the Institute of State and Law under the USSR Academy of Sciences; Fedor Burlatsky, chief of the Philosophy Department of the Social Sciences Institute in Moscow; Academician Tatyana Zaslavskaya, department head, Institute of Economics and Organization of Industrial Production, Siberian Department, USSR Academy of Sciences, and president of the Soviet Sociological Association. Georgiy Shakhnazarov, chairman of the Soviet Association of Political (State) Studies, was appointed to the Central Committee Secretariat as chairman of the Department for Liaison with Communist Parties of Socialist Countries in October 1986 and became a personal aide to Gorbachev in March 1988; and Evgeny Primakov, the director of the Institute for World Economics and International Relations under the USSR Academy of Sciences, a member of Gorbachev's inner circle, was elected to candidate membership in the Central Committee in March 1986 and was promoted to candidate membership in the Politburo in September 1989. See Central Intelligence Agency, Directorate of Intelligence, *Directory of Soviet Officials: National Organizations* (Washington, D. C., 1989), pp. 4, 18; Sergei Voronitsyn, *A Directory of Prominent Soviet Economists, Sociologists, and Demographers by Institutional Affiliation* (Munich: Radio Liberty, 1987), pp. 4, 6, 10; *New York Times*, 21 September 1989, p. 6.

45. See Alexander Rahr, "Gorbachev's Personal Staff," *Radio Liberty Research Bulletin*, RL 216/88 (30 May 1988).

46. *Pravda*, 9 May 1985.

47. Gorbachev, *Izbrannye rechi i stat'i*, vol. 3, p. 162.

48. *AS* No. 5785.

49. *Pravda*, 19 February 1988, p. 1.

50. See Christian Schmidt-Häuer and Maria Huber, *Russlands zweite Revolution: Chancen und Risiken der Reformpolitik Gorbatschows* (Munich: Piper, 1987).

51. *Pravda*, 19 February 1988, p. 1.

52. *Materialy plenuma Tsentral'nogo Komiteta KPSS 27-28 ianvaria 1987 goda* (Moscow: Politizdat, 1987), p. 8.

53. *Pravda*, 6 February 1988, p. 1.

54. *Pravda*, 10 July 1988, p. 1.

55. *Literaturnaia Rossiia*, no. 24 (17 June 1988), pp. 2-3, 8-9.

56. See Lev Trotsky, "Novyi kurs," *Molodoi kommunist*, no. 8, 1989, pp. 51-58.

57. Gorbachev, *Izbrannye rechi i stat'i*, vol. 5, p. 217.

58. See "Gorbachev in Siberia," *Radio Liberty Research Bulletin*, RL 412/88, p. 5.

59. *Pravda*, 14 February 1987, pp. 1-2.

60. Dudintsev's novel appeared in *Neva*, nos. 1 and 2 (January and February 1987). Akhmatova's poem was published in *Oktiabr*, no. 3 (March 1987); Shatrov's play was published in *Novyi mir*, no. 4 (April 1987); Rybakov's novel was serialized in *Druzhba narodov*, beginning in April 1987.

61. See *Oktiabr*, no. 7, 1988 (back cover); *Literaturnaia gazeta*, no. 30, 1988, p. 7.

62. For samples of Gorbachev's contributions to the Lenin cult, see his book *Perestroika*, passim.

63. The novel appeared in *Oktiabr*, no. 6 (June 1989). For the "commentary," see G. Vodolazov, "Lenin i Stalin," in ibid., pp. 3-29. Citations from p. 3.

64. See the interview of Zalygin by David Remnick, in *Washington Post*, 21 April 1989, pp. C1 and C9. For a detailed account of the episode, see John B. Dunlop, "Solzhenitsyn Begins to Emerge from the Political Void," *Report on the USSR*, vol. 1, no. 36, pp. 1-6, and Douglas Smith, "Reappraisal of Solzhenitsyn in the USSR," ibid., pp. 6-9.

65. See *Novyi mir*, no. 7 (July 1989), and no. 9 (September 1989).

66. Bill Keller, "The Life of a Soviet Censor," *New York Times*, 18 July 1989, p. A6.

67. See the interview with Sergei Zalygin in *Moskovskie novosti*, no. 29 (1989), p. 13.

68. See Vasiliy Selyunin, "Istoki," *Novyi mir*, no. 5 (May 1988), pp. 162-89. Three years earlier (in *Novyi mir*, no. 8, 1985), Selyunin had trained his guns on Soviet labor policy, questioning the meaning of "no unemployment" in the Soviet Union "if we only half-work." He also co-authored a devastating critique of the USSR Central Statistical Administration (*Novyi mir*, no. 2, 1987). In an article published in *Literaturnaia gazeta* (no. 44, 1987), he claimed that the Soviet welfare state has turned Soviet citizens into "social dependents" incapable of managing their own affairs. In 1988, Selyunin called into question Gorbachev's economic strategy, arguing that he had to make a choice between increasing economic growth (*uskorenie*) and restructuring the economy (*perestroika*). See "Tempy rosta na vesakh potrebleniia," *Sotsialisticheskaia industriia*, 5 January 1988, pp. 2-3.

69. *Izvestiia TsK KPSS*, no. 2, 1989, pp. 209-87; no. 3, 1989, pp. 128-70.

70. *Literaturnaia gazeta*, 2 July 1986, as cited in Robert C. Tucker, "Gorbachev and the Fight for Soviet Reform," *World Policy Journal*, Spring 1987, pp. 188-89.

71. See the interview of N. I. Efimov, first deputy editor of *Izvestiia*, in *La Repubblica*, 21 June 1986. Cited in Thane Gustafson, "The Crisis of the Soviet System of Power and Mikhail Gorbachev's Political Strategy," in Bialer and Mandelbaum, *Gorbachev's Russia and American Foreign Policy*, p. 203.

72. *Izvestiia*, 22 March 1988.

73. At the outset, Gorbachev had spoken of "crisis phenomena" only in reference to the Brezhnev era. (See, for example, *Materialy plenuma Tsentral'nogo komiteta KPSS 27-28 ianvaria 1987 goda*, p. 8). Six months later, he acknowledged that the "pre-crisis" extended into his own administration (*Pravda*, 26 June 1987).

74. See the figures cited by A. N. Komin, first deputy chairman of the USSR State Committee on Prices, in *Sovetskaia Rossiia*, 18 October 1987, p. 3.

75. *Pravda*, 19 February 1988, p. 1.

76. See, for example, Arkadii Vaksberg, "Komu eto nuzhno?" *Literaturnaia gazeta*, no. 4, (21 January 1987), p. 12.

77. See "V pol'zu spravedlivosti," *Literaturnaia gazeta*, no. 47 (19 November 1986), p. 13.

78. See V. Z. Rogovin, "Sotsial'naia spravedlivost' i sotsialisticheskoe raspredelenie zhiznennykh blag," *Voprosy filosofii*, no. 9, 1986, pp. 3-20. Citation from p. 8.

79. T. Zaslavskaya, "Chelovecheskiy faktor razvitiia ekonomiki i sotsial'naia spravedlivost'," *Kommunist*, no. 13, 1986, pp. 61-73.

80. Vaksberg, "Komu eto nuzhno," p. 12.

81. Yakovlev, "Dostizhenie...," p. 16.

82. Ibid., p. 17.

83. Julia Wishnevsky, "Politburo Calls for Restructuring of Legal Bodies," *Radio Liberty Research Bulletin*, RL 386/86 (9 October 1986), p. 1.

84. This formulation was used at the Nineteenth Party Conference. See Gorbachev's opening speech and the resolution on legal reform, in *XIX Vsesoyznaia konferentsiia Kommunisticheskoi Partii Sovetskogo Soiuza. Stenograficheskiy otchet* (Moscow: Politizdat, 1988), vol. 1, p. 68, and vol. 2, p. 174.

85. See the interview of Ivan Kazmin and Albert Pigolkin, legal experts from the All-Union Research Institute of Soviet Legislation, in *Izvestiia*, 17 October 1986.

86. See *Vedomosti Verkhovnogo Soveta SSSR*, no. 37, 1986.

87. See the collection of laws and decrees in *O korennoi perestroike upravleniia ekonomiki. Sbornik dokumentov* (Moscow: Politizdat, 1987).

88. For the text of the law, see *Pravda*, 2 July 1987, p. 3. The law went into effect on 1 January 1988.

89. *Izvestiia*, 24 May 1987. For a discussion of the referendum issue, see Sergei Voronitsyn, "What Happened to the Draft Law on Referendum?" *Radio Liberty Research Bulletin*, RL 266/87 (13 July 1987).

90. Radio Moscow, 2 February 1988, as cited in Julia Wishnevsky, "Soviet Government Refuses to Entertain Anonymous Denunciations," *Radio Liberty Research Bulletin*, RL52/88 (3 February 1988), p. 1.

91. *Literaturnaia gazeta*, no. 23, 8 June 1988.

92. For the text of the resolution, see *XIX Konferentsiia...*, vol. 2, pp. 172-75.

93. Statement by Anatoliy Lukyanov, then a secretary of the CPSU Central Committee, at a conference on legal reform. (See *Moscow News*, no. 26, 1987, p. 4). Lukyanov studied law at Moscow State University together with Gorbachev and was appointed first deputy chairman of the Presidium of the USSR Supreme Soviet (vice-president of the USSR) in October 1988.

94. The term *nomenklatura* has come to mean both the "ruling class" and the "elite recruitment system" in the Soviet Union. See Michael Voslensky, *Nomenklatura: The Soviet Ruling Class. An Insider's Report* (Garden City, NY: Doubleday & Company, 1984); Bohdan Harasymiw, *Political Elite Recruitment in the Soviet Union* (New York: St. Martin's Press, 1984); T. H. Rigby and B. Harasymiw, eds., *Leadership Selection and Patron-Client Relations in the USSR and Yugoslavia* (London: George Allen & Unwin, 1983).

95. On the genesis of the *nomenklatura* system, see T. H. Rigby, "The Origins of the Nomenklatura System," in Inge Auerbach, eds., *Felder und Vorfelder russischer Geschichte. Studien zu Ehren von Peter Scheibert.* (Freibach: Rombach Verlag, 1985), pp. 241-54.

96. Thane Gustafson and Dawn Mann, "Gorbachev's Next Gamble," *Problems of Communism*, vol. 36, no. 4 (July-August 1987), p. 31. Percentages calculated.

97. Ibid., p. 34. Percentages calculated.

98. G. Razumovskiy, "Partiinuiu rabotu—na uroven' zadach perestroiki," *Partiinaia zhizn'*, no. 12 (June 1987), p. 12.

99. *Pravda*, 11 May 1988, p. 1. See also "Printsipy kadrovoi politiki partii v usloviiakh perestroiki," *Partiinaia zhizn'*, no. 11 (June 1988), p. 12.

100. See *Materialy Plenuma Tsentral'nogo Komiteta KPSS 27-28 ianvaria 1987 goda*, passim. English translation: Michael Gorbachev, *Reorganization and the Party's Personnel Policy* (Moscow: Novosti Press Publishing House, 1987).

101. *Materialy Plenuma Tsentral'nogo Komiteta KPSS 27-28 ianvaria 1987 goda*, pp. 31, 41.

102. Razumovsky, "Partiinuiu rabotu—na uroven' zadach perestroiki," p. 12.

103. I have borrowed this formulation from Professor S. Dzarov, who applied it to the party as a whole (*Sotsialisticheskaia industriia*, 22 May 1988).

104. See Anatoly Akhutin, "Communicate and Take Responsibility," *Moscow News*, no.30 (24 July 1988), p. 3.

105. T. Samolis, "Oshishchenie: Otkrovennyi razgovor," *Pravda*, 13 February 1986, p. 3.

106. See the speeches of Gorbachev, Yeltsin, Ligachev, Gromyko, etc., at the Congress (*Pravda*, 26-28 February 1986).

107. Even Ligachev agreed that there had been a "lack of control" of cadres, complained about "parochialism and localism" in the party, and called for the rethinking of "some aspects of our personnel policy." See *Pravda*, 27 February 1986, pp. 2-3, and 28 February, p. 4.

108. *Materialy Plenuma Tsentral'nogo Komiteta KPSS 27-28 ianvaria 1987 goda*, pp. 12, 13.

109. *Pravda*, 27 May 1988, p. 2. For an analysis of the conference, see Rolf H. W. Theen, "The Nineteenth All-Union Conference of the Communist Party of the Soviet Union: A Milestone in the Development of Perestroika," *World & I*, vol. 3, no. 10 (October 1988), pp. 657-83.

110. *Pravda*, 29 June 1988, pp. 6, 4.

111. For the text of the resolution, see *Pravda*, 5 July 1988, p. 2.

112. See Kevin Devlin, "Soviet Journalist Describes El'tsin's Struggle Against Party 'Mafia,'" *Radio Liberty Research Bulletin*, RL 206/88 (20 May 1988); Timothy J. Colton, "Moscow Politics and the El'tsin Affair," *The Harriman Institute Forum*, vol. 1, no. 6 (June 1988).

113. The new departments are the Agrarian Department, the Ideological Department, the Socioeconomic Department, and the State and Legal Department. The continuing departments are: Administration of Affairs, Defense Industry, General, International, Organizational Party Work (renamed Party Building and Cadre Work). The commissions are: Agrarian Policy, Ideological, International Policy, Legal Policy, Party Building and Cadre Policy, and Socioeconomic Policy.

114. See Rolf H. W. Theen, "Democracy Soviet Style," *World & I*, vol. 4, no. 6 (June 1989), pp. 98-103.

115. For a discussion of the "crisis of confidence" in the CPSU, see Rolf H. W. Theen, "Party-State Relations under Gorbachev: From Partocracy to 'Party' State?" in Mel Gurtov, ed., *The Transformation of Socialism: Perestroika and Reform in the Soviet Union and China* (Boulder, CO: Westview Press, 1990), pp. 73ff.

116. *Pravda*, 21 July 1989, pp. 1-4. Ryzhkov's criticism is found on p. 3.

117. Ibid., p. 2.

118. Ibid., pp. 2, 3.

119. *Pravda*, 19 July 1989, p. 3.

120. Leonard Schapiro, "The Party and the State," *Survey*, no. 38 (1961), p. 111. See also V. I. Lenin, *KPSS o rabote partiinogo i gosudarstvennogo apparata* (Moscow: Izdatel'stvo politicheskoi literatury, 1976).

121. For a discussion of the historical evolution of party-state relations, see Theen, "Party-State Relations under Gorbachev."

122. *Pravda*, 29 June 1988, p. 4.

123. *Pravda*, 21 July 1989, p. 3.

124. See Tass, 25 April 1989; Elizabeth Teague, "Fall in Representation of Party Apparatus in

CPSU Central Committee," Radio Liberty, *Report on the USSR*, vol. 1, no. 19, 1989, p. 4.
125. *Pravda*, 19 July 1989, p. 3.
126. Ibid., pp. 1-3. Citation from p. 1.
127. Ibid., pp. 1, 2.
128. Ibid., p. 3.
129. Ibid., p. 2.
130. John Loewenhardt, "Politburo Zasedaet: Reported and Secret Meetings of the Politburo of the CPSU," *Nordic Journal of Soviet & East European Studies*, vol. 5, no. 2 (1988).
131. *Sovetskaia kul'tura*, 15 July 1989.
132. *Mezhdunarodnaia zhizn'*, no. 9, 1988.
133. For a recent synthesis of Gorbachev's thinking, see M. Gorbachev, "Sotsialisticheskaia ideia i revoliutsionnaia perestroika," *Pravda*, 26 November 1989, pp. 1-3.
134. *Pravda*, 20-22 September, 1989. For the CPSU's draft "platform" on nationalities policy, see ibid., 17 August 1989, pp. 1-2.
135. *Izvestiia TsK KPSS*, no. 6 (June 1989), p. 81.

3. THE SOVIET ECONOMY IN TRANSITION: A RESURGENCE OF REFORM

Susan Linz

After five years of experimenting with a variety of "radical" reform proposals, Soviet efforts to restructure their economy *(perestroika)* to increase the
quantity and improve the quality of goods and services produced
appeared to shift into high gear. At the end of the eighties, Gorbachev's
top economic advisers were describing the Soviet Union as facing a severe
economic crisis — of a magnitude similar to the economic crisis in the
United States during the Great Depression. At the first meeting of the new
Presidential Council on March 27, 1990, perhaps to avoid workers' strikes
and to dissuade individual republics from pressing for immediate independence, Mikhail Gorbachev proposed a batch of thirty-some draft laws
(zakony) and decrees *(postanovleniya)* which had the potential to stimulate
Soviet economic development.[1] The "new and improved" economic
reform package coordinates proposed changes in different sectors of the
Soviet economy, and, more importantly, addressed virtually all the main
economic problems facing the Soviet Union today.

Of the proposed laws, four stood out: one moves on the transition to a
market economy, a second called for a reform of the price formation
mechanism, a third affected the banking system — imposing a "hard bud-

get constraint" on firms and financial institutions, and finally, a fourth proposes a framework for 100 percent foreign ownership of enterprises in the USSR. The decrees, among other things, called for the establishment of cost-of-living adjustments to soften the impact of the inevitable price increases on low and medium income families. These elements were also included in the reform initiatives announced in October 1990.[2] While this list is not complete, it does give a flavor of the type of economic changes being proposed to speed up the transition to a more decentralized economic structure. More importantly, the proposals address the elements of the Soviet economy which need to change in order to allow for the transition to a market-oriented environment. Such elements as price reform and private property ownership have never before been part of a reform initiative. Introducing these two elements will effectively eliminate centralized control over the majority of production and distribution decisions and thus have a significant impact on the distribution of income and power in the USSR. The absence of these two elements in previous reform programs undermined their prospects for success.

Will *perestroika* succeed? If one measures its success as a function of increased production and improved quality, and if the time frame includes at least a decade, *perestroika* will no doubt be counted as successful. As Soviet leaders appear to have recognized, the success of *perestroika* depends upon greater enterprise autonomy and thus reductions in the size and power of the economic bureaucracy, more effective input utilization, an increase in the non-state sector of the economy, and an expanded share of exportable manufactured goods. This paper highlights the elements of *perestroika* that will contribute to its success. In particular, it focuses on how *perestroika* will convert the Soviet economy from a *sellers' market,* which coincides with persistent and pervasive shortages, to a *buyers' market,* one responsive to consumer demand.

Perestroika Shifts into High Gear

It appears that for the first time since the New Economic Policy of the 1920s, Soviet leaders are actively establishing the comprehensive legal, economic, political, and social foundations required to facilitate the transition from a centrally planned economy to an economy dominated by market allocation. Such a transition effectively moves the loci of decision-making over a wide range of goods and services from political leaders and bureaucrats to individual consumers and producers. That is, centralized control over production targets, purchasing, and price formation is to be abolished for most industrial sectors and for construction. Firms will be granted extensive rights to freely seek their own customers and suppliers and to trade at contract-negotiated prices. Under the proposed new economic system, ministry control over enterprise operations will diminish and ministry evaluation of enterprise performance will disappear. Denationalization *(razgosudarstvlenie)* of state property is to occur through leasing of production facilities and the sale of shares. Restrictions on small-scale private enterprise are to be lifted. Work collectives are to become the effective owners of industry.

The goal of the hybrid "planned market economy" proposed in the reform initiatives in 1990 is identical to that stated in conjunction with all previous reform efforts over the past three decades: improve the technological level of Soviet industry and increase efficiency in the use of productive inputs in order to expand the supply of goods available to Soviet consumers and to enable Soviet manufacturers to compete more effectively in world markets. That all previous reform efforts have failed to increase the quantity and improve the quality of production is evident in even a cursory glance at current economic conditions in the USSR.

Why the sudden rush to move full-speed ahead with the most controversial and thus most difficult elements of economic reform? Prior to the meeting of the Presidential Council, Leonid Abalkin, deputy prime minister for economic reform and one of Gorbachev's main economic advisers, called for an immediate change in the Soviet economic structure to promote the transition from the centrally administered economy to a decentralized but regulated market-oriented economy. Abalkin stressed the necessity of introducing by the end of 1990 measures originally planned for gradual adoption in 1992–1993, pointing out that further delays in introducing the required changes in the Soviet economic system would only postpone the inevitable and increase costs of transition.[3] This observation could just as easily been made two to three years earlier. More than likely, dramatic political developments in the first half of 1990 — defeats suffered by Communist party functionaries in local elections in March, independent economic policies being pursued in Baltic and Transcausasian republics — have caused Soviet leaders to see the dilemma posed by working within a decentralized political decision-making structure to successfully put in place policies that will inevitably, if only temporarily, disrupt the economic well-being of a large segment of the population. Without a significant change in both the political and economic decision-making structures, however, it is unlikely that economic conditions will improve.

Current Economic Conditions: A Crisis Situation?

When asked in 1989 if they thought the coming year would be better, worse, or the same, more than one-third of those polled in the USSR expected the coming year to be better, 13 percent thought it would stay about the same and 6 percent thought it would get worse. In 1990, *Ogonek* published the results of a follow-up survey.[3] This time only 4 percent of those polled expected the coming year to be better, 22 percent thought it would stay the same, and 14 percent anticipated the situation worsening.

Why the pessimism among the Soviet population? Economic conditions do not appear to have improved with *perestroika*. In many aspects, economic conditions may even have deteriorated more rapidly under Gorbachev's reforms than under previous reform efforts. For the past three decades, Soviet leaders have faced declining output growth rates, pervasive shortages, poor quality production, and the inefficient use of resources. Gorbachev has been facing, in addition, macroeconomic instability in the form of rising inflation, growing unemployment, and substantial domestic and foreign trade budgetary deficits. The situation is further compounded by popular demands to deal with serious environmental issues. Thus Gorbachev is struggling to adopt a reform package that will overcome microeconomic inefficiency combined with macroeconomic instability, and at the same time resolve the difficult choice between production and pollution, both of which appear to be generating serious health problems for a major segment of the population. The following discussion highlights the scope of these problems.

Declining Growth

The Soviets have traditionally used *net material product* (NMP) as the official measure of aggregate economic activity, which, unlike gross national product (GNP), excludes most services. While NMP is consistent with Marxian analysis, it nonetheless underestimates the actual size of the economy. Official records report a growth in NMP of 8 percent per year for the second half of the sixties, 4 percent per year in the late seventies, and less than 3 percent per year in the eighties. Recent estimates by Soviet economists suggest that economic growth stopped in the mid 1970s.[5] Given reports on growth in the defense sector, this would mean that the non-military sector of the economy has in fact been shrinking for over a decade.

While aptly characterized as trudging on a treadmill of economic reforms for the past three decades, Soviet leaders have failed to reverse or even slow down declining output growth trends.[6] To date, *perestroika* has failed to have a significant impact on economic performance. Figures released by the State Committee for Statistics (Goskomstat) show decreased aggregate output for 1989 and the first quarter of 1990, despite efforts to increase supply by expanding cooperative and private sector activities over the past 3 years.[7] Sectors where production gains were reported in 1989–90 were insufficient to boost overall production figures. Part of the reason is that economic performance in 1990 for the first time was measured in terms of *volume* of production rather than *value* of production as has been the practice in the past. Using production *volume* statistics precludes the possibility of using price increases to create the type of artificial increase in performance made possible when production *value* statistics are used.

Declines in industrial production in 1989 and 1990 may be attributed to disruptions in work (4.5 million workdays lost through strikes in January 1990 alone, compared with 7 million for the whole of 1989),[8] a reduction in defense production which was not offset by increased civilian production, and the halting of production in sectors identified as having environmentally harmful consequences (more than one thousand major production lines were closed by local soviets in 1989 in response to popular pressure).[9] Output in heavy industry enterprises, traditionally a high-priority sector in the Soviet economy, fell by some 3 percent in 1989–90 in comparison with previous years.

Although the data suggest that consumer goods production rose in 1989 and early 1990 — more electronic and durable goods were produced as defense plants were converted to civilian production — the overall trend of declining growth rates and deteriorating economic performance had not been arrested by the numerous reform programs implemented in the first five years of Gorbachev's tenure. Housing construction has been particularly problematic.[10]

Several basic elements in the Soviet economy associated with the supply of and demand for energy, labor, and capital have contributed to the relatively poor performance in the past and these elements have yet to be significantly changed by *perestroika*. In the energy sector, oil and coal production fell in 1988 and 1989, in part because of strikes and in part because of transport bottlenecks. The oil refineries of Bashkiria, for instance, were either shut down or at nearly zero-level production, yet farm machinery elsewhere in the USSR stood idle due to a lack of fuel. Refineries have the capacity to produce the required diesel fuel but transportation shortages delay deliveries to users. The energy sector is also plagued with rising exploration and extraction costs: in coal production, for example, these higher costs are associated with greater depths, thinner seams, and a higher methane content. Coal that cost 150 rubles per ton to get out of the ground in 1960, cost 800 rubles in 1985.[11] To date, higher costs have not been matched with higher prices to encourage conservation or more efficient utilization. Consequently, energy capacity has not increased as fast as demand.

Policies resulting in the inefficient use of energy also apply to the use of capital and have contributed to poor economic performance for the past several decades. Soviet industries use nearly two times as much capital per unit of output as comparable industries in the United States, in part because of artificially low capital charges and in part because of decisions by Soviet managers to self-supply necessary inputs rather than rely upon deliveries from firms specializing in the production of those requisite inputs. In the machine building industry, for example, 70 percent of the enterprises produce their own castings, 65 percent produce their own finished metal plates, 50 percent produce their own instruments rather than waiting for firms subordinate to other ministries to deliver necessary inputs.[12] Experience has shown that firms manufacturing *"defitsit"* materials supply first to other firms subordinate to the same ministry, regardless of plan directives. When supplies are scheduled to be delivered by firms subordinate to a different ministry, deliveries are rarely made in a timely manner — even in high-priority sectors. Thus, self-supply has been a rational strategy by pursued by virtually all Soviet plant managers. Such duplication and lack of specialization drives up production costs and results in an inefficient use of resources. It may also help to explain why construction projects that would be completed in two to three years in the United States take up to twelve years in the Soviet Union and why despite a fivefold increase in capital investment in agriculture between 1965 and 1988 agricultural output grew by only 20 percent.[13]

Centralized allocation and pricing policies created an environment where Soviet managers were not motivated to use capital efficiently. Nor were they motivated to upgrade or retool the capital stock in a timely manner. Capital replacement in the United States occurs at a rate of 5 percent per year; in Japan, 10 percent of the capital stock is replaced each year. By comparison, in the USSR only 2 percent of the capital stock has been replaced each year. Consequently, Soviet managers now must meet production quotas using an aging capital stock — nearly half of which has been in place for more than twenty-five years.[14]

Shortages: Persistent and Pervasive

Although the level and rate of Soviet economic growth in the past few decades has been a matter of some debate, all agree that Soviet leaders, from Khrushchev to Gorbachev, have been unable to simultaneously maintain their military commitment and fulfill their promises to improve consumer living standards. Despite recent reductions in Soviet defense expenditures, from 77.3 billion rubles in 1989 (about 9 percent of GNP) to 70.9 billion rubles in 1990, and an estimated 66.3 billion rubles in 1991, shortages of goods and services, from food to transportation, pervade everyday life in the Soviet Union.[15] Food production failed to significantly increase in response to high levels of investment each year in the agricultural sector. Indeed, unfavorable pricing policies brought about a shortfall in (above-plan) grain deliveries to the state in 1989 and 1990. Farmers elected to sell their above-plan output to cooperatives at higher (market-based) prices. Typically, state prices have not covered production costs, causing farmers to feed "surplus" grain to livestock rather than deliver it to state trading agencies.[16] While these decisions are rational from the farmers' point of view, inputs to state-sector food processing plants is not expanding at the rate necessary to stock the shelves of state-retail stores.

Perhaps the most worrisome feature of the large cash overhang is the negative impact it tends to have on work incentives. A cash overhang in excess of the value of consumer goods traded means that, theoretically, Soviet consumers need not work to earn money to make purchases — in fact, they would be better served by spending their time in queues rather than at work. Planners have responded to the cash overhang by using rationing, queues, and waiting lists for the *defitsit* goods rather than allowing prices to adjust to eliminate the shortages.

To date, Soviet leaders have been unable to change the economic environment where consumers queue endlessly for basic necessities. In fact, Soviet leaders for the past four years have contributed to the situation where "too many rubles are chasing too few goods" by printing money to finance wage increases in excess of productivity increases. In the first six months of 1989 alone, the average monthly salary of workers and salaried officials in the state sector increased 10 percent — from 215 rubles to 236 rubles per month — while overall labor productivity increased by only 2.8 percent.[17] Wage increases not supported by productivity increases, plus higher incomes earned in the cooperative sector where goods and services sell for prices three to five times higher than in state retail-stores, have contributed to a "cash overhang" estimated at an amount approximately equal to nine months' earnings of the entire state-sector workforce — an amount more than equal to the retail trade turnover in a single year.

This excess demand environment has necessitated the rationing of basic foodstuffs in several republics and the auctioning of consumer goods at individuals' workplaces. The shortage environment has also caused Soviet managers to continue to employ armies of specialized personnel *(tolkachi)* to seek out and obtain by whatever means necessary the requisite materials to fulfill production quotas.

While all members of the Soviet population agree that shortages are the main economic problem, they recognize that each year an enormous amount of resources and effort go into the production of goods that fail to meet anyone's needs. Production plans are fulfilled and bonuses received for goods that no one will voluntarily purchase. Inventories of unwanted goods fill warehouses at the same time consumers spend hours trying to purchase basic necessities. The failure to match production with user needs is especially problematic for firms that require intermediate goods with particular specifications. When specifications are not met, production is delayed until suitable adjustments are made or substitutes are found. The persistence of an environment in which supply of intermediate and consumer goods perpetually falls short of demand is frequently referred to as a *sellers' market.*

Macroeconomic Instability

Whether Gorbachev is successful in implementing a reform package that resolves the microeconomic inefficiences in production and distribution decisionmaking will depend in large part on how successful he is at reducing the macroeconomic instability in the Soviet Union. Inflationary pressures, growing deficits, and unemployment — standard problems in market-oriented economies that are addressed by a combination of monetary and fiscal policies — have worsened considerably in the USSR in the past few years. To date, the Soviet economy functions without the financial institutions necessary for coordinating a monetary and fiscal policy response. The prospect of resolving the macroeconomic instability in the absence of such institutions is rather slim.

Inflationary pressures did not begin with the Gorbachev era.[18] In fact, inflationary pressures were an important cause for the initial adoption of the centrally planned economy in the late twenties. Inflationary pressures have persisted in the Soviet economy, as in other socialist economies, in part because decisions by firms for capital and other inputs are not subject to a "hard budget constraint" that motivates managers to use resources efficiently or face bankruptcy. In part, inflationary pressures are caused by financing wage increases by printing money, rather than linking wage increases to productivity increases. This policy, combined with higher incomes earned in the cooperative sector, has contributed to a "cash overhang" in the Soviet economy estimated at 170 billion rubles in 1989.[19] Various estimates suggest that if prices were allowed to adjust, at least 70 percent of all goods sold in the USSR would double in price within a year.

Several factors relating to policies implemented under *perestroika* are contributing to growing budget deficits which are financed by borrowing (Gosbank lent 63.4 billion rubles to the government in 1989 at zero interest) and printing money, which in turn contributes to inflationary pressures in the economy. Expenditures have been increasing to cover higher pension payments, unemployment compensation, and excess (unplanned) construction and investment costs — between 1986 and 1988 the latter totaled nearly 19 billion rubles. Revenues have been falling as a consequence of declining oil prices in world markets and reduced state-sector sales of alcoholic beverages (prior to the anti-alcohol campaign, alcohol sales accounted for one-sixth of all state-retail sales).[20] These and other factors generated a budget deficit that rose from 21 billion rubles in 1985 (2.6 percent of GNP) to 100 to 120 billion rubles in 1989 (about 11 to 14 percent of GNP). While the United States deficit grew substantially during the eighties, it stayed under 5 percent of GNP.[21]

First, on the expenditure side, recognizing that a significant share of the elderly population live in conditions of poverty — 50 percent of the pensioners received payments of less than the 75 rubles per month designated as poverty level — the USSR Supreme Soviet approved a pension bill in 1989 that establishes a minimum pension payment of 70 rubles per month, which will increase pension payments made by the state by an average of 40 percent. More than 20 million former *kolkhozniki* and state workers will be affected by this legislation, at an additional cost to the state budget of some 29 billion rubles per year.[22]

Second, on the revenue side, Gorbachev's anti-alcohol campaign reduced production and therefore state revenues from the sale of alcoholic beverages. Indeed, tax revenues fell by 6.2 billion rubles in 1985-86 (about 6 percent), and, according to one Soviet economist, the revenue shortfall was covered by printing more rubles.[23] Productivity increases associated with reduced alcohol consumption do not appear to have increased output in other sectors to cover the lost revenue from the reduction in alcohol production. It is not clear whether the link between medical care costs and alcohol consumption has had a positive or negative impact on state revenues: if alcohol consumption went down when state production was reduced, medical care costs may also have declined. It may be, however, that alcohol consumption remained the same, with private sector (illegal) production maintaining the supply of alcoholic beverages.[24] Medical care costs would vary according to the relative quality of private- versus state-produced alcohol.

Revenues also fell as a consequence of the decline in oil prices, which contributed to a foreign trade deficit in 1989 of 3.3 billion rubles, the first trade deficit in fourteen years.[25]

The final element of macroeconomic instability that Gorbachev cannot ignore is the growing level of unemployment. Soviet estimates put state-sector industrial unemployment at 1.3 million people. Total unemployment estimates reach some 4 to 5 million. These figures suggest a nation-wide unemployment rate of 1.8 to 2.4 percent, although most of the unemployed are concentrated in the Central Asian republics and the Caucasus. Western estimates of unemployment range from 5.6 to 8.4 million, about 6.2 percent of the working-age population. The unemployment situation will worsen during the transition from a centrally planned to a regulated market-oriented economy as workers either are "released" from state-owned firms that go bankrupt or have different labor requirements, or voluntarily leave the state sector to look for employment opportunities in the cooperative sector.[26] "Released" workers are to be assisted by placement bureaus in finding employment in new state sector jobs.[27] Yet despite these employment bureaus and the options some workers have to move into the cooperative sector, unemployment is rising. Additional layoffs are also projected as *perestroika* streamlines the economic bureaucracy. Estimates put 12 to 16 million people in these three categories of unemployed during the transition period. Demobilized troops from Eastern Europe and the Chinese border will no doubt contribute to the problem of unemployment.

Soviet leaders see a twofold cost of unemployment. First, the loss in output that would be available if all able-bodied working-age people were fully employed. Second, unemployment is frequently associated with popular discontent. Politicians in democratic societies learned early on that popular support is more likely to come from people who have jobs and satisfactory living conditions than from those whose future is uncertain. Gorbachev faces the likelihood of strikes and other work disruptions instigated by those whose situations have worsened.

Further compounding the unemployment situation is the impact on output of regional labor shortages. In 1989, some 2.5 million vacant positions (particularly in energy-related sectors) were reported in the Far East in the RSFSR. The likelihood of growing numbers of unemployed in European Russia voluntarily going to regions experiencing labor shortages is rather slim. In the past, social and cultural factors have outweighed economic incentives in the decision not to migrate voluntarily from local regions for employment reasons. Inadequate housing and other social infrastructure elements no doubt contributed to the decision. One option for resolving the problem is to reassign demobilized troops to labor shortage regions for the duration of their conscription period, if only to work on the construction of housing, roads, sanitation facilities, and so forth.

As if these problems were not enough, Gorbachev now faces an increasingly vocal population regarding the condition of the environment. In many instances, environmental concerns form the basis for various political groups in different republics. The extent of popular concern is illustrated by the mass demonstrations in March 1990 over suspected radiation leakage at an experimental nuclear reactor in Mtskheta.[28] The Institute of Nuclear Physics of the Georgian Academy of Sciences decided to close the site, no doubt calculating that the costs of closing were minimal compared to political benefits in terms of public approval.

Environmental Problems

Glasnost has disclosed the fact that the deterioration of the physical environment in the USSR has reached crisis proportions. Given a situation characterized by a shortage of pollution cleanup equipment and inadequate technology for pollution-free production, Soviet leaders confront the difficult trade-off between production and pollution. In the pharmaceutical industry, the decision to temporarily terminate production at a single facility created an emergency situation with respect to an adequate supply of medicine. The following discussion offers a brief overview of current environmental conditions and factors contributing to the deteriorating situation.

Policies favoring rapid industrial and agricultural development have had significant consequences for the quality of the physical environment in the USSR. This is particularly evident with respect to water resources. Centralized allocation and pricing policies contributed to the inefficient use of water, generating a situation where more than a quarter of the water used in the agricultural sector is irretrievable and where nearly 50 million acres of land not intended for irrigation are being swamped each year because of water transmission losses.[29] These same policies have created a situation where the extent of water pollution is so severe that production costs are being driven up in some industries, and other formerly lucrative industries (fishing, tourism, and so forth) are simply being eliminated.

Unfortunately, these policies have not been matched by adequate investment in water pollution control or cleanup equipment. Consequently, the State Committee for the Protection of the Environment (Goskompriroda) reports that only 3 percent of the contaminated water is treated adequately; 50 percent is improperly purified, and 20 percent is dumped directly into local water supplies without any treatment whatsoever. These figures are clearly only lower-bound estimates because the magnitude of the water pollution problem is masked by the amount of illegal dumping and accidents that occur each year which are not included in official statistics. Soviet press reports indicate that in 1989 alone, some 2,000 accidents had "serious negative effects" on the land, water, and air.[30] Moreover, official statistics fail to include untreated run-off in agricultural regions (pesticides and chemical fertilizers) and industrial centers (petrochemical and other pollutants at industrial sites that are improperly stored or treated) that goes directly into storm drainage systems and ultimately into local water supplies.

The water pollution problem is best illustrated by considering three examples.[31] First, the drinking water in Moscow. Because water treatment facilities are inadequate (too few in number, using inappropriate technology), the water in Moscow is permitted to have more than 100 times the level of DDT recommended by the World Health Organization. Second, the Volga River basin. Some 40 percent of the polluted waste water flows into the Caspian Sea from the Volga each year. Economic losses from environmental disruption in the Volga-Caspian system are estimated at $2 to $3 billion per year (of which $1 to $2 billion stem from lost fishing activity — the Caspian used to hold 90 percent of the USSR's sturgeon stock). Finally, the Black Sea. Ninety percent of the Black Sea has been declared dead as a result of (i) industrial waste — it is estimated that 4,300 tons of nitrogen compounds, 900 tons of petroleum products, 600 tons of lead, and 200 tons of detergents flow into the Black Sea each year; (ii) agricultural waste — flushing of pesticides and fertilizers from the Danube and Dnieper; and (iii) naval operations — which leave a lasting (if untreated) petrochemical residue. Inadequate sewage capacity and improperly treated waste has caused bacteria counts at resort beaches to reach 100 to 200 times the norm.

Water pollution is only part of the environmental disruption story. The 217 million rubles spent in 1988 on land protection and reclamation projects made little headway in reversing the erosion, desertification, and salinization of the land.[32] Despite priority to expand agricultural production, policies were pursued in the sixties and seventies which contributed to the area of salinized land's almost doubling in one decade, and nearly 15 million acres of productive agricultural land was lost to erosion and desertification. Irresponsible agricultural development — negligence in pesticide and fertilizer use stemming from improper training, improper use, and a lack of equipment to properly disperse the chemicals — contributed to land damage, as did the use of over-heavy tractors that packed down the land and required additional plowing (and increased fuel use) and fertilizer to maintain targeted levels of wheat production.

Environmental conditions are not helped by the 9 billion tons of solid waste per year deposited in the 6,000 official landfills — half of which fail to meet sanitary standards because of the shortage of bulldozers and other grading equipment to cover the waste. In Moscow alone, of the 6 billion tons of refuse generated per year, 1 million tons are dumped illegally (in unmonitored dumps) because they fail to meet sanitary norms.[33]

As with the water pollution example above, the magnitude of the waste disposal problem is distorted by the absence of reliable statistics. Given the relative costs and benefits involved, Soviet managers are no doubt pursuing strategies that result in significant on-site improper storage or illegal dumping of hazardous waste.

Soviet environmental officials may have no idea what has been buried or disposed of in the less populated regions of the USSR. Moreover, the pace of industrial and agricultural development may require environmental officials to ignore the information they do have. In Estonia, nearly 300 children attending two kindergartens experienced a significant loss of hair. The cause was determined to be the fact that the schools were built on a radioactive waste dumpsite with little separating the buildings from the radioactive material.[34] One wonders about the health of the construction workers.

The accident at Chernobyl' also contributed to Soviet environmental disruption problems.[35] The total volume of radioactive material released after the accident at Chernobyl' in 1986 was about ninety times that released in Japan in 1945. More than 2 million acres of land were contaminated (50 percent of the total territory of Zhitomir *oblast)*, with a population of some 360,000 people affected. Cleanup costs have reached 8 billion rubles, of which 2.3 billion were spent on Chernobyl' alone; the rest went to provide housing, medical care, and so forth for the relocated people. Four years after the accident, untested areas still remain. For many reasons, it will be hard to calculate the long-term health and environmental consequences of the Chernobyl' incident.

Centrally planned socialist economies have a greater potential than market-oriented economies to minimize environmental disruption. Yet socialist economies appear to have worse environmental problems than capitalist economies at similar levels of economic development. Why such serious environmental disruption in the Soviet Union?

Centralized resource allocation and price formation policies have kept the price of raw materials artificially low, thereby eliminating the incentive for managers to recycle or to find alternative energy sources or inputs. It is not surprising to learn, for example, that even with a command structure which identified recycling as priority in 1980, after eight years only 27 percent of the paper/cardboard production in the USSR uses recycled materials.[36] Policies which impose no cost for pollution and minimal costs for waste disposal combined with a shortage of machinery and equipment for pollution cleanup have all contributed to the current environmental problems. Perhaps most unfortunate is the absence of investment in technology for pollution-free production. Thus Soviet leaders now face, and will face for at least the next decade, the difficult choice of production or pollution. The Soviet economy has no excess production capacity in many sectors and is therefore unable to compensate for plant shut-downs by shifting production to less controversial facilities. Thus, plant closings of the most severe polluters — fertilizer, pharmaceuticals, copper smelting, pulp and paper mills — will have a negative impact not only on agricultural production and on health care provision, for example, but also a more general impact on unemployment.

By most measures, current economic conditions in the USSR have indeed reached crisis proportions. To maintain the political support required to implement the latest elements of economic reform, Gorbachev needs to win the support of the general population. Their support will be more freely given if they feel their material well-being is improving. In order to visibly improve their standard of living, the pervasive and persistent shortage situation must be resolved.

The Soviet Sellers' Market

Shortages in the Soviet economy stem from a combination of systemic, policy, and institutional factors. The organization of the economic bureaucracy, a three-tiered vertical hierarchy with the State Committee on Planning (Gosplan) at the apex, not only prolongs the time it takes to make initial production and distribution decisions, but also eliminates any possibility of efficiencies associated with "spot decisions" in response to local conditions where production or distribution has been disrupted. The absence of property ownership rights that permit individuals to gain from efficient resource use or better production techniques has also undermined the motivation of Soviet managers and workers. Thus, given the same quantity and quality of inputs, the Soviet centrally planned economy has produced fewer goods and services than would be produced in a decentralized, market environment in a similar time frame.

Since the initiation of the centrally planned economy in the Soviet Union in the late 1920s, planners have typically set output targets high relative to the firms' productive capacity. That is, planners consistently send down to firms *taut* plans in an effort to maximize output. Managers are required by law to make every effort to fulfill all aspects of the plan: production targets, cost targets, sales targets, productivity targets, delivery targets, quality targets, input utilization targets, and so forth. In past years, plant managers faced up to one hundred different production-related targets. Because Soviet planners cannot possibly monitor the activities of the more than 50,000 plant managers, planners established bonuses that reward managers for fulfilling the major elements of the production plan. Traditionally, the most important target to meet has been output (measured in *value* of production). Only when output targets were completed in a timely manner were bonuses paid to managers, bonuses equivalent to 30 percent or more of their monthly salary. Complicating the taut planning situation was the policy by planners that based next year's output targets on a fixed percentage increase over the production targets fulfilled this year — what Soviet economists term "planning from the achieved level" and Western economists describe as the "ratchet effect."

The combination of the bonus policy, the taut planning policy, and the "ratchet effect" caused Soviet managers to engage in a variety of activities contrary to the objectives of the planners. Managers, for example, tended to underreport productive capacity, overorder inputs, produce poor quality goods, and falsify plan fulfillment documents in order to be assured of receiving their bonuses. Furthermore, in an environment where supplies were frequently late or inadequate, where plan targets are difficult to achieve, and where bonuses were only paid when production quotas are met, managers were reluctant to initiate innovation. Risks associated with introducing a new product or a new production technique far outweighed any rewards to the manager. Although the plan often included a target associated with the introduction of new technology, the contribution to the bonus for fulfilling this aspect of the plan was minimal.

These systemic and policy factors contributed to an environment in which neither managers nor workers were motivated to improve production performance. Moreover, neither managers nor workers were penalized for poor performance. If production quotas were met, regardless of quality or cost, bonuses were paid. In this environment, planners consistently demanded more output, managers responded with ever higher demands for materials, labor, and equipment, and neither worried about efficient resource utilization or cost. When production costs exceeded centrally administered prices, planners provided subsidies: Valentin Pavlov, minister of finance, reports that the state annually spent 5 billion rubles to support 8,000 loss-making state-owned enterprises. Other Soviet sources suggest that one in seven firms operated at loss.[37] Thus Soviet managers faced a "soft budget constraint" rather than the "hard budget constraint" of bankruptcy that managers in capitalist economies face.

Consequences of a Sellers' Market

Persistent, pervasive shortages have generated numerous negative consequences in the Soviet economy, causing Soviet leaders to describe current economic conditions as having reached crisis proportions. In a sellers' market environment, product quality deteriorates.[38] Managers feel no pressure to respond to consumer demand. The shortage situation is so severe in the Soviet Union that everything produced is sold, regardless of whether it satisfies particular requirements by users.[39] Consequently, a significant amount of time, energy, and resources are devoted to refashioning intermediate goods, especially machinery and equipment, to meet firm-specific requirements. With regard to innovation or adopting new technology, managers operating in a sellers' market are reluctant to actively pursue this option for expanding productive capacity or improving production processes because they have little recourse if the innovation fails to perform up to specification. Furthermore, managers have a strong incentive when operating in a sellers' market to self-supply as many inputs as possible. The loss of specialization and duplication of effort associated with self-supply drives up production costs.

Consumers have responded to the sellers' market environment, where 243 of 276 basic consumer goods are reported in short supply (defitsit), by hoarding non-perishable goods. A typical example of unwarranted mass purchasing was reported by the Soviet press in the fall of 1989. Soap production in 1989 rose by 6 percent, bringing domestic production levels up comparable to Finland and Japan, to the equivalent of 7.88 kilograms (nearly seventy bars) of soap for every man, woman, and child in the Soviet Union.[40] Despite increased production, despite diverting soap destined for commercial use to household use, and despite imports of some 3 million tons of soap in 1989 alone, 40 percent of Soviet consumers reported at the end of 1989 that they were less likely to find soap in state-retail stores than they were to find meat or sugar — goods previously identified as "impossible to find."

Is there a shortage of soap? When rumors spread in Yaroslav that soap might soon be unavailable, consumers stampeded the stores, and sales of soap soared fortyfold in two days. For those who lived through the difficult days of World War II, such behavior is not uncommon. The Soviet press reports one elderly woman purchasing more than three dozen bars of soap even though she had no way to carry them home. Panic buying spilled over to salt, matches, flour, and other non-perishables. A prominent Soviet economist, Nikolai Shmelev, described one of his friends purchasing enough soap to do laundry for seven years. Official statistics suggest that Soviet consumers have hoarded at least a ten-week supply of soap; doctors report having treated growing numbers of patients who experienced upper respiratory irritation from storing large quantities of soap in their small apartments.

Persistent and pervasive shortages distort the decisionmaking of producers and consumers, which further contributes to the shortage environment and results in the inefficient use of resources and time.

Converting a Sellers' Market Into a Buyers' Market

Gorbachev faces three options for converting the sellers' market to a buyers' market in the Soviet economy. *Perestroika* addresses all three: increasing supply, decreasing demand, and introducing price reform, that is, allowing prices to adjust to surplus or shortage conditions.

Increasing Supply

Perhaps the most "radical" elements of *perestroika* are associated with efforts to increase supply. Supply increases are to result from improved performance of state-owned firms as managers are given more autonomy over production and distribution decisions. The 1986 Law on State Enterprise, for example, granted managers of state-owned firms more autonomy in production, employment, and investment decisions, simultaneously giving them more responsibility for the profitability of their firms. Supply increases are also to result from entry of new firms: cooperatives, joint ventures with foreign companies, foreign firms located in the USSR, and small-scale private enterprises.[41] The change in ownership rights has been designed to strengthen the link between performance and pay. Removing the state monopoly over property ownership effectively eliminates centralized control over resource allocation and production and distribution decisions. While this reduces the state's ability to achieve mission-oriented projects in particular sectors of the economy, it enhances the efficiency of decisionmaking overall as managers have greater possibilities for making "spot decisions" in response to local conditions.

Property ownership rights were revised in 1987 to permit cooperatively owned firms to compete with state-owned firms in producing goods and services. At the end of September 1989, 172,000 of the 236,000 registered cooperatives were actively engaged in production or distribution activities, employing some 4 million people. Despite lack of popular support and

obstacles by local officals, growth in the cooperative sector as been significant. In the first year, retail trade turnover in the cooperative sector
reached 2 billion rubles, grew to 6 billion in 1988, and totaled some 25 to
30 billion rubles in 1989. Cooperative sector turnover is expected to reach
more than 50 billion rubles in 1990.[42] While growth in the cooperative sector initially was most rapid in consumer services and consumer goods production, by 1989 cooperatives had expanded into housing construction
and agricultural production. Popular discontent about the magnitude of
cooperative sector incomes to date has far outweighed popular support
for cooperative sector activities: about twice as many people responded
with negative attitudes toward cooperatives and private trade in 1989. The
negative attitude is particularly pronounced among individuals who have
not participated in cooperative sector activities and among individuals living in the Central Asian republics, where three to four times as many people were opposed to the expansion of cooperative and private-sector activities.[43] Obstacles to the formation of cooperatives by local officials has further impeded the expansion of production and distribution in this sector
of the Soviet economy.[44]

Privately owned firms are to be legalized in July 1990 as a result of the
March 1990 vote of the the Soviet parliament: 350 to 3 to allow citizens to
own the "means of production" and establish small-scale factories. The law
is designed to permit individuals to gain from their work in handicrafts,
farming, the provision of services for the public, and "other forms of individual activity that serves the interests of society."[45] It is unclear whether
land ownership is possible under the new law, but long-term leasing of
agricultural land is evidently permitted.

As radical as changes in property rights has been the conversion of
defense plants to civilian production to increase the supply of consumer
goods.[46] Defense plants, traditionally receiving the best materials, the most
highly skilled personnel, and the latest technology, have been successful in
producing at quality standards comparable to advanced industrialized
countries. Gorbachev no doubt hopes that similar success will be achieved
by the military-industrial complex (*voenno-promyshlennyi kompleks, VPK*) in
civilian consumer goods production. He authorized the spending of four
billion rubles in 1990 to facilitate the shifting of existing industrial capacity within VPK from defense production to civilian production, the transfer
of investment resources within VPK from military to civilian production,
and the reassignment of civilian firms/ministries to VPK (e.g., enterprises
of Ministry of Machine Building for Light and Food Industry and
Household Appliances). The conversion is to result in the use of more
high-tech equipment in the production of consumer goods, the reduction
of any idle productive capacity in the defense sector, and the extension of

civilian sector management skills. As a point of information, the nine defense ministries have for a long time produced consumer durables: washing machines, refrigerators, vacuum cleaners, for example. The 1990 production schedule calls for VPK to produce 40 percent of its output for civilian needs; by 1995, it is to produce 60 percent of its output for civilian needs.[47] The conversion of defense plants is to focus on the manufacture of medical equipment, equipment for light industry (food processing equipment, for example), fishing boats, civilian aircraft, and the social infrastructure (housing, hospitals, schools).

In addition to the entry of new firms and the conversion of defense plants to civilian production, supply is to increase as a result of an aggressive import policy. Imports totaling some $15 billion worth of consumer goods in 1989–1990, plus an additional $5 to $6 billion per year for the following three years are to be financed in part by reducing imports of machinery and equipment, in part by savings from reduced aid to Latin American countries, in part by reduced imports of agicultural products, and in part by borrowing.[48] Soviet sources indicate a stock of uninstalled equipment totalling $8 to $10 billion, thus the ability to cut back annual imports of machinery and equipment until this stock is put in place. Savings from reduced sugar subsidies to Cuba are estimated at $800 million per year in hard currency. Agricultural imports can be reduced if domestic production increases. To stimulate domestic agricultural production, proposals call for paying Soviet farmers hard currency for above-plan production, at a price some fraction of world market price, the savings to be used for financing imports of consumer goods. It is not clear how transportation, storage, and processing bottlenecks will be resolved if domestic agricultural production does respond to this new incentive.

Decreasing Demand

At the same time that Gorbachev is implementing policies to increase supply, he is also attacking the shortage situation by decreasing demand for goods and services from households and government. Soviet consumers had accumulated in bank accounts by the end of 1989 savings in an amount equal to nearly one year's earnings, with perhaps as much stuffed in pillows and under mattresses. Under the auspices of *perestroika*, Gorbachev is pursuing a series of policies to reduce the cash overhang. For example, more foreign travel has been permitted, and the official exchange rate for obtaining hard currency has been increased significantly. Income taxes are to increase, as are penalties for tax evasion.[49] Gorbachev also has called for restoring state alcohol production to previous levels in order to (i) absorb some of the excess income, (ii) reduce

possibilities for earning excessive incomes from the sale of illegally produced alcohol, (iii) raise state revenues from taxes levied on sales of alcohol. In addition, *perestroika* includes not only the sales of state-owned physical assets (housing, tractors, trucks, and so forth) to individuals, but also
the sales of financial assets: government bonds that at maturity can be
turned in for gold, goods (a car, for example), or rubles.[50] To reduce government demand for goods and services, Gorbachev has called for a 10 to
15 percent reduction in defense expenditures, a 40 percent reduction in
investment in the energy sector, and a 30 percent reduction in all other
centrally funded investment expenditures. Reform initiatives have included the discussion of options such as raising interest charges on excess
inventories and reducing ministry subsidies by at least 30 percent (non-
farm subsidies were planned at 11 billion rubles for 1989). Policies to
reduce Soviet aid to Cuba and a number of other Latin American countries over the next few years have been discussed, as has a penalty tax on
firms that increase average wages by more than 3 percent per year (firms
producing consumer goods are to be exempt). Goskomstat figures suggest
that wage growth remains high relative to productivity increases: in
January 1990 wages were about 15 percent higher than in January 1989,
while labor productivity declined by about 1 percent during this same
period. This combination contributes to inflationary pressures.

Policies to absorb excess cash balances and increase the supply of consumer goods will reduce inflationary pressures in the Soviet economy.
Reducing inflationary pressures will minimize the disruptions associated
with the transition to a market-oriented economy and increase the likelihood that a successful transition will be made.

Price Reform

The most politically sensitive aspect of *perestroika* is price reform. Under
the current system, the majority of prices are centrally administered on
the basis of a "cost-plus" pricing rule, where managers have no incentive
to minimize or even to reduce production costs. Rather, the firm's situation improves as production costs rise because profits are calculated as a
fixed percentage of cost and profits are the source of the fund from which
bonuses are paid.

Even though *perestroika* began in earnest in 1986, price reform was not
scheduled to occur until 1992. Planners delayed official price reform
because of inflationary pressures in the Soviet economy which, if prices
are allowed to adjust freely, would cause prices to skyrocket, generating a
politically unacceptable situation.[51] However, there are sectors of the
Soviet economy emerging as a consequence of *perestroika* where prices do

respond to supply and demand conditions. Goods and services produced by joint ventures (over 1,500 joint ventures have been registered since 1987), cooperatively owned firms, and those in the agricultural sector are sold at prices established by supply and demand conditions rather than by the State Committee for Prices (Goskomtsen). By allowing prices in specific sectors of the economy to respond to market conditions, Gorbachev is preparing Soviet consumers for the inevitable and substantial increase in prices that will come with the reform initiatives.[52] Moreover, by limiting the introduction of flexible prices, policymakers have an opportunity to resolve difficulties associated with higher prices on fixed income groups — pensioners, for example.

Both Soviet and Western economists, and the majority of the Soviet population, are predicting a significant rise in prices to occur in conjunction with the transition to a market-oriented economy. In order to lessen the impact of the price explosion, central planners will continue to set prices of basic inputs (oil, gas, coal, electricity, metals, and freight tariffs, for example), taking into account world market prices. A second group of goods would be subject to regulated prices — price ceilings would be imposed, and prices would no doubt rise immediately to that limit. Finally, a third group of goods would have prices determined by market conditions. Six months after the initiatives were announced, the list of goods to be included under these categories of pricing mechanisms still had not been made publicly available.

To prevent the social unrest associated with the anticipated 150 to 200 percent rise in consumer goods prices, all incomes are to be indexed against a basket of "necessities" — particularly food, which accounts for 50 percent of family budgets. Additional measures will be taken to protect income of people on pensions and fixed incomes, salaried employees in the "nonproductive" sector, and workers in sectors where central planning controls remain in place. To minimize the disruption associated with introducing more flexible prices, production and distribution decisions will be governed by state orders and supply limits in defense industries, export industries, industries producing products for low-income groups in the population, and other "strategic" sectors, state orders *(goszakazy)* and supply limits will remain in force. Proposals call for more aggressive use of credit and interest rates to regulate enterprise borrowing and encourage saving in a further effort to minimize excess demand for resources, goods, and services.

This latest round in price reform proposals still falls far short of what needs to be done to facilitate the successful transition to a decentralized decisionmaking environment. In part, however, any true price reform proposal is contingent upon the existence of several institutional arrangements which are currently absent in the Soviet economy. Price reform and market transactions require well-defined property rights. Price reform is unlikely to succeed without the simultaneous establishment of financial and capital markets in the Soviet Union.[53] Moreover, price reform in an environment characterized by persistent and pervasive shortages, an environment lacking institutions to implement monetary and fiscal policy, can result in little more than rampant inflation. Currently, Soviet consumers have the option of queuing (at a high nonmonetary cost, unless forgone earnings are included) for goods in the lower-priced state-retail stores or shopping in the "second economy" where prices, typically set by supply and demand conditions, are two to five times higher. Price reform will close the gap between state-sector and private-sector prices. Without a compensation scheme for low-income families, price reform will impact adversely upon a major segment of the Soviet population. Gorbachev is no doubt concerned that this impact may significantly undermine *perestroika*.

Prospects for Success

When Gorbachev came to power in March 1985, he clearly had no idea of the magnitude of the economic problems he faced (even the CIA has only recently revised its assessment of the economic conditions!), and he attempted to offset declining growth rates by calling for workers to improve and increase their performance. Since that time, *glasnost* has generated an onslaught of evidence and discussion about deteriorating environmental and health conditions, about the rapidly growing technological gap with the West, about the pervasiveness of the shortage situation. Stop-gap policies to reverse declining output trends simply exacerbated the budget deficit and contributed to inflationary pressures. By the end of the eighties, little progress in improved economic performance was evident.

Will *perestroika* succeed? If the success of *perestroika* is measured by its ability to increase the quantity and improve the quality of goods and services produced in the Soviet Union, yes, I think *perestroika* will succeed. For the first time, the reform proposals are addressing the aspects of the Soviet economy that must change for performance to improve: the size and power of the central economic bureaucracy, flexible pricing, per-mance-based pay, and property ownership. It is unfortunate, however, that these changes will impact on the entire population in both positive and negative ways, and thus undermine popular support for *perestroika*. The Soviet people will gain from higher wages, more housing, better health care, and greater accessibility to better-quality goods and services. They will face higher prices, the prospect of unemployment, and a drastically reduced social welfare program. *Perestroika* will succeed if its unanticipated political and social consequences do not undermine Gorbachev's efforts to push it to successful fruition.

Notes

1. *Izvestia*, 28 March 1990. For further discussion, see J. Tedstrom, "What to Expect in the New State of Economic Reform," *Report on the USSR*, 20 April 1990, pp. 1-3.
2. See, for example, Stanislav Shatalin's reform proposal. *Perekhod k rynky. Kontseptsiya i programma. Chast' I* (Moscow, September 1990).
3. Leonid Abalkin, *Pravitel'stvennyi vestnik*, no. 13 (1990), pp. 6-7. For further discussion see P. Rutland, "Abalkin's Strategy for Soviet Economic Reform," *Report on the USSR*, 25 May 1990, pp. 3-6.
4. In a year-end survey of public opinion in Moscow, 71 percent of the respondents favored *perestroika* even though 82 percent thought the Soviet economy had deteriorated significantly under *perestroika* [see *Moskovskie novosti*, no. 2 (1990), p. 9]. A report on the opinion poll results published in *Ogonek* (no. 15, 1990) are cited in "Opinion Polls Show Pessimism," *Report on the USSR*, 27 April 1990, pp. 35-36.
5. Leading Soviet economist Abel Aganbegyan discusses the lack of growth in "Programma korennoi perestroika," *EKO* 18, no. 11 (November 1987), pp. 3-19 (see especially p. 7), and *The Economic Challenge of Perestroika* (Bloomington, IN: Indiana University Press, 1988), p. 2. See also estimates by V. Selyunin and G. Khanin, "Lukavaya tsifra," *Novy mir* 63, no. 2 (February 1987), pp. 194-95. For additional discussion see Michael Ellman, *Collectivization, Convergence and Capitalism: Political Economy in a Divided World* (London: Academic Press, 1984), pp. 135-46.
6. Gertrude Schroeder,"Soviet Economy on a Treadmill of Reform," in Joint Economic Committee, *Soviet Economy in a Time of Change* (Washington, DC: Government Printing Office, 1979).
7. *Izvestia*, 28 January and 7 April 1990, p. 1.
8. In the first six months of 1989, 2 million person-days were lost as a result of strikes; in July-November 1989, 5.5 million days were lost during miners' strikes and ethnic unrest. For an excellent discussion, see Elizabeth Teague, "Worker Unrest in 1989," *Report on the USSR*, 26 January 1990, pp. 12-13.
9. *Planovoe khoziaistvo*, no. 10 (1989), p. 7. It is estimated that plant closings will reduce output in several key industries in 1990, including 5.2 million tons of fertilizer, over 250,000 tons of synthetic rubber, and 500,000 tons of polymers. In January 1990 the Nairit Scientific Production Association in Erevan, a major manufacturer of heart medicines, painkillers, vitamins, ammonia, fertilizer, and chloroprene rubber, was shut down. Protests by environmentalists also halted production of pharmaceuticals at the Azot plant in Kemerovo. In some cases, these were the only plants in the Soviet Union producing essential medicines. Government plans to improve the supply of medicines by constructing new pharmaceutical plants have been delayed in part because of environmental protests and in part because local officials refuse to allocate requisite land to the Ministry of Pharmaceutical Industry. For excellent discussion, see D. J. Peterson, "Medicines, Newspapers and Protecting the Environment," *Report on the USSR*, 23 March 1990, pp. 10-13.

10. In Gorbachev's first two years of power, housing construction rose by more than 20 percent — from 1.9 million apartments in 1985 to 2.3 million in 1987. However, at the end of 1988, some 14 million urban families were on waiting lists for better housing — a million more than in 1987 — and another 5 million people were living in slums (*trushchoby*). Both the shortage of apartments and the housing allocation system contribute to the problem. See Henry W. Morton, "Who Gets What, When, and How? Housing in the Soviet Union," *Soviet Studies*, no. 2 (1980), pp. 252-57; and A. Trehub, "*Perestroika* and Social Entitlements," in J. Tedstrom, ed., *Socialism, Perestroika, and the Dilemmas of Soviet Economic Reform* (Boulder, CO: Westview Press,1990), pp. 207-31.

11. For a recent survey of the energy situation, see Leslie Dienes, "Energy: From Bonanza to Crisis," *Report on the USSR*, 1 December 1989, pp. 1-5.

12. "The Soviet Economy: The Hard Road from Capitalism to Capitalism," *Economist*, 18 November 1989, p. 21.

13. For a discussion of long construction periods and overinvestment in agriculture, see V. K. Faltsman, *Proizvodstvenny potentsial SSSR: voprosy prognozirovaniya* (Moscow: Ekonomika, 1987), pp. 12, 83. For a discussion of the traditional reaction to long construction periods —higher investment rates — see D. Chernikov, "Intensifikatsiya i proportsionalnost ekonomicheskogo rosta," *Planovoe khoziaistvo* 63, no. 6 (June 1986), pp. 63-72. For a concise summary, see J. Tedstrom, "The Soviet Economy: Planning for the 1990s," *Report on the USSR*, 22 December 1989, pp. 1-7.

14. For a discussion of scrapping rates and rising repair costs see T. Khachaturov, "Perestroika v sfere kapitalnykh vlozheni," *Voprosy ekonomiki* 60, no. 1 (January 1988), pp. 3-11; Boris Rumer, "Some Investment Patterns Engendered by the Renovation of Soviet Industry," *Soviet Studies* 36, no. 2 (April 1984), pp. 257-66; D. M. Palterovich, "Tekhnicheskaya rekonstrucktsiya narodnogo khoziaistva," *Voprosy ekonomiki* 60, no. 1 (January 1988), pp. 117-26; and K. K. Valtukh and B. L... Lavrovski, "Proizvodstvenny apparat strany: ispolzovanie i rekonstruktsiya," *EKO* 17, nol. 2 (February 1986), pp. 17-32. For a discussion of equipment shortages contributing to low retirement ratios, see F. Kushnirsky, "The Role of Industrial Modernization in Soviet Economic Planning," in Joint Economic Committee, vol. I, *Gorbachev's Economic Plans* (Washington, DC: Government Printing Office, 1987), pp. 257-73.

15. The extent of unsatisfied consumer demand is indicated by the 41 billion ruble (14 percent) increase in personal savings in 1989. For estimates of Soviet military spending, see G. Weickhardt, "Recent Discussion of Defense Economics," *Report on the USSR*, 9 March 1990, pp. 9-13.

16. Don Van Atta,"Soviet Agricultural Performance," *Report on the USSR*, 23 February 1990.

17. Wage and salary data are available in *Sotsialisticheskaya industriia*, 22 January 1989, p. 1; *Trud v SSSR* (Moscow, 1988), p. 146; *Argumenty i fakty*, no. 35 (1989); *Izvestia*, 29 July 1989, p. 1.

18. For a discussion of consequences of inflationary pressures in the Soviet economy, see A. Shmarov and N. Kirichenko, "Inflatsionnyi `vsplesk' masshtaby i prichiny," *Ekonomicheskaya gazeta*, no. 13 (1989), p. 12.

19. Monthly wages of blue- and white-collar workers average between 220 and 240 rubles; employees working in cooperatives earn an average of 500 rubles per month. At the end of 1989, more than 337 billion rubles were in savings accounts. More than 41 billion rubles were added to accounts during the course of 1989, a 14 percent increase in one year. A Goskomstat report indicates that the imbalance between purchasing power and available goods has created a situation where meat, sausage, and butter were rationed in 90 of the 445 cities they surveyed in 1989.

20. The campaign against alcohol was one of the first measures adopted by the Politburo

after Gorbachev became general secretary in 1985. During the campaign, alcohol sales were limited from 2:00 to 7:00 p.m.; the number of shops selling alcohol was reduced by half; many cafes were closed or lost their rights to serve alcohol; sales to people under the age of twenty-one were prohibited; large fines were levied on workers who showed up for work drunk. According to *Pravda* (18, 14, and 26 January 1986), the immediate impact of the anti-alcohol campaign was pronounced: Alcohol sales fell by 25 percent during the last seven months of 1985 and 37 percent in 1986, followed by a further reduction of 13 percent in 1987. By the end of 1987, the volume of state sales of alcohol was 46 percent below the 1980 level. The Soviet press reports a sharp reduction in alcohol-related diseases, crimes, and accidents (*Izvestia*, 10 March, 2 June, and 3 December 1987), plus an increase in life-expectancy (*Pravda*, 18 January 1987), but fails to mention any positive impact on economic performance such as higher labor productivity.

21. Data on Soviet budget deficits from 1982 to 1989 are available in *PlanEcon Report*, 1 September 1989; see also V. Treml, "A Note on the Soviet Budget Deficit," *Report on the USSR*, 22 September 1989, p. 12. For discussion of the deficits, see V. Panskov, "Kak preodolet' defitsit byudzheta," *Ekonomicheskaya gazeta*, no. 5 (1989), pp. 5-15, and P. Hanson, "Inflation versus reform," *Report on the USSR*, 21 April 1989, pp. 13-18.

22. For an excellent discussion, see D. J. Peterson, "Supreme Soviet Adopts Emergency Pension Measures," *Report on the USSR*, 18 August 1989, pp. 7-10.

23. P. Hanson, "USSR — Puzzles in the 1985 Statistics," Radio Liberty Research Bulletin RL 154/88 (20 November 1986), and J. Vanous, "The Dark Side of *Glasnost*: Unbelievable National Income Statistics in the Gorbachev Era," *PlanEcon Report* 3, no. 6 (13 February 1987); N. Shmelev, "Novye trevogi," *Novy mir* 64, no. 4 (April 1988), p. 163.

24. According to *Izvestia* (10 March 1987), the militia confiscated 900,000 distillers by the end of 1986, and the number of sentences for *samogan* producers rose more than sixfold from 1984 to 1986. Shmelev estimates, however, that the reduction in state alcohol production was made up for by moonshiners. See N. Shmelev, "Novye trevogi," pp. 162-63.

25. *Ekonomika i zhizn'* reported a foreign-trade deficit in 1989 of 3.3 billion rubles. Goskomstat figures reported in *Pravda* (28 January 1989) suggested an anticipated deficit of at least 2 billion rubles. The trade deficit combined with the net hard currency debt — estimated at $8 billion in 1989 — will not strengthen Gorbachev's hand as he goes out to seek major new credits.

26. Gosplan economist V.Kostakov estimated in 1986 that between 13 and 19 million manufacturing jobs would be eliminated if *perestroika* is successful in increasing labor productivity at the targeted rate. See Vladimir Kostakov, "Odin, kak semero," *Sovetskaya kul'tura*, 4 January 1986. He argued in 1989 ("Pogolovnaya zanyatost' i rynok truda," *Izvestia*, 11 January 1989) that a significant number of employees — at least 10 million people — are on enterprise payrolls to assist with production at the end of the plan period and will be "freed" as enterprises shift to full economic accounting (*polnyi khozraschet*).

27. Soviet officials estimate that one-third of the working population will ultimately be affected by *perestroika*. *Voprosy ekonomiki*, no. 2 (1989), p. 27. Employment bureaus are to minimize the disruption. For an excellent discussion of the formation and role of employment bureaus, see Aaron Trehub, "*Perestroika* and Social Entitlements," pp. 207-31.

28. Elizabeth Fuller, "Georgian Nuclear Reactor to Close in Wake of Public Protest," *Report on the USSR*, 20 April 1990, pp. 17-18.

29. *Izvestia*, 7 February 1990, p. 3. For an excellent discussion of water pollution problems and sources see M. Rozengurt, *Water Policy Mismanagement in the Southern USSR: The Ecological and Economical Impact*, National Council for Soviet and East European Research, November 1989, and D. J. Peterson, "The State of the Environment: The Water," *Report on the USSR*, 16 March 1990, pp. 14-19.

30. *Izvestia*, 28 January 1990, p. 3. Also see, State Committee for the Protection of the Environment, *Sostoyanie prirodnoi sredy v SSSR v 1988 godu*, Moscow, 1989.

31. Rozengurt, *Water Policy Management*, p. 45.

32. D. J. Peterson, "The State of the Environment: Solid Wastes," *Report on the USSR*, 11 May 1990, pp. 11-15.

33. *Izvestia*, 26 July 1989, p. 6.

34. Peterson, "State of the Environment: Solid Wastes," p. 13.

35. For an excellent analysis of the consequences of the Chernobyl' accident, see D. Marples, *Chernobyl' and Nuclear Power in the USSR* (New York: St. Martin's Press, 1986), and *The Social Impact of the Chernobyl' Disaster* (New York: Macmillan Press, 1988).

36. *Sostoyanie priorodnoi sredy v SSSR*, p. 66.

37. V. M. Ivanchenko estimates that in 1984 as few as 12 percent of Soviet industrial and agricultural enterprises could have successfully operated on a self-financing basis — that is, earning revenues sufficient to cover operating costs. *Ekonomicheskaya gazeta*, no. 32 (1986), p. 8.

38. The relationship between quality and shortages is discussed by A. Bim and A. Shokhin, "Sistema raspredeleniya: na putyakh perestroiki," *Kommunist* 63, no. 15 (October 1986), p. 69. Quality deteriorates as production intensifies at the end of the planning period to fulfill output quotas ("storming"). Shmelev estimates that only 17 to 18 percent of Soviet manufactured goods meet quality standards required for export. See N. Shmelev,"Avansy i dolgi," *Novy mir* 63, no. 6 (June 1987), p. 154. There is also an incentive for plant managers to misreport the quality of merchandise in a shortage environment where goods classified as "rejects" can be sold at prices higher than those paid by state trading agencies.

39. In-depth interviews with recent emigrants from the Soviet Union who formerly held managerial positions in heavy and light industry enterprises describe producing merchandise to fulfill plan targets that was unacceptable to local customers because of quality or design and which they could "send to the provinces" (rural areas). Managers also describe unloading unwanted inventories as part of a package negotiated with *tolkachi*: if you want X amount of *defitsit*, you must take Y amount of surplus (useless) goods. For further discussion, see S. Linz, "Managerial Autonomy in Soviet Firms," *Soviet Studies*, April 1988, pp. 175-95.

40. See, for example, *Izvestia*, 29 October 1989; *Trud*, 19 September 1989; *Pravda*, 11 August and 15 September 1989. Soap production figures are given in *SSSR v tsifrakh v 1988 godu* (Moscow 1989). For further discussion, see D. J. Peterson, "Soap in the Soviet Union: Portrait of a Shortage," *Report on the USSR*, 17 November 1989, pp. 1-6.

41. Soviet reports indicate that more than 1,200 joint ventures were registered with the Ministry of Finance by the end of 1989, although many have failed to start operations or have already gone bankrupt. Half of the joint ventures are light industry and service establishments, another 20 percent are in industrial services, and about 15 percent are in heavy industry and machine tools. Legal, financial, and organizational problems have plagued establishment of joint ventures, as have lack of supplies and market prices, and transportation, communication, and storage facilities. For further discussion, see "Joint Ventures Accelerated in the U.S.S.R.," *International Economic Review*, December 1989, pp. 8-9.

42. Data on the cooperative sector is available in *Pravital'stvennyi vestnik*, no. 19 (1989), p. 10; *Ekonomika i zhizn'*, no. 1 (1990); J. Tedstrom, "The Soviet Cooperative Movement: An Update," *Report on the USSR*, 13 October 1989, pp. 3-7.

43. For an excellent survey of Soviet opinion poll results, see Anders Aslund, *Gorbachev's Struggle for Economic Reform* (Ithaca, NY: Cornell University Press, 1989), chapter 6.

44. According to *Izvestia* (22 December 1987 and 17 January 1988), local authorities refused to register cooperatives whose orientation they disliked. Thus, every tenth cooperative had been refused registration and many more had been delayed. For an excellent survey of cooperatives, see J. Tedstrom, "The Reemergence of Soviet Cooperatives," in J. Tedstrom, ed., *Socialism, Perestroika, and the Dilemmas of Soviet Economic Reform*, pp. 104-34.

45. Excerpts from the new property law were published by the *New York Times*, 8 March 1990. For a discussion of the property ownership debate, see P. Hanson, "Ownership and Economic Reform," Radio Liberty/Radio Free Europe #154/88 (6 April 1988); "The Question of Ownership," *Report on the USSR*, 8 December 1989, pp. 6-7; and "The Ownership Debate: Are There Any Taboos Left?" *Report on the USSR*, 19 January 1990, pp. 5-7.

46. See J. Tedstrom, "Managing the Conversion of the Defense Industries," *Report on the USSR*, 16 February 1990, pp. 11-18; "Conversion and the Problem of Industrial Science," *Report on the USSR*, 25 August 1985, pp. 19-20; and "Is the Contribution of the Defense Complex to Civilian Production Growing?" *Report on the USSR*, 16 June 1989, pp. 1-3.

47. Weickhardt, "Recent Discussion of Defense Economics," pp. 9-13. It will be interesting to compare the timetable of the conversion process with what occurred after World War II.

48. Shmelev, "Novye trevogi," pp. 160-75. Discussion of ways identified by Soviet officials to finance imports of consumer goods is found in S. Whitlock, "Shmelev's Program to Rectify the Soviet Financial Crisis," *Report on the USSR*, 30 June 1989, pp. 8-11; P. Hanson, "Economic Stabilization Plans," *Report on the USSR*, 27 October 1989, pp. 9-12; and S. Foster, "Convertible Currency Payments for Above-Average Sales of Farm Produce," *Report on the USSR*, 10 November 1989, pp. 13-15.

49. See discussion in J. Tedstrom, "New Draft Law on Income Taxes," *Report on the USSR*, 16 June 1989, pp. 8-10.

50. *Stroitel'naya gazeta* reported that, in what appears to have been the first housing auction, a one-room apartment with a list price of 8,500 rubles went for 18,500 rubles, a two-room apartment in Kiev sold for 23,000 rubles and a three-room apartment for 34,000 rubles. The privatization of the Soviet housing market was announced in December 1988 (see *Trud*, 6 December 1988, and *Pravda*, 12 December 1988). The decree enabled tenants to purchase their apartments with a down payment of 50 percent of the state price, with the balance to be paid over ten years. For further discussion, see A. Protsenko, "Kuplyu Kvartiru, v kotoroi zhivu," *Izvestia*, 9 March 1989, p. 2, and P. Hanson, "Inflation versus Reform." For discussion of bond sales, see Oleg Bogomolov, *Literaturnaya gazeta*, no. 16 (September 1987), and N. Shmelev, "Novye trevogi," p. 169.

51. See A. Deryabin, "Snachala ispravim tsenoobrazovanie," *EKO*, no. 3 (1989), pp. 41-56; M. Bornstein, "Soviet Price Policies," *Soviet Economy*, no. 3 (1987), pp. 96-134; A. Shokhin, A. Guzanova, and L. Liberman, "Prices through the Eyes of the Population," *Problems of Economics*, no. 2 (1989), pp. 6-13; V. Rutgaizer, I. Glinkin, P. Filenkov, and A. Shmarov, "On the Question of Reforming Consumer Prices and the Monetary Incomes of the Population," *Problems of Economics*, no. 2 (1988), pp. 75-90.

52. V. Rutgaizer, A. Shmarov, and N. Kirichenko, "Reforma roznichnykh tsen, mekhanizm kompensatsii i razvitie potrebitel'skogo rynka," *EKO*, no. 3 (1989), pp. 58-70; V. D. Belkin, "Uriki proshlogo," *EKO*, no. 3 (1989), pp. 71-77; V. Slepov, M. Kokorev, and V. Naumov, "Problemy perestroiki systemy roznichnykh tsen v SSSR," *Voprosy ekonomiki*, no. 2 (1989), pp. 104-112.

53. For an excellent survey of the literature, see Perry Patterson, "Prospects for Commodity and Financial Exchanges," in J. Tedstrom, ed., *Socialism, Perestroika, and the Dilemmas of Soviet Economic Reform*, pp. 177-91.

4. RURAL REFORM IN THE SOVIET UNION

Don Van Atta

For more than fifty years, no agricultural enterprises other than collective and state farms, organized according to a single model and governed by a hierarchy of political and administrative agencies centered in Moscow, have existed in the Soviet countryside.[1] Central agencies have allocated supplies and equipment to the farms at government-set prices. What and when to grow have been determined by the plan "sent down" to the farm from party and state authorities. Almost all produce has been delivered to off-farm state agencies, which then pay official government prices for it. The peasants have worked in large brigades organized and paid along industrial lines. Although the *kolkhoz* is theoretically a member-owned cooperative, wages for collective farmers have been guaranteed by the state since the mid-1960s and issued whether or not the farm produced anything.

The March 1989 plenary session of the CPSU Central Committee proclaimed a series of agricultural policy changes, collectively referred to as the "New Agrarian Policy," intended to alter every aspect of Soviet command agriculture. If the new policy is effectively implemented, it will change the countryside as radically as Stalin's collectivization did.

The reforms will allow many kinds of farms, including the existing *kolkhozy* and *sovkhozy*, newly created cooperative farms, and single-family holdings. A new land law approved at the end of February 1990 permits peasants to hold and work land individually and to pass it on to their heirs (but not to sell or exchange it freely), a return to the land tenure norms of the 1920s. Under the reform proposals, the family will once again become an important work group, and peasants will be paid according to the quality and quantity of their harvests. Equipment and supplies will be sold by competing suppliers to individual farmers, collective and state farms, or to voluntary cooperatives representing them. Agricultural producers will be free to sell what they grow to the highest bidder. Farmers and farms will be able to organize to defend their political interests.

This summary, however, makes the new policy seem much more coherent, and more likely to be effective in the short term, than it really is. The reform proposals evolved as individual changes produced consequences seemingly unanticipated by the political leadership. Marketization, cooperativization, and the restoration of the family as the basic agricultural work unit can be carried out in many ways. Different Soviet leaders and groups in Soviet society clearly have quite different ideas about what these concepts mean in practice. Simply because a party or state decision requires something to be done does not mean it will happen in practice. The structure of the Soviet party-state creates many opportunities for resistance by both officials and the peasants themselves. Because agricultural policy directly involves the basic role of the party in Soviet society, the changes cannot be carried out as neatly as their sponsors might wish. For the New Agrarian Policy to be really innovative and successful, much of the existing rural order must be altered, and that will be neither easy nor quick.

The 1989 reforms mark a new stage in policy disputes in which the issues and alternatives have remained relatively consistent since the mid-1960s. At the March 1965 Central Committee plenum, the new, post-Khrushchev collective leadership agreed that the countryside needed more capital investment than had been provided by either Stalin's rapacious policies or Khrushchev's mobilizational ones. Everyone agreed that more money for the countryside was necessary, but there was less agreement on how it should be spent. Some members of the leadership, especially Gennadii Voronov and Aleksei Kosygin, argued that if the increased resources were to be effectively used, they would have to be accompanied by changes in farm organization and management to decentralize production decisions and allow them to be made by the peasants themselves.[2] Leonid Brezhnev, who won the power struggle in the late 1960s, denied that decentralized management was needed. To the degree he undertook any organizational reforms, they served to increase the power of party and state authorities or to centralize production.

The current debate echoes this earlier struggle. Since becoming general secretary, Mikhail Gorbachev's expressed views on agrarian policy have shifted from an emphasis on "perfecting" the existing system to calling for its radical alteration, even though the shell of *kolkhoz* and *sovkhoz* organization is to be retained.[3] The current Soviet leadership retains the commitment to high levels of agricultural investment made in the 1960s. But Gorbachev has come to realize, as Khrushchev and Voronov had before him, that without organizational reform, simply investing more money in the countryside will not solve the country's food problems. In late 1987, when the general secretary spoke at a meeting on accelerating the development of the food-processing industry, he asserted that the farms already had all they needed to perceptibly improve food supplies within two to three years. The *kolkhozy* and *sovkhozy* had begun to master intensive techniques of cultivation, which could ensure high and stable yields. But such methods had to be accompanied by reorganization of production, because, as he said, it was

> important that the human being really should be included in the production process and run [*upravlial*] and manage it himself. This is the main thing. Frankly speaking, both the use of the accumulated potential and the mastery of new techniques will likewise rely on this [human factor], since in the final analysis everything must go through the human being.[4]

Making the farmer able to manage his own work has turned out to be much more difficult than these words might suggest. The fight that will determine the success or failure of Gorbachev's rural reforms concerns reorganization of the farms and the agencies that supply, buy from, and control them so that the peasant may become "master on the land."

A conservative position, generally represented by CPSU Central Committee Agriculture Commission Chairman Egor Ligachev, argues that the basic problem of Soviet agriculture is not so much the need to produce more as it is to get what is grown onto the store shelves. The enormous waste of agricultural products can be cut only by more state investment. If the good farm managers are allowed to run their farms properly and the poor managers learn to run theirs equally well, then the existing *kolkhoz* system can achieve miracles of increased productivity. From this viewpoint, basic reorganization as Gorbachev has envisioned it is unnecessary and even undesirable.

His opponents clearly believe that pursuing Gorbachev's agrarian policy threatens the bases of the Soviet political system and party power. The general secretary is willing to run this risk because of the urgency of improving the nation's food supplies and the need to cut expenditures of hard currency on agricultural imports. But even if he can overcome resistance in the party and state elite, the obstacles to reform in the countryside will be formidable. After briefly examining agrarian policy during the

Brezhnev era, this paper summarizes the rural reform measures that have been advanced since 1985. It then examines the conservative counterarguments and the political implications of the struggle over change in the countryside for the overall process of *perestroika*.

The Brezhnev Legacy

Brezhnev greatly increased both direct state investment in agriculture and the prices paid by the state for produce. By the 1980s about one-third of all Soviet capital investment went to agriculture and associated sectors of the economy. The ministries that built agricultural equipment and the Ministry of Land Reclamation and Water Resources, responsible for land reclamation and hydroelectric and flood-control work, grew fat on this money.[5] Equipment prices rose steadily, although quality remained low and farms could not obtain either complete sets of equipment or spare parts for the machinery they had. Seven years after mass production began, the newest Soviet combine harvester, the Don-1500, which sells to a farm for more than 40,000 rubles,[6] has a mean time between failures of only thirty operating hours.[7] The area of reclaimed land continuously expanded, but much of it turned out to be only marginally productive. Agricultural economist Vladimir Tikhonov calculated that the 43.9 billion rubles spent on land improvement in 1981–1985 will pay for themselves in increased net profits in 109 years.[8] The poorly built new irrigation systems wasted water and demanded costly maintenance. In response, the regime initiated ever-greater water projects, culminating in the ambitious plans for irrigation, including work to reverse the flow of Siberian rivers, approved by Konstantin Chernenko (Brezhnev's chosen heir) in late 1984.[9]

Brezhnev's policy partially succeeded. By increasing the income of some peasants and extending social benefits to all of them, it helped to bind many farm workers to the regime. A substantial fraction of rank-and-file peasants do not favor reform because of their stake in the existing system. The vast flows of money bought the general secretary the support of regional party officials and central ministers, helping him to consolidate his personal power against Politburo rivals in the 1970s. Those crucial local officials, in turn, used the state's resources to strengthen their own positions. Investment, combined with increasing grain imports to support the enlarged herds of cattle, steadily improved urban food supplies (or at least consumer perceptions of them) through about 1978.

But in a more fundamental sense, Brezhnev's policy was a dismal failure. By the late 1970s, the concentration of meat and milk production in large, high-cost complexes without adequate feed supplies threatened to create new meat and milk shortages like those of 1969. Grain imports became standard procedure to obtain enough feed and high-quality wheat for macaroni and bread, draining the state's hard currency.[10] Investment bought higher-cost output without much expansion in the total amount of produce. Much of the money was stolen or wasted. The overall quality and quantity of Soviet arable land declined under Brezhnev's leadership.

Young, able-bodied peasants, often uprooted anyway by half-completed rural reconstruction schemes that knocked down their old villages and promised a new one sometime later, flocked to the cities, leaving some areas of the Russian heartland empty except for the old and the alcoholic. For instance, in Pskov *oblast'*, only 10 percent of the 850,000 rural residents are able-bodied workers. One-fifth of the province's villages have no able-bodied residents at all.[11] A million hectares of agricultural land has gone out of production in Pskov since the end of World War II because there is no one left to work them.[12]

The vast reclamation schemes contributed to an ecological crisis. Irrigation works built without proper drainage made bogs or salt marshes out of plowland — for instance, some 20 percent of the irrigated area in Volgograd *oblast'* has become unusable swampland.[13] Half of the crop land in the Syr-Dar'ia *oblast'* of Uzbekistan has been damaged by salt from excess irrigation.[14] So much water for irrigating cotton was drawn from the rivers which flow into it that the Aral Sea has all but dried up, threatening the environment of all of Central Asia.[15] Reduced volumes of water have concentrated pollutants in the Don and Volga Rivers, threatening to destroy commercial fisheries and posing increasing health hazards.[16] Overuse of pesticides and defoliants has led to an incredible rate of birth defects and disease among Central Asians, especially among the children who are herded out into the fields each year to pick the cotton crop by hand.[17]

These policies not only waste investment and people, the loss of agricultural products is enormous as well. Poor farming practice greatly reduces the harvest. All the country's fields are infested with weeds, which "steal" ten to 12 million tons of nutrients annually, reducing the harvest by as much as 40 percent of what should be grown.[18] In the late 1970s, it was claimed that 35 to 40 million tons of grain grown were never harvested because of lack of equipment or the slowness of harvest work.[19] The situation seems not to have improved since.

A quarter to a third of Soviet agricultural produce that is raised never reaches the consumer.[20] Only one-third of the potatoes grown on *kolkhozy* and *sovkhozy* eventually find their way to the country's dinner tables.[21] Grain dropped from the cargo boxes of open trucks on the way to the elevators turns the roadsides white as snow at harvest time. In Astrakhan *oblast'*, students brought from school to harvest the tomato crop get packing boxes by dumping out already-picked tomatoes that have rotted in their packaging while awaiting transport from the field.[22] The centralized fruit and vegetable warehouses found in every city are renowned for their characteristic rotten stench. Half of the potatoes stored in Moscow's warehouses rot.[23] Twenty to thirty percent of all the fruits and vegetables delivered to the stores from farms in the Russian far north and far east are written off because of spoilage before being sold.[24] Because of the shortages, managers and sales clerks divert more foodstuffs to sell under the counter. As a result of all these difficulties, Soviet consumers see little food in the state stores. The situation has worsened in the past few years as the old system's authoritarian controls have gradually weakened while market forces have not yet been felt. Thirty percent of respondents to a poll reported in February 1990 said that they cannot get enough food.[25]

Not all the reasons for massive waste are peculiar to agriculture. Underinvestment in transportation facilities has left the USSR with an antiquated and broken-down railroad system. There are almost no refrigerated warehouses, freight cars, or trucks available to move perishable goods to market. The highway network is woefully inadequate. Despite its much greater area, the Soviet Union has only one-third the aggregate mileage of roads found in the United States.[26] Most rural roads are still dirt. During rains or the spring thaw they become seas of mud passable only on tractors. Until recently, farms were responsible for building their own roads, leaving them subject to the difficulties of obtaining materials, manpower, and equipment which plague all construction by *kolkhozy* and *sovkhozy*. Slow, poor-quality construction work is normal for procurement agencies as well. Not only has storage space for the crops been inadequate, but many existing facilities are so badly built that stored produce quickly spoils.

To a great extent, infrastructural difficulties result from the concerns of the state planners. Farms must turn in most of their grain. Then they can buy some of it back from the processing agencies as mixed feed for their animals. Not only must they pay more for the processed item than they received for the grain they sold, but the mixed feed they get back is often much worse in quality. A Ukrainian *kolkhoz* chairman, for instance, complains that he sells the state select wheat for 9.4 rubles a centner, but then has to pay 18 to 20 rubles a centner for feed that often includes salt and clay.[27] Simply cutting the procurement plans and allowing farms to keep more of their own produce would significantly reduce transportation expenses and increase meat production.

Since the *kolkhoz* system was designed to extract as much food from the villages as possible, procurement and processing stations were deliberately built at a distance from the farms. Stalin forbade farms to build or use·their own food processing facilities, even going so far as to destroy peasant hand mills for grinding grain. As a result of the lack of local processing facilities, much produce that is blemished or perishable is never put to use. Farms have been allowed to conduct primary food processing only since 1985. Construction of more on-farm storage space really began only recently.[28]

Investment in better transportation and storage facilities certainly can help cut waste and improve food supplies. Official policy has recognized these difficulties for more than a decade. The July 1978 Central Committee plenum mandated major investments in agricultural transportation and storage facilities. Then-Prime Minister Nikolai Tikhonov announced plans to increase investments in agricultural transportation and storage of agricultural produce by 60 percent (to some fifteen billion rubles) in his speech on the five-year plan at the Twenty-sixth Party Congress in February 1981. The USSR Food Program, adopted in May 1982, declared an intensified war on agricultural waste. Yet another attempt to improve infrastructure was ordered in an eight-year program approved in October 1987.[29] In early October 1989, the CPSU Agrarian Policy Commission discussed further measures to reduce waste and losses.[30] No one doubts that the enormous losses must be cut. How to do so is another matter.

Current Reform Proposals

Gorbachev most fully laid out the New Agrarian Policy at the March 1989 Central Committee plenum.[31] The entire program was, and is, clearly quite controversial. Plans for the plenum were first announced in August 1987, but it was repeatedly postponed, apparently because of policy disagreements within the leadership.[32] An unusual, expanded Politburo meeting was held before the plenum to discuss proposals brought in by the party agrarian policy commission, headed by Ligachev, but the proposals were sent them back for further work, another sign of elite discord.[33] The plenum's final resolution was less radical than the general secretary's report, and it took an unusually long time to be published, suggesting behind-the-scenes bargaining.[34] At the post-plenum press conference, Ligachev explained away, rather than just explaining, the plenum's decisions.[35] Gorbachev himself gave his ideas a more radical twist in a meeting with representatives of the media at the end of March 1989.[36]

Since then, the party's policy guidelines have been fought over repeatedly as the new Congress of People's Deputies has struggled with the Soviet Union's multiple crises. General legislation on leasing of state and *kolkhoz* assets, land tenure, and property has been approved. But struggles over the meaning of the new laws continue within the party even as bureaucratic resistance and administrative obstacles make change slow and uneven.

The following discussion summarizes the institutional changes in the Soviet countryside which have taken place since the Twenty-seventh Party Congress in 1986. Until then, Gorbachev's agrarian policy largely continued measures adopted by his predecessors. Since the congress, declared Soviet agricultural policy has increasingly broken with the traditional system of command agriculture instituted by Stalin in the 1930s. Although it received its name at the March 1989 plenum, the New Agrarian Policy has evolved and continues to do so.

The reforms can be analytically broken down into two parts: first, changes in the farms' external environment, involving reorganization or abolition of the party and state agencies which administer the farms and alterations in the farms' economic environment, and, second, changes within the *kolkhozy* and *sovkhozy* themselves. Taken together, these reforms suggest a new model of Soviet agriculture, although none of them is as yet working well and some may never do so.

Changes in the Farms' External Environment

A vast, hierarchical apparatus of parallel party and state agencies exists to administer the *kolkhozy* and *sovkhozy*. Orders descend to the farms from the all-union authorities in Moscow through union-republican, *oblast'* or *krai* (province), and *raion* (district) authorities before finally reaching the harassed *kolkhoz* chairmen and *sovkhoz* directors. Every action of the farms, whether determining what and how much to plant, when to harvest, or how much to pay the farm workers is governed by directives from above (although successful farms develop many ways to get around those directives).

Apparatus directives are essential to command agriculture. In the absence of market forces, centrally mobilized "campaigns" are the principal means both of fulfilling routine economic tasks and introducing organizational innovation in Soviet-type political systems.[37] The bureaucracy manages farm work so closely that failure to fulfill the day's sowing or harvesting plan can get a farm manager an urgent summons to the district center and an unpleasant hour with the district party secretary.

This apparatus has been reorganized repeatedly since it was first established during Stalin's collectivization of agriculture in the early 1930s. But its basic outlines and functioning have remained constant. The New Agrarian Policy seeks to free the farms from much of this dead weight and transform what remains from agencies that govern the farms into ones that can provide specialized services and assistance.

Because of their subordination to a plan calculated in terms of volumes of output and the endless availability of "soft" state funds to cover any bookkeeping deficits, the *kolkhozy* and *sovkhozy* have been little affected by changes in their economic environment such as output prices. As in the rest of the economy, an unfavorable economic situation could most expeditiously be altered by appropriate representations to the administrators who set conditions. The New Agrarian Policy seeks to replace this command agriculture with one in which farms will have to respond to market signals. So altering the administrative system and introducing more of an agricultural market are inextricably bound together.

Abolition of the USSR State Agro-Industrial Committee

Created in late 1985, Gosagroprom unified the central agricultural management organs, embracing a number of formerly separate and competing ministries.[38] It quickly became a bureaucratic monster in its own right. A USSR Council of Ministers decree implementing the March 1989 plenum's decisions officially abolished it,[39] although a Gosagroprom "elimination commission" was still operating in January 1990.[40]

The Congress of People's Deputies established a new USSR Council of Ministers' State Commission of Food Supplies and Procurements to take over some of Gosagroprom's tasks in June 1989.[41] Although it is not supposed to reincarnate the old ministerial system, it is not yet clear that the commission is more than a new version of the old USSR Gosagroprom.

Other functions previously performed in Moscow were given to republic-level agencies.[42] State Agro-Industrial Committees still exist at the republic level. *Oblast'*-level agroindustrial associations (some are now being renamed agricultural unions with no apparent change in function or powers) also continue to exist. To a great extent, the centralized managerial functions and style of Gosagroprom have not been eliminated. Instead, the republic and *oblast'* agricultural authorities have taken them over. Instead of one centralized directive organ, now several dozen competing ones continue to try to do the same things the one big committee was supposed to handle before.

Abolition of the RAPO

The local branches of the central ministries have always been as narrowly interested in fulfilling their own plans as their parent agencies in Moscow. Creation of *raion* agroindustrial associations (RAPOs) in each of the country's rural districts in 1982 was supposed to end this competition and unite all the farms and their service agencies in a harmonious whole.

The original RAPO, formed in the 1970s in the Abasha district of Eduard Shevardnadze's Georgian SSR, used private-plot contracting, economic rewards, and local party control of suppliers to reorient agriculture to market production and incentives. The RAPO that was generally introduced after the May 1982 Central Committee plenum, however, streamlined rather than subverted the existing system of farm management by administrative command. The power of local party officials over their farms increased. Farms have to deal with several dozen independent procurement, supply, repair, and construction agencies, each of which tries to fulfill its own plan and so squeezes as much as possible out of the farms. Although these service agencies were supposed to be subordinated to the RAPO, most retained their independent plans and ministerial allegiances in Moscow. So the creation of the RAPO changed little.[43]

The April 1989 Council of Ministers resolution implementing the March plenum's decisions mandated replacement of the RAPO with an "agrocombine" (APK) or "agroindustrial association" (APO). The new *raion*-level agencies, unlike the RAPOs, are supposed to be voluntary and reduce their district service and management staffs to a minimum. They are also supposed to work as single enterprises and break even on their operations.[44]

The first agrocombine, the APK "Kuban" in Krasnodar *krai*, was established as an experiment in 1984.[45] It transferred all the district specialists to consulting cooperatives that work on contract for the farms and demolished most of the district- and farm-level management apparatus. The combine's director, Mikhail Lomach, claims that if all farms were to begin to process their output on site as he does, assortments and sales of many foods could be doubled or tripled within three years.[46]

The model agroindustrial association, the APO "Novomoskovskii" in Tula *oblast'*, was inaugurated in early 1987 at a ceremony attended by then-Central Committee Secretary for Agriculture Viktor Nikonov.[47] Supposedly, the APO is more democratic than either the old RAPO or the agrocombine.[48] Apparently that means that the farm managers have more control over the association than the local party authorities. So far it is difficult to see that the new names have affected the operation of most district authorities.

Replacement of the State Plan by "Goszakazy"

Since the 1930s, Soviet farms, whether nominally state enterprises (*sovkhozy*) or cooperatives (*kolkhozy*), have been subject to capricious, always-too-high plans for produce deliveries to the state. Farm plans were set from above, and neither managers nor farmers have had much say in determining their assignments. Fulfilling the plan was the farmers' "first commandment," and they often sinned. Farms that succeeded in meeting their plans were frequently hit with additional requirements to make up for others' shortfalls, and local and regional authorities often dictated what, where, and how much individual farms could grow, destroying any possibility of rational crop rotations or effective regional specialization. These problems were repeatedly condemned by the authorities, but little changed in practice.

Gorbachev hinted that this situation might change by making a favorable reference to Lenin's "tax-in-kind" *(prodnalog)* in the "Political Report" he delivered at the Twenty-seventh Party Congress in early 1986. During the Civil War of 1918–1921, urban food detachments had simply seized the peasants' produce. As a major part of the conciliatory New Economic Policy he instituted in 1921, Lenin ended this food requisitioning, replacing the armed detachments with relatively low and stable delivery quotas paid for at relatively reasonable prices. Gorbachev's revival of the *prodnalog* implied that farms would be freed from intermediate plan indicators and given lower delivery quotas. Plans would be stable over the whole five-year-plan period (a promise always previously violated).[49] To emphasize the change, the old "plan assignments" were later rechristened "state orders."

So far, however, *goszakazy* have not freed the farms from arbitrary and capricious planning. The state orders, like the old plan targets, are set by administrators with little reference to farms' productive possibilities. Complaints that the *goszakazy* cover the farms' entire output and more are numerous. Courts have determined that the *goszakazy*, like the old plans, have the force of law, so farms are subject to sanctions for failure to fulfill them.[50]

The high *goszakazy* are one reason farm managers are reluctant to lease land to peasants, let alone give a peasant a plot to work as an independent farm. An individual peasant or cooperative just getting a farm set up may be reluctant to take on a part of the farm's burden, especially when the farm itself often fails to fulfill its state order but pressures the lease-holder to do so anyway.[51]

A recent amendment to the 1987 Law on the State Enterprise strips ministries of the power to issue *goszakazy*, reserving it to the State Planning Committee. If this change affects agricultural planning, and if it is effective, then the farms' position may improve somewhat since they will have to answer to only one superior.[52] However, the basis of Soviet planning remains administrative orders, not market signals, so the situation has not fundamentally changed. As of May 1990 it was still true that, as agricultural journalist Igor Abakumov observed in a commentary on a state decision to raise the prices it pays for grain, "even though formally *goszakazy* aren't sent down to them, not every [*sovkhoz*] director or [*kolkhoz*] chairman can resist the *raion* and *oblast'* authorities."[53]

Creation of Union-Republic and Oblast' Food Stocks

Since collectivization, procurement agencies have taken as much of the farms' produce as they could get. Procurements were then redistributed according to the central authorities' orders. Farms might get some of their own grain returned as animal feed, meaning it had been uselessly hauled away from the farm and back. While in storage awaiting disposition the crops might spoil. Central agencies might also order produce shifted from one part of the country to another, sometimes depriving both the producing region and the consignee of the produce, which spoiled in transit.

Control of food stocks was decentralized to encourage regional self-sufficiency and cut cross-hauls.[54] The plan for deliveries to the central food stocks was lowered. Above-plan procurements of are retained by the union republics and individual provinces to use as they see fit. These changes were expected to give local authorities reason to push for increased production because the results could be seen in the food stores of their own area.[55]

Although the all-union plan for procurements was cut, it is unlikely farm plans were cut. Republics and provinces failed to meet their plans for deliveries to the all-union stocks in 1989, instead holding on to agricultural produce for local use.[56] Since no region is self-sufficient, this decentralization exacerbates shortages in other parts of the country that would normally be supplied from the all-union stores. Instead of the central government's setting food-distribution priorities, each union republic or *oblast'* is doing so.

Until 1986, farms were expected to sell any output they produced in excess of their plan targets to the state procurement agencies at higher "above-plan" purchase prices. In August 1986, the Politburo permitted farms to sell some of their fruit, vegetable, and potato output in Moscow and Leningrad *kolkhoz* markets.[57] This was later generalized into permission for the farms to sell up to 20 percent of their planned and all their above-plan fruit and vegetable output on the *kolkhoz* markets or elsewhere at whatever prices the market would bear.

The hope was that direct sales would stimulate farms to cut waste by actually marketing more of what they grow and expanding production. But these new rights were little used. A year after the initial permission for sales in Moscow and Leningrad was given, the Central Committee criticized everyone concerned for failing to improve food supplies there.[58] In

January 1989, Gosagroprom Chairman Vsevolod Murakhovskii explained that farms were still often given plans for all their produce, effectively negating their right of free sales.[59] The much-publicized offering of hard currency to farms for above-plan grain sales begun in mid-1989 had, as of January 1990, also elicited little response, for similar reasons.[60]

The March 1989 plenum provided that farms were eventually to make all, or almost all, their sales on a free market. At the post-plenum press conference, however, Egor Ligachev explained that this would happen only after the consumer food market had been put in balance and shortages ended. Since for the reformers the point of introducing the market is to end shortages by allowing supply and demand to operate, Ligachev's statement amounted to saying that farms would not be allowed more free sales.

Creation of "Agrofirms"

Conflicts of interest between subunits of ministries and departments and farms within a particular geographical area were supposed to have been solved by the establishment of the RAPO and the other territorial agroindustrial committees. Such horizontal integration did nothing to solve problems in coordinating different agencies involved in moving produce from field to consumer. The "agrofirm" vertically integrates the farm producers, procurement, food processing, transportation, storage, and food retailing agencies to eliminate bureaucratic barriers.

Unlike the agrocombines and APOs, the agrofirms do not encompass all the farms and related enterprises in a district, instead adding processing, transportation, storage, and retail sales outlets to a successful farm. Most agrofirms are located near major cities. The major drive for their creation unfolded in 1987 and 1988, probably in part because of the failure of the earlier resolution allowing free sales on the *kolkhoz* markets to improve urban food supplies.[61] The agrofirms, unlike regular farms, possessed the resources to move their output to the cities and sell it once there, difficulties that probably contributed to the lack of response to the earlier above-plan sales decision. Moreover, because they included all the intermediate agencies, their state delivery plans (state orders) clearly included the in-town sales.

The most successful agrofirm is the "Adazhi," located near the Latvian capital, Riga. Reportedly, some of its success can be explained by its unusual access to hard currency — the farm has been selling luxury furs on the international market for years. The chairman of the "Adazhi" agrofirm, Albert Kauls, is a member of the new USSR Presidential Council.[62]

The agrofirm concept obviously cannot be applied throughout Soviet agriculture. Much of the agrofirms' success depends on their good fortune in being located near major cities. But, like truck-farming operations anywhere, they can serve an immediate urban need.

Equipment and supplies have traditionally been distributed to the farms on the basis of allocation orders issued by the central planners. As with their own production plans, the farms' supposed ability to influence distribution decisions by ordering needed materials and equipment from the ministries that produced them did not work in practice. Monopoly producers found many ways to force the farms to buy what they wished to sell rather than what the farms needed. The obvious response to this situation is the creation of wholesale markets in production inputs.

Planned as part of the general economic reform in 1987–1988, there is little evidence that wholesale trade in equipment, supplies, or other production needs has been instituted as yet. Organization of a farm equipment sales and service cooperative in one rural *raion* was recently reported as a major event. In that case, the head of the state repair agency in the district favored creating a competitor, a benign attitude unlikely to be shared by most of his colleagues.[63] Peasants who have taken land on leases can usually get needed equipment and supplies only from the farm from which they have subcontracted, so that the farm sets prices arbitrarily and high.[64] The opening of the first retail store in the Urals *oblast'* selling small implements and other necessities directly to leaseholders was reported as an unusual event.[65]

Increasing Retail Food Prices

The subsidy represented by the difference between the price paid to the farm and the retail sales price is very high.[66] In 1984, some 44.3 billion rubles were spent to subsidize meat and dairy products.[67] In early 1989, milk sales were subsidized by 20 kopeks a liter, meat sales by 3.2 rubles a kilogram.[68] The current subsidy system, in combination with state plans that require all farms to produce a little of every crop, pays farms to produce crops for which they are not well suited by location or natural endowment.

Production costs are high in large part because the prices farms must pay for their inputs are arbitrarily set. Much of the increase in purchase prices in the past twenty years passed through the farms to suppliers of fuel, equipment, and other supplies. As the economist Nikolai Shmelev suggests, there is a cycle of price increases. To meet higher costs, the farm arranges to have the prices the state pays it increased. Then the supplier of production inputs, seeing that the farm can afford to pay more, arranges to have its prices increased.[69] So the state subsidy to cover the difference between production costs and retail price grows. As long as the prices are administratively set and subject to negotiation by the enterprise, the cycle will continue. The subsidies will not be eliminated just by changing purchase prices. Rationalization of the prices farms pay for their equipment and supplies will be needed as well.[70]

A general price reform was planned as part of the 1987 economic reform package. Agricultural input prices, however, continue to increase. The leadership backed away from tampering with the subsidy on consumer food prices, clearly fearing the political consequences if prices were raised. Gorbachev ruled out general increases in retail food prices in his speech at the March plenum.

A year later, as part of the discussion of "radical reform," the regime did begin to attack the problem of retail food prices by announcing a planned tripling of the price of bread and baked goods effective July 1, 1990. Bread prices, which have not changed since the early 1930s, are set so low that it is profitable for peasants to buy bread in the stores to feed to their cattle on their private plots. Even this minimal measure set off panic buying in the country's food stores and contributed to the perception that Gorbachev's popularity at home had fallen precipitously, although the announcement of the increase had promised "full compensation for the whole population" (in which case it is difficult to see how the price increase will improve the state's financial position).[71]

Ending Direct State Subsidies for Kolkhozy and Sovkhozy

Many farms have relied on state subsidies to meet their wages bills and other current expenses. Although these subsidies are formally bank loans, getting them seems to be a sheer formality and repayment is unlikely. In 1970–1987, more than fifteen billion rubles in bank credits to collective and state farms and other enterprises in the agricultural sector were written off as uncollectable. At the beginning of 1988, more than seventy-two billion rubles in credits were not being paid back on schedule — and almost certainly never would be paid.[72]

Subsidies are to be ended through the introduction of "full economic accounting" *(polnyi khozraschet)* and "self-financing" *(samofinansirovanie)*. Full *khozraschet* simply means that farms should keep track of all their costs, profits, and losses. Since the entire economic environment has been administratively regulated, there has been little reason for farms to do so seriously. "Self-financing" allows farms to keep their profits rather than turning all or most of them over to the state for redistribution as the state sees fit.

Farms under full *khozraschet* and self-financing will be denied state credits except on a commercial basis and allowed to go bankrupt if they cannot meet their expenses. Estonia seems to have been the first large area to adopt these conditions[73] — the Baltic states' relatively more developed agriculture served as a test bed before the change was introduced elsewhere. A September 1987 agricultural resolution required all farms to adopt self-financing by 1988–1989.[74] It is not clear that they actually did, although the Ukraine, at least, claimed to have done so.[75]

Sovkhozy supposedly adopted *khozraschet* in the late 1960s. But because many of them are always planned to be unprofitable, the change was never effective. The state has never been willing to allow unprofitable farms to cease operations. Until it does, neither *khozraschet* nor self-financing will have much effect.

Converting Bankrupt Farms into Subsidiaries of Industrial Enterprises

Industrial enterprises have been encouraged to organize their own "agroshops," or subsidiary farms. The produce these farms provide is then used in the enterprise's cafeterias or distributed to employees on concessionary terms. Although some subsidiary farms have been organized on waste land, in other cases unprofitable *sovkhozy* or *kolkhozy* have been taken over by a successful factory. In this way, unprofitable farms are made to seem solvent, although such "profitability" is largely a bookkeeping exercise. The underlying purpose is to maintain the rural community around which the farm was organized. Because it allows farms to go bankrupt without being physically liquidated, Soviet officials prefer to reorganize farms as subsidiaries.

In September 1987, provincial and republican Soviet executive committees were given the power to attach unprofitable farms to successful industries in their territory. Farms that went bankrupt under *khozraschet* and self-financing could be saved in this way. According to Viktor Nikonov, then CPSU Central Committee secretary in charge of agriculture, by May 1989 some 180 of the country's 1,700 unprofitable farms had been reorganized into "cooperatives of cooperatives" (see below) or subsidiary farms.[76]

The social policy embodied in the subsidiary farm idea may be commendable, although it is also unfair since it relies on the farm's luck in being taken over by a strong enterprise rather than in being provided with unemployment insurance or relocation assistance. However, it is not entirely clear why industrial enterprises should want to take on the burden of unprofitable farms. As the economic reforms affect industry it seems likely they will less and less want to do so. The obvious result will be a return to administrative pressure on industrial enterprises from the local and central party authorities to save the bankrupt farms by accepting them as subsidiaries. Nor is it clear that industrial enterprises have any particular expertise or interest in running farms.[77]

Internal Changes in the Farms

Sovkhozy and *kolkhozy* engage in two kinds of agricultural production. "Social" production is work done for wages by the farm workers on the farm's own fields and in its own livestock sheds. "Private" production, on the other hand, is done by those same workers on their small "personal subsidiary farms," or private plots, for their own use.

From the 1930s until the mid-1960s, most farmers actually lived on the produce from their private plots. Earnings from *kolkhoz* or *sovkhoz* work were so small that farm labor often became nothing more than a price paid for the privilege of having the private plot. After guaranteed wages were introduced in the mid-1960s, earnings from the farm increased and private plot production began to decline as the farm population shrank and aged and the plot became less important as a source of family income.

Kolkhozy and *sovkhozy* are organized hierarchically, with the farm workers doing their jobs in large "brigades" run by an overseer. Since the peasants not only work for but also live on the farm, their lives are subject to a great deal of control by the farm management (which, although theoretically elected on *kolkhozy*, is really appointed by higher officials). Until the late 1970s, *kolkhoz* peasants' internal passports were held in the farm office and issued to them only when needed for approved trips, so they could not legally leave the farm, even for a short time, without permission. (Quitting the *kolkhoz* for good requires permission by a vote of the membership.)

Changes in the internal structure of the *kolkhozy* and *sovkhozy* under the New Agrarian Policy are intended to integrate the private and public sectors so that farm workers will work better for the farm, and to give the farm workers more independence and autonomy at work and in their daily lives.

The size of private plots has been closely regulated by both farm and higher authorities. Farmers were discouraged from selling too much produce, and they often had it confiscated on the way to market by unsympathetic officials with quotas to fill.

In 1982, farms were allowed to contract with their workers for livestock. The farm provided young animals and feed, and the farmer then sold the mature animal back to the farm to be marketed. However, the restrictions on the size of private plots, and the number of animals a family could keep, were lifted only in 1987.[78] Not all restrictions are gone yet; each farm can still decide on an appropriate size of private holdings for local conditions. Since 1987, the party-state has urged that private plots be more tightly integrated with the collective sector in both production and marketing.

Some local officials have continued to oppose expanded private plots. In Volgograd *oblast'* the party first secretary organized gangs to smash private greenhouses because too many farmers were making too much money producing tomatoes. Most of those affected were retirees, who lived on their profits since the pensions they receive from their lifetime of farm work are so small. No tomatoes can be found in the state stores in Volgograd.[79]

Changing the Pay System for Farm Work

Until recently, the state guaranteed the piece-rate wages paid to *kolkhoz* and *sovkhoz* peasants. Whether the farm was profitable or not, every worker got paid the state-approved rate for every operation done. The bank gave the farm the money to cover the wages if needed. Not only did this system create an incentive to do more of the easy or highly paid operations than needed while avoiding low-paid, difficult jobs, it also meant that the peasants had little reason to care whether or not the farm was profitable. A complicated bonus system for overfulfilling plans, economizing on inputs, and so forth was supposed to reward them if the farm was profitable, but because of the arbitrariness of the plans received from above did not do so.

Now, farm wages are to be paid based on the gross income of the farm after current production costs are paid *(ot valovogo dokhoda)*.[80] In theory, unprofitable farms will have no money for wages. Since state credits to pay for wages are no longer to be issued, this change was forced by the *khozraschet* and self-financing reforms described earlier.

First permitted in industry (as so-called "second-model *khozraschet*" in 1987), pay from gross income in agriculture was ordered to become standard in the Council of Ministers' resolution implementing the March plenum decisions.[81] The extent to which it has been adopted is still unclear.

Since collectivization, family groups have not been allowed to work together in social production because they might come to think of part of the *kolkhoz* or *sovkhoz* as "their" land, surreptitiously restoring private farming. This ideologically motivated prohibition was repeatedly challenged by farm managers, agricultural economists, and even some members of the elite because it clearly destroyed a major motivation for better work. But until Gorbachev mentioned family labor approvingly at the Twenty-sixth Party Congress, an approval repeated in the March 1986 resolution on agriculture, the prohibition stood.

The use of family groups as work units on *kolkhozy* and *sovkhozy* was strongly urged in a December 1986 CPSU Central Committee resolution.[82] Families were permitted to engage in some consumer services enterprises in the Law on Individual Labor Activity that took effect in mid-1987.[83] The 1988 Law on Cooperatives allowed them to organize as independent co-ops.[84] The peasant family's economic rights are completely rehabilitated in the 1990 Law on Property, which provides that, in the absence of other legislation, peasant family property is to be held in common by the household.[85] This stipulation restores pre-collectivization peasant law, which was based on the household rather than the individual.

Allowing Leasing of Land and Equipment from the Farm

As long as they are effectively day laborers, *kolkhoz* peasants and *sovkhoz* workers have little incentive to economize on inputs, increase labor productivity, or care for the land. Allowing individuals or voluntarily organized groups to get land and equipment from the farm on a lease *(arenda)*, in return for either a specified volume and quality of produce or a share of the lessee's profits, restores this incentive.

Most commonly, these leases are internal, between the farm authorities and some of their own peasants, so the agreement is technically a "lease subcontract," or *arendnyi podriad,* and treated as a labor contract. Under these conditions the contracting parties are not equal. The lessees have no rights to appeal to a court of law to enforce their contract or to hold their own bank account, a mark of legal independence. The farm pays for the produce and then markets it as its own.

Individuals or agricultural cooperatives may also lease land directly from the local soviet, outside of the *kolkhoz* or *sovkhoz*. In this case they are an independent organization able to conclude contracts, open their own bank account, and market their produce themselves. But like urban cooperators they are outside of any of the administered systems for distributing production supplies and equipment and subject to regulation and taxation by the soviets.

Initially legalized by a Supreme Soviet Presidium decree in April 1989, a formal Law on Leasing was approved near the end of that year.[86] Leases are to be effective for up to fifty years, and may be inherited by relations who have been working on the land. Neither the land nor the lease may be sold.

The 1989 Law on Leasing indicated that territory not assigned to a collective or state farm could be leased by the local soviet to individuals or cooperatives. The 1990 Law on Land provides that anyone who wishes to leave a *kolkhoz* or *sovkhoz* may do so, receiving in the process an enclosed tract as good as the farm's average land that is then to be held on a life-time lease from the local soviet.[87] The contradiction between the two laws has not yet been resolved.

Allowing Independent Peasant Farms and Production Cooperatives

For the first time since collectivization destroyed all individual farms and imposed a uniform system of *kolkhozy* and *sovkhozy* throughout the USSR, the new land law allows different forms of farming. Independent peasant farms may be set up on land leased from the local soviet or created from disbanded *kolkhozy* or *sovkhozy*.

Independent farms may be run by individual families, in which case they are called peasant farms or, following a vogue for things Western, "farmers' farms" *(fermerskie khoziaistva)*. The 1988 Law on Cooperatives also permits small, newly organized agricultural production cooperatives of several families or unrelated individuals to take over peasant farms. They have the same legal status as individual peasants.

Individual peasant farming has appeared mostly in Latvia, Lithuania, and Estonia and depopulated areas of the Russian Republic's non-black earth zone and far north.[88] Leasing from *kolkhozy* and *sovkhozy (arendnyi podriad)* has not been widely adopted in the Baltic states, however. Lithuanian agricultural economist and former prime minister Kazimiera-Danuta Prunskiene explained to a Moscow conference on economic reform that it would be neither fair nor politic to lease land to people when descendants of the owners from whom the farm was taken by collec-tivization are still alive, know its boundaries, and very likely want it back.[89] As part of their drive for independence, the three Baltic states are clearly preparing for full decollectivization. But the Baltic region differs from most of the rest of the USSR in its tradition of individual farms and the shorter time since collectivization was carried out there.

According to the State Statistics Committee, at the end of 1989 there were about 4,000 peasant farms in Latvia, just over 1,000 in Lithuania, and 800 in Estonia. The peasant farm movement was reportedly growing in the RSFSR and the Ukraine, but no numbers were reported, suggesting that only a few individual farms had as yet been established in those areas.[90] In January 1990, agricultural economist Gelii Shmelev, in a slash-ing rebuttal of fears that peasant farming would destroy the *kolkhoz* system, claimed that in most provinces of the Russian Republic no land at all had yet been given to peasants, whether on lease subcontract from farms or as peasant proprietors.[91] At the end of May 1990, Central Committee

Agricultural Secretary Egor Stroev claimed there were about twenty thousand peasant farms in the entire USSR.[92]

Neither leasing nor peasant farming has gained wide use as yet, partly because the peasants do not trust the authorities to keep their bargains. Many peasants fear that some future regime might decide, as Stalin did in 1929, to take the land away again or even to repeat the process of "liquidating the kulaks as a class," destroying peasant farmers and their families. The various laws enacted in 1989–1990 are supposed to provide guarantees against such a catastrophe, but only time and a reformed political system will convince the peasants that these laws are more meaningful than most of the legislation they have lived with for the last fifty years.

Transforming Existing Farms into "Cooperatives of Cooperatives"

Rather than breaking up all the existing *kolkhozy* and *sovkhozy* into peasant farms, something that may be neither desirable nor possible, the New Agrarian Policy proposes that in most cases they should be transformed into "cooperatives of cooperatives." This model, originated by the martyred experimenter Ivan Khudenko in the 1960s, envisions that each subunit of a *sovkhoz* or *kolkhoz*, such as a farming brigade, machine shop, warehouse, or management, will be related to the others only on a monetary basis. Each small group sells its products and services to the others and buys what it needs from them.[93] The *kolkhoz* or *sovkhoz* continues to exist, but "it isn't the same: it has neither brigadiers, livestock-farm heads, nor timekeepers — only those who are indispensable remain."[94] The reorganization of *kolkhozy* and *sovkhozy* in this way was proposed in Gorbachev's speech at the Fourth Congress of Collective Farmers in March 1988.[95]

To raise more capital and increase their workers' stake in results, some farms have begun to reorganize as joint-stock companies *(aktsionernye obshchestva)*, as they are permitted to do under the Law on Cooperatives and the new Model Farm Charter adopted in 1988.[96] Workers may buy shares *(aktsii)* at a fixed price from the farm. They receive annual payments from the farm's profits based on the number of shares they hold. The *aktsii* apparently may not be resold unless the farm buys them back at the issue price. It is not clear whether the annual dividend paid on the shares changes if farm profitability increases, but it seems that if the farm goes bankrupt or is reorganized as a subsidiary farm the workers' investments can be lost. So these *aktsii* are perhaps more like participation in a profit-sharing plan or a cooperative employee stock ownership plan than the usual Western stock shares.

Towards a Mixed Agriculture

If all these ideas are actually implemented, a patchwork of *kolkhozy*, *sovkhozy*, subsidiary farms, leased individual farms, and freehold farms will emerge in the Soviet countryside. The hierarchy of party and state organs concerned with controlling the farms will be replaced by market forces. Despite conservative claims, no reform spokesman has argued in print that all the *kolkhozy* and *sovkhozy* should be replaced by individual farms, although the "cooperatives of cooperatives" might leave very little of the existing farm management in place. No one doubts that large, mechanized farms are needed to feed what is now a highly, even over-urbanized population. Opponents of the New Agrarian Policy, however, tend to conveniently forget these cautions, ascribing to the reformers views that they do not actually advocate.

The Conservative Response

The conservative position in the current debate rejects most of the policy changes enumerated above. Conservatives hold that the *kolkhoz* system needs only minor changes. If capital investments to reduce waste are properly made and the management is allowed to do its job without interference, the existing system can solve the country's food problems and eventually increase agricultural production dramatically. Peasant farming and private plots cannot supply the country. They can serve only as minor adjuncts to the country's real producers, the large-scale state and collective farms. Leasing should be contained within the existing farms and their basic internal structure retained. There is no need for more than strictly limited autonomy of work groups within the existing farms; to give them more control over their own resources and sales would lead to a total breakdown of the food supply system.

The managers of the 10 percent or so of Soviet farms that are successful under existing conditions characteristically argue that what they need most is greater authority to manage their own enterprises. Their favorite reform is the APO. Vasilii Starodubtsev, chairman of the "Novomoskovskoe" APO, seems to express views typical of such successful leaders. A long-time model *kolkhoz* chairman, Starodubtsev frequently suffered from the rules and regulations imposed by the party-state administrators because of his efforts to get things done for his farm.[97] His APO exemplifies the good *kolkhoz* chairman's concept of how agriculture should be organized, allowing him to run things at the local level without interference from the party or the state.[98]

Like many chairmen of good *kolkhozy* (and many entrepreneurs in market economies), Starodubtsev wants a kind of control over his workers that he does not want applied to himself. He is not particularly fond of workers' participation in management. He has, for instance, spoken out against the election of managers, which he says tends to become simply a popularity contest.[99] As might be expected, Starodubtsev is vehemently opposed to breaking up the *kolkhozy* and *sovkhozy* to create individual peasant farmsteads.[100]

A Soviet farm worker's productivity is about one-fifth that of an American farmer.[101] Conservatives see two ways to improve it. The first is to provide the *kolkhozy* and *sovkhozy* with more and better equipment. Although Soviet production of agricultural equipment is the highest in the world, farm managers regularly complain about both quality and availability of needed machinery. Their situation is growing worse because as the agricultural equipment industry has begun to operate under the economic reform's conditions, prices have risen sharply, threatening to bankrupt the farms.[102]

Changing wage schemes to give farmers more incentive would also improve productivity. Therefore many conservatives are willing to introduce the lease contract to make individual peasants bear the cost of their equipment and land, paying them in accord with results. The farm would then take the difference between what it pays the peasant contractor for his produce (the internal, or *raschetnyi*, price) and the state purchase price it receives. Conservatives contend that leasing must be contained within the farms to provide the lessees with adequate housing and other amenities as well as supply, repair, marketing, and other services. Such leases shift the burden of uncertainty about production results from management to the worker, since the peasant must pay if management fails to provide contracted-for inputs or cannot sell his produce.

Egor Ligachev has been the primary exponent of these views in the leadership. His statements probably reflect the demands of his principal rural constituents, the managers of "good" farms, as well as his own ideological preferences and his authority-building strategy in elite competition. He has repeatedly called for spending more on "non-productive" items, which largely means rural development to hold the labor force.[103] He claims to favor land leasing, but only within the collective and state farms. Under his leadership, the CPSU Agrarian Policy Commission has devoted much of its attention to the struggle with waste.[104] In December 1989 at the Congress of People's Deputies, he summarized the conservative position on resources while answering a rhetorical question about why Soviet agricultural labor is so unproductive.

The reason is clear, comrades. It is the inadequate provision of equipment to the agroindustrial complex and the inadequate social infrastructure in the Soviet countryside....

I asked our specialists to make some calculations. They show that if we managed to raise the level of the weak farms' equipment provision and social infrastructure to the level of the farms that are working well or even in the middle rank, the food supply in the country would be normal and the problem would disappear. But this would require 270 billion rubles in capital investments.... This is a little less than was planned to be channeled into the agroindustrial complex during the current five-year plan.[105]

This may sound at first like the voice of sweet reason. He asks for only as much more money as is already being spent, and promises that then all the problems will disappear. The difficulty with Ligachev's proposal is that the country does not have the money to maintain the high levels of agricultural investment mandated in the 1986–1990 five-year plan without greater returns than it received from that investment. Even if it did, these "calculations" offer no guarantee at all that the money would actually buy the increased food production promised. In the same speech, he argued for retail and wholesale price reform. Urging the creation of a "a support mechanism for price parity in agricultural and industrial products," he apparently had in mind another round of procurement price increases to match higher equipment costs.[106] The May 1990 increase in grain prices clearly responded to this demand.[107] Yet in the absence of other changes, increased purchase prices can only add to the Soviet budget deficit and fuel further inflation.

The high-cost structure of Soviet agriculture provides a further argument against fundamental agrarian reform. Opponents of peasant farming and leasing claim that establishing peasants as independent farmers would cost astronomical sums for equipment, buildings, roads, and other necessities of life.[108] These arguments are not quite convincing, since they assume the level of prices and capital utilization according to current standard planning norms, which are certainly inflated. Experimental lease collectives and peasant farms have generally used much less equipment, fewer and less costly structures, and economized on other production inputs. (The allowances for equipment allocation and usage, designs for structures, and norms for using such things as seed and fertilizer are all determined by the agencies which produce these inputs. They have never had much reason to economize.) Nor, if the cost involved is building everyone a farmhouse, is it clear why farmers would necessarily have to move out to "their" land. The existing infrastructure of housing, village services, and transportation should be adequate or inadequate, whether peasant proprietors are travelling to their land or *sovkhoz* workers are. Equipment and repair cooperatives could be set up on the basis of existing farm garages.

These calculations of the cost of setting up peasant farms assume that all the existing farm population would want to become individual farmers. Ligachev told a Swedish interviewer that "he considers it would cost far too much and take far too long to turn all unprofitable *sovkhozy* and *kokhozy* into private farms."[109] No one really expects, though, that all the unprofitable *kolkhozy* and *sovkhozy* would be broken up into individual farms. Many of them are unprofitable because they are producing very little at very high cost and should simply be abandoned as farms altogether. (The real concern may be that even the "good" existing farms will not be competitive in a market economy, in which case many more farms would be unprofitable.) Nor would all the existing labor force remain farmers. Reorganization would release under-utilized labor into new subsidiary enterprises, such as food processing, rural construction, or services. In some cases excess workers might have to be pensioned off or given unemployment compensation.[110]

The potential unemployment created by agricultural reform is a real concern among farm workers and managers. Many peasants have a strong interest in retaining the existing system. Rural pensioners and the manual workers who are still the majority of the farm labor force are usually left out of leasing schemes. The *kolkozy* and *sovkhozy* guarantee them minimal employment. The average age of the Soviet rural population is over fifty, so most farmers have a substantial stake in *kolkhoz* or *sovkhoz* services and pensions.[111] If the *kolkhozy* and *sovkhozy* are dismantled, or if the farms' incomes are sharply reduced, those people may lose their livelihood. Similarly, many managers clearly fear reform because they cannot imagine how they would operate in a marketized system.[112]

Ligachev has another reason for defending the existing *kolkhoz* order as well. He argues in ideological terms that

> Some people... demand the establishment of small peasant farms instead of kolkhozes and sovkhozes. Others even say that it is necessary to introduce private property in land. In this regard, I ask what this will mean for our homeland. It will mean no more nor less than, if we are to look truth in the eye, a radical change in the social base in the village. You will agree, comrades, that this is a different social system.[113]

If peasant farming is permitted in the countryside, he says, then capitalism will have been restored in the USSR. Challenging the dominance of

the existing collective farms means capitalism victorious, not a mixed
economy that is still socialist. As far as Ligachev is concerned, there can be
no socialism with individual farming.

Political Implications

The New Agrarian Policy has fundamental implications for the structure
of the Soviet party-state and the process of creating a socialist state of laws.
If the current reform proposals are fully implemented, they will fundamentally change the organization of Soviet agriculture and the distribution of managerial power within it. Implementing those policies requires
radical changes in the structure of the Soviet state, something that the
existing party and state apparatus fiercely resists. Because it implicitly
rejects Stalinist collectivization, the New Agrarian Policy also threatens the
claim to rule of the Communist party and perhaps even the legitimacy of
the Soviet state as a whole. But continued failure to solve the country's
food problems are at least equally threatening to the country's stability
and the party's power.

Gorbachev has accepted the need for radical changes in the organization of Soviet agriculture. On all the usual Kremlinological indicators of
having outmaneuvered and ousted rivals he is in extraordinarily good
shape. He has steadily reduced Ligachev's position, and coerced the party
elite into giving up much of its power.

Yet the agrarian reform has not gone very far yet. In many respects, the
drive to introduce the New Agrarian Policy parallels previous administrative campaigns to introduce organizational innovations. The general secretary finds himself in a bind. His only effective lever for enforcing
change is the administrative apparatus. Yet that apparatus is not capable of
changing; it can only report that things have been done. It does so, but in
fact all that is different on the farm is a label and the number on the
farm's statistical reporting form. The Soviet state Stalin built is curiously
weak: its "strong fingers" can kill millions, but it does not possess the
"thumbs" that would allow it to influence its citizens' behavior in less catastrophic ways.[114]

The leadership's inability to implement changes in the countryside is a
direct result of the great political strength of the rural district and *oblast'*
first secretaries. As "prefects," they intervene on behalf of their farms —
and to prevent outsiders from affecting their farms' operation.[115]

Gorbachev recently described the party apparatus' coordinating role:

For a long period the party was built into the administrative-command system for the rule of society and lived according to the laws of that system. And it was not merely built into it, but, in essence, towered over everything, monitored all processes of state, economic and ideological life, supplanting and bypassing everyone else, issuing indisputable directives and commands to state and economic organs and social organizations.[116]

In rural areas, the role of party secretaries in obtaining and distributing resources, protecting favored clients, and punishing those who dared oppose them grew during the Khrushchev and Brezhnev years. The regional secretaries were increasingly able to evade central control and twist central directives to suit their own purposes.[117]

Repeated replacement of the incumbent provincial officials since Gorbachev came to power in 1985 has not affected the power inherent in the position of provincial or district party first secretary. The replacements often quickly begin to act like the men they took over from. In January and February 1990, a wave of popular uprisings led to the ouster of *oblast'* first secretaries in Chernigov, Volgograd, Tiumen', and elsewhere.[118] Once again individual leaders changed while the system did not.

The reforms begun with the constitutional changes of October 1988 and initially implemented in the March 1989 elections to the Congress of People's Deputies help to secure Gorbachev's own position. They lessen his dependence on the party by giving him an independent power base. But more importantly for his reform program, they also create new institutional instruments for implementing policy and governing Soviet society that are not controlled by the old party-state elite.

The new requirement that the *oblast'* or *raion* first secretary simultaneously chair the corresponding soviet allows some popular control over those leaders, since they must be elected to the chairmanship by the soviet itself. But so far local party secretaries have generally won those elections, suggesting that they are maintaining control. The new land law provides that local Soviets, rather than the *kolkhozy* and *sovkhozy* themselves, control the allocation of land to peasant farms and agricultural cooperatives. But as long as the same people from the party apparatus dominate the soviets, that change will not help people who want their own plots very much.

Reforming party and state institutions to make them work more effectively will do little good if most of the population comes to reject the basic premises on which their overall legitimacy is built. The conservatives defend the *kolkhozy* as a defense of the policy of forced collectivization. If the collective farms cannot be made to work efficiently, then Stalin's decision to create them wholesale using force and famine is finally proven wrong. If all of the blood spilled and hardship endured in the countryside at the party's orders were in vain, what remains of its claim to exercise the leading role in society? Rethinking Soviet agrarian history threatens the Communist party's contemporary political power.[119] For Ligachev, his alter ego Nina Andreeva,[120] and perhaps for many other professional party *apparatchiki*, command agriculture is not so much an economic mechanism as evidence of party authority. Altering or abolishing the *kolkhoz* system threatens the party's right to rule.

If food supplies are not speedily improved, however, the legitimacy of party rule will be in danger because the *kolkhoz* system has not been changed. The informal "social contract" between the regime and the population hinges on guaranteed and slowly rising social welfare in return for political quiescence.[121] In a country where "spending on food approximates... the purchasing patterns found in less developed countries rather than developed countries,"[122] food supplies are a crucial part of that tacit bargain. Economic reforms that require more effort from the population with little immediate return are threatening enough to this balance. If food supplies fail, or if prices are sharply increased, the specters of the 1962 Novocherkassk food riots and the sudden development of the Polish Solidarity movement in 1980 could quickly materialize into real threats to the existing regime. The demands for increased food supplies at state prices made by striking coal miners in the Ukraine and Siberia in the summer of 1989 are recent reminders of this danger.

Conclusions

Soviet agriculture cannot continue to be conducted as it has been in the past. Despite the arguments of conservatives like Ligachev, the resources for further extensive growth are no longer available, and promises that just a little more investment will finally bring results are no longer credible. Available resources must be used more efficiently, which makes reform inevitable.

The magnitude of the Soviet food crisis and the obvious national security issues raised by dependence on foreign states for food imports suggest that, in the long run, Soviet agricultural organization must change. The seriousness of the situation also implies that even if Gorbachev himself is removed from the scene by party conservatives, agricultural changes will continue. In the short run of the next five to ten years, however, Soviet agriculture will still perform relatively poorly as the reforms are slowly introduced. Moreover, agricultural reform depends on industrial changes just as industrial reform requires successful agricultural change.

Administrative campaigns to manage the farms will disappear, replaced by more market-oriented mechanisms. With the end of agricultural management campaigns, the rural party apparatus that existed to conduct them will also disappear. But as the officials in that apparatus become convinced of the inevitability of change, they are likely to use their remaining control over political and economic resources to adapt themselves to the new system. (For example, managers of farm divisions seem often to become heads of newly independent cooperatives formed from those divisions, a way of keeping their positions in new circumstances.) Some of these officials may convert their political control of economic resources into economic wealth.[123]

The party itself is likely to split. Even before the first meeting of the Congress of People's Deputies in mid-1989, Vasilii Starodubtsev raised, in veiled terms, the possibility of a peasant party (by which he meant a political organization to defend the existing large farms).[124] Boris Oleinik, a deputy chairman of the USSR Supreme Soviet, has urged the formation of a separate political party to defend farmers' interests and act as a "reliable partner of the Communist Party" during the debate on the new land law.[125] The Association of Peasant Farms and Rural Cooperatives of Russia (AKKOR), an organization of Soviet individual farmers to defend their interests against the state, has already been set up.[126] A USSR Peasant Union, dominated by administrators and managers of existing successful farms, is also being created.[127] At least two organizations, one made up of individual peasants and cooperators and the other uniting people who have benefited from the existing system, seem likely to emerge in the countryside.

There is little reason to think that the agricultural reforms will lead to Western-style capitalism in any direct way. Like farmers in other developed countries, neither the *kolkhozy* and *sovkhozy* nor the new peasant farmers want to face the market as isolated individuals. Gorbachev's plans to create voluntary cooperatives are intended to provide some shelter from market forces. As the reforms proceed, the farmers will certainly become more vocal in demanding that, as a current Soviet catch-phrase has it, the city's debt to the country be paid. Rather than subsidizing cheap food for the cities, the state will eventually have to reform all prices and then put some of the realized resources back into agricultural development — but never again so generously as during the great years of investment and waste in the 1970s and early 1980s.

Different kinds of farm organization will come to dominate various regions of the country. The *kolkhozy* and *sovkhozy* will certainly be broken up in some areas, especially in the Baltic states, the Transcaucasus, much of the Ukraine, and the northwestern part of European Russia (the non-black earth zone). These are areas where collectivization was not done as long ago as the rest of the country (the Baltics and Western Ukraine, annexed by the USSR after World War II), or where geography makes large-scale farming economically infeasible, or areas which have lost so much population that the only hope for putting the land back into cultivation is through individual farmers. In the Russian central black earth zone, historically overpopulated, the fate of large farms is uncertain. Such farms are much more likely to survive in the steppes of southern Russia, western Siberia, and the former virgin lands areas of Kazakhstan, where relatively small population and more recent development together with extensive, mechanized, agriculture make larger farms a more economic proposition.

The Soviet countryside cannot simply return to what it was under the New Economic Policy of the 1920s, when individual peasant farms were paramount. Population shifts and the industrialized nature of modern farming make such a simple reversal of collectivization impossible. Instead, a patchwork of various kinds of farms will emerge. The era of managing Soviet agriculture by a common pattern set in Moscow is nearly over. Although its death agonies may be protracted and difficult, command agriculture will not long be mourned.

Notes

1. The author thanks Lynn Erin McNeil for research assistance and Karl-Eugen Wädekin for comments on this paper.

    The collective farm, or *kolkhoz*, is formally a cooperative of its members. The state farm. or *sovkhoz*, is a state enterprise distinguished from industry only by the circumstance that its output is agricultural products. Although the distinction between the two was at one time a very important ideological matter, there has been little practical difference between them since the mid-1960s when *kolkhozy* were ordered to begin paying guaranteed wages to all their members. The various plans for reform being discussed do not distinguish between *sovkhozy* and *kolkhozy*.

2. Werner G. Hahn, *The Politics of Soviet Agriculture 1960–1970* (Baltimore: Johns Hopkins University Press, 1972).

3. On the evolution of Gorbachev's views on the lease contract and family farming, see Don Van Atta, "'Full-Scale, Like Collectivization, but without Collectivization's Excesses': The Campaign to Introduce the Family and Lease Contract in Soviet Agriculture," *Comparative Economic Studies* 32, 2 (Spring 1990), pp. 109–443.

4. "Pererabatyvaiushchei promyshlennosti — uskorennoe razvitie: Soveshchanie v Tsentral'nom Komitete KPSS," *Sel'skaia zhizn'*, 20 October 1987, p. 1.

5. Brezhnev-era water policy is examined by Thane Gustafson, *Reform in Soviet Politics: Lessons of Recent Policies on Land and Water* (Cambridge: Cambridge University Press, 1981).

6. K. Mozhin, "Tseny, zatraty i rynok," *Ekonomicheskaia gazeta*, 6 (February 1989), p. 11.

7. Iu. Balanov, "Samoednyi kombain," *Don*, 3 (March 1989), pp. 122–28.

8. V. Tikhonov, "Chtoby narod prokormil sebia," *Literaturnaia gazeta*, 31 (3 August 1988), p. 10.

9. "O Dolgovremennoi programme melioratsii, povyshenii effektivnosti ispol'zovaniia meliorirovannykh zemel' v tseliakh ustoichivogo narashchivaniia prodovol'stvennogo fonda strany," *Izvestiia*, 27 October 1984, pp. 1–2.

10. The cost of imports has become one of the major arguments in favor of reform. See Erik Whitlock, "Critics Cite Wastefulness of Agricultural Import Policy," *Report on the USSR* 1, 27 (7 July 1989), pp. 1–3.

11. V. Grigor'ev, "Povernut' ekonomiku k nuzhdam sela," *Partiinaia zhizn'*, 12 (June 1989), pp. 9–10.

12. V. Vorob'ev and V. Somov, "Pytalovskii proryv: Arenda vozvrashchaet liudei sela k polnokrovnoi zhizni, vedet k prodovol'stvennomu dostatku," *Pravda*, 5 September 1988, p. 2.

13. Igor' Gamaiunov, "Pretendent: V kom ishchet svoego voploshcheniia mechta o 'krepkoi ruke,'" *Ogonek*, 1 (January 1990), pp. 6–8.

14. M. Isakulov, "Zaboty khlopkoroba," *Sel'skaia zhizn'*, 2 July 1987, p. 2.

15. "Novye podkhody k resheniiu vodnykh problem strany: obsuzhdaiut akademiki B.N. Laskorin i V.A. Tikhonov," *Kommunist*, 4 (February 1988), pp. 90–100.

16. D. J. Peterson, "The State of the Environment: An Overview," *Report on the USSR* 2, 8 (23 February 1990), pp. 13-17.

17. M. Volkov, "Khlopkovyi Molokh prodolzhaet pozhirat' vremia, sily, zdorov'e detei," *Pravda*, 24 November 1988, p. 2.

18. A. A. Nikonov, "Realizatsiia sistem vedeniia sel'skogo khoziaistva v usloviiakh intensifikatsii proizvodstva i uskoreniia nauchno-tekhnicheskogo progressa," *Vestnik sel'skokhoziaistvennoi nauki*, 2 (February 1986), pp. 9–18, at p. 13.

19. V. Tikhonov, "Sel'skoe khoziaistvo i mezhotraslevye sviazi," *Ekonomika sel'skogo khoziaistva*, 2 (February 1978), pp. 18–27, at p. 25.

20. V. Tikhonov, "Reforma ekonomiki: Mnenie uchenogo: S chego nachinaetsia samostoiatel'nost'," *Izvestiia*, 17 December 1987, p. 2, says one-fourth of agricultural produce grown is wasted, as did N. I. Ryzhkov in a speech to the Supreme Soviet in June 1989. He also reported then that some 77 billion rubles had been allocated (presumably in the current five-year plan) to improve and reequip food-processing plants. See "O programme predstoiashchei deiatel'nosti pravitel'stva SSSR," *Pravda*, 8 June 1989, pp. 2–4. G. Kulik, "Krest'ianin — ne izhdivenets: Prioritetnoe razvitie selu nuzhno na dele, a ne na slovakh," *Pravda*, 1 September 1989, p. 2, says up to a third of all production is wasted in the RSFSR.

21. Aleksei Klimenko, "...I privet gorodu: Prodovol'stvennyi kompleks: Defitsit produktov ili defitsit poriadka?" *Pravda*, 2 July 1989, p. 2.

22. M. Gusev. "Astrakhanskaia gor'kaia osen': Razmyshleniia v kontse ogorodnoi strady," *Sovetskaia Rossiia*, 20 September 1989, p. 4.

23. V. Tikhonov, "Kontseptsiia radikal'noi perestroiki khoziaistvennogo mekhanizma APK," *Planovoe khoziaistvo*, 4 (April 1987), pp. 12–22, at 13.

24. V. Pishchulin, "Ekh, iablochko... vo chto prevrashchaiutsia svezhie ovoshchi i frukty, poka 'dokatiatsia' do severa i dal'nego vostoka," *Ekonomicheskaia gazeta*, 22 (May 1988), p. 24.

25. "'Za i protiv: Obeshchaniiami syt ne budesh,'" *Ogonek*, 5 (February 1990), inside front cover, p. 1. No information about the date of the survey or the number of respondents is available.

26. Elizabeth M. Clayton, "Soviet Rural Roads: Problems and Prospects," *Studies in Comparative Communism* 20, 2 (Summer 1987), pp. 163–74, at p. 167.

27. N. Mironov, "Uiti ot 'prodrazverstki': Predsedatel' kolkhoza razmyshliaet o tom, kak skoree reshit' prodovol'stvennuiu problemu," *Pravda*, 28 January 1989, p. 2.

28. M. Kriukov, "Rostovskie bliznetsy," *Pravda*, 18 May 1989, p. 4; V. Somov, "Bez posrednika i bez poter'," *Pravda*, 24 June 1989, p. 1; A. Ternovskii, "Minielevatory i kombinaty," *Agropromyshlennyi kompleks Rossii*, 12 (December 1989), p. 33. For an overview of the food-processing industry's difficulties, see Erik Whitlock, "Problems with Food Processing Persist," *Report on the USSR* 1, 25 (23 June 1989), pp. 12–14.

29. "Soveshchanie v Tsentral'nom Komitete KPSS," *Sel'skaia zhizn'*, 18 October 1987, p. 1; "Pererabatyvaiushchei promyshlennosti — uskorennoe razvitie: Soveshchanie v Tsentral'nom Komitete KPSS," *Sel'skaia zhizn'*, 20 October 1987, pp. 1–3. The second report mentions that the defense industry will be expected to help reequip food processors, perhaps the first time this task was publicly assigned.

30. "V Komissii TsK KPSS po voprosam agrarnoi politiki: Sokrashchenie poter' — kratkii put' narashchivaniia prodovol'stviia," *Pravda*, 10 October 1989, p. 2.

31. "Ob agrarnoi politike KPSS v sovremennykh usloviiakh: Doklad General'nogo sekretaria TsK KPSS M.S. Gorbacheva na Plenume TsK KPSS 15 marta 1989 goda," *Pravda*, 16 March 1989, pp. 1–4; "Zakliuchitel'noe slovo M.S. Gorbacheva na Plenume TsK KPSS 16 marta 1989 goda," *Pravda*, 18 March 1989, pp. 1–2. See Dawn Mann and Elizabeth Teague, "Gorbachev Calls for a 'Green Revolution,'" *Report on the USSR* 1, 13 (31 March 1989), pp. 1–6; and Erik Whitlock, "Soviet Agriculture after the March Plenum," *Report on the USSR* 1, 17 (28 April 1989), pp. 5–7.

32. "Perestroika izmeriaetsia delami: Vstrechi M.S. Gorbacheva s sel'skimi truzhenikami Podmoskov'ia," *Pravda*, 6 August 1987, pp. 1.

33. "V Politbiuro TsK KPSS," *Pravda*, 4 March 1989, pp. 1–2.

34. "Postanovlenie plenuma tsentral'nogo komiteta KPSS ot 16 marta 1989 goda: Ob agrarnoi politike KPSS v sovremennykh usloviiakh," *Pravda*, 1 April 1989, pp. 1–2.

35. Foreign Broadcast Information Service, *Daily Report: Soviet Union* (hereafter FBIS-SOV), 20 March 1989, pp. 47–51.

36. "Na perelomnon etape perestroiki: Vystuplenie M.S. Gorbacheva," *Pravda*, 31 March 1989, pp. 1–2. For an analysis, see Elizabeth Teague, "Gorbachev Meets the Press," *Radio Liberty Research*, 31 March 1989.

37. Cynthia S. Kaplan, *The Party and Agricultural Crisis Management in the USSR* (Ithaca, NY: Cornell University Press, 1987); Don Van Atta, "The USSR as a 'Weak State': Agrarian Origins of Resistance to Perestroika," *World Politics* 42, 1 (October 1989), pp. 129–49; and Van Atta, "Why Do Models Succeed? Introducing Organizational Innovation in Agricultural Work," pp. 185–201, in Karl-Eugen Wädekin, ed., *Communist Agriculture: Farming in the Soviet Union and Eastern Europe* (London and New York: Routledge, 1990).

38. Rolf H.W. Theen, "Hierarchical Reform in the Soviet Economy: The Case of Agriculture," in Susan J. Linz and William Moskoff, eds., *Reorganization and Reform in the Soviet Economy* (Armonk, NY: M.E. Sharpe, 1988), pp. 73–87.

39. "O korennoi perestroike ekonomicheskikh otnoshenii i upravleniia v agropromyshlennom komplekse strany," *Pravda*, 12 April 1989, p. 2.

40. Aleksandr I. Ievlev, a former first deputy chairman of Gosagroprom, was identified as the head of this body in a Radio Moscow report of a session of the all-union Kolkhoz Council in January 1990, as translated in FBIS-SOV, 23 January 1990, p. 100.

41. "Goskomissiia po prodovol'stviiu i zakupkam pristupaet k rabote," *Vestnik agroproma*, 35 (August 1989), p. 2.

42. Don Van Atta, "Further Reshuffling of Agricultural Management," *Report on the USSR* 1, 38 (22 September 1989), pp. 9–11.

43. See Jim Butterfield, "Soviet Local Agriculture and the RAPO Reforms" (Ph.D. dissertation, Notre Dame University, August 1989).

44. N. Liaporov, "Porozn' voz ne vyvezti," *Pravda*, 8 March 1989, p. 2.

45. "V Politbiuro TsK KPSS," *Sel'skaia zhizn'*, 8 June 1984, p. 1.
46. K. Aksenov, "Pered plenumom TsK KPSS: Chem 'lechit" defitsit," *Pravda*, 4 March 1989, p. 2.
47. "Po puti integratsii," *Pravda*, 11 April 1987, p. 3.
48. A. Artem'ev, "Na kooperativnoi osnove," *Partiinaia zhizn'*, 12 (June 1989), pp. 15-19.
49. "Politicheskii Doklad Tsentral'nogo Komiteta KPSS," pp. 23–121 in *XXVII S"ezd Kommunisticheskoi Partii Sovetskogo Soiuza: Stenograficheskii otchet* (Moscow: Izdatel'stvo politicheskoi literatury, 1986), pp. 52–53.
50. Iurii Shpakov, "Gore lukovoe," *Pravda*, 26 April 1989, p. 2.
51. V. Ryzhkov, "Kooperativ — Dobryi partner pokupatelia," *Pravda*, 9 June 1989, p. 5; Ivan Vasil'ev, "Vremia vlasti, bremia vlasti," *Sovetskaia Rossiia*, 10 September 1989, p. 2.
52. Vasilii Parfenov, "Politicheskii dnevnik: 'Vtoroi dukhanie' zakona," *Pravda*, 6 August 1989, p. 2.
53. I. Abakumov, "Kommentarii 'Izvestii,'" *Izvestiia*, 8 May 1990, p. 1.
54. CPSU Central Committee and USSR Council of Ministers resolution, "O dal'neishem sovershenstvovanii ekonomicheskogo mekhanizma khoziaistvovaniia v agropromyshlennom komplekse strany," *Pravda*, 29 March 1986, p. 2.
55. This rationale was explicitly stated by Gorbachev in his 1987 Murmansk speech, in *Pravda*, 1 October 1987, as translated in the *Current Digest of the Soviet Press* (hereafter CDSP) 39, 40, p. 2.
56. "V Sovete Ministrov SSSR," *Pravda*, 21 October 1989, p. 2.
57. "V Politbiuro TsK KPSS," *Pravda*, 22 August 1986, p. 1.
58. *Izvestiia*, 23 July 1987, p. 1, as translated in CDSP 39, 29, p. 21.
59. "V Sovete Ministrov SSSR," *Pravda*, 15 January 1989, p. 3.
60. "V Sovete Ministrov SSSR," *Sel'skaia zhizn'*, 11 August 1989, p. 1; Christian J. Foster, "Convertible Currency Payments for Above-Average Sales of Farm Produce," *Report on the USSR* 1, 45 (10 November 1989), pp. 13–15. On the lack of response, see, for instance, K. Aksenov, "Krest'iane uchatsia schitat': Obozhgla sinitsa ruki...," *Pravda*, 5 January 1990, p. 2.
61. Kapitolina Kozhevnikova, "Firma ili forma?" *Literaturnaia gazeta*, 30 (27 July 1988), p. 11.
62. "Chleny Prezidentskogo soveta SSSR," *Izvestiia*, 29 March 1990, p. 1.
63. M. Mel'nikov, "Vtorzhenie 'Servis-Dona,'" *Ekonomika i zhizn'*, 11 (March 1990), p. 16.
64. For one of many instances, Galina Chernogolovina, "Krutye ovragi: chto meshaet arendatoru zakrepit'sia na zemle," *Pravda*, 10 October 1989, p. 2.
65. D. Gutenov, "Pokupai, arendator!" *Pravda*, 28 January 1990, p. 4.
66. Karen Brooks reports that budget subsidies to cover the difference between prices paid to farms by the state and prices paid by consumers were 14 percent of the whole Soviet state budget in 1986, the last year for which those data are available. The subsidy has risen from 57.9 billion rubles in 1986 to 88 billion rubles in 1989 (current prices for each year, presumably overstating the increase because of inflation). Karen M. Brooks, "Soviet Agriculture's Halting Reform," *Problems of Communism* 39, 2 (March-April 1990), pp. 29–41, at p. 37.
67. A. Kalnins, "Puti sovershenstvovaniia khoziaistvennogo mekhanizma APK," *Voprosy ekonomiki*, 10 (October 1986), pp. 64–72, at 70.
68. K. Mozhin, "Tseny, zatraty i rynok."
69. Nikolai P. Shmelev, "Rethinking Price Reform in the USSR," *Soviet Economy* 4,4 (October-December 1988), pp. 319–27, at 323–24.
70. I. Lukinov, "Zatraty i tseny v sel'skom khoziaistve: Pochemu oni rastut?" *Kommunist*, 3 (February 1989), pp. 24-30.
71. Radio Moscow, 1500 GMT, 23 May 1990, as translated in FBIS-SOV, 24 May 1990, p. 58;

Esther B. Fein, "Rising Food Prices Stir Panic Buying among Muscovites," *New York Times*, 26 May 1990, pp. 1, 5.

72. V. Semenov, "Khozraschet i samofinansirovanie," *APK: ekonomika, upravlenie*, 3 (March 1989), pp. 3-15, at p. 7.

73. "V Politbiuro TsK KPSS," *Sel'skaia zhizn'*, 16 October 1987, p. 1.

74. CPSU Central Committee resolution, "O neotlozhnykh merakh po uskoreniiu resheniia prodovol'stvennogo voprosa v sootvetstvii s ustanovkami iiun'skogo (1987 g.) plenuma TsK KPSS," *Pravda*, 25 September 1987, pp. 1–2.

75. Petr Buthel, TASS (1125 GMT, 23 January 1989), as translated in FBIS-SOV, 30 January 1989, p. 70.

76. Oszkar Ruzes, "The People Determine the Deadline," *Népszabadság*, 6 May 1989, p. 6, as translated in FBIS-SOV, 18 May 1989, pp. 58–60.

77. Vladimir Pavlovich Karpenko, "Pod novoi vyveskoi," *Ekonomika i zhizn'*, 6 (1 February 1990), p. 8.

78. CPSU Central Committee and USSR Council of Ministers resolution, "O dopolnitel'nykh merakh po razvitiiu lichnykh podsobnykh khoziaistv grazhdan, kollektivnogo sadovodstva i ogorodnichestva," *Sel'skaia zhizn'*, 25 September 1987, pp. 1–2.

79. Igor' Gamaiunov, "Pretendent," p. 6.

80. Karl-Eugen Wädekin, "The Re-emergence of the Kolkhoz Principle," *Soviet Studies* 41, 1 (January 1989), pp. 20–29.

81. "O korennoi perestroike ekonomicheskikh otnoshenii i upravleniia v agropromyshlennom komplekse strany," *Pravda*, 12 April 1989, p. 2.

82 CPSU Central Committee resolution, "O neotlozhnykh merakh po povysheniiu proizvoditel'nosti truda v sel'skom khoziaistve na osnove vnedreniia ratsional'nykh form ego organizatsii i khozracheta," *Pravda*, 18 December 1986, p. 1.

83. "Zakon Soiuza Sovetskikh Sotsialisticheskikh Respublik: Ob individual'noi trudovoi deiatel'nosti," *Pravda*, 21 November 1986, pp. 1, 3.

84. "Zakon Soiuza Sovetskikh Sotsialisticheskikh Respublik: O kooperatsii v SSSR," *Pravda*, 8 June 1988, pp. 2–5.

85. "Zakon Soiuza Sovetskikh Sotsialisticheskikh Respublik: O sobstvennosti v SSSR," *Pravda*, 10 March 1990, p. 4.

86. "Ukaz Prezidiuma Verkhovnogo Soveta SSSR: Ob arende i arandnykh otnosheniiakh v SSSR," *Pravda*, 9 April 1989, p. 2; "Osnovy zakonodatel'stva Soiuza SSSR i soiuznykh respublik: Ob arende," *Izvestiia*, 1 December 1989, p. 3. For analyses, see John Tedstrom and Philip Hanson, "Supreme Soviet Issues Decree on Leasing," *Report on the USSR* 1, 18 (5 May 1989), pp. 6-8; and Erik Whitlock, "The Soviet Agricultural Leasing Debate," *Report on the USSR* 1, 28 (14 July 1989), pp. 10–11.

87. "Osnovy zakonodatel'stva Soiuza SSSR i soiuznykh respublik: O zemle," *Pravda*, 7 March 1990, pp. 3,5.

88. *Pravda*, 6 May 1989, p. 3 reports passage of the Latvian law on peasant farming. The Latvian law was amended to remove the time limit on tenure at the end of the year. See *Pravda*, 12 November 1989, p. 3. The Estonian law on individual farmsteads *(khutora)*, reported in *Pravda*, 7 December 1989, p. 2, also provides for unlimited tenure. The Lithuanian law, which limits peasant holdings to fifty hectares, is reported in *Pravda*, 7 July 1989, p. 3.

89. V. Badov, A. Kolesnichenko, A. Nikitin, and A. Fedotov, "Ekonomicheskaia reforma na perevale," *Pravda*, 6 November 1989, pp. 1–2 at 2.

90. Radio Moscow, 1200 GMT, 1 February 1990, as translated in *FBIS-SOV*, 2 February 1990, p. 116.

91. Gelii Shmelev, "Fakty — upriamaia veshch', ili o 'fermerskoi ugroze' kolkhozam i sot-sializmu," *Izvestiia*, 10 January 1990, p. 2.

92. A. Platoshkin, "Krest'ianin — Eto obraz zhizni: Pochtu 'Pravdy' kommentiruet sekre-tar' TsK KPSS," *Pravda*, 22 May 1990, pp. 1–2.

93. M. Makulbekov, "Zhizn' posle zhizni: Eshche raz o sud'be idei ekonomista i khleboroba Ivana Khudenko," *Izvestiia*, 27 December 1989, p. 3.

94. "Razdum'ia: Iskat', deistvovat', utverzhdat': S kandidatom v chleny Politbiuro TsK KPSS, pervym sekretarem TsK Kompartii Gruzii E.A. Shevardnadze vstretilis' korrespondenty 'Izvestii' T. Chanturiia i E. Iakovlev," *Izvestiia*, 12 January 1984, p. 3.

95. M.S. Gorbachev, "Potentsial Kooperatsii — Delu perestroiki," *Sel'skaia zhizn'*, 24 March 1988, 2–4.

96. M. Lapshin and I. Kononov, "God raboty aktsionernogo obshchestva," *APK: Ekonomika, upravlenie*, 4 (April 1989), pp. 36–39.

97. Vladimir Shvetsov, "Vozvrashcheniia k 'Vozvrashcheniiu': Po sledam odnogo ocherka," *Pravda*, 24 July 1989, p. 3.

98. See the description of how the APO came to be organized in A. Artem'ev, "Na koopera-tivnoi osnove."

99. Iurii Makhrin, "Zametki publitsista: Demokratiia i distsiplina," *Pravda*, 16 November 1987, p. 2.

100. O. Stepanenko, "Zashchitite krest'ianstvo: Tak stavit vopros V. Starodubtsev," *Pravda*, 6 January 1990, p. 2.

101. Viktor Dolgov, "Krest'ianstvo i perestroika," *Volga*, 11 (November 1988), pp. 151–71.

102. N. Mironov, "Ul'timatum," *Pravda*, 8 October 1989, p. 2.

103. E.K. Ligachev, "Chelovecheskii faktor, khozraschet i perestroika v agropromyshlennom komplekse," *Kommunist*, 4 (February 1987), pp. 28–42, at 31.

104. See the interview with Ligachev broadcast by Radio Moscow on 9 October 1989, as trans-lated in *FBIS-SOV*, 10 October 1989, pp. 77–81.

105. *Izvestiia*, 15 December 1989, p. 10, as translated in CDSP 41, 52, p. 23.

106. *Izvestiia*, December 15, 1989, p. 10, as translated in *FBIS-SOV-Supplement: USSR Congress of People's Deputies*, 7 February 1990, pp. 1–3, at p. 2.

107. "Novye zakupochnye tseny na zerno," *Izvestiia*, 8 May 1990, p. 1. In an accompanying commentary, correspondent Igor Abakumov argues the increase will most benefit peas-ant farms and lessees who are not bound by state orders and can change their output mix and produce more of what the new prices make most profitable. This is true, but the increase still raises the total amount of the agricultural subsidy, doing little about the underlying economic problems of pricing and incentives.

108. N. Avdeev, "Ne zovite menia na khutor," *Pravda*, 13 November 1989, p. 2.

109. Aasmund Wilersrud, "The Soviet Union's Farmers Live in Poor and Miserable Conditions," *Svenska Dagbladet*, 1 February 1990, p. 5, as translated in FBIS-SOV, 8 February 1990, pp. 109–11, at 109.

110. There are now occasional reports of collective farms that provide their members with unemployment payments. For instance, I. Iakovchuk, "Posobie po bezrabotitse: Ego ustanovili v kolkhoze, perestroivshem svoiu ekonomiku," *Izvestiia*, 28 August 1989, p. 2.

111. A. Morgachev, "K diskussii v Verkhovnom Sovete SSSR: Nuzhna li muzhiku volia," *Sel'skaia zhizn'*, 12 October 1989, p. 3.

112. A. Platoshkin, "Sovetskii fermer? Pochemu by net?" *Pravda*, 4 July 1988, p. 2.

113. *Izvestiia*, 15 December 1989, p. 10, modifed from the translation in *FBIS-SOV-Supplement*, 7 February 1990, at p. 1.

114. This description of Soviet-style party-states comes from Charles E. Lindblom, *Politics and Markets* (New York: Basic Books, 1977).

115. Jerry F. Hough, *The Soviet Prefects: The Local Party Organs in Industrial Decision-Making* (Cambridge: Harvard University Press, 1969).

116. "Perestroika raboty partii — vazhneishaia kliuchevaia zadacha dnia: Doklad M.S. Gorbacheva na soveshchanii v TsK KPSS," *Pravda*, 19 July 1989, p. 1.

117. Local officials in the Soviet Union can use their power to manipulate resources and buy support in ways similar to those described by Robert H. Bates, *Markets and States in Tropical Africa: The Political Basis of Agricultural Policies* (Berkeley: University of California Press, 1981).

118. Dawn Mann, "Authority of Regional Party Leaders Crumbling," *Report on the USSR* 2, 8 (23 February 1990), pp. 1–6.

119. See Thomas Sherlock, "Politics and History under Gorbachev," *Problems of Communism* 37, 3–4 (May-August 1988), pp. 16-42, at 19–23; R.W. Davies, *Soviet History in the Gorbachev Revolution* (Bloomington: Indiana University Press, 1989); and Thomas Sherlock and Vera Tolz, "Debates over Number of Stalin's Victims in the USSR and in the West," *Report on the USSR* 1, 36 (8 September 1989), pp. 10–14.

120. Publication in early 1988 of Nina Andreeva's "letter," a document full of anti-semitism, crude Russian chauvinism, and historical errors, was universally understood in the Soviet Union as a Ligachev-inspired salvo against Gorbachev's reforms. Nina Andreeva, "Pis'mo v redaktsiiu prepodavetelia leningradskogo vuza: Ne mogu postupat'sia printsipami," *Sovetskaia Rossiia*, 13 March 1988, p. 3. A history of this curious document is given by Giuletto Chiesa, "Secret Story behind Anti-Gorbachev Manifesto," *L'Unità*, 23 May 1988, as translated in *FBIS-SOV*, 31 May 1988, pp. 55–58. For a general analysis, see Michel Tatu, "19th CPSU Conference," *Problems of Communism* 37, 3–4 (May–August 1988), pp. 1–15.

121. On social welfare measures as a strategy for increasing the Soviet regime's political support, see George W. Breslauer, *Five Images of the Soviet Future: A Critical Review and Synthesis* (Berkeley: Institute of International Studies, University of California, 1978); Peter Hauslohner, "Gorbachev's Social Contract," *Soviet Economy* 3, 1 (January-March 1987), pp. 54–89; and Walter D. Connor, *Socialism's Dilemmas: State and Society in the Soviet Bloc* (New York: Columbia University Press, 1988).

122. Stephen K. Wegren, "Food Prices in the USSR," *Report on the USSR* 2, 12 (23 March 1990), pp. 13–15, at 13.

123. Jean C. Oi's studies suggest that some rural party cadres in the People's Republic of China have successfully converted their political control into economic dominance. See her articles "Communism and Clientelism: Rural Politics in China," *World Politics* 37, 2 (January 1985), pp. 238–66; "Peasant Households Between Plan and Market: Cadre Control over Agricultural Inputs," *Modern China* 12, 2 (April 1986), pp. 230–51; and "Market Reforms and Corruption in Rural China," *Studies in Comparative Communism* 22, 2–3 (Summer-Autumn 1989), pp. 221–33.

124. O. Stepanenko, "'Semeinoe delo' Starodubtsevykh," *Pravda*, 25 May 1989, p. 3.

125. Reported by John Tedstrom, "Land Law a Symbolic Step Forward," *RFE/RL Daily Report*, 21 February 1990.

126. Don Van Atta, "Russian Peasants' Association Founded," *Report on the USSR* 1, 33 (18 August 1989), pp. 10–11; V. Virkunen, "Pravo na zemliu i voliu: Zamatki s krest'ianskogo s"ezda Rossii," *Sel'skaia zhizn'*, 25 January 1990. p. 2.

127. The draft rules of this new body have been published: "Proekt: Ustav krest'ianskogo soiuza SSSR," *Sel'skaia zhizn'*, 22 April 1990, p. 2.

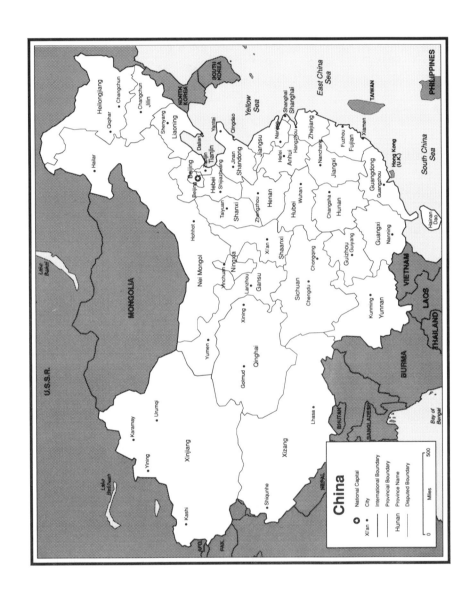

China

- ✦ National Capital
- Xi'an • City
- International Boundary
- Provincial Boundary
- Hunan Province Name
- Disputed Boundary

0   Miles   500

5. POLITICAL REFORM IN CHINA

Parris H. Chang

To some China analysts, developments in the People's Republic of China (PRC) since 1978 constituted a "second revolution."[1] The reforms instituted by Deng Xiaoping, they thought, would generate revolutionary changes in the Chinese economic and political systems, changes that might represent a clean break with Mao's legacy and with communist orthodoxy.

The violent crackdown against the pro-democracy movement in June 1989 belied such an optimistic prediction, notwithstanding the pledges by Deng and other Chinese Communist party (CCP) leaders that the policy of the open door and the reform programs remain unchanged. In fact, long before the student demonstration began in mid-April 1989, in the wake of the death of former CCP General Secretary Hu Yaobang, there had already been unmistakable signs that Deng's "second revolution" was in trouble.

The reform attempted by the Dengists, like reforms elsewhere, has generated controversy — it may have solved some problems but has created new ones in the process. It also entails redistribution of resources (power, positions, jobs, perks) and results in winners and losers. For these and other reasons, Deng's reform efforts have been opposed and resisted by losers and vested interests from all directions, as well as from the conservatives and ideologues.

This essay is about the politics of reform under Deng. Specifically, it will focus on political reform and analyze what Deng has tried to do, the motivations behind the reform proponents and opponents of the intended changes, and the consequences.

Deng's Quest for Control

A group of veteran CCP leaders who have run China in the post-Mao era were victims of Mao's purge during the Great Proletarian Cultural Revolution. They were rehabilitated politically in the wake of Mao's demise in September 1976. For instance, Deng was reinstated as CCP vice-chairman, vice-premier, and People's Liberation Army (PLA) chief of staff in July 1977, only after a fierce political battle that Deng's allies and supporters waged against Hua Guofeng, who inherited Mao's mantle as CCP chairman in October 1976, and other Maoists in the leadership.[2]

In order to secure Hua's consent, Deng did confess his political errors and even pledged to support Hua,[3] but once back in office, he lost no time in challenging Chairman Hua for leadership. Indeed, there was a continuing struggle over power and policy in the CCP leadership, involving a test of strength during 1977–1981 between groups and individual leaders supporting Hua, on the one hand, and those supporting Deng, on the other. Likewise, the struggle between the Dengists and anti-Dengists in attempts to control and shape the reforms has continued since 1981.

The coalition under Hua consisted of two diverse elements. One was the leftist "whatever faction," whose members rose to political prominence during the Cultural Revolution and had numerous followers among the rank and file of the party. Another was the "petroleum faction," a group of economists and technocrats who ran the Chinese economy under the late Premier Zhou Enlai's stewardship during 1966–76, who were credited with the remarkable development of China's petroleum industry and were strongly represented in economic ministries of the State Council. Li Xiannian, CCP vice-chairman from 1977 to 1982, is said to be its behind-the-scenes leader. In addition, the Hua coalition had also drawn support from such elder statesmen as Marshal Ye Jianying and from a few army leaders.

This coalition was in ascendancy during 1976–77 and largely controlled the policy councils until the spring of 1978. Indeed, the political line of the Eleventh Party Congress in August 1977 and the ten-year National Development Plan sanctioned by the Fifth National People's Congress (NPC) in March 1978 bore the mark of the coalition's influence.

The coalition behind Deng, on the other hand, consisted of several groups of veteran officials, great numbers of whom were victims of the Cultural Revolution. Many of them were long-time associates of Deng (for example, Hu Yaobang and Wan Li), some were Deng's peers and political allies (such as Chen Yun and Peng Zhen), and some were coopts into Deng's group (like Zhao Ziyang and Yang Dezhi). While these groups shared intense antagonism toward Mao's legacy, they differed on the ways and means of reform and the program of the "four modernizations."

It seems appropriate here to note parenthetically that these and other leadership groupings or factions were based neither on institutions (like the army or secret police) nor on historical associations (such as field army ties). Perhaps with the exception of the petroleum faction, which was composed primarily of economic planners and "technocrats," other groupings drew their members from across the major institutional lines and field army affiliations. Whereas allegiance to Mao's tradition seems a crucial ingredient that held together the "whatever faction" and set it apart from other factions, as a rule Chinese factionalism is not ideologically oriented.

Nor are China's factions mainly policy oriented, although they do entertain certain policy preferences, and such preferences could increase or damage support for competing factions or affect factional alignments in Chinese politics. Instead, the personal relationships of cadres, as an insightful study by Lucian Pye has pointed out, has been the primary basis for factions in China since the Cultural Revolution.[4] In addition to dimensions of Chinese personality and attitudes about authority, trust, dependency, and other sentiments that Pye attributes to the lingering influence of Chinese culture, which impels the Chinese to form close personal networks, Chinese communist cadres have also learned from the abrupt and unpredictable policy and political changes in the past decade and a half that personal ties and mutual help — and not correct ideological stance or institutional loyalty — best protect their careers and enhance political power.

Having close ties with many powerholders in the party and the PLA and being highly experienced in domestic and external affairs, Deng clearly possessed personal and political assets unmatched by Hua or other Chinese leaders. Besides, his modernization program seemed to better represent the national mood and enabled him to win political support. Thus, in the course of leadership infighting, the balance of power gradually but steadily shifted in favor of Deng's coalition.

Deng's struggle for control commenced soon after he won official rehabilitation in July 1977. Although Chairman Hua and his supporters dominated the Eleventh CCP Congress in the following month, Deng was able to place several of his men in strategic posts. For example, Hu Yaobang became head of the powerful Organization Department of the party and engineered important personnel changes that not only would shift the balance of power in favor of the Deng camp but would also accelerate Hu's own political ascendancy in subsequent years. Hu did essentially three things: (1) he pushed hard for the reinstatement of numerous cadres victimized by the GPCR, (2) he placed supporters and allies in major leadership posts and enlisted supporters through dispensing patronage, and (3) he carried out purges to remove the Maoists and the recalcitrant cadres opposed to reforms.

A concerted campaign against the so-called "wind faction," the "slippery faction," and "the quakers" began in early 1978.[5] Its targets were those cadres who had once supported or collaborated with the Gang of Four and had then lined up behind Hua after October 1976. Over the objection of Hua Guofeng, the campaign resulted in 1978 in the dismissal of eight provincial-level first secretaries and numerous lesser cadres. While not each and every one of the newly appointed belonged to the Deng camp, the majority of them did.[6]

In retrospect, it was in the Central Work Conference and the Third Central Committee Plenum during November-December 1978 that the coalition led by Deng achieved a decisive political breakthrough. Four veteran leaders, Chen Yun, Deng Yingchao (Mrs. Zhou Enlai), Hu Yaobang, and Wang Zhen, who could be counted on to back Deng on most issues, were elected to the Politburo. The plenum also named nine veteran cadres to the CC; among them were Huang Kocheng, Hu Qiaomu, and Xi Zhongxun, and all of them, like Deng Xiaoping, had been victims of the Cultural Revolution.

Moreover, Chen Yun was also elected party vice-chairman — a position he had held during 1956-1966. A seasoned economist and outspoken critic of Mao's radical Great Leap Forward, Chen Yun replaced Li Xiannian as the top economic policy maker and became head of the ad hoc Financial and Economic Group in the spring of 1979. One of the group's specific tasks was to map out a three-year readjustment program to replace the ten-year National Development Plan, which was formulated chiefly by Hua, Li Xiannian, and Yu Qiuli and announced to the NPC in March 1978, but which had to be discarded because it was highly unrealistic in target-setting and unsound in its emphasis and allocation of resources. In addition, Hu Yaobang was named secretary-general of the Central Committee, to be in charge of daily work at headquarters and to supervise party organizations at all levels.

Several Politburo members of the whatever faction came under fire at the meetings and lost much of their political influence. Vice-Chairman Wang Dongxing, who was concurrently director of the Central Committee

General Office (which oversees vital party files) and thus was able to block political rehabilitation of such ranking leaders as Peng Zhen, was forced to yield the job, which went to Yao Yilin, a close friend of Chen Yun and Peng Zhen. Wang was also relieved of his control over the 8341 Army Unit, a sort of Praetorian Guard, which was in charge of the leaders' security but operated outside the regime's established security apparatus and even ran its own espionage network.[7] Although Hua Guofeng retained the party chairmanship, he lost much of his power, for those leaders who supported or joined with him and the party machinery now came under the control of Hu Yaobang and Yao Yilin.

The Dengists in Ascendancy

Deng's ascendancy was evident once again when the Fifth Plenum met behind closed doors from February 23 to 29, 1980, to deliberate on major policy and personnel matters. The meeting approved the posthumous rehabilitation of Liu Shaoqi and made sweeping leadership changes: it ousted four leaders of the whatever faction (Wang Dongxing, Wu De, Chen Xilian, and Ji Dengkui) from the Politburo and elevated two close associates of Deng, Hu Yaobang and Zhao Ziyang, to the ruling Politburo Standing Committee. And it reestablished the party's Central Committee Secretariat, with Hu Yaobang as the general secretary, to manage daily affairs of the party.

The four diehard Maoists of the whatever faction had been targeted for removal by Deng since 1978, and they came under strong attack at the Third Plenum, as previously noted. Deng had temporized then, possibly because he had lacked sufficient power or because he had wanted to avoid a divisive leadership fight that could endanger resolution of more pressing issues. However, the efforts to preserve an appearance of leadership unity at that time and the resurgence of the left the following spring produced a curious sense of political uncertainty in the party ranks and emboldened many cadres to oppose or drag their feet on the programs the Deng group wanted to pursue. Hence, Deng decided to strike against them rather than wait until the next party congress (scheduled for 1981, though it did not take place until 1982).

It must have been obvious to Deng that many cadres had adopted a wait-and-see attitude toward his pragmatic programs because of his advanced age. They were reluctant to come on board because they feared that, just as the post-Mao leadership had done away with Mao's programs, the leadership coming after Deng could scrap his "revisionist" line and punish those who implemented it. To remove such doubt once and for all and forestall his adversaries from taking over the leadership in the future, Deng sought to structure his succession in advance and put into positions of power a group of possible successors who are committed to his cause and will continue his policies.

For example, Deng installed his closest comrade-in-arms, Hu Yaobang, as head of the Central Committee Secretariat and packed it with supporters who would hold aloft the Deng banner after he was out of the political picture. As the day-to-day decision-making body, the Secretariat would run the party and preempt Hua's functions as party chairman. Deng's intention was to dilute Hua's control over policy and the party organization and eventually to ease him out of the party chairmanship.

In the same vein, Deng steadily packed the State Council with his own supporters and ousted his opponents. One of Deng's goals was to force Premier Hua Guofeng out of the State Council and replace him with Zhao Ziyang. Zhao was a highly pragmatic and experienced provincial official and had established a very successful record as the chief executive of Sichuan, China's most populous province, with a population of over 100 million. Although he was not too closely associated with Deng before the Cultural Revolution (unlike Hu Yaobang, Wan Li, and others), Zhao's pragmatism, his good record in Sichuan, and especially his strong support for Deng's programs apparently impressed Deng a great deal; hence he was coopted into the Deng camp.

Thus, to no one's surprise, the NPC in September 1980 approved Hua's resignation as premier and appointed Zhao as his replacement. The session also accepted the resignations of six vice-premiers: Deng Xiaoping, Chen Yun, Li Xiannian, Xu Xiangqian, Wang Zhen, and Wang Renzhong. The departure of these veteran officials was engineered by Deng himself to strengthen Zhao's control over the State Council. The departure of Li Xiannian was particularly critical, because he was China's highest-level economist until 1978, and he did not fully support the modernization programs promoted by Deng and Chen Yun. According to sources inside China, Li was the leader of the petroleum faction, which had stonewalled the Deng-Chen readjustment efforts.[8] In Deng's calculation, Li's departure from the State Council would weaken the influence of the petroleum faction and correspondingly strengthen the position of the Deng forces.

As a matter of fact, in the summer of 1980 several officials identified with the petroleum faction came under heavy fire from the Deng camp. Vice Premier Yu Qiuli, who was also director of the powerful State Planning Commission, was moved to the lesser State Energy Commission and yielded his former post to Vice-Premier Yao Yilin. Deng's supporters also seized on an oil-drilling incident (the capsizing of an offshore oil rig in 1979, which left seventy-two workers dead) to mount a strong attack on officials of the petroleum faction. Consequently, the petroleum minister, Song Zhenming, was summarily dismissed, Vice-Premier Kang Shien received a "demerit of the first grade" (a severe public reprimand), and Yu Quili had to make a humiliating self-criticism.[9]

Apparently inspired by the Deng camp, delegates to the September 1980 NPC session and a spate of newspaper articles criticized the gigantic Baoshan steel project and other major construction undertakings for waste, faulty investment plans, and other deficiencies. It was perhaps no accident that officials responsible for these projects were associated with the petroleum faction. Furthermore, the alleged backstage boss of the faction, Li Xiannian, was not spared. He was the target of an attack in the Central Work Conference in November-December; he was compelled to recant his errors, and the text of his lengthy self-criticism was subsequently disseminated.[10]

In addition, Deng, who undoubtedly believes Mao's celebrated dictum that political power grows from the barrel of a gun, made special efforts to establish control over the military. Soon after his reinstatement as PLA chief of staff in the summer of 1977, he began to place his supporters in key military posts. For example, Wei Guoqing was appointed director of the General Political Department; Luo Ruiqing was made secretary-general of the Military Affairs Commission; and Yang Yong was named deputy chief of staff. (Yang Chengwu, who had served as de facto chief of staff prior to Deng's return but had not been close to Deng, was transferred to the post of Fuzhou Military Region commander.) At the same time, Deng undertook to purge many PLA officials (such as Chen Xilian) who had collaborated with the Gang of Four or had opposed his policies, and to replace those he considered inept or too old. Indeed, many old PLA cadres were relieved of their leadership positions and served only as advisers to various military bodies.[11]

To bring the PLA into line, Deng employed a variety of means. He launched one campaign after another to strengthen political work and "ideological education" among PLA officers and soldiers. In early 1980, Deng stepped down as PLA chief of staff and promoted Yang Dezhi, then commander of the Kunming Military Region, as his successor in an attempt to win over a senior PLA leader who was not previously close to the Deng camp. Most important of all, Deng effected sweeping leadership changes in the PLA hierarchy, from the center out to the provinces. For instance, commanders in ten out of the eleven military regions were replaced during 1978-1980 (the only Mao-era holdover was Li Desheng, of

Shenyang Military Region), and new political commissioners were sent to all of the eleven Military Regions.

Reforms Launched

It is highly remarkable that within three years of Deng's formal reinstatement in July 1977 he had succeeded in establishing control over China's political scene. In spite of continued opposition, Deng and his allies dominated the decision-making councils and called the shots. By the summer of 1980, the Dengists were confident enough of their political strength to begin to initiate major political and institutional reforms.

For instance, Deng and his supporters convened an enlarged Politburo meeting during August 18–23, 1980, to deliberate on reform of the party and state leadership systems. On August 18, Deng gave the keynote speech, in which he called for (1) reforms, among others, against bureaucracy, life tenure of cadres, and overconcentration of power; (2) steps to promote democracy, collective leadership, and strengthening the socialist legal system; and, most important of all, (3) a large-scale program to cultivate and promote cadres who were young, better educated, and professionally more competent.[12]

To make room for the younger cadres in the leadership councils, according to Deng's proposal, veteran party leaders in the Central Committee and Politburo would move to a central advisory committee (to be established upon the revision of the CCP constitution), which would perform mainly advisory and supervisory functions. A similar advisory body would also be created in the State Council for aging governmental officials.

In addition, Deng also proposed reform of the economic system. For example, changes were to be made in the economic structure and in the excessive control over economic decisions by the party organizations, and enterprises would be granted greater power. Other reforms included a greater emphasis on experts, new management setups, and greater participation by workers with a view to improving efficiency and productivity as well as to strengthening accountability.

According to a Central Committee circular, participants in the enlarged Politburo meeting had "many good supplementary and amendatory opinions."[13] Subsequently, on August 31, a revised text of Deng's speech was approved by the Politburo and on September 11 issued as a Central Committee document (No. 66) for dissemination and discussion in party ranks. The latter were urged to convey their views and suggestions to the party center by October 15, so that the Central Committee, the NPC Standing Committee, and the State Council could incorporate their inputs in the course of enacting new laws or regulations. In the fall of

1980, China's media went on a campaign to publicize and promote Deng's reform proposals.[14] Many Deng brain-trusters also went around to various forums to explicate and promote his reform program.[15]

Muddling through:
Deng's Reform Measures

Notwithstanding the efforts by the Dengists to push various reform programs, they found themselves compelled to postpone and/or water down their initial plan as the political opposition emerged and coalesced in the winter months of 1980–81. For example, the highly publicized plan to reform the leadership system — to do away with the life tenure of cadres and to fix the length of time the leading cadres could serve — had to be shelved for the time being. A shrewd politician, Deng knew when and how to compromise. After considerable hard bargaining among the factions, the Sixth Central Committee Plenum was called into session for three days in the last week of June 1981, following a ten-day "preparatory meeting."

The plenum adopted the Resolution on Questions in Party History Since 1949 and approved the demotion of Hua Guofeng and the elevation of Hu Yaobang and Deng Xiaoping to the party chairmanship and Military Affairs Committee (MAC) chairmanship, respectively. These were major gains for the Dengists, but they had to settle for much less than what they had hoped for. The plan to set up a central advisory commission and to "kick upstairs" Ye Jianying and other "old guard" leaders failed to materialize.

Under such circumstances, it is not difficult to understand why Deng placed unusual emphasis on the Twelfth CCP Congress, which was convened during September 1–12, 1982. In fact, he termed it the most crucial party meeting since the Seventh CCP Congress of 1945, which had ushered in the era of Mao. Obviously, Deng sought to introduce the Deng era through the 1982 congress. More specifically, Deng wanted to accomplish three major objectives: (1) to reaffirm the Deng ideological and policy line; (2) to reorganize the leadership bodies at the top and down to the local levels, so as to remove the old guard and the remnant Maoists and establish a power structure controlled by the Dengists; and (3) to adopt a host of reform measures and a comprehensive rectification campaign to weed out the opposition.

While Deng and his supporters accomplished much of what they sought, they did not get everything they wanted. Despite the vigorous campaign by Deng Xiaoping and his followers to remove the old guard from the levers of power and promote younger cadres with greater profes-

sional competence into leadership positions, their efforts were only partially successful. At the party congress, 172 veteran officials (both Deng's
supporters and his opponents) willy-nilly stepped down from the
Politburo, the Central Committee, and other front-line positions of leadership and took back seats in the newly established Central Advisory
Commission. Marshal Liu Bocheng, a close friend of Deng's who had
been ill for years, resigned from the Politburo and the Central
Committee, and was specifically commended by the party.[16] However,
numerous other leaders remained in the party's top policy-making councils, Deng's pressure notwithstanding.

Out of the twenty-five Politburo members elected at the congress, eigh-
teen were holdovers, and out of these, six were already in their eighties
and five more in their late seventies. The seven newly elected members
were not much younger, with six of them over seventy years old and one
sixty-seven. All of the six members of the Politburo Standing Committee,
the party's topmost decision-making body, were also reelected, including
Marshal Ye Jianying (eighty-five) and Li Xiannian (seventy-four), who had
opposed Deng's policies.

Perhaps to counter Deng's pressure, Ye told the party congress on
September 6 that he was already eighty-five, senile, ailing, and weak, and
that he had requested on many occasions to withdraw from the leadership
posts, but that until the Central Committee approved his retirement, he
would continue to do his best to serve until the day he died.[17] As if to justify the reluctance of the old guard to step down, another veteran leader,
Chen Yun, declared to the congress on the same day that, since the ranks
of cadres showed a gap between the old and the young, the old comrades
could not leave the leading bodies all at once and, in accordance with circumstances and practical needs, some would still remain at the "front
line" for the time being. Instead of handling the heavy day-to-day business,
Chen added, the veteran cadres should devote their energies mainly to
"helping and guiding younger cadres, passing on experience to them, giving advice on major issues, and keeping a close watch on the basic orientation of the system."[18]

The refusal of senior leaders to retire from positions of power also
watered down the institutional reforms which Deng had sought to implement, resulting in a compromise: He would control the three leadership
organs, the Central Committee, the Central Commission for Discipline
Inspection, and the Central Advisory Commission. Such a setup established a system of collective leadership, division of labor, and checks and
balances, thus forestalling excessive concentration of power and making a
recurrence of anything like the Cultural Revolution highly unlikely. The
proposed organizational changes were designed largely to induce the vet-

eran cadres to abdicate their posts at the front line and move to the Central Advisory Commission (CAC), which would have only limited power. The new party constitution (Article 22) made it quite clear that the Central Advisory Commission could only act as "political assistant and consultant" to the Central Committee. Deng himself also conceded that the existence of the Central Avisory Commission would be only temporary and predicted that it would be abolished in ten years, or would last "at most not more than 15 years." He was the chairman of the Central Advisory Commission during 1982–87.

In the wake of the Twelfth Congress, the Dengists sought to present the new setup in the best possible light and spoke of "three echelons" of the leadership elite, largely in terms of seniority.

Thus, according to Hu Yaobang, the first echelon of leaders were Deng, Ye, Li Xiannian, Chen Yun, Peng Zhen, Deng Yingchao, Nie Rongzhen, and Xu Xiangqian, who were in their late seventies and eighties but continued to decide "China's major policies."[19] The second-echelon leaders were somewhat younger and carried out the "day-to-day administration of policy." Hu placed himself, Premier Zhao Ziyang, and Vice-Premier Wan Li in this category. As a matter of fact, members of the CCP Secretariat and top officials of the State Council were on the second rung and constituted the backbone of China's "high command." But most of these leaders were in their sixties and some were over seventy; hence, according to Hu, special efforts were made to cultivate and build up the third echelon of leaders, who were in their fifties and younger. The three-echelon leadership was presented as a great innovation to ensure smooth transition of power and continuity of policy and leadership stability;[20] it actually disguised a retreat from Deng's design to push for an earlier retirement of the veteran leaders.

Measures for Political Reform

In addition to rejuvenating the leadership personnel, that is, removing the cadres who were too old and/or in opposition to Deng's reform programs, the Dengists made substantial efforts to carry out political reform. It should be emphasized that such reform was designed to accomplish specific utilitarian objectives, and democracy has not been among them.

In ideological terms, political reform has been justified on the grounds that the superstructure must correspond to the development of the productive forces. Inasmuch as the prevailing political system was mostly copied from that of the Soviet Union with the addition of the Chinese Communist party's legacy accumulated during the revolutionary period, and since modernization calls for a big increase in the productive forces, "changes in those relations of production and in the superstructure which do not correspond to the development of the productive forces" were necessarily entailed.[21] Thus, political reform is seen as a means, an instrument to facilitate economic modernization — the central task of the regime.

For Deng, political reform also serves another important purpose — to prevent a repetition of the tragic and traumatic Cultural Revolution. Talking about the catastrophe of the Cultural Revolution, Deng said, "I do not mean that the individuals concerned should not bear their share of responsibility, but rather that the problems in the leadership and organizational system are more fundamental, widespread and long-lasting, and they have a greater effect on the overall interest of our country."[22] He added, "Without political restructuring, it is impossible to protect the fruit of reforms in the economic structure and to continue its progress."

Whereas Deng seems to be clearly aware of the linkage between reform and economic modernization, and on a number of occasions he has told foreign visitors that political reform was necessary for economic modernization, when the crunch came he elected to slow down political reform in order to save and continue economic reform. His basic mistake was to believe that economic reform and modernization could be separated from the fifth modernization — democracy.

Some efforts were made to carry out political reform during the 1980s. Concrete measures that were put into effect included separation of the functions of the party from government, decentralization of power, streamlining of the administrative structure, and reforming of the personnel (cadre) system. These measures were designed chiefly to combat the overconcentration of power in the party organizations and in the party and government organizations at top levels and to effect proper division of labor in order to improve administrative efficiency.

Below, we will briefly outline the motivation or rationale behind each of these measures, pointing out the sources of opposition and the outcome of the reform efforts.

1. Separation of the Functions of the Party from Government

In his report to the Thirteenth Party Congress, then General Secretary Zhao Ziyang defined the party's functions as follows:

> The Central Committee (CC) should make policy decisions on such important questions as China's internal affairs, foreign affairs, the economy and defence, recommend persons for leading posts in the supreme state organs and exercise political leadership in all fields. The local Party committees at the provincial, municipal and county levels

should exercise political leadership in local work, carrying out the line formulated by the CC and ensuring that the decrees of the central government are implemented. Their principal responsibilities should be to carry out directives from higher Party organizations and from the CC, to ensure the implementation in their local areas of directives from governments of higher levels and from the State Council, to propose policy decisions on important local issues, to recommend cadres for key posts in local state organs, and to co-ordinate activities of the various local organizations."[23]

On an earlier occasion, Deng stated the principle of division of labor between the party and the government: "The Party's main functions are to work out its own guidelines and state policies and exercise overall leadership. Through legal processes, the organs of state power convert the Party's political line into state intentions and are responsible for this implementation and administration."[24] He said, furthermore, "The problem of the confusion of responsibility between the Party and government and of the usurpation of government functions by the Party has existed for a long time in China's system of leadership." And he termed it "the root cause of over-centralization of powers and a major reason for bureaucracy and administrative inefficiency."[25]

Zhao concurred and emphatically stated that "until the problem [the lack of distinction between the party and government] is solved, Party leadership cannot be strengthened and *other reform measures cannot be smoothly carried out. Therefore, the key to reforming the political structure is the separation of Party and government.*"[26] Much was made of the issue of the separation of the party from the government, before and after the Thirteenth Party Congress in 1987. However, partly due to the opposition of many party cadres, especially those who have no particular expertise or have been trained for ideological propaganda and political work and could thus lose some of their power and privileges, the results are mixed, and the problem of the overlap of party functions with those of the government has not been solved. It is true that now the party and the government at all levels are physically separated, but they are not functionally separated. As has often been the case, at all levels the real functions of the party head and the government administrator vary from one work unit to another. They depend particularly on the leader's sources of power and personality; in some work units the party leader might be more powerful than his government counterpart, while in others the government leader wields more power than his party counterpart.

In the wake of the violent crackdown against the pro-democracy movement and the ascendence of conservative forces, the new trend is to place greater emphasis on the "leadership of the Party" and strengthen the power of party officials at all levels. In short, the political turmoil since the spring of 1989 has further set back the reform of separating the functions of party and government.[27]

2. Decentralization of Power

In order to effect better division of labor between central and local authorities, changes have been made to delegate power to local authorities and enterprises. Zhao Ziyang defined these changes as follows:
   a. Delegating power to local governments. "Local matters will be handled by local authorities, while central authorities determine major policies and exercise supervision."
   b. Delegating power to enterprises and institutions. "To delegate powers of operation and management to the enterprises and institutions so as to let them manage their own affairs with full authority. The function of the government is to provide service for enterprises and to supervise, in accordance with laws, the regulations and policies."
   c. Delegating power to mass organizations. "It is essential to give full play to mass organizations and to self-managed mass organizations at the grass-roots level (i.e., residents' and villagers' committees) so that the people will handle their own affairs always in accordance with the law."[28]

These changes were clearly intended to overcome red tape and stimulate initiative at lower levels. As Zhao said, "Our leading organs have taken charge of many matters which they should not and cannot handle, or cannot handle efficiently, getting bogged down in routine work. On the other hand, the grass-roots units lack the power to make decisions, and it is hard to fully arouse the initiative of the people."[29]

Decentralization of power itself is a less controversial issue, but the extent to which power should be decentralized is controversial. Those who favor the centrally planned economy are understandably reluctant to delegate power to lower levels, especially to enterprises, for fear of political and economic anarchy.

Much effort has been made to delegate power to lower levels, and considerable results have been obtained. In fact, decentralization of power stems from the gradual introduction of a market economy, which requires that local governments and enterprises respond to environmental (marketplace) and organizational changes, instead of to blind directives from the higher levels. Creating a number of special economic zones and open cities and allowing them to establish their own legislation and regulations is proof of delegating power to local governments; the dynamism and vitality of coastal regions and enterprises underlie the rationality of this reform.

It is undeniable that decentralized power is sometimes abused at lower levels — hence corruption, evasion of taxes and customs tariffs, and other illegal practices. These undesirable consequences gave the advocates of the centrally planned economy a pretext for taking back delegated powers. Since the summer of 1988, and especially since the crackdown of June 1989, the trend has been to re-centralize control.

3. Streamlining the Administrative Structure

In line with the efforts to improve efficiency and cut down on red tape, another area of reform has been to streamline the administrative structure and simplify procedures. According to Zhao, the government should change from direct to mainly indirect control of enterprises. Thus, "We should reduce and merge departments that are in charge of managing enterprises and do the same with specialized sections in departments that are charged with overall responsibilities."[30] He also called for "institutionalizing administrative management through administrative legislation."

The motivations behind the reform are not difficult to understand. In the words of Deng, "The leading bodies at all levels are unwieldy and overstaffed. The extra hands look for something to do. The worst consequences of this are debilitating delays, slow policy decision-making and ineffective problem-solving, hampering any effort to motivate the lower levels."[31] In the same vein, added Zhao, "Overstaffing, overlapping and unwieldiness of government organs, confusion of their responsibilities and buck-passing are also major causes of bureaucratism."[32]

In the beginning of 1982 the Chinese leadership embarked on an "administrative revolution" as a way of streamlining the administrative structure. In a report to the Standing Committee of the National People's Congress on March 3, then Premier Zhao Ziyang said that reform of China's bloated and inefficient bureaucracy would start with the State Council (the executive branch of the central government), and he made public some details of the reform.[33] According to Zhao's report and other sources in the Chinese media, the measures proposed to overhaul the bureaucracy included the following: (a) the 98 ministries, commissions, and agencies of the State Council would be reduced to 52; (b) vice-premiers, numbering 13 until recently, would be reduced to 2; (c) restructuring would begin in 12 ministries and commissions, these would be merged into 6, and their departments cut from 180 to 112; (d) the number of

ministers and vice-ministers in these organizations would be cut from 117
to 27, a reduction of 77 percent; and the number of department directors
and deputy directors would be halved and staffs cut back by 33 percent.

Despite the assurance by Deng Xiaoping that trimming the bureaucracy was only "a revolution against the administrative system and not against
any one person,"[34] as many as 200,000 of the 600,000 administrative workers in the central government apparatus, and a much higher percentage
of the 1,000 ministers and vice-ministers and 5,000 department directors
(most of them quite old) would be cut during 1982–83. The aged executives were encouraged to retire — at age sixty-five for ministers and sixty
for vice-ministers and department (bureau) chiefs — at full pay for life
and with the same political treatment as when they were in office. The
problem of overstaffing was no less serious in provincial and local government; the work of streamlining these organizations was to begin in 1983
and was likely to affect more cadres, probably millions.

The bureaucracy has been a serious obstacle to China's modernization:
it is overstaffed with office holders who are either unwilling or unable to
assist in China's modernization. Therefore, in order to improve work efficiency, strengthen discipline, and strive for China's modernization, the
regime must streamline the bloated bureaucracy and cut out the dead
wood. However, such motivations alone did not account for the new measures. Rather, the campaign was largely intended to cope with opposition
in the leadership and obstructionists in the bureaucracy. Trimming the
bureaucracy is a great cause that few can openly challenge, and it is thus a
formidable political weapon that Deng and his associates can use to solicit
compliance and remove opposition. Targeted for removal were a large
number of Maoist "upstarts" who rose as a result of the Cultural
Revolution during 1966–76; cadres in the party, government, and the PLA
who were either too old or opposed to Deng's programs; and those
unlucky corrupt officials who got caught.

The projected overhaul and reshuffle could adversely affect millions of
positions throughout the nation. Although those who lost their jobs, especially the aging cadres, would continue to draw full pay, what matters most
to them is the loss of their positions and the power and privileges that go
with them. (They know too well that when you have power, you have
everything.) While pensions and other compensations might soften the
blow for some of those affected, strong opposition to the new purge
spread as many of the potential victims fought for survival. The results of
the reform appear to be mixed. Many cadres who were supposed to have
retired or to have lost their jobs found ways to retain power and privilege.
The only change has been that they have different titles and use different
stamps.

Take the example of the State Council. At one time, there were as many as thirteen vice-premiers; in 1983, the number was cut to two (Li Peng and Tian Jiyun), but other vice-premiers were given a different title — state councilor — with the same perks and power. Currently, there are three vice-premiers and nine state councilors, most of them in their sixties and seventies. In the State Planning Commission, in addition to the minister there are twelve vice-ministers, far exceeding the number (three to five) recommended by Premier Zhao Ziyang in 1982. Likewise, the drive to cut the bloated bureaucracy has had only limited success; the ninety-eight State Council ministries, commissions, and agencies were reduced drastically in the first years of the campaign but were later restored with the same names or under different names, and there are now ninety-two of them (forty-two ministries, twenty-six commissions, and twenty-one agencies and ad-hoc bodies).

To some critics, the party's new drive to streamline the administrative structure notwithstanding, the old cycle of "streamlining-swelling-streamlining-reswelling" has been repeated once more. In addition to political opposition, China's economic system presents a real obstacle. Unlike in a capitalist country, in China there is no real private sector to attract government employees and thus there is no real employment solution to the problems of overstaffing and overlapping.

4. Reforming the Personnel System Relating to Cadres

In order to recruit and maintain better qualified cadres, the Chinese leadership has put forth the idea of creating a civil service system. According to Zhao Ziyang,

> This means formulating laws and regulations for the scientific management of government personnel who exercise the administrative power of the state and perform official duties. These public servants are to be classified in two categories: those handling political affairs and those doing professional work. Public servants in the political affairs category, whose tenure in office will be for a specified period of time, must be managed strictly in accordance with the relevant provisions of the Constitution and the Organic Law and be subjected to supervision by the public. Public servants in the professional work category, whose tenure in office is to be permanent, will also be managed in accordance with the law governing public servants. For posts in this category, people will have to pass a statutory examination in open competition. The job responsibilities of such public servants will be clearly defined and their performance will be evaluated in accordance with statutory standards and procedures.[35]

The Chinese civil service system has a long tradition and was historically well institutionalized. It recruited through examinations the "best and the brightest" from all walks of life and was regarded as a fair system that provided equal opportunities to all.

When the Communist party seized power in China in 1949, it discarded the old system altogether but never established a new one in its place. The CCP did set up a spoils system in which all the communists who participated in the revolution were assigned positions of responsibility, regardless of their qualifications and ability. As pointed out earlier, Deng has sought the retirement of the takeover generation of communist cadres, who had held onto their positions but were found wanting and incapable of leading and managing a changing and modernizing society.

As a matter of fact, most of them have finally stepped down from key administrative positions or retired from the bureaucracy. Since May 1985, for example, those party secretaries who head China's thirty provincial-level party committees are cadres in their fifties and are college educated. In line with the policy to select and promote officials who are youthful, better educated, and competent, not a few engineers and scientists have been appointed governors and vice-governors.

On the other hand, however, the old guard does not give up easily. They have strived to create a "new class" by putting their offspring in their places. They have used the campaign to promote younger, better educated, and professionally proficient cadres to positions of leadership in the past decade to install their own relatives, whether or not they are qualified, and this has seriously alienated and demoralized a large number of rank-and-file cadres.

To establish a public civil service system as outlined by Zhao Ziyang requires strong political will and discipline. It means setting up fair, objective, and explicit criteria to recruit and promote talent from all strata of society (including children of former landlords and capitalists). Until now, recruitment and promotion in the personnel system has lacked well-defined standards and is too politicized, and those in charge of job placement at all levels have been too powerful and arbitrary. The ills of such a "system" are numerous — nepotism is only one of them. It is highly questionable that a genuine civil service system will be established in the aftermath of the Tiananmen incident.

Conclusion

In the preceding pages, this essay has analyzed the politics of reform in China and examined the pros and cons and the results of several reform measures. We should emphasize once again that, in the perception of

Chinese leaders such as Deng Xiaoping and Zhao Ziyang, political reform is designed primarily to enhance efficiency and economic modernization, not to promote democracy as we understand it in the West. Chinese communists like Deng do not believe in the "consent of the governed" and their accountability to the people. In fact, Deng has often criticized the American system of checks and balances (even though he speaks in favor of the separation of party and government to prevent overconcentration of power).

Long before the crackdown on the pro-democracy movement in June 1989, Deng had closed down the pro-democracy wall, suppressed the free speech movement, and outlawed the underground publications' agitation for democracy and human rights. In a polity in which the state controls the economy and the private sector is weak, the odds against political reform, even when it is promoted by political leaders from the top, are enormous. Compared with the process of democratization in Taiwan and Korea, where the private sector is large; the countervailing economic, social, and political forces are strong and growing; and the people and ruling elite alike accept the notions of representative democracy and accountability, the prospects for democracy in mainland China seem rather remote.

The leadership reshuffle and the political changes since Tiananmen have arrested and even set back modest reform efforts. Jiang Zemin has replaced Zhao Ziyang as the CCP general secretary. Hu Quili, a reform-minded member of the Politburo Standing Committee who was in charge of the regime's propaganda, was dropped for siding with Zhao in opposing martial law and was succeeded by Li Ruihuan, mayor of Tianjin.

Jiang and Li are "technocrats," who understand the importance of the open door policy and have done fairly well as administrators of Shanghai and Tianjin, respectively. They were promoted by Deng Xiaoping to the leadership nucleus to balance off conservatives like Premier Li Peng and Vice-Premier Yao Yilin. Their outlook is quite different from that of Zhao and Hu, as they were quite ruthless in the suppression of student movements in their municipalities.

As a matter of fact, not a few officials who were reputed to be advocates of reform and supporters of Zhao have been ousted. Among them are Yan Mingfu, a member of the CCP Secretariat and director of the United Front Department: Wang Meng, minister of culture; and Liang Xiang, governor of Hainan. Bao Tong, a key aide to Zhao, and most of Zhao's brain-trusters who conceived and initiated many of the reform measures are under arrest.

Meanwhile, the influence of Yang Shangkun, president of China and vice-chairman of the CCP Military Affairs Committee, who was closely involved in the decision to use force against the demonstrators last June, is on the rise. In late October 1989, he was promoted to first vice-chairman of the MAC and strengthened his hold on this very powerful body. Although Jiang Zemin takes over the MAC chairmanship vacated by Deng Xiaoping, he has no military experience and lacks leadership stature: hence, the real power in the military sphere is likely to lie in Yang's hands. Moreover, Yang's brother, Yang Baibing, director of the PLA General Political Department, has also been promoted to the post of MAC secretary-general, enabling the Yang family to consolidate control over the PLA.

Yang Shangkun, eighty-three but in robust health, seems to aspire to Deng's leadership status. For years he has been waiting in the wings for the day when he could emerge from Deng's shadow and come to center stage himself. That does not portend well for the reform cause, because Yang is fairly conservative and has played an important part in the downfall of two reform leaders, Zhao and Hu Yaobang.

In China, every policy change is accompanied or preceded by a change in ideology. In the wake of the Tiananmen crackdown, the regime has been propagating new ideological themes that justify the repression and economic retrenchment, as well as reaffirming the "four cardinal principles" (leadership by the CCP, dictatorship of the proletariat, socialism, Marxism-Leninism/Mao Zedong Thought), on the one hand, and attacking bourgeois liberalization and those views promoting "total Westernization," on the other.[36]

Before Deng launched the reform movement, a national discussion, "What is the criterion of the truth?," was inspired by Deng's supporters to destroy Mao Zedong's ideological authority and remove constraints on the reform programs. As Deng became the dominant leadership figure, his version of Marxism became the "true" Marxism.

The importance of ideology in both political and economic reforms can be seen in the Thirteenth Party Congress activities of November 1987. In order to legitimize both political and economic reforms, Zhao put forth a new ideological concept called "the primary stage of socialism" as the basic line of the party. In his report to the party congress, he said:

> China is now in the primary stage of socialism.... We must proceed from this reality and not jump over this stage.... To believe that it is possible to jump over the primary stage of socialism, in which the productive forces are to be highly developed, is to take a utopian position on this question, and that is the major cognitive root of left mistakes.... During this stage we shall accomplish industrialization and commercialization, socialization, and modernization of production, which many countries have achieved under capitalist conditions.

In Zhao's logic, if China is still in the primary stage of socialism, not yet in the stage of socialism, then China should be allowed to do what other countries have done under capitalist conditions.

Now all of this has been reversed. In addition to emphasizing communist orthodoxy, primacy of ideology, and Maoist revolutionary values in policy, a "red" (revolutionary) outlook rather than expertise has been used in selecting and promoting party officials. In a front-page commentary in the *People's Daily* on January 24, 1990, for instance, the party organ quotes CCP General Secretary Jiang Zemin as saying, "In choosing people, in assigning people, in educating people, we must take a revolutionary outlook as the prerequisite, to insure that party and government leaders at every level are loyal to Marxism."[37] It seems obvious that ideological rectitude has now been placed over ability, education, and competence, qualities that were assigned primary importance prior to the spring of 1989.

Notes

1. E.g., Harry Harding, *China's Second Revolution: Reform after Mao* (Washington, D.C.: Brookings Institution, 1987).

2. See Parris H. Chang, "Chinese Politics: Deng's Turbulent Quest," *Problems of Communism*, vol. 30, no.1 (January-February 1981), pp. 1–21.

3. Deng wrote two letters addressed to Chairman Huo Guofeng and the Central Committee in late 1976 and March 1977, pleading for his reinstatement.

4. Lucian W. Pye, *The Dynamics of Factions and Consensus in Chinese Politics: A Model and Some Propositions* (Santa Monica, CA: The RAND Corporation, July 1980), pp. 6–7.

5. See *Renmin Ribao*, 6,10, and 15 January 1978.

6. For a detailed analysis of the political tug of war between Deng and his rivals, see Chang, "Chinese Politics: Deng's Turbulent Quest," pp. 1–4.

7. See Parris Chang, *Power and Policy in China*, 2d ed. (University Park, PA: Pennsylvania State University, 1978), pp. 234-36.

8. Lo Ping, "The NPC Session (1980)and the Hu Yaobang-Zhao Ziyang Leadership Structure," *Chengming*, no. 34 (August 1980), pp. 5–7.

9. "A Profound Lesson," *Renmin Ribao*, 27 August 1980. Although the news that Yu Qiuli made a self-criticism was not publicly divulged, it has been known to many inside China.

10. Pi Yun, "Required Readings for the Party Cadres: Speeches of the Four Top Party Leaders," *Chengming*, no. 40 (February 1981), p. 15.

11. By the summer of 1980, more than 10,000 PLA ranking cadres, including such officials as Deputy Chief of Staff Li Da, Deputy Air Force Commanders Xue Shaoqing and Kuang Rennong, and Fuzhou Military Region Political Commissar Li Zhimin, had stepped down from the leadership posts and become "advisers." See Huang Jung-yueh, "Military Cadre Problems," *Studies on Chinese Communism* (Taipei), 15 August 1980, p. 117.

12. Deng Xiaoping, "The Reform of the Party and State Leadership System" (18 August

1980), *Selected Important Documents*, vol. 1 (Beijing: People's Publishing House, 1982), pp. 510–34.

13. See *Studies on Chinese Communism* (15 July 1981), pp. 106-107.

14. For examples, see Special Commentator, "An Important Reform on the Party and State Leadership System," *Renmin Ribao*, 28 October 1980, and "Discussions on Promotion of Systemic Reform" in *Guangming Ribao*, 16, 17 and 19 October 1980.

15. See a speech by Feng Wenbing (vice-president of the CC Party School), "On Questions of Socialist Democracy," *Renmin Ribao*, 24 November 1980. (A condensed version is also in *Review*, 26, January 1981, pp. 17–20, 28, under the heading, "Reforming the Political Structure.") See also a speech by Liao Gailong (member of the Office of Policy Research of the CC Secretariat) entitled, "The Historical Experience and the Path of Our Development," addressed to a "Forum on CCP History" attended by theoreticians from the party schools across the nation (section 4 of his lengthy speech is published in *The Seventies*, no. 134, [March 1981], pp. 38–48).

16. See "The Letter of Salute from the 7th Plenum of the 11th CC to Comrade Liu Bocheng" and "The Letter of Salute... to Comrade Cai Zhang," *Selected Important Documents*, vol. 2, pp. 1306-10.

17. *Renmin Ribao*, 7 September 1982, p. 2.

18. Ibid.

19. Parris H. Chang, "Interview with Hu Yaobang," *Problems of Communism*, vol. 32, no. 6 (November-December 1983), p. 69.

20. An Zhiguo, "Three Echelons of Leading Cadres," *Beijing Review*, no. 27 (July 1983), p. 4.

21. *Beijing Review*, vol. 22, no. 5 (January 1979), p. 7.

22. "Why Deng Stresses Political Restructuring," ibid., vol. 30, no 38 (21 September 1987), p. 15.

23. Ibid., vol. 30. no. 45 (9–15 November 1987), pp. 38–39.

24. "Deng's Ideas on Political Restructuring," ibid., vol. 30, no. 39 (28 September 1987), p. 14.

25. Ibid.

26. Ibid., vol. 30, no. 45 (9–15 November 1987), p. 38. Emphasis added.

27. After Shanghai CCP Secretary Jiang Zemin was promoted to CCP general secretary in June 1989, Mayor of Shanghai Zhu Jung-gi also held concurrently Jiang's party post in Shanghai, thus reversing the trend of separating the two functions.

28. *Beijing Review*, vol. 30, no. 45, p. 39.

29. Ibid.

30. Ibid.

31. Ibid., vol. 30, no. 39, p. 14.

32. Ibid., vol. 30, no. 45, p. 39.

33. "Restructuring the State Council," ibid., vol. 23, no. 9 (1 March 1982).

34. *Renmin Ribao*, 19 February 1982.

35. *Beijing Review*, vol. 30, no. 45, p. 40.

36. For example, Wu Shuqing (president of Peking University), "The Course for China's Reform and Opening," *Beijing Review*, vol 45, no. 1 (1–7 January 1990), p. 18.

37. See Nicholas D. Kristof, "Chinese Paper Places Ideology over Ability," *New York Times*, 25 January 1990, p. 10.

6. ECONOMIC REFORM IN CHINA

Joseph Fewsmith

Following the watershed Third Plenum of the Eleventh CPC Central Committee in December 1978 that brought Deng Xiaoping to power, China undertook an economic reform effort that—until the tragic events of June 1989 in Tiananmen Square on the one hand and the recent, dramatic unfolding of political change in Eastern Europe and the Soviet Union on the other—were as sustained and far-reaching as any in the socialist world. Despite the difficulties and setbacks that that reform effort currently faces—and those problems are considerable—this decade of reform has materially bettered the lives of millions of people and will be of lasting historical significance.

A decade ago, when the Deng regime came to power, the Chinese economy faced a wide variety of problems. Not the least of these was the very considerable ideological problem that most of the reform measures then under consideration had long been considered "capitalist," not only in the ten years from the beginning of the Cultural Revolution to the fall of the Gang of Four but also in the seventeen years that had preceded the Cultural Revolution. That is to say, despite periods of reform in the mid-1950s and early 1960s, there was little in the ideological canon of the Communist Party of China (CCP) to justify the far-reaching measures of the decade about to unfold.

The scale of the crisis faced by the CCP, however, justified unprecedented efforts to reform the way China was ruled and the way the economy operated. On the one hand, the extremes to which the Gang of Four had taken Marxist-Leninist/Mao Zedong Thought had not only discredited the radical interpretation of that ideology but also much of what had been accepted as mainstream understanding of socialism in the period before the Cultural Revolution. This discrediting of official ideology—and the near shattering of the party's prestige that went with it—opened up new ways of thinking about the relationship between the polity and the economy. On the other hand, the enormity of the economic problems China faced in that period justified radical new measures simply in the hope of restoring the economy.

At the time the Dengist reforms were launched, the economic problems facing the country were formidable indeed. The long-standing practice of favoring heavy industry at the expense of agriculture had left the countryside in dire straits. Peasant incomes had barely risen in the thirty years of the People's Republic of China, and agricultural growth rates could not supply raw materials for the continued growth of industry. At the same time, light industry had been similarly starved for the benefit of heavy industry, and the nation faced a severe shortage of consumer goods. In addition, urban incomes had also failed to rise significantly over the history of the PRC, leaving workers feeling underpaid and unmotivated. It should be added that the so-called "little leap outward" under Hua Guofeng, in which major industrial plants were imported with little regard either to the local ability to run them or to the country's foreign exchange capability, did perhaps more harm than good in correcting the underlying imbalances of the Chinese economy.

In the decade since then, the Deng regime has undertaken an extensive reform program in an effort to address the underlying problems of the economy. This effort has not been guided by any set blueprint but rather has followed the pragmatic route of "feeling the stones while crossing the river." This reform strategy, given the lack of consensus on reform issues at any one time and the need to negotiate with the interests to be affected, was probably necessary. Still, as will be seen below, it has had its costs, and those will have to be faced.

The Dengist reforms have done much to address the most blatant problems of the economy. The 1979 decision to raise the procurement price for grain substantially and to allow individuals to reap the benefits of their efforts provided an immediate and dramatic stimulus for the rural economy. The dramatic growth of rural enterprises, which now employ some 90 million people, has provided an important new source of income for rural workers and has greatly increased the output of light industrial goods.

At the same time, the state has delegated important economic decision-making authority to enterprises and local governments, thereby reducing its direct interference in the economy and giving lower-level organizations an incentive to develop. This delegation of authority has been accompanied by a significant reduction in the amounts and kinds of materials distributed by the state. In the past decade, the types of raw materials centrally distributed by the state decreased from 256 to 26, and the types of products distributed by the state were reduced from 120 to 60.[2] These steps have allowed market forces to play a much greater role in the Chinese economy; some estimate that about half of all transactions at present are carried out under market conditions.

These reforms have stimulated an unprecedented growth of the Chinese economy. Gross value of industrial output (GVIO) has increased by an average of more than 11 percent per year, and GNP has grown from 348 billion yuan in 1978 to 1,300 billion yuan in 1988—an average annual rate of 9.6 percent—which compares favorably with the average annual rate of 6.1 percent from 1953 to 1978.[3] Foreign trade has grown from a mere $15 billion in 1977 to more than $100 billion in 1988, making China one of the top dozen or so trading nations in the world.[4] At the same time, the establishment of Special Economic Zones (SEZs) in Guangdong and Fujian Provinces (and more recently the establishment of Hainan Province, which enjoys even more favorable policies than the SEZs) has played a major role in opening up the coastal economy to foreign trade and drawing in foreign capital. Shenzhen, the most developed of the SEZs, has grown from a small town of 20,000 to 30,000 people in the late 1970s to a thriving city of half a million people a decade later, with a gross social output value of over 17 billion yuan in 1989.[5]

Reflecting this economic growth, the incomes of both peasants and urban residents have climbed steadily. The average per capita income of the rural population has risen from 134 yuan in 1978 to 545 yuan in 1988, while that of urban workers has increased from 316 yuan to 1,119 yuan in the same period.

Despite these and other achievements of the Dengist period, there is little doubt that the process of reform—one that was intended to minimize economic dislocation and political conflict—has nevertheless led to a series of economic difficulties that have engendered political conflict. Though the political conflict that erupted so tragically in Beijing in the spring of 1989 has manifold origins in popular demands for more freedom, anger over inflation and corruption, the precipitous decline in the party's prestige, ideological conflict, intraparty struggle, and so forth, it is also apparent that deep disagreement over economic issues was an important factor. This was reflected in a torrent of commentary in the summer of 1989 that focused particularly on the problems of inflation, deficit spending, "privatization," and neglect of China's "backbone" enterprises—issues that were blamed on former General Secretary Zhao Ziyang.

Throughout the decade decisionmakers have—both by design and through the compromises forged in the course of policymaking—pursued a strategy of reform that has attempted to maximize beneficiaries and minimize losers. Reform has been incremental, challenging ideological tenets and entrenched interests only when necessary, and it has sought to protect both inefficient industries and the populace—particularly urban residents—from the logical consequences of market forces.

The approach of "feeling the stones while crossing the river" and the policy of "delegating authority and granting benefits" (*fang quan rang li*) have been central to this reform process. The former expression refers to a process of incremental reform rather than following a set blueprint, while the latter connotes a policy of providing incentives by allowing local authorities and enterprises to reap many of the benefits of increased production. Although this strategy has minimized opposition and produced notable economic results, it has also entailed serious costs. In particular, this strategy has promoted the development of a set of interlocking interests that have distorted investment and consumption and that have to date prevented reform from creating an economic mechanism that can allocate economic resources efficiently. Moreover, this strategy has in many ways weakened the ability of central authorities to deal with the problems generated by reform even as the number and obstinacy of those problems have mounted.

The difficulties generated by economic reform, as the following sections show, are evident in tensions between large state-owned enterprises and smaller, locally operated enterprises, strains between central and local interests, a distorted consumption structure, inflationary pressures, and the corruption that has emerged in the course of price reform.

The Legacy of the Pre-1978 Economic Structure

The difficulty of the reform task in China stems in large measure from the administrative structures and economic imbalances bequeathed by the centralized system of state ownership as it had developed over the three decades before reform was initiated. Although the Chinese economic system was never as centralized as that of the Soviet Union and efforts to break away from a Stalinist model of development started with the Great Leap Forward in 1958, it is nevertheless true that a large number of so-called "backbone" enterprises that were critical to China's economic life were subject to direct control or supervision from Beijing. These backbone enterprises are composed of about 10,000 enterprises—out of some 400,000 industrial enterprises in China—that account for about two-thirds of all industrial capital assets and some 70 percent of all tax payments to the central government. These industries are the most technologically advanced in China, and enhancing industrial efficiency—not to mention filling Beijing's coffers— does depend to a large extent on these industries.

This structure of backbone enterprises has been built up and supported by an economic-administrative structure that is designed to extract revenue from society by controlling flows of labor and capital. One of the central ways in which this was done was by imposing a surprisingly rigid separation of the urban and rural economies. Rural production costs were kept artificially low by prohibiting land sales and internal migration from rural to urban areas, thus removing land as a cost of production and ensuring an overabundance of rural labor. In 1978, some 75 percent of China's labor force continued to work in agricultural production even though agriculture accounted for only about 35 percent of the nation's economic output. Certain forms of economic activity, including cash cropping, sideline activities, and itinerant peddling, were restricted or forbidden, thus keeping opportunity costs low. In addition, the "circulation channels" for the procurement of agricultural products and the sale of agricultural inputs were monopolized by the state. These measures enabled the state to extract surplus from the countryside to support the building of industry through the "scissors effect"—a total of 600 to 800 billion yuan over some thirty years.[6]

China's rural policies also ensured a steady supply of low-cost grain to the urban areas, allowing the state to maintain a low-wage policy in the cities; urban wages remained basically unchanged from 1952 to 1978. This was accomplished in part through a rigid employment system that virtually prevented labor mobility. Thus, productivity gains redounded to the state's benefit. This low-wage policy was further supported by a cradle-to-grave welfare system. Thus, the harsh conditions of employment were ameliorated by job security, full employment, free health care, free schooling, and nearly free housing. One of the side-effects of this system was that enterprises were turned from economic units into social units, and enterprise heads became more mayors than managers.[7]

The existence of this system has blocked and distorted thoroughgoing reform in a number of ways. The most obvious way in which it has produced difficulties for reform is that it institutionalized a highly distorted price structure. Prices for agricultural produce were too low, as were prices for basic industries including raw materials, energy resources, and transportation. Secondly, this system cultivated an urban working class that, relative to its worth, is pampered and protected. Despite being poorly paid for thirty years, the system of subsidies and guaranteed lifetime employment have protected workers from the rising cost of grain and other goods as well as from being laid off as enterprises seek to rationalize. Third, this structure has bequeathed a set of entrenched interests that has made the adjustment of interests extremely difficult and have made abuse of reforms inevitable.

The Evolving Center-Local Relationship

The Dengist reforms, like previous efforts to overcome the deleterious effects of overcentralization in 1957 and 1971, began by delegating authority to lower organizational levels. In contrast to those efforts to decentralize economic authority, the Dengist reforms were based on using economic rather than ideological incentives to spur production. Moreover, the Dengist reforms, taking heed of those earlier attempts, sought to delegate decision-making authority directly to the enterprises rather than to local authorities. The first effort has by and large been successful; the second has not. The result has been to spur localism, which has increased and distorted investment, accelerated the expansion of processing industries relative to basic industries, created barriers against the free movement of goods, and undermined the effectiveness of centrally imposed economic levers.

The centerpiece of the government's efforts to "delegate authority and grant benefits" was to greatly expand the percentage of profits that enterprises were allowed to retain for investment and rewards for workers. From 1979 to 1986, the retained profits of enterprises grew from 3.7 percent of total profit to some 20 percent (after various taxes had been paid). At the same time, enterprises were given greater control over depreciation funds. Whereas originally the depreciation fund was turned over to the state, this was changed so that 70 percent remained with the enterprise and 30 percent with the responsible local bureau. Later, enterprises were allowed to retain the entire amount.[8] Such changes have given enterprises much greater control over their own financial affairs.

At the same time that local enterprises were given greater economic decision-making authority, the central government also attempted to enlist the support of local authorities for economic development. To this end, it gave local governments greater authority over economic policy and reformed the tax system in ways that would benefit the localities. Thus, local governments have been given greater authority to approve investment decisions. By 1988 localities could approve construction projects up to 30 million yuan. More important, the central government in 1980 reformed the existing tax system of "unified collections and unified disbursements" by allowing local governments to keep a proportion of the revenue collected, a system popularly known as "eating in separate kitchens" (*fen zao chi fan*). This system often encourages localities to preserve uneconomic enterprises because tax payments are not based on profits but rather on the circulation tax, which is based on output value. Thus, even if an enterprise is not very profitable, or even if it has a deficit, local authorities are likely to have an incentive to keep it open.[9]

Although the intention of delegating greater economic decision-making authority to local governments appears to have been to provide incentives for them to support economic development—and thus to complement the devolution of decisionmaking authority to enterprises—the effect in practice has been to foster a symbiotic relationship between local enterprises and governments that undermines efforts to separate economic and political authority. Both local enterprises and governments have strong incentives to forge such a relationship. On the one hand, because markets are neither open nor efficient, enterprises often seek the help of local government in obtaining scarce raw materials and marketing output. On the other hand, local governments have an interest in protecting local industry in order to enhance their tax base and to attain social goals such as full employment.

This mutually beneficial relationship leads local government to intervene in various ways to protect local enterprises. They can use their political connections to plead with the central government for new investment or reduced tax burdens, and they can use their control over local banks to secure new funding or to defer repayments. Such interventions mean that local enterprises are not operating under hard restraints. When economic problems are encountered, they do not have to find ways to improve efficiency, or to lay off workers, or even to go bankrupt; rather, they can seek relief from the local authorities.

This symbiotic relationship between local enterprises and government has been further strengthened by changes in the political system that have significantly reduced the functions and authority of the central government. In previous periods of economic decentralization before 1978, the political relationship between the center and localities had always remained distinctly hierarchical. Even when management over enterprises has been greatly decentralized, the central government has maintained

control over the planning and the distribution of materials.[10] The political
center had also always maintained firm control over appointments to local
leadership positions, so that local leaders remained responsive to the top.
Moreover, in the past the primary impetus for decentralization had come
from the top.

Reform has changed this relationship in important ways. The delegation of authority and the encouragement of local investment has made the
localities much more important economic units in the system. The magnitude of this change is suggested by two figures. On the one hand, the balance between in-plan investment by the central government and out-of-
plan investment by local authorities has shifted greatly in favor of the latter. By 1985, of the 254.3 billion yuan of total investment in fixed assets,
only 44.88 billion yuan were within the state budget.[11] On the other hand,
the percentage of revenue accruing to the central government has
declined rapidly. Whereas central revenue accounted for 60 percent of all
government revenues in the 1970s, it now accounts for less than 50 percent. Similarly, the proportion of government revenues in the national
income has dropped from 32 percent in 1979 to about 19 percent in
1989.[12]

At the same time, the system of local people's congresses has been
strengthened, making officials more responsive to local needs. In elections that took place in twenty provinces, municipalities, and autonomous
regions in early 1988, 190 candidates were put forward by petition. Fifty-
four of these were listed as formal candidates, and eight were elected. In
general, the top leadership posts in localities are still centrally appointed,
but some deputy heads are put forward at the local level. A notable case
was in Henan Province, where Liu Yuan, son of Liu Shaoqi, was nominat-
ed by local supporters and eventually elected vice-governor.[13] These
changes have given the localities the economic resources and political
capacity to pursue their own interests more effectively, and so, in contrast
to the past, the impetus for decentralization comes largely from the bottom.

Localities have used their enhanced sense of local self-interest and their
increased political and economic power to direct much of their investment to the processing industry, which, given China's distorted price
structure, yields great profits. However, because investment is carried out
locally in protected markets, much of this investment is duplicative and
wasteful. For instance, China's watch industry expanded rapidly from 64
plants turning out 22 million watches in 1980 to 366 plants turning out
some 73 million watches in 1986. However, in 1986, only 58 million watches were sold, and by mid-1987 there were some 35 million watches in ware-

houses. Because of this overproduction, by 1986 38 plants were running deficits. The following year, apart from a few plants making famous-name brand watches that continued to make good profits, one-third were running deficits and many others were said to be close to the margin.[14]

Other consumer goods industries encountered similar problems. The number of motorcycle plants grew from 24 to 177, and the number of deficit plants grew from 4 to 43, while the amount in arrears grew from several tens of thousands yuan to over 19 million yuan in 1986. In 1980, China had few plants producing household appliances, but by 1986 there were 906 such plants, of which 199 were running deficits totaling 147 million yuan. By 1988, China had 41 plants with a capacity to produce over 10 million refrigerators, but demand was estimated at only 4 to 5 million. Nevertheless, there were another 50 plants under construction. By 1986, the production capacity for washing machines had similarly overreached the market. China's plants were capable of producing 12 million washing machines, but actual production was only 8.93 million, 74 percent of capacity; nevertheless, some 1.7 million washing machines—19 percent of actual production—could not be sold and were stored in warehouses.[15] According to one recent report, more than two-thirds of the productive capacity is idle in recently introduced color television and refrigerator lines.[16]

This tendency to build economically inefficient plants with excessive production capacity has contributed to enterprise losses. In 1986, China's independent accounting plants ran deficits totalling 7.24 billion yuan—78.7 percent more than the preceding year. In 1987, the figure was more than 9 billion yuan.[17]

The Consumption Structure

This tendency of local authorities and enterprises to engage in duplicative construction of economically inefficient plants is reinforced by a distorted pattern of consumption that is, in turn, supported by the rapid increase in urban incomes and the continuation and even strengthening of China's traditional welfare system. This distorted pattern of consumption has both exacerbated economic problems by spurring the rapid growth of light industry, thus driving up prices for scarce inputs, and created political difficulties by raising expectations beyond a level that the Chinese economy is likely to be able to satisfy.

China's consumption structure is distorted in that urban residents in particular spend their income to sustain a much higher quality of life than

would be expected given China's level of development. In the earlier period of reform, as urban incomes were beginning to rise, there was great
demand for the "three old things"—sewing machines, bicycles, and watches. In recent years, as urban incomes have continued to rise, there has
been tremendous demand for the "four new things"—color televisions,
washing machines, recorders, and refrigerators—and other high-grade
consumer goods. As a result, from 1984 to 1986, the retail sales volume of
durable consumer goods in China grew at an average rate of 41.9 percent,
of which color television sets increased by 69.3 percent, refrigerators by
157.3 percent, and washing machines by 77 percent.[18]

Whereas at the end of 1983 every hundred households in cities and
towns owned 2.5 color television sets, 1.7 refrigerators, 2.91 washing
machines, and 27.1 recorders, by the end of 1986, these figures had risen
to 27.4 color television sets, 12.7 refrigerators, 59.7 washing machines, and
51.6 recorders. As a result of this rapid popularization of the "four new
things," the level of ownership in China by the end of 1986 had reached
or surpassed the level attained by Japan, the Soviet Union, and South
Korea when their per capita GNP was $1,000.[19]

Underlying this distorted pattern of consumption is the long-ingrained
system of subsidies. As noted above, under the economic structure that
had grown up since 1949, governments and enterprises had provided
urban residents with a complete cradle-to-grave welfare system, including
free medical care, free schooling, food subsidies, and nearly free housing,
not only when they are working but also when they are retired. This pattern of welfare was a direct result of the economic structure that paid
workers little and kept wages basically frozen over the thirty years from the
1950s until reform was launched in the late 1970s. In exchange for the
severe restrictions which the state imposed on workers—particularly low
wages and no freedom to choose place of employment—the state provided lifelong job security and free benefits.

Rather than being abandoned in the course of reform as a relic of the
old system and as rising wages made such subsidies seem less necessary,
the welfare system has expanded rapidly. Part of the reason for retaining
this system appears to be habit. The institutionalization of the welfare system under the pre-1978 economic structure had fostered the expectation
that prices would remain stable, and that expectation was not easily
changed. In part this was because the socialist system had developed a
moral commitment to the welfare of the workers—subjecting them to
unemployment and rising costs seemed unsocialist. A more important reason for the continuation and expansion of the system was the continuing
effort to carry out reform without creating losers. Opposition from urban

consumers who were forced to pay more for grain and other consumer goods would have threatened social stability and fed political resistance. As one economist put it:

> To reduce resistance to the reform, measures have been adopted to protect vested interests and to offer new benefits such as job allowance and retirement allowance. As a result, the size of social consumption provided by the free supply system has been expanded day by day, and the tendency of paying in kind has been further exacerbated with the sharp increase in the number of new officials and also with the ever upgrading of the physical goods supplied at public expense.[20]

Thus, when economic reform began and more power was delegated to the enterprise level, there was a strong tendency for enterprises to use their new-found discretionary power to distribute more wages and more welfare benefits to their workers. This tendency has been strengthened since 1985, when the economy overheated, and as structural imbalances have worsened and the inflation rate has picked up.[21]

The central pillar in this welfare system has always been the subsidization of the cost of grain to urban consumers—a policy that has the perverse economic effect of retarding grain production even while it promotes grain consumption. When the state decided in 1979 to raise procurement prices in the countryside in order to stimulate agricultural production, it also decided to maintain the price of grain in the cities by subsidizing the difference. This pattern has not changed in the ten years since, and currently the state provides 0.34 yuan and 1.6 yuan for every kilogram of grain and every kilogram of peanut oil, respectively, consumed by urban residents.[22] At the same time, as inflation has mounted, the state has begun subsidizing the cost of meat to urban consumers and now provides a subsidy of about 10 yuan per month to urban workers to compensate for the increased cost of meat. These subsidies alone add up to approximately 30 billion yuan a year.

At the same time, the cost of housing is heavily subsidized so that the average urban resident currently pays only 0.87 percent of his monthly income on housing. As a proportion of income, the cost of housing is now even less than it was in 1952, when it was 2.32 percent of income, and in 1964, when it was 2.61 percent of income.[23] In addition, governments and enterprises provide urban residents with free medical care—which cost 10 billion yuan in 1987—and free schooling.

The burden of subsidies is heavy. In Beijing, the most heavily subsidized city in China, the average per capita subsidy in 1988 was 530 yuan, almost half the annual salary for an average employee.[24] Altogether, price subsidies for the whole country were estimated to be over 50 billion yuan in 1987. This does not include the amount paid for maintaining superfluous workers in factories. It is estimated that there are some 20 million excess workers, who cost the economy 50 to 60 billion yuan per year.[25]

In addition, since welfare payments of various sorts are far more extensive than wage differentials within enterprises, there has been a tendency for egalitarianism to grow, despite the state's efforts over the past decade to encourage paying more productive and more skilled workers at a higher rate.

One effect of this life-long welfare system is that urban residents have little expectation of risk, which means that they are less likely to save for a rainy day and more likely to save for consumption. As a result, people do not exhibit the life cycle changes in savings rates produced by people in other nations. The corollary of this is that savings tend to be short term; people basically save to purchase consumer goods, particularly consumer durables.[26]

This distorted consumption structure has had a number of adverse effects on China's development, including most of all the pressure that it has put on local governments to produce consumer goods, thus skewing the investment structure toward processing industries.[27] Hence, the pattern of subsidies—a relic of the pre-1978 economic structure—has stimulated a pattern of consumption that has reinforced the tendency of local governments to expand their tax bases by investing in and promoting processing industries.

While this demand for consumer durables has stimulated the development of various light industries, local protectionism has interfered with the development of larger, more efficient industries. Thus, high demand for consumer durables coexists with the underutilized production capacity and overproduction of consumer goods discussed above. Moreover, the demand for consumer durables has not, generally speaking, stimulated the development of other sectors of the economy. Because Chinese technology is not generally at the level of producing the equipment needed to turn out high-grade consumer goods, there are few "backward linkages" in the Chinese economy. Instead of stimulating the growth of the machine tool and other industries, the demand for consumer durables is translated into a demand for importing processing lines from abroad.

Furthermore, because consumer durables production is capital intensive and has few backward linkages, it does not do as much as more labor-intensive industries would do to draw labor off the land. Thus, the rise of urban consumption has done less than would be expected in transforming the traditional rural economy into a modern economy.[28] In addition, such consumer durables as refrigerators and washing machines take the place of service employees who might be expected to increase as the urban standard of living has increased. Thus the development of the service sector has lagged behind.[29]

Inflationary Pressures

This mutually reinforcing structure of decentralization, localism, demand for consumer goods, duplicative construction, and cradle-to-grave welfare has contributed to inflationary pressures in Chinese society by stimulating the growth of industry and urban consumption beyond the capacity of the agricultural sector to supply raw materials and high-quality foodstuffs. In the last decade in general and the last four years in particular, the industrial economy has grown at a much faster rate than the rural economy. From 1979 to 1984, the agricultural economy grew at an average annual rate of 7.8 percent while industry grew at an average rate of 9.6 percent. Thus, the ratio between agricultural and industrial growth was maintained at 0.81:1. But since 1984, agricultural growth has largely stagnated while industrial growth has accelerated. In the four years from 1985 through 1988, agriculture grew at an average rate of 4 percent, while industry averaged 16 percent, dropping the ratio of agricultural growth to industrial growth to only 0.25:1. The resulting pressure on agricultural prices from industries dependent on agricultural raw materials and from China's growing population has forced prices up, and about two-thirds of all inflation from 1985 through 1988 is attributable to rising agricultural prices.[30]

Moreover, the rapid growth of town and township industries has contributed to inflation in at least three ways. First, the movement of labor from agricultural production to nonagricultural production has reduced agricultural input, contributing to a decline in output, at the same time that it has placed new demands on the agricultural sector for inputs. Second, the rapid growth of local enterprises has placed new strains on basic industries, driving prices for energy and raw materials up. Third, many town and township industries have been supported by an expansion of bank credit, which has contributed to the overall expansion of credit and growth of the money supply.

Furthermore, decentralization of decisionmaking about wages to enterprises that are not bound by hard-budget restraints has led to an expansion of consumption funds. From 1978 through 1983, productivity and wages grew 3.6 and 7.2 percent, respectively, while national income grew at an average annual rate of 7.1 percent. In 1984, however, wages and bonuses grew 22.3 percent while national income increased only 12 percent.[31] This trend has continued since then, and in 1988 wages and bonuses grew 23.1 percent while national income grew only 11 percent.[32]

This expansion of consumption funds is not due so much to loose monetary policy per se as it is to the nature of the state-enterprise relationship. In a system in which, on the one hand, enterprises are "responsible for profits but not for losses"— that is, because there is no effective mechanism for declaring enterprises bankrupt, banks inevitably have to extend new credit — and where, on the other hand, enterprises function not to maximize profits but to maximize the welfare of the enterprise community, there is an inevitable tendency for enterprises to distribute earnings to workers in the form of wages, bonuses, or welfare and to rely on the state and banks for new investment funds and credit.

The state's inability to control the growth of wages and bonuses has been paralleled by its failure to hold down "group consumption"—purchases by administrative units, social organizations, enterprises, and institutions. By 1988, such expenditures stood at 95.6 billion yuan, 1.6 times their level in 1983.[33]

The high rate of industrial growth and the rapid expansion of town and township industries reflects in part the state's inability to impose financial restraint on localities that are pursuing their own interests. This inability to exercise macroeconomic control is reflected in the state's repeated failure to restrain investment. For instance, in 1984 the state decided that investment should remain at about the same level for the next three years, but it in fact increased by about 80 percent. In 1988, total social investment was originally planned to be 300 billion yuan, but in fact it was over 400 billion yuan.[34]

At the same time, many enterprises are highly inefficient, absorbing state and local funds to little economic benefit. It is estimated that some 300,000 enterprises ran in the red in 1988, absorbing some 40 billion yuan of subsidies.[35] In addition, many enterprises that claim to make profits continue to operate simply by bank credit.

The increased cost of subsidies and demands for investment have put great pressure on state finances. In the six-year period from 1979 to 1984, the state's income increased 34 percent, while the amount of subsidies increased by 480 percent; 69.7 percent of increased revenues were used for subsidies.[36]

In short, the decentralization of the economy, which has been accompanied neither by the formation of adequate capital or labor markets nor by the establishment of unified financial controls, has continuously pressured the state to loosen controls over money and credit. Between 1977 and 1987, the volume of money in circulation grew more than 600 percent, about six times the rate of growth of national income.[37] In each of the last six years, the money supply has grown at a rate at least twice, sometimes three times, as great as the growth of the economy.[38] In 1988, the original plan called for issuing an additional 20 billion yuan in currency, but in reality an additional 67.9 billion yuan was issued.[39] In part because of this, the gap between supply and demand has been widening in the course of reform. According to one estimate, from 1978 through 1986 China produced a cumulative output of 3.25 to 3.75 trillion yuan worth of goods, but demand was in excess of 5.4 trillion yuan—a cumulative gap of 1.65 to 2.15 trillion yuan.[40]

Price Reform and Corruption

Perhaps nowhere is the tension between the socialist economic structure as it had existed before 1978 and reform more obvious than in the relationship between reform and corruption. One of the legacies of China's economic structure before reform was that the products of basic industries such as coal, oil, and transportation were priced low, while other products, including those of the processing industry, could reap large profits because of a favorable price structure. While this problem was recognized early in the Dengist period, it was difficult to address for several reasons. First, raising the price of raw materials would increase the production costs of enterprises, forcing some of them to incur deficits and causing others to be less profitable, thus increasing government expenditures while reducing its revenues. Second, the price structure in existence represented a de facto distribution of interests in the society. Changing that price structure was inherently redistributional and hence opposed by many interests. Third, it was feared that readjusting the price structure would cause inflation and that inflation would create social disorder.

Despite the inherent difficulties of price reform, the state made repeated efforts in the early 1980s to rationalize the price structure to a certain extent—the increase of grain procurement prices being the outstanding example. Moreover, as urban reform got under way in earnest in the mid-1980s, price reform was considered the "key" to reform. Nevertheless, price reform efforts in late 1984 and early 1985 caused the economy to overheat, with the result that such efforts were halted as retrenchment policies were adopted in 1985. Although there have been repeated attempts to promote a comprehensive price reform since then, including fully drafting a plan that was to be put into effect in 1987, fear of opposition and inflation have caused such reforms to be postponed.

In the meantime, unable to move ahead with a comprehensive price reform, the state has since the mid-1980s phased in a "dual track" price system under which the prices of in-plan materials continue to be bought and sold at state-set prices while out-of-plan goods are sold at negotiated prices. The intent was to gradually create a market structure by slowly increasing the percentage of goods permitted to be sold at negotiated prices, thus reunifying prices at market-set levels.

This attempt to carry out gradual price reform has stalled for several reasons. First, the rising costs of production under this system did not, as hoped, spur enterprise efficiency but led, on the contrary, to increased enterprise deficits, reduced tax revenues, and increased ex-factory prices. Second, given the ability of enterprises to negotiate for favorable treatment with the relevant government departments, higher prices for some goods did not generally lead to a redistribution of resources or to the closure of inefficient enterprises but rather to the reestablishment of the original price structure at a higher level. Thus, the rise of out-of-plan prices tended to pull along in-plan prices, contributing to inflation.

Moreover, despite the tendency for in-plan prices to rise in the wake of out-of-plan prices, the latter were soon far above the former. This system virtually invited corruption on a grand scale. According to one recent estimate, the aggregate difference between the state-set price of capital goods and the negotiated price at which they are actually sold amounts to 200 billion to 300 billion yuan annually. Figuring conservatively that 20 percent of this difference is illicitly siphoned off, the authors suggest that corrupt profits amount to 20 billion to 40 billion yuan annually.[41]

Widespread corruption has evoked strong resentments, which were given poignant expression in a strongly worded speech by senior economist Qian Jiaju to the Chinese People's Political Consultative Committee session in the spring of 1988. According to Qian, "Honest people can barely make a living, whereas opportunists and the corrupt live in abundance and are envied by others. Nothing corrupts the moral climate in society more than this."[42] A year later, opposition to corruption became a central motivation in the demonstrations of millions of people throughout China.

Political Dilemmas of Economic Reform

One of the great ironies of Chinese economic reform is that, proceeding from a strategy that in terms of economics, politics, and ideology was designed to offend as few interests as possible, reformers were nevertheless led over the course of a decade into a situation from which it was very difficult to escape. The strategy of economic decentralization expressed by the phrase *fang quan rang li* (delegating authority and granting benefits) had stimulated investment and growth, but it had also led to new strains in the economy, including excess investment, duplicative and economically inefficient plant construction, shortages of energy, raw materials, and transport capacity, and inflation.

The solution to such problems was by no means easy. In part because of the legacy of China's socialist economic and political system and in part because of the particular strategy adopted during the course of economic reform, China lacked the institutional, economic, and political resources to deal with its economic problems as well as manage the popular discontent that was growing in response to inflation, corruption, and perceived inequalities of income.

On an institutional level, reform had, perhaps inevitably given the weakness of China's economic and government structures by the end of the Cultural Revolution, concentrated more on stimulating economic growth than on building functionally differentiated economic organizations. This was a long-term problem of state-building that involved sorting out complex relations of interest, separating economic functions from political functions and central authority from local authority. Powers such as banking and taxation needed to be appropriately centralized, while basic investment and other economic decisions needed to be decentralized.

Doing this was no easy matter given the background of a Leninist system, the complex relations that evolved during the Cultural Revolution, and perhaps China's political culture. At least since 1949, economic functions have adhered closely to political power. Thus, as noted above, it is difficult to decentralize economic power without also decentralizing political power, and, conversely, it is difficult to recentralize such economic functions as banking and taxation without also reimposing the sort of all-controlling political power that had distorted and disrupted China's economic development since the founding of the PRC.

This weak institutional structure was a major contributor to the proliferation of corruption in China. As one Chinese economist has recently argued, by opening up the overly centralized process of decisionmaking economic reform was successful in reducing the irrationality inherent in the old structure of power but it increased the conflict between the public policy decisions and the private interests of decisionmakers. The old, centralized economic structure effectively prevented the widespread privatization of public power and corruption because it sharply curtailed the number of people involved in decisionmaking. The cost of this, however, was "enormous efficiency losses, such as the economy lacking a driving force, information being incomplete, and operation being rigid."[43] Opening up the system, however, has increased the privatization of public power and stimulated corruption.

China also lacked the political institutions to adequately cope with popular pressures. If such institutions had been stronger, they might have become effective channels for bringing public pressure to bear, for building consensus on policy decisions, or at least for defusing popular complaints about the ill effects of economic reform, such as corruption and inflation.

These institutional weaknesses were compounded by a lack of economic resources for dealing effectively with the strains that had emerged. In part, because the state had "bought off" resistance to reform by subsidizing affected interests, by the late 1980s it did not have the financial strength either to support major new investments in basic industries and agriculture or to offset the disruptions that would inevitably accompany a major overhaul of the price system. Thus, as economic difficulties mounted in the late 1980s, the state found itself unable either to adequately support such sectors as agriculture, energy, and raw materials that lagged behind or to push through the sort of radical measures that might have allowed economic forces to bring about a new equilibrium.

On another level, it might be said that the greatest problem economic reforms in China faced—and this applies even to the period before the suppression of the pro-democracy demonstrations in Beijing and the ouster of Zhao Ziyang—was the lack of political will to continue. Whereas reform in the early 1980s could garner support and allay detractors by adopting the pragmatic approach of "feeling the stones while crossing the river," because it could bring immediate benefits to various groups, by the late 1980s there was no longer a natural constituency for reform. Without such a constituency it is increasingly difficult to implement any reform measure, no matter how important or successful, in the face of entrenched interests that have little to gain from it and perhaps a great deal to lose.

When the reform program began, reformers could point to an important constituency—the peasants—that would benefit from the reforms. They could also point with justified pride to the increased income of the peasants and the abundant harvests that soon followed as proof that reform was worth the cost. Likewise, as reform moved into the urban economy, the process of "delegating authority and granting benefits" to local authorities and enterprises could win reform adherents at the local level and raise the income of urban workers. The economic growth that followed seemed to prove the correctness of reform.

In recent years, however, these initial gains have given way to a more difficult and more uncertain process in which the benefits of reform are less obvious. The rapidly rising costs of agricultural inputs have wiped out much of the benefit that peasants enjoyed from the early years of reform, and then inflation threatened the new-found wealth of urban workers. Public opinion surveys showed that people were much less satisfied with reform and less optimistic about its chances for success. Moreover, the state, having granted substantial subsidies already, no longer had the wherewithal to grant new concessions to the localities and to maintain the livelihood of peasants and workers as it undertakes new reforms. The peasants clearly need higher procurement prices for their grain, but such costs could not be passed on to urban workers without risking either social disorder or production slowdowns. Efforts to recentralize authority would certainly evoke local resistance. In short, the strategy of "feeling the stones while crossing the river" faced diminishing returns.

The absence of adequate institutional, economic, and political resources to deal with the economic and political strains brought about by decentralization and an opening up of the decision-making structure perhaps accounts for the approach that then General Secretary Zhao Ziyang and other reformers pursued after 1986, but particularly in 1988. In this period, Zhao pursued a policy of loose money and high economic growth in the apparent hope that, on the one hand, popular discontent could be alleviated by continually increasing incomes while, on the other hand, higher growth rates would mean higher tax revenues for the state. This strategy was brought to a rapid halt in the fall of 1988 as inflation, then running at an annual rate of about 30 percent, forced the adoption of retrenchment measures.

Economic retrenchment is intended to deal with the problems facing the Chinese economy by imposing sharp controls on the money supply and credit to slow inflation, by diverting greater resources to basic industries so as to bring about a better balance between those industries and the processing industries, and by recentralizing economic resources in the hands of the state.

Such measures, while beneficial in some respects, carry heavy costs. In China, the effect of tight monetary policies is quite different than in market economies. Because of the social contract between enterprises and workers, enterprises cannot, generally speaking, cut salaries or lay off workers. At the same time, many of their capital costs remain constant, in part because of the near absence of a secondary market for capital goods. Assets that are not being employed by enterprises must still be maintained by them because there is no easy way to dispose of them—and no assurance of their being able to acquire the same type of equipment in the future if the need arises. By the same token, enterprises that could employ such capital goods are not able to acquire them. With capital costs and wage costs fixed, enterprises have little choice but to cut technological innovation, that is, to reduce their long-term efficiency.

In addition, because enterprises depend on bank loans for their normal operating expenses, the imposition of tight monetary policies forces enterprises to respond by delaying payments to other enterprises, by not repaying loans to banks, by stockpiling goods, and by cutting production sharply—all of which increases the needs for funds at the same time that fewer funds are available. Production tends to fall faster than consumption, creating more, not less, inflationary pressure. Thus, unlike the result in market economies, where a tight money supply can reduce inflationary pressures and make the economy more efficient by forcing a more efficient allocation of assets throughout the economy by stimulating technological innovation and by bringing supply and demand into equilibrium, a tight monetary policy in China tends to make the economy less efficient while not reducing and perhaps even exacerbating inflationary pressures.[44]

Moreover, efforts to control the money supply by instituting credit quotas fall disproportionately on the efficient industries and on the state sector, those that rely most heavily on central government financing and hence are most responsive to government cutbacks—a result known as "whipping the fast ox." This tends to hurt precisely those industries that are intended to lead the economy. In addition, lowering production of such key state industries cause tax revenues to fall. These were, some economists argue, precisely the effects of the contractionary policies adopted in 1985 and the reason they were abandoned in early 1986.[45]

The difficulties with retrenchment policies lead inevitably to pressures to loosen them—and by the spring of 1990 it became apparent that China was once again taking some measures to increase the money supply and stimulate production. Whether or not this will lead to a new round of loosening and tightening is not yet clear, but it is apparent that unless China can find both the resources and the will to confront some of the underlying difficulties in the economy—including the restraints on the movement of capital assets and labor, the confusion surrounding property rights, and the irrational price structure—then it runs the risk of either recreating the overly centralized economic system from which it has tried so hard to escape or exacerbating the conditions that brought about the imposition of retrenchment. Avoiding such outcomes will require difficult political choices, choices made all the more difficult by the decision to suppress the pro-democracy demonstrations in June 1989.

Conclusion

Over the past decade, the Dengist reforms have significantly addressed many of the long-standing problems plaguing the Chinese economy. Particularly in the early 1980s, reformers worked to correct serious imbalances in the economy by trying to adjust the proportions among heavy industry, light industry, and agriculture. In doing so, they greatly stimulated the growth of rural enterprises, providing an outlet for millions of workers who could no longer work productively in the agricultural sector as well as for new workers entering the labor force. They have also substantially reduced the amount of state intervention in the economy, allowing market forces to play a much greater role. Decentralization of economic and political authority has given local enterprises an incentive to develop. Despite the inflation in recent years, both urban workers and rural peasants are substantially better off than they were a decade ago.

In spite of these important gains, however, it is clear that the Chinese economy faces substantial difficulties. Perhaps the most serious problem is that reform has failed to create a mechanism whereby resources can be efficiently distributed. Political interests and ideological strictures have hindered the development of clear-cut notions of ownership or property rights. Without such rights being adequately defined and defended, there is no way to clearly assess what belongs to the state and what belongs to the enterprise. It is thus impossible to make enterprises truly responsible for their own profits and losses. At the same time, without a clear notion of property rights, there is no way that enterprises can be allowed to go bankrupt. It is also impossible for enterprises to sell off equipment that they are not using or to acquire equipment that they need on a capital market. Even more basic, unless enterprises are viewed more as economic units and less as social units, it will be impossible to reduce the number of superfluous workers. Until such measures are taken, there can be no efficient movement of either capital or labor and hence little likelihood that structural imbalances can be corrected or that productivity can be significantly enhanced.

Moreover, the decentralization of authority has created difficulties for the state in its efforts to create an efficient market-oriented economy. The relationship that has evolved between the state and the localities has not only given the latter important leverage over the banking and taxation systems but has also given local authorities a whole range of powers by which they are able to thwart the policies of the central government. The problem is not that decentralization cannot help promote economic development, but that over the previous thirty years the state had created mechanisms centered around political mobilization and neglected institution building. The difficulty that China faces, as noted above, is that it is difficult to centralize authority over such economic functions as banking and taxation without recreating the overly centralized, stifling economic-political system which reform was initiated to overcome.

Precisely this problem is underscored by the retrenchment program that has been underway since fall of 1988. Although apparently not intended to reinstitute a full-scale planning system, the state has nevertheless attempted to strengthen control over critical industries. The functions of the old State Economic Commission, abolished in 1988, have been revived under the auspices of the new State Council Production Commission that was established in January 1990. Although this commission is only intended to coordinate the production of some 200 industries—including such huge industrial enterprises as Anshan Iron and Steel and the Daqing Petroleum Field—the reimposition of direct state control over such industries raises anew critical and controversial questions about the relationship between plan and market and between large-scale state-owned enterprises and the large number of smaller enterprises that make up the bulk of the Chinese economy. The new official formulation touting the "integration" of plan and market does not appear to provide an adequate framework for the answer to such questions.

In addition, the ability of the Chinese government to deal effectively with the economic problems that it faces appears to have been substantially undermined by the events of June 1989. Although in some ways the authoritarian measures taken suggest an ability to act decisively and to take unpopular measures—as the government did in selling bonds to workers and in raising transportation fees—it seems likely that continuing divisions within the government will undermine the formation and execution of coherent economic policy. Moreover, the campaign to criticize some of the economic policies pursued under Zhao Ziyang as capitalistic, even though it has began to fade in late 1989 and early 1990, is likely to make both the open discussion of economic reform and the vigorous pursuit of important reform measures very difficult. As of early 1990, it appears that the need to revive the market, reduce unemployment, and alleviate unemployment is bringing about a loosening of retrenchment, but the political atmosphere seems unlikely to open up sufficiently to allow vigorous pursuit of such measures as clarifying property rights, establishing the People's Bank of China as an independent central bank, and implementing thoroughgoing price reform.

Most critical, however, has been the loss of public confidence. As noted above, reform has reached a point at which hard choices involving the redistribution of interests are needed. Without public confidence that present sacrifices will be recompensed by long-term economic growth, it seems unlikely that the state can secure sufficient cooperation to push through significant reforms—assuming that it has the desire to do so. In the face of these ideological and political problems, it seems likely, at least in the short run, that China will try to rely on a mix of policies, including strengthened planning over critical industries, some loosening of the money supply to dampen popular discontent, and continued pursuit of local reform efforts, particularly in provinces along the southeast coast.

More fundamental reform measures will likely have to await a significant change in the political situation.

Notes

1. For a critique of the economic problems facing China in that period, see Ma Hong and Sun Shangqing, eds., *Zhongguo jingji jiegou wenti yanjiu* (Economic structural problems in China) (Beijing: Renmin Chuban She, 1981).

2. Wang Huning, "Zhongguo bianhua zhong de zhongyang he difang zhengfu guanxi: zhengzhi de hanyi" (The relationship between central and local government in the course of change: the political implications), *Fudan xuebao*, May 1988, p.4.

3. Pang Jinju, "On the Damages, Causes, and Remedies of China's Inflation," *Nankai Jingji Yanjiu* (Nankai economic studies), no. 1 (February 1989), trans. in JPRS-CAR-89-041, 9 May 1989, pp. 15-21, and He Jianzhang, "Firmly Adhere to the Socialist Course of Reform," *Guangming Ribao*, 27 October 1989, p. 3, trans. in Foreign Broadcast Information Service, China *Daily Report* (hereafter cited as FBIS-CHI), 3 November, 1989, pp. 43-48.

4. Nicholas R. Lardy, "Debate over Reform of China's Foreign Trade System," paper presented at the annual meeting of the Association for Asian Studies, Washington, D.C., March 1989.

5. *Renmin Ribao*, 11 September 1989, trans. FBIS-CHI, 2 October 1989, p. 57.

6. Chen Xiwen, "Zhongguo nongcun jingji: chao changgui zengzhang zhuan ru changgui zengzhang" (China's rural economy: the change from supranormal growth to normal growth), *Jingji Yanjiu*, December 1987.

7. The noneconomic aspects of China's enterprise structure are discussed in Andrew G. Walder, *Communist Neo-Traditionalism: Work and Authority in Chinese Industry* (Berkeley: University of California Press, 1986).

8. Wang Huning, "Zhongguo bianhua zhong ...," p. 3.

9. Xie Duo, "Wenti yu tansuo: Zhengdun zhili shenhua gaige" (The problem and its tentative solution: rectify control and deepen reform), *Shijie Jingji Daobao*, 21 November 1988, p. 12.

10. Wang Huning, "Zhongguo bianhua zhong...," p. 2.

11. Wang Huning, "Zhongguo bianhua zhong...," p. 4.

12. "Financial Situation Dire: Wang Bingqian," Xinhua, 31 August 1989, trans. FBIS-CHI, 1 September 1989, pp. 15-16.

13. Wang Huning, "Zhongguo bianhua zhong...," p. 6.

14. Wang Yuan, "Chanye jiegou, 'fen zao chi fan,' touze zhuti" (Industrial structure, "eating in separate kitchens," and investment entities), *Jingji Guanli*, September 1989, p. 56.

15. Ibid.

16. Pang Jinju, "On the Damages, Causes, and Remedies of China's Inflation."

17. Wang Yuan, "Chanye jiegou...," p. 56.

18. Resident's Behavior Group, Economics Institute, Chinese Academy of Social Sciences, "Zhumin de xiaofei xuanze yu guomin jingji chengzhang" (The consumption choices of residents and the development of the national economy), *Jingji Yanjiu*, no. 1, January 1988, pp. 26-42.

19. Ibid. See also "Jingji zengzhang yu chanye jiegou de biandong" (Economic growth and

changes in the production structure), *Shijie jingji daobao*, 27 April 1987, p. 5.

20. Zhao Renwei, Chen Dongqi, and Wang Zhongmin, "Shichanghua gaige jincheng zhong de shiwuhua qingxiang" (The tendency of paying in kind in the course of market-oriented reform], *Jingji Yanjiu*, April 1989, pp. 3-16.

21. Ibid.

22. Liu Yuanda and He Xiaolin, "Cong wujia kan guoqing" (Looking at the national conditions from the point of view of prices), *Beijing Ribao*, 22 June 1988.

23. Zhao Renwei, Chen Dongqi, and Wang Zhongmin, "Shichanghua gaige...."

24. Xinhua, 17 July 17 1989, in FBIS-CHI, 21 July 1989, p. 32.

25. Liu Guangdi, "Lun yizhi tonghuo pengzhang de daijia he cuoshi" (On the price of and measures for controlling inflation), *Guangming Ribao*, 11 March 1989. See also Xie Zhenjiang, "Jiage butie nali qule?" (Where have price subsidies gone?), *Jingji Ribao*, 27 February 1989.

26. Residents' Behavior Group, "Zhumin de xiaofei...."

27. Tian Yuan, Ma Jiantang, and Wang Yukun, "Options for Checking Inflation—Analysis and Policy Concepts," *Jingji Cankao*, 21 March 1989, p. 4, trans. FBIS-CHI, 3 April 1989.

28. Residents' Behavior Group, "Zhumin de xiaofei...." See also, Liu He, Liang Junping, and Yang Huanchang, "General Thoughts on Implementation of China's Industrial Policy," *Jingji lilun yu jingji guanli*, no. 2 (28 March 1989), pp. 14-19, trans. JPRS-CAR- 89-068, 3 July 1989, pp. 15-21.

29. Residents' Behavior Group, "Zhumin de xiaofei...."

30. Yang Qixin, "Lun zhili jingji huanjing yu shenhua gaige" (Improving the economic environment and deepening reform), *Zhongguo jingji tizhi gaige*, no. 12 (December 1988).

31. Wang Mengkui, "A Question that Merits Attention during the Present Economic Development," *Jingji Wenti*, July 1985, trans. JPRS-CEA-86-053, 2 May 1986, pp. 1-2.

32. *Zhongguo tongji nianjian* (Statistical yearbook of China), 1989 (Beijing: Zhongguo Tongji Chuban She, 1990), pp. 125 and 21.

33. Ma Jiantang, "Does Not Consumption Inflation Exist in China?" *Jingji Cankao*, 27 June 1989, trans. FBIS-CHI, 13 July 1989, pp. 42-44.

34. Yang Qixian, "Lun zhili jingji...."

35. Yan Kalin, "Make Full Preparations for Eliminating 300,000 Enterprises," *Jingji Ribao*, 17 August 1988, p. 2, trans. FBIS- CHI, 2 September 1988.

36. Dai Yuanchen, "On the New Inflationary Inertial Motion Caused by the Policy of Dealing with Inflation," *Jingji Yanjiu*, December 1988, trans. FBIS-CHI, 28 February 1989.

37. The volume of money in circulation in 1978 was 21.2 billion yuan. It was more than 145 billion yuan in 1987. See Wang Mengkui, "Certain Questions on Curbing Inflation," *Qiushi*, no. 7 (1 October 1988), pp. 12-17.

38. Pang Jinju, "On the Damages, Causes, and Remedies of China's Inflation."

39. Wang Dacheng, "The Predicament Confronting Reform and Construction, and the Way Out," *Guangming Ribao*, 3 June 1989, p. 3, trans. FBIS-CHI, 24 July 1989.

40. Xiang Zhongwei, "Bringing China's Inflation under Control," *Jingji Yanjiu*, no. 6 (June 1988).

41. Economic Situation Analysis Group under the Economics Institute of the Chinese Academy of Social Sciences, "Near-Term Measures for Freeing Reform from Its Current Difficulties," *Jingji Yanjiu*, July 1989.

42. "Qian Jiaju Discusses Prices, Reform, and Social Mood," *Wen Wei Po*, 4 April 1988, trans.

FBIS-CHI, 12 April 1988, p. 39.

43. Fan Gang, "Inherent Conflicts in Reform, Inflation, and State Ownership," *Jingjixue Zhoubao*, 22 January 1989, trans. JPRS-CAR- 89-032 (10 April 1989), p. 30.

44. Hu Haiming, "Zhuyi jinsuo yingen hou de fu xiaoying" (Pay attention to the negative effects following monetary retrenchment), *Shijie Jingji Daobao*, 28 November 1988, p. 12. For a very good anaylsis of the inefficiencies created by a tight monetary policy, see Microeconomic Situation Analysis Group, "Economic Growth Under Retrenchment: A Report on the Analysis of the Microeconomic Situation in the First Half of 1986," in Gary Zou, ed., *The Debate on China's Macroeconomic Situation (I)*, published in M.E. Sharpe's series, *Chinese Economic Studies*, Winter 1989.

45. Zhang Wenzhong and Zhu Jun, "Yi jiu ba wu nian jinsuo zhengce de jiaoxun" (Lessons from the 1985 retrenchment), *Shijie Jingji Daobao*, 2 January 1989, p. 11.

7. Rural Reform in China

Thomas P. Bernstein

Introduction:
The Significance of Decollectivization

More than a decade ago, the Chinese leaders initiated a reform process, which transformed agriculture in less than five years. Having been collectivized in the middle fifties, Chinese peasants returned to a form of family farming, though still on the basis of the collective ownership of land. Decollectivization was a highly significant instance of reform in Marxist-Leninist systems. Household contracting represented a break with the core assumptions of radical Maoism; but even more important, it implicitly or even explicitly repudiated Marxist-Leninist orthodoxy concerning the superiority of collective agriculture. With regard to radical Maoism, the reforms legitimated the idea of individual or family enrichment ahead of others, though in a context of a continued commitment to common prosperity; and they broke with Maoist ideals of self-sufficiency and self-reliance. With regard to Marxist-Leninist orthodoxy, decollectivization was an admission that collective farms, that is, the people's communes, had not succeeded in solving the problem of motivating peasant labor. This implied that the goal of subjecting agriculture to the procedures of the industrial assembly line, which is at the heart of the Marxist vision, is much more problematic than Marxists had long believed.

The distinctive incentive problem of agriculture consists of the temporal separation between work and result. Whether or not work is done well in the spring may not be apparent until the agricultural cycle is completed at harvest time. Even carefully calculated and measured piece rates cannot adequately cope with this problem. Incentives are needed that motivate agricultural laborers not just to meet particular job specifications but that motivate them to keep in mind the final result. Performance improves when individuals, groups, or households are put in continuous charge of a plot of land, the reward being based not on specific-task performance but on the harvest. The household is a readily available and convenient unit to achieve the goal of linking remuneration with output.[1] This line of reasoning suggests that household farming is compatible even with highly modern agriculture.

Reform-minded scholars in China have pointed to the examples of efficient household-based agriculture in the advanced world, as in the United States, Western Europe, and Japan, to show that traditional Marxist-Leninist assumptions about the backward nature of family production and the necessity of establishing large-scale agricultural units have to be qualified, if not abandoned.[2] The thesis of the viability of the family farm has not been officially adopted, and much concern has been voiced in the Chinese popular and academic press that the holdings of Chinese peasants—one-half hectare per family, on average, as of the late 1980s—are simply too tiny to be economical. The more conservative leaders and their academic supporters have seized on this situation to advocate some kind of recollectivization.[3] But the decade-long existence of household contracting speaks for itself as a repudiation of long-standing Marxist-Leninist dogma.

This chapter will examine the process of reform, the problems that have emerged, and the issue of the permanence of the reforms.

The Process of Reform, 1978-1982

Household contracting emerged from an incremental process in which leaders felt their way along from step to step searching for solutions, metaphorically described by Chinese economists as *mozhe shitou guohe*, crossing a brook by groping for stones on which to step.[4] This is not to say that the leaders did not have goals. The major one was and still is the achievement of rural modernization. Specific goals include securing of steady increases in output, productivity, and incomes; elimination of rural poverty; and release from agriculture of several hundred million laborers, primarily by means of rural industrialization. These goals, in the view of the reform leaders who came to power in 1978, were not being achieved under the commune system. They believed that the commune system itself was restricting the further development of the productive forces. Reformers were committed to change and were willing to experiment, in accord with the slogan, "Practice is the sole criterion of truth." There is little evidence that the outcome as it emerged by 1982-83, that is, the restoration of family farming, was foreseen, planned, or even desired in 1977 or 1978.

The most important impetus for change was that the reform leaders led by Deng Xiaoping diagnosed an acute crisis in agriculture. Output had risen but only barely kept up with population growth. Peasant living standards had stagnated since the mid-1950s, and acute poverty persisted. A 1978 Central Committee document spoke of 150 million peasants whose rations were inadequate, that is, who did not have enough to eat.[5] A report on Liyuan Commune in Anhui Province showed that loss of human and animal life during the Great Leap Forward (1958-61), combined with ongoing oppressive political campaigns, had so depleted resources that begging had become a chronic means of survival:

> In normal years, more than a third of the population left to beg for food.... In the winter of each year, one to three thousand people, carrying or leading the children, were driven from their villages to go begging in Jiangsu, Zhejiang, Hunan, Hubei, Fujian, or Guangdong provinces.

The central TV station made a "restricted reference film" of life in Liyuan Commune. "Conditions were so bad that they had to be seen for one to believe that villages could be so poor and the commune members so miserable this many years after Liberation."[6]

The persistence of hunger and poverty damaged the rulers' legitimacy. They had, after all, come to power with peasant support and with a commitment to improve the lives of the people. Hence, the reforms were undertaken to regain support and legitimacy in the countryside. Moreover, the leaders shared the traditional concept that peasants constituted the foundation of the state. As the senior leader Chen Yun put it, "Without grain there will be chaos" *(wu liang zi luan)*. In 1978, Chen Yun predicted that if the agricultural situation were not improved, "branch party secretaries will lead their teams to go begging in the cities," thereby causing general instability.[7]

The perception of crisis, accompanied by the political triumph of the reform coalition at the Third Plenum, resulted in a series of policy changes, including increased imports in order to reduce the procurement burden on peasants, sharp increases in procurement prices to restore incentives to peasants, and anti-leftist measures to restore a workable balance between the collective and private sectors, such as return and enlargement of private plots, removal of restrictions on sideline activities and on markets, as well as restoration of payment according to labor. The production team, the lowest and smallest of the three commune divisions, was reaffirmed as the basic unit of distribution. The system of labelling deviants as class enemies was largely abolished, thus ending three decades of the creation of outcasts. Among these policies, the procurement price increases played a central role in motivating peasants to produce more. Indeed, it is doubtful that household contracting would have succeeded without this crucial corollary measure.

These remedial policies assumed the continued existence of the communes, albeit in rationalized form. But even while drastic steps were taken to improve the collectives, household contracting was already being practiced in some localities, despite prohibition by the central authorities. The origins of household contracts go back to the crisis of the Great Leap Forward, when famine raged and agricultural output hit bottom. Some national and local leaders had permitted peasants to practice *bao chan dao hu*, assignment of output quotas to the household. Deng Xiaoping's famous quip that it didn't matter whether a cat was black or white as long it caught mice was made in July 1962 about household contracting, Deng saying that it might be an appropriate solution to the current crisis.[8] After Mao decisively intervened in August 1962, contracting to the household became a capitalist deviation for which officials were purged. According to some reports, however, remote villages continued to practice household farming surreptitiously.[9]

Now, in the post-Mao period, when the political climate had moderated, some local party secretaries allowed family farming, especially in acutely poverty-stricken areas, probably with the behind-the-scenes tolerance of reform-minded central leaders. Peasants took to the practice with great enthusiasm, and production increased. Until the fall of 1979, household contracting was officially prohibited, however, even while various "responsibility systems" were permitted that linked reward to output in the case of individuals and groups. In September 1979, a national decision lifted the blanket prohibition on family farming, but only for the very poorest areas. From then on, but amid fierce controversy, reform-minded officials became more and more receptive to household contracting, leading to the progressive lifting of restrictions. By the spring of 1982, all forms of household contracting were given the imprimatur of socialist legitimacy. This included the most radical form of family farming, *da baogan*, comprehensive household contracting, which in contrast to a more collectivist version did away not only with collective deployment of labor but also with unified distribution of the proceeds according to a system of work points. Under *da baogan*, which by 1983 had become the predominant form of farming, the household's obligations to state and collective consisted in paying the land tax, selling quota grain under the state procurement system, and paying a fee to the collective. Whatever remained could be freely disposed of by the household, thereby providing a major incentive to maximize output as well as a substantial degree of autonomy to the peasants.

How did this transformation come about?[10] First, reform-minded leaders sought to create a political climate in which change was legitimate and Maoist orthodoxy discredited. A Chinese version of *glasnost* was launched in 1979, which sought systematically to expose the errors of the past. Articles, short stories, and statistics exposed the bitter sufferings of the peasants. "Leftist interference," recurrent efforts to introduce more radical forms of socialism, had in many places reduced peasants to dire poverty, either because of excessive investment, arbitary imposition of irrational farm practices, or because "capitalist tails" (that is, sidelines, an important source of household income) had been "cut off."[11] Maoist policies of local self-sufficiency, such as "grain as the key link," had robbed areas specializing in other crops of their comparative advantage, causing them to be impoverished. The immense famine of 1959-61 was publicly described for the first time, and numerous indictments were published on harsh and mindless bureaucratic abuse of peasants under the guise of leftism.[12] The message of these indictments was summarized in a remark made to me in 1985 by a county party secretary in Anhui who said that agricultural policies had been correct from 1949 to 1955, in error from 1955 to 1978, and once again correct only since then, thereby writing off twenty-three years of the PRC's history.[13]

Second, decision makers were apparently won over to this change as evidence became available of its capacity to increase output not only in the poverty-stricken areas but also in the better-off places. Grain output rose from 304.8 million metric tons in 1978 to 407.3 in 1984. This evidence appears to have convinced them that household contracting could not only help solve the problem of rural incomes and urban food supply, but also reduce pressure on the national budget. The sharp increase in agricultural procurement prices announced in 1979 had burdened the state budget with very large subsidies, since the government was afraid to pass the increase on to the urban consumer. The leaders had also promised in 1978-79 that state investment in agriculture would increase, which would have enlarged budgetary outlays even more. Now the success of household farming seemed to make it possible for the leadership to shift the investment burden to the peasants. They reduced agricultural investment as a proportion of state investment from about 10.6 percent of state investment in capital construction in 1979 to 3 percent in 1986, the absolute amounts dropping from 5.8 billion yuan to 3.5 billion.[14] State investment in agriculture was confined to large irrigation projects, energy development, and major transportation projects. The state expected that peasant money would provide funding for virtually all local needs, including schools, local roads, and agricultural infrastructure. One 1983 *People's Daily* article spoke of the "huge amounts of money" needed for rural development:

> Where should this money come from?...Rural construction should mainly rely on local communes and brigades...with state assistance as a supplement. Funds used for the peasants mainly come from the peasants....At present the countryside has become much richer and the peasants are holding more than 80 billion yuan in their possession.[15]

As will be noted below, peasants have not been willing to invest in agriculture, and this is one of the major sources of the difficulties that beset agriculture in the second half of the 1980s.

A second explanation looks to the dynamics of elite conflict. Decollectivization was controversial. Many high officials had in the past been penalized for supporting "rightist" policies and hence suffered from a "lingering fear" of retaliation should a line change occur, as had happened so frequently in the past. Others probably opposed decollectivization because of ideological convictions. And still others were members of factions that resisted reform policies for reasons of the power struggle. The political process during which decollectivization came to prevail was thus conflictual and characterized by strong opposition, particularly in the case of several provincial party secretaries. In order to overcome resistance, reform leaders made adherence to the policy of household contracting into a matter of line, that is, a test of whether or not an official was in support of the current leadership and its policies. It was defined as a "profound education in the ideological line." "Stern criticism" was directed at those who disregarded mass demands for the new system.[16] Mobilization of this kind of ideological pressure helps account for the fact that household contracting swept over the entire country in 1982-83. All along, change was supposed to take place in accordance with local conditions (*yin di zhi yi*). But in fact, decollectivization was pushed everywhere, in a manner reminiscent of Maoist mass campaigns, using "one stroke of the knife" (*yi dao qie*).

A third explanation focuses on mass demands and asks about the role of the peasants in decollectivization. Some studies of peasant responses suggest that peasant attitudes were mixed. For instance, those whose households were short of labor power preferred the security of the collective system, whereas those with ample labor power opted for family farming.[17] Others feared future penalties should the reform leaders fall and a reversal take place. But by and large, peasants responded with enthusiasm to the change, and this enthusiasm may well have been a critical ingredient in the decision of the top leaders to support household contracting. As a knowledgeable Chinese official explained, leaders had originally intended to confine the rural reform to the establishment of "responsibility systems" that linked reward to final output (*lienchan zirenzhi*) but did not give the family control over the land. But the peasants wanted a responsibility system that contractually linked reward to final output (*lienchan chengbao zirenzhi*), in which they were put in full charge of the land, and it was this pressure from below to which the leaders yielded.

Mass enthusiasm, even if not by any means unanimous, still leaves open the question of local leadership and control. After all, a strong presence of the party in the villages has always been a distinctive feature of the Chinese political system. To this day about half of the party membership of about 45 million serves in the countryside. As in the case of higher-level officials, village party cadres, too, had for decades been subjected to intense indoctrination and to political "struggle" when found to be deviant. Many were therefore afraid to lead in the establishment of household contracting for fear that the next change in line would result in punishment. This fear, reinforced by whatever Maoist convictions they had and by the prospect of losing power and authority should decollectivization prevail, led to hesitation and obstruction in carrying out the new line. Thus, there are a good many accounts of local cadres resisting the new practices in the face of mass demands, or of their simply abdicating leadership.[18] This pattern, in other words, was one in which the central leaders signalled to the peasants that household contracting was acceptable and even desirable and the peasants felt empowered to pressure the cadres.

But there was also another situation, in which the pressure exerted by villagers, who, after all, were the relatives and neighbors of the party cadres, was effective in motivating them to act in favor of the new system. When these pressures prevailed, party cadres would take the lead in the transition, sometimes in the face of conservative higher-level criticism without accompanying higher-level sanction. And sometimes party cadres, "fearing neither dangers, rumors, or slanders," took the lead in implementing the change against mass opinion.[19]

Probably the most widespread circumstance was that, as the central leaders made an increasingly firm commitment to household contracting, they signalled to the village cadres that the new policy was legitimate and had to be implemented. In such circumstances, the new policy might well be imposed on the peasants.[20]

In sum, it cannot be said that the local party leadership controlled the process of conversion in the same sense that previous social or economic campaigns had been controlled. But it is also not accurate to say that the establishment of household contracting was the product of the peasants' spontaneous desires. The presumption that decollectivization was a process that took place under local party leadership is strengthened by the fact that village party organizations survived the transition. Many village branches were, to be sure, damaged by decollectiviztion. Some became paralyzed, and some party cadres became so disoriented by the change that they withdrew from political and administrative work.[21] But the rural party organizations as a whole survived the change and continued to be in charge of village affairs, even after the peasants gained a certain degree of independence.

Follow-up Reforms

The establishment of household contracting necessitated further reforms on the principle that he who says A must also say B. For instance, almost as soon as household contracting was in place, the issue of the length of the land contract arose. Initially, a peasant household contracted for land use for only one or two years. Short-term tenure gave rise to "predatory land use."[22] Peasants who knew that somebody else might soon be farming their plot did not bother to maintain soil fertility or improve the land. Hence, security of tenure became an immediate issue that had to be dealt with. Already in 1984, contracts were extended to 15 years and, in the case of orchards, forests, or fish ponds, for even longer periods. Because the problem persisted of motivating peasants to invest in the land, consideration was given to even more drastic extensions of leaseholds. As one source reported in 1987, "To encourage long- term investment in farming, the period for which land is contracted will remain unchanged at 50 years and children may inherit the contracted land."[23] However, it appears that this change was not implemented, apparently because of concern that it might perpetuate the parcelization of land.[24]

Extension of land contracts was one example of follow-up changes necessitated by the initial change. Probably the need to lengthen land-tenure contracts was an unanticipated consequence of the reforms. It is doubtful whether those who favored household contracting in 1979 or 1980 were aware that more and more concessions would have to be made to the private interests of peasants and that they were embarking on a slippery slope towards the de facto and perhaps de jure restoration of private property in land. However, had thought been given to the implications of household contracting, the issue could not have been brought out into the open during the transition, since doing so would have given opponents the ammunition with which to charge that the reformers were giving away the "socialist store."

A similar need for follow-up reforms arose with regard to transfer of land contracts. As a family moved through the life cycle, the availability of labor was bound to vary, necessitating a mechanism for decreasing or increasing family holdings. Agricultural planners favored contract transfer because they hoped to spur the concentration of land in the hands of specialized grain farmers, whose scale of operations would be enlarged, as would their level of commercialization. They also wanted to encourage the growth of rural industry, and to this end, too, a mechanism was needed that would allow peasants to relinquish the land to someone else. Transfer of contracts was consequently permitted in 1984, including payment of compensation for land improvements but not for the land itself, since land continued to be a collective asset not subject to purchase or sale. Few peasants transferred contracts in this way. Peasants often held onto contracted land for security when family members took up other occupations, following a pattern of diversification seen on Taiwan. In order to stimulate concentration of land in the hands of specialist-farmers, thought began to be given in the middle eighties to the creation of a quasi-land market in collectively owned land by allowing the purchase and sale of contracts.[25] As of 1989, this possibility had not materialized.

Still another reform was the formal abolition in 1984 of the people's communes and their replacement by township governments and village committees. Township governments, *xiang* or *zhen* (small towns), replaced commune-level administrations. Village committees were set up on the territory of the former production brigades. The production teams, the lowest level of the old three-tiered commune system, essentially disappeared, although a cadre of the former team, which usually had been a small village, maintained liaison between the village committee and the peasants. The production teams, which used to organize the labor of their members on collective fields, thus became the main organizational casualty of the reforms. In addition, the establishment of the village committees and *xiang* governments signified the end to the merger of the collective and governmental authorities that had taken place during the Great Leap Forward of 1958. At the village committee level, economic functions, that is, the management of village-owned assets including industry, large agricultural machinery, irrigation, as well as the administration of land contracts, was vested in a separate economic committee. At the *xiang* level, too, separate economic committees were put in charge of industry and other economic activities. However, it appears that this differentiation was formal and symbolic. Economic and governmental units usually work closely together. Most important, the true center of power, the party committee and its party secretary, was not affected by these changes. Although much has been written about the importance of differentiating government from party, in the rural areas little progress was made in securing a change in this sphere. Nor was much progress made with regard to ensuring accountability of local political leaders and organizations to the peasants.[26]

Finally and most important, a series of reforms aimed at the development of a "commodity economy." Reformers wanted to get away from the self-sufficiency orientation of the communes and promote development via market exchange, diversification, specialization, and the spread of entrepreneurship. Because an estimated 70 percent of farm labor may be released from agriculture in the next decades, new employment opportunities needed to be created in industry, the service sector, and specialized agricultural undertakings.[27] To this end, once household contracting was in place a series of policies were promulgated to relax or abolish restrictions on individual enterprise. To facilitate the emergence of "specialized households," those who engaged full time in a particular line of work, peasants were empowered to invest in a wide range of enterprises, including manufacturing, retail and wholesale commerce, and services such as transportation, first locally and later nationally. Private ownership of the means of production such as tractors and trucks was permitted in 1983 and 1984. Peasants could start their own businesses, sell shares to raise capital, or contract to operate village-owned enterprises, either by sharing profits with or paying a fixed fee to the village committee, which owned village industry. To facilitate mobility, peasants were permitted to work temporarily in large cities and to set up businesses in the small towns (*litu bu li xiang*).

In addition, restrictions were relaxed on the hiring of labor, a central issue in any socialist state. Initially, in 1983, euphemisms were used. Peasants could engage in "labor exchange," take on "assistants," "apprentices," or "helpers."[28] At the Thirteenth Party Congress in 1987, private enterprise was named a "necessary" supplement to the predominantly socialist economy, and in 1988 the state constitution was amended to permit limited private enterprise, defined by law as businesses employing more than eight laborers. Hiring of labor, which had rapidly exceeded the restrictive boundaries set in 1983, had been in a gray area of legality and was thus now officially permitted.[29] However, even afterwards, hiring of labor was viewed with suspicion by quite a few party cadres, though others themselves engaged in the practice! After the Tiananmen events in 1989, private business was harshly criticized for tax evasion and corruption, and hiring of labor became more and more suspect, certainly so when party members did the hiring.[30]

The core idea behind this set of reforms was marketization. Hostility to the market is a basic part of Marxist-Leninist orthodoxy. Reformers enthusiastically embraced the market and the idea that it was legitimate to make a profit from market transactions. Reformers believed that the circulation of commodities required diverse channels, because the monopoly over trade held by the state and its agents, the nominally independent supply and marketing cooperatives, could not meet the needs of a diversifying agricultural and urban economy. Reports showed that peasant households specializing in transport—a critical bottleneck in the Chinese economy— were satisfying real needs in supplying agricultural and sideline products. Moreover, flourishing markets gave rise to new industries to serve the market, such as catering and communications.[31] Reports quoted peasants as saying that these new markets had "solved problems which many state and collective commercial, financial, and trade departments could not solve for a long time."[32] Hence, advocates of reform called for further steps towards marketization:

> What should be done in the second step in the rural reforms is mainly to straighten out market relations and build up a good market mechanism, and let it spontaneously regulate the relationship between production and consumption, readjust the production structure, and promote the circulation of labor power, land, capital, technology, and other important factors in agricultural production.[33]

However, the market-oriented reforms were not completed. The key factors of production were not freed fully from administrative control. Land could not be bought and sold, labor became only partially mobile, and capital also did not circulate freely. The reforms were thus only partial in nature.

Appraising the Reforms

Rural reforms were highly successful from 1979 to 1984. During the first years, they produced dazzling results. Agricultural output rose rapidly. Productivity increased, and peasant incomes more than doubled. Rural poverty declined sharply, although pockets of poverty remained even in wealthy areas, and in general the western and northwestern provinces lagged behind. The coastal provinces, especially Guangdong and Fujian, did especially well in developing markets and enterprise. The successes of the first five years, it is important to reiterate, were due not simply to household contracting but also to the increase in procurement prices. In addition, ten large fertilizer plants built in the 1970s began to produce and greatly improved the supply of this crucial input. Agriculture also benefited from the capital construction undertaken during the Mao period, even as the "learn from Dazhai" campaigns of the 1960s and 1970s were harshly criticized. But whatever the sources of success, the agricultural sector gave a boost to reform in the country as a whole. In striking contrast to the Soviet Union under Gorbachev, successful rural reform in China provided an immediate payoff in terms of improved food supply and a higher standard of living in both town and country. General support for reform increased among both the elite and the masses. A sense of optimism and forward momentum was generated, which found concrete expression in the urban-industrial reform initiatives adopted in 1984.

Since 1985 the picture has been much more mixed. Agriculture became caught up in the general problems of the Chinese economy, especially inflation, as well as in growing corruption, which stemmed to a significant degree from the fact that the marketizing reforms were incomplete, leaving officials in charge of crucial commodities but with new options to "use their power for private gain" (*yi quan mou si*). Most important, grain output, which rose from 305 million metric tons in 1978 to 407 million metric tons in 1984, since then has fluctuated below this peak. Outside observers believe that the increases of the preceding period cannot be sustained, mainly because the current level of technology has reached its limits and yields cannot rise without a new technological breakthrough. Even more important, agricultural investment has declined while price scissors resulting from inflation lowered incentives.

What mattered most to the regime was that output of the most crucial agricultural commodity of all, grain, ceased to increase. China's leaders were mesmerized by the problem of feeding over a billion people. The population grew more rapidly than anticipated, reaching 1.1 billion in April 1989, thus confronting the leaders with the prospect of feeding even millions more than they had counted on. This was to some extent an unanticipated consequence of household contracting, which disrupted the rural part of the birth limitation program both by weakening organizational effectiveness and by raising family interest in having more children, both for the household economy and to provide for old age.[34]

Lagging incentives and lagging investment were two of the core problems of agriculture from the mid-1980s on. The incentive problem arose in part because the prices of commodities such as grain continued to be set by the state. In 1985, the old compulsory system of purchase and sale of agricultural goods, established in 1953, was abolished and replaced by contractual purchases at state-set prices. But these contractual sales by peasants were in fact "assignments by the state" rather than freely negotiated bargains.[35] Because of inflation, selling grain to the state became unprofitable for the peasants, especially since the market price of essential industrial outputs rose sharply, leading to a scissors effect. Making peasants grow grain thus required renewed and widespread resort to administrative pressure, since peasants preferred to grow other, more lucrative crops. The state's need for cheap grain meant that peasants were not nearly as free to decide on which crops to grow as is implied by the idea of household contracting. The government sought to improve incentives, raising grain procurement prices for the first time in many years in 1989, but only by about 15 percent. The government also tied the sale of key inputs, such as fertilizer, diesel oil, and plastic sheeting, to the grain contracts, thus making these inputs available at the low state price rather than at the higher market price. Peasants did not always benefit from these preferences, however, since local officials often diverted these goods to the lucrative free market.[36] In thinking about these issues, it is worth keeping in mind that in other countries farmers do necessarily benefit from a free market, as shown by the fact that many governments subsidize agriculture. But Chinese peasants did not have the political clout to compel their government to subsidize them. Also, the Chinese government could not pay adequate prices to the peasants without fundamentally restructuring its budgetary allocations, a step that it was unable to take because of the weight of the bureaucratic interests involved.[37]

As noted earlier, state investment in agriculture sharply declined in the 1980s in the expectation that the new peasant wealth would offset the reduction. However, in the 1980s peasant investment in agriculture declined together with that of the state. One indicator of this was that the foundation laid during the Mao period in farmland capital construction eroded. In 1957, 27 million hectares of arable land were irrigated and in 1979, 45 million, but since then there has been no further growth but instead shrinkage, to 44.2 million hectares.[38] The press criticized "poor maintenance of water conservancy installations in recent years [which] aggravated the losses caused by natural disasters in some localities."[39] The number of mechanized tube wells dropped. Soil fertility declined in "some localities," and soil eroded. Drainage facilities deteriorated. Experts warned even in 1986 that the decrease in investment in farmland capital construction could lead to stagnation in output. "The central leaders hold that this opinion is worth noting."[40] A campaign to revitalize rural capital construction started in the fall of 1989 under the auspices of the conservative leadership that gained ascendancy in June 1989.

When peasants, or for that matter local governments or collective organizations, invested in productive activity, it was less often in agriculture
than in commercial and industrial enterprise. The rates of return from
such activities as transportation far exceeded the profits to be made from
growing grain. Rural industry, whether leased or owned by individuals, by
the village committees, or by township governments, grew throughout the
1980s at extremely high rates, ranging from 11 percent in 1980 to 68 percent in 1984 and 21 percent in 1986.[41] Rapid industrial expansion in the
rural sector gave employment to millions of peasants. By 1986, 75 million
workers labored in rural industry, up from 28 million in 1978. Rapidly
growing rural industry created major imbalances with agriculture, causing
the government to ask local governments to divert profits from industry in
order to help agriculture.[42]

Lagging investment in agriculture indicated that the rural reforms had
not yet been put on a stable foundation. Part of the investment problem
was institutional. Household contracting and associated reforms that
aimed at stimulating enterprise and marketization weakened the collective
capacity to invest and to supply collective goods and services that the
household itself could not easily provide. The successor institutions to the
production brigades and the communes—the village committees and
township governments—were supposed to provide the services that the
communes had supplied. But in the initial period of the change to household contracting, these services, ranging from birth control to education
to the supply of collective inputs such as water, were often disrupted or
even abolished as collective assets were redistributed. How to supply adequate services to the peasant households has been an issue frequently discussed in the press. Part of the problem was resources: while peasants paid
a fee to the village committee (tiliu), it was not necessarily adequate for
collective investment, and extracting money from each household proved
more difficult than withholding it from collective distribution. Peasants
often bitterly complained that local authorities extracted miscellaneous
funds from them for frivolous purposes such as cadre meetings. Lack of
accountability in the management of local funds caused popular distrust
and unwillingness to contribute.[43]

Part of the problem was lack of effective leadership over agriculture by
the county down to the xiang (township) and the village committee, since
the main interest of local officials lay in fostering industrial growth.
Zouping County, Shandong, was an exception. There, the Agricultural
Bureau drew up a plan in 1985 to balance household contracting with unified management in each of the county's 842 villages. This included common cropping; collective plowing, sowing, and irrigation; and common
measures for plant and soil protection. As of 1985, only half of the villages

provided for these collective services and functions. In about 30 percent of villages, there were no collective services at all, and these tended to be the poorer villages in the hills rather than the plains. But it seemed doubtful how widespread such cases of vigorous leadership were.[44]

The questions of how to increase investment and how to provide services that the individual household could not supply were closely bound up with the questions of socialism and collectivism. In early 1989, for instance, Premier Li Peng said that "developing the collective economy is conducive to increasing agricultural investment."[45] Some scholars and officials believed that cooperatives should be established that would provide services to the household for all stages of the production process. But when peasants heard the word "cooperative" (*hezuo she*), they were reminded of collective farming, which was called by the same name. Their concern was not misplaced, because some officials worried not only about essential services but also about the size of the family farm, believing it to be too small to be viable and that it was a drag on technical progress. In their view, the scale of operations needed to be enlarged, particularly in the advanced agricultural areas.[46]

New cooperative groupings initiated by peasants did in fact appear and much publicity was devoted to them. They were called *nongcun jingji lien-heti* (village economic combines). As of 1986, there were 478,000 such combines, with 4.2 million participants. Peasants actually organized most of these for industrial purposes, for transportation, for construction, and for operating fisheries. Only a few were involved with crop cultivation.[47] It is not likely that these combines will be the solution to the problem of services.

Because peasants were fearful that household contracting might be abolished, they preferred to invest in building houses or to search for a quick payoff from commerce or industry rather than put their earned surplus into agriculture. During the 1980s, a truly astonishing housing boom swept through rural China. Entire villages were rebuilt. This bespoke not only long unmet needs and revival of peasant customs, but also peasant insecurity with regard to the future of the reforms. Unlike other assets, peasant houses were not socialized during the collective era and hence were seen as a secure investment.[48] Peasants also acquired television sets, refrigerators, and other consumer durables at sharply rising rates, often to the chagrin of urbanites who resented newly rich peasants' carting off such valued goods to their villages. But the important underlying problem was not only the unprofitability of investment but also peasants' fears that long-term investments were an insecure proposition. Short-term maximizing behavior was a widely observed phenomenon in rural China in the 1980s.[49]

Because peasants feared for the future of household contracting, the leaders kept reassuring them that they did not intend to coerce peasants into amalgamating their holdings and that all options were open, including reliance on large, specialized households (*zhuanye da hu*)to provide services. But official fears were also voiced that peasants might become dependent (*yi fu*) on a small number of rich and powerful specialized households.[50] At the 1988 Agricultural Work Conference, Politburo member Tian Jiyun said that household contracting still had "great vitality," but also stressed development of "socialized services" for the households for all parts of the production process. He called for establishment of a multi-tiered, diverse service system to provide information, technology, capital, plant protection, mechanization, storage, circulation, and administrative services.[51]

A year later, similar formulations were offered, but with a new addition, namely, that while household contracting would remain in most villages, in advanced areas "an appropriate scale of management can safely be promoted."[52] This formulation seemed to suggest official sanction for partial recollectivization. Remarkably, this formulation was similar in method to the policy adopted in 1979 and 1980, when it was said that the collective system would remain but that in very poor areas household contracting could be tried. As of early 1990, it was not clear how much of an impact this amendment to ongoing policy will have, but it is a sign that peasant worries have not been unfounded. Central leaders keep assuring the peasants that change will not be imposed from above. Perhaps they will let a new system evolve on the basis of the evolution of economic forces, technological needs, peasant self-interest, and guidance by government policy. But peasants have had ample experience with programs that were introduced voluntarily and quickly became compulsory. The cooperativization campaigns of the 1950s were an excellent example.

Conclusion:
The Question of Permanence

The rural reforms are in trouble, and the leaders are not sure what to do about the difficulties. The party-state could try to recollectivize. Some officials believe that in view of stagnant grain output, household contracting has outlived its usefulness. But the leaders are afraid of the peasants, knowing that they can resist by slowing down and letting productivity drop and that they can engage in vigorous protest, as has already happened.[53] The leaders have repeatedly assured the peasants that nothing will be done against their will. Besides, the regime is now constrained in its choices by a great many situational factors, including declining capacity to enforce decisions in the localities.[54] Drastic steps such as recollectivization are thus not at all likely.

At the same time, the regime is dissatisfied with the existing system, and the greater the problems, the greater the temptation to take drastic steps to change it. Hence the peasants' oft-voiced fear, "Will policy change?" is not in principle unjustified.[55] The underlying reality is that the reforms are not anchored in an accountable political system or in law or in constitutional guarantees. They are anchored in the pragmatic rule, "Practice is the sole criterion of truth," which means that the reforms are vulnerable to judgments concerning their efficacy. Conversely, of course, judgments also have to be made concerning the costs of abrogating reforms. If the rulers believe the reforms are not effective, they can in principle try something else. A recent example pertains to labor mobility, which the reforms had encouraged, and which is a vital ingredient of any economy with a signficant market component. In 1988, when policy makers decided on economic cutbacks in order to check inflation, the scale of urban construction was curtailed and far fewer peasants were needed. "Stringent measures" were announced to reduce the flow of rural labor into the cities. A strict "registration and licensing system" was to be introduced, with emphasis on local absorption of rural surplus labor.[56] Thus, liberalized labor mobility, an important aspect of the reforms, was curtailed by administrative fiat. When the preferences of policy makers change, or when the political balance shifts, the reforms can be affected. Peasants understand this well and act accordingly in making investment decisions.

Pragmatism is not the only decision rule governing the reforms. There also are the Four Principles, to which the country is supposed to adhere and which were announced by Deng Xiaoping in the spring of 1979. They are the dictatorship of the proletariat, party leadership, Marxism-Leninism/Mao Zedong Thought, and the socialist road. They logically contradict the pragmatic principle of "practice is the sole criterion of truth," which judges policy by a test of effectiveness and is in principle unprejudiced.

As in the case of pragmatism, what counts in determining what is or is not socialist is the political balance and the judgment of those in power. Those who have had the power to interpret the doctrine in the last decade have favored reform and have introduced a wide range of practices normally associated with capitalism. But this does not mean that the leaders only pay lip service to the Four Principles and that pragmatism is their only guide. The record of Chinese reform suggests that the socialist road—or more precisely, the initial stage of socialism—does impose constraints on the choices that are made, for instance, with regard to the primacy of public ownership. For example, there may well be sound non-ideological reasons for not turning land into a commodity, but judging from the record, the ideological obstacle does carry weight. In terms of political conflict, the fact that China's leaders claim to be adhering to the socialist road enables any claimant for power to charge that socialism is being sold out or is in jeopardy. In society at large, the continued existence of the socialist principle means that an aura of illegitimacy and uncertainty attaches to many private business activities, from hiring labor to making a large profit. Those who do business under such conditions feel vulnerable and may have to take out various kinds of political insurance in order to protect themselves.[57] When the political climate becomes less benign, as it did in the summer of 1989, the status of private entrepreneurs becomes even more precarious. Thus, even if the Four Principles do not presage the demise of private or semi-private enterprise in the near future—after all, the initial stage of socialism is to last until the middle of the twenty-first century—they do shape the environment in which the changes initiated since 1978 operate. The rural reforms, in other words, operate in an environment in which limits of uncertain scope prevail.

Notes

1   A succinct statement on this issue applicable to China is M. E. Bradley and M. Gardner Clark, "Supervision and Efficiency in Socialized Agriculture," *Soviet Studies*, vol. 23, no. 3 (January 1972), pp. 465-73.

2. See, for instance, Zhang Luxiong, "The Family Operation in Socialist Agriculture," *Guangming Ribao*, 2 July 1984, *Foreign Broadcast Information Service-Daily Report, PRC* (henceforth abbreviated as FBIS-CHI) no. 139, 18 July 1984, pp. K8-9.

3. *South China Morning Post*, 7 September 1989, in FBIS-CHI no. 172, 7 September 1989, pp. 38-39.

4. Remarks by Liu Guogang, a prominent Chinese economist, made at Columbia University, September 1984.

5. "Decisions of the Central Committee of the CPC on Some Questions Concerning the Acceleration of Agricultural Development (Draft)," 11 January 1979, *Issues and Studies*, July 1979, pp. 104-5.

6. See "Starving to Death in China," introduction by T. Bernstein and anonymous co-author, in *New York Review of Books*, vol. 30, no. 10 (16 June 1983), pp. 36-38. This is a translation of an internally published article, "Zhengce fangkuan: qiong she fanshen" (Policies have relaxed; a poor commune turns over), *Nongye Jingji Congkan*, no. 6 (25 November 1980), pp. 18-19.

7. Chen Yun, "Tiaozheng guomin jingji, jianchi an bili fazhan" (adjust the national economy; persist in developing according to proportions), 21 March 1979, in *San zhong chuan hui yilai* (Since the Third Plenum) (Beijing: Renmin Chuban She, 1982), vol. 1, p. 74.

8. Deng's speech was partially published in the summer of 1989. See *Nongmin Ribao*, 2 August 1989, FBIS-CHI no. 171, (6 September 1989), pp. 28-30.

9. See, e.g., *Renmin Ribao*, 5 June 1982, FBIS-CHI no. 112, 10 June 1982, pp. K5-8, on Guizhou.

10. For one informed overview, see David Zweig, "Content and Context in Policy Implementation: Household Contracts in China, 1977-1983," in David Lampton, ed., *Policy Implementation in the Post-Mao Era* (Berkeley: University of California Press, 1987), pp. 253-83.

11. A concise summary is Li Xuechang, "Ping nongcon gongzuo zhong di zuoqing cuowu,"(Leftist errors in village work), *Shanghai Shehui Kexue*, no. 1 (1981), pp. 26-32.

12. Cf. Penny Kane, *Famine in China, 1959-61: Demographic and Social Implications* (London: MacMillan Press, 1988). Excess mortality ranged between 14 and 27 million.

13. In the summer of 1985, I spent four months in China doing research on rural reform, including field research in Zouping County, Shandong, and Fengyang County, Anhui. Much of this paper draws on data gathered in 1985.

14. *Zhongguo Tongji Nianjian, 1987* (China Statistical Annual, 1987) (Beijing: Guojia Tongji Chuban She, 1987), p. 477.

15. *Renmin Ribao*, 22 April 1983, FBIS-CHI no. 80, 25 April 1983, p. K8.

16. *Renmin Ribao*, Observer, 23 January 1983.

17. Cf. Jonathan Unger, "The Decollectivization of the Chinese Countryside: A Survey of Twenty-Eight Villages," *Pacific Affairs*, vol. 58, no. 4 (Winter 1985-86), pp. 585-606.

18. *Zhejiang Ribao*, 14 December 1980, FBIS-CHI no. 8, 13 January 1980, pp. 6-8, and *Renmin Ribao* Observer, 23 January 1983, and accompanying articles in this issue.

19. E.g., *Ban Yue Tan*, no. 1, 10 January 1986, FBIS-CHI no. 31, 14 February 1986, pp. K3-6.

20. See Unger, "The Decollectivization of the Chinese Countryside," and *Renmin Ribao*, 2 March 1981, FBIS-CHI no. 41, 3 March 1981, p. L24.

21. John P. Burns, "Local Cadre Accommodation to the 'Responsibility System' in Rural China," *Pacific Affairs*, vol. 58, no. 4 (Winter 1986), pp. 607-625, especially p. 615.

22. Du Runsheng, head of the party secretariat's Rural Policy Research Center, used this term. See *Xinhua*, Beijing, 28 December 1983, FBIS-CHI no. 1, 3 January 1984, pp. K12-14.

23. *Beijing Review*, vol. 22, no. 1 (1 January 1987), p. 24.

24. Information from scholars interviewed in Beijing in late December 1989.

25. Du Runsheng, in *Xinhua*, Beijing, 30 October 1987, FBIS- CHI no. 210, pp. 25-26.

26. See the author's "The Limits of Rural Political Reform," in Victor Falkenheim, ed., *China in a New Era: Politics* (New York: Paragon Press, 1989), pp. 299-336.

27. *Xinhua*, Beijing, 13 March 1984, FBIS-CHI no. 53, 16 March 1984, pp. K17-18.

28. See "Dangqian nongcon jingji zhengce de rogan wenti— zhaiyao" (Summary of several questions of current rural policy), *Renmin Ribao*, 10 April 1983.

29. Peng Kehong, "Dui wo guo muqian gugong wenti chutan," (Preliminary discussion of the current problem of hired labor in China), *Makesi Zhuyi Yanjiu*, no. 2, 1986, pp. 176-86.

30. See *Renmin Ribao*, 14 July 1989, FBIS-CHI no. 144, 28 July 1989, pp. 11-17.

31. See *Renmin Ribao*, 25 September 1985, FBIS-CHI no. 198, 11 October 1985, pp. K22-27, for a report on the activities of 2.2 million households in 7 provinces, who had gone into commercial work.

32. *Renmin Ribao*, 26 May 1985, FBIS-CHI no. 194, 4 October 1985, pp. K16-18.

33. *Nongmin Ribao* Commentator, 30 June 1985, FBIS-CHI no. 135, 15 July 1986, pp. K4-5.

34. See Judith Banister, "Population Policy and Trends in China, 1978-83," *China Quarterly*, no. 100, pp. 717-41.

35. This was a term used by cadres in Anhui in 1985. It was also used in the media, e.g., *Nongmin Ribao*, 6 October 1988, FBIS-CHI no. 203, 20 October 1988, pp. 20-22.

36. *Renmin Ribao* Commentator, 16 September 1988.

37. An excellent analysis is in Joseph Fewsmith, "Agricultural Crisis in China," *Problems of Communism*, vol. 37, November-December 1988, particularly pp. 83ff.

38. *Zhonguo Tongji Nianjian, 1987*, p. 139.

39. *Xinhua*, Beijing, 15 January 1986, FBIS-CHI no. 11, 16 January 1986, p. K2.

40. *Nongmin Ribao* Commentator, 22 July 1986, FBIS-CHI no. 148, 1 August 1986, pp. K15-16.

41. See Christine P. Wong, "Interpreting Rural Industrial Growth in the Post-Mao Period," *Modern China* , vol. 14, no. 1 (January 1988), pp. 3-30.

42. Commentator, "Do Not Forget to Take Agriculture as the Foundation," *Liaowang*, Beijing, no. 6, 10 February 1986, FBIS-CHI no. 38, 26 February 1986, p. K6.

43. For one of many articles on peasants' "unreasonable burdens," see Chen Yimin, "Nongmin fudan ji de jiangqing," (It is urgently necessary to reduce peasant burdens), *Nongcun Gongzuo Tongxun*, no. 4, 1983, pp. 19-20.

44. Information collected in Zouping in 1985. The other county studied that year, Fengyang, Anhui, did not have such a plan.

45. *Xinhua*, Beijing, 8 February 1989, FBIS-CHI no. 26, 9 February 1989, pp. 10-11.

46. *Xinhua*, Beijing, 11 May 1988, FBIS-CHI no. 92, 12 May 1988, pp. 38-39.

47. See *Zhongguo Tongji Nianjian, 1987*, pp. 211-14.

48. *Nongmin Ribao*, editorial, 28 March 1987, FBIS-CHI no. 73, 16 April 1987, pp. K19-20.

49. See, e.g., *Renmin Ribao*, 17 February 1987, FBIS- CHI no. 40, 2 March 1987, pp. K21ff.

50. Zhou Yueli, "Lun nongcon de jingji lienhe," (On amalgamation in the rural economy), *Hongqi*, no. 11, 1986, pp. 11- 15.

51. *Renmin Ribao*, 17 December 1988.

52. *Renmin Ribao*, Observer, 22 October 1989.

53. Since 1985, 7,000 protest actions against taxation have been reported. See *South China Morning Post*, 19 June 1989, FBIS- CHI no. 116, 19 June 1989, p. 14.

54. See "Beijing Authority Being Undermined by Local Powers," *New York Times*, 11 December 1988, p. 1.

55. For one such report of peasant fears, see *Renmin Ribao*, 19 April 1986.

56. *Xinhua*, Beijing, 9 December 1988, FBIS-CHI no. 238, 12 December 1989, p. 31.

57. Zouping County's most prominent enterpreneur did this by endowing a monument to revolutionary martyrs, building a school, paying a schoolteacher's salary for life, and building a road. Such contributions are reminiscent of those made by the gentry in Qing times but have a clear political motivation.

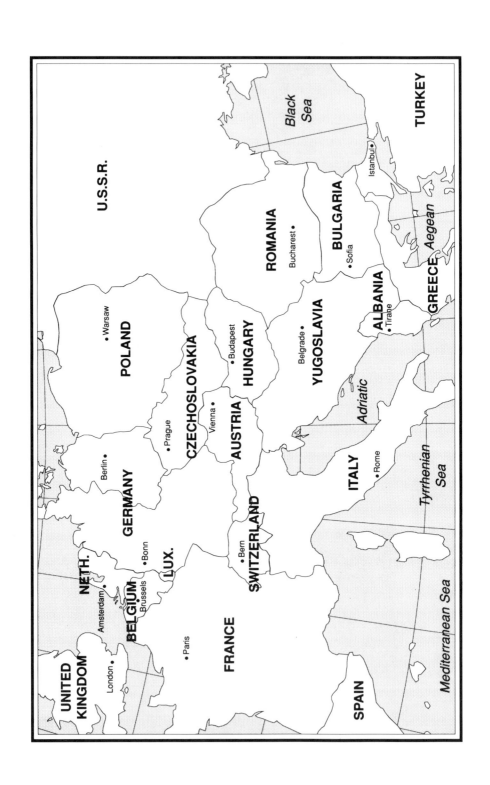

8. REVOLUTIONARY CHANGE IN EASTERN EUROPE

The Societal Basis of Political Reform

Alexander C. Pacek
and
Roger E. Kanet

The year 1989 proved to be one of monumental importance for the Soviet Union, the countries of Eastern Europe, and the entire international community. At the beginning of the year Soviet leader Mikhail Gorbachev found only limited support among the political elites of Eastern Europe for his conception of political reform. Only the Communist party leaderships in Poland and Hungary could be viewed as committed reformers. Elsewhere, the concept of reform received little more than lip service in Bulgaria, was generally criticized in Czechsolovakia and the GDR, and was most strongly condemned in Romania. Even in Poland and Hungary the pace of reform was slow and seemed on the verge of stalling. By the end of the year a Solidarity government ruled Poland, the Berlin Wall had fallen and German unification was but a matter of time, Ceausescu's dictatorship had been overthrown in Romania, and a world-renowned dissident playwright, Vaclav Havel, had been elected president in Czechoslovakia. Revolutionary change — in the full sense of "revolutionary" — was in process throughout the region, as the basic structures of domestic political power (including the formal institutions of governance) and the foundations of the European inter-state system were radically changing.

Only four times during the past two centuries have events of such importance for the nature of domestic and international political relationships occurred in Europe: (1) during the French Revolution and the Napoleonic wars, when France attempted to destroy the old political order and replace it with a French-centered system of nominally democratic states; (2) after the defeat of Napoleon in 1815, when the old order was in large part reestablished by the victors; (3) after World War I, when the traditional European empires collapsed and were replaced by a number of small states in Central Europe and a regime in Soviet Russia committed to revolutionary change; and (4) after World War II, when the geographic and political map of Europe was changed and the USSR and the United States emerged as the dominant actors in Europe and the world. The changes initiated during 1989 promise to have consequences comparable to those associated with the four earlier periods of revolutionary "restructuring."

Though the economic and political tensions of forty years of Soviet domination, autocratic rule by local communist elites, and economic mismanagement and corruption were increasingly apparent throughout Eastern Europe, there was little overt evidence in early 1989 that events of such great import were about to occur — though social pressures were building that would explode later in the year. Central to the dramatic changes throughout the region that resulted by the end of 1989 in the establishment of Eastern Europe's first noncommunist governments since the 1940s was the new attitude of the Gorbachev leadership toward the area. In the past any movement toward reform had met with strong Soviet resistance. By 1989, however, Soviet policy had shifted to the point where it encouraged reform and was even willing to accept the reality of expanded pluralism and the demise of communist dictatorships as the price for economic efficiency and political stability in the region and enhanced long-term stable political and economic relationships with the West.

Yet the radical changes that occurred in Eastern Europe during the last six months of 1989 must be viewed within the overall context of state socialism as it was institutionalized in the area and of the recent emergence of autonomous social groups. As developed in the Soviet Union in the 1930s under Stalin and in Eastern Europe after its imposition in the late 1940s, state socialism consisted of a highly centralized economy that emphasized heavy industry, authoritarian political structures meant to ensure political control by minuscule and illegitimate Communist party elites, and a strong dependency or patron-client relationship between the

USSR and the smaller communist states of Eastern Europe. However, almost immediately after Stalin's death in 1953 and throughout the ensuing years evidence mounted that demonstrated both the political and the economic weaknesses of the system. Sporadically, and unsuccessfully until 1989, attempts were made in several of the countries concerned to reform portions of the state socialist system inherited from Stalin.

After the signing of the Helsinki Accords in 1975, organized movements committed to the protection of political and human rights were active (and under pressure) in a number of European communist states. Usually these groups based their demands for political reform on the commitments made by their governments in Helsinki and on the guarantees of the constitutions of their respective states.

Evidence also mounted throughout much of the region concerning the stagnation of economic growth and the fact that the socialist economies were falling behind their capitalist counterparts, including the East Asian NICs, in the development and adaptation of modern technology to the production process. In addition, the inability of the state to meet implied social commitments — for example, the growing shortages of consumer goods and housing, and the inability to halt the degradation of the environment — contributed to increased dissatisfaction with the existing political system and to the demand for major political change to extend effective political participation beyond the narrow circle of the Communist party elite.

Even before the emergence to political prominence of Mikhail Gorbachev and "new thinking" in the USSR, there was a growing awareness of the fundamental nature of the problems facing communist states, the imperatives of initiating economic and political reform, and the increased flexibility in relations between the USSR and its European allies. Thus, prior to spring 1985, when Gorbachev was elected the new head of the CPSU, the situation throughout much of the region was ripe for political change. Thus, prior to spring 1985, when Gorbachev was elected the new head of the CPSU, the situation throughout much of the region was ripe for political change. Thus, prior to spring 1985 have the efforts at reform expanded to the point where one can speak of the dismantling of key elements of the traditional state socialist system — from the dominance of central planning to the emergence of officially sanctioned pluralism and the decline of the dominant role of the communist *nomenklatura*.

The major concern of this chapter will be to provide a background and overview of developments throughout Eastern Europe that have contributed to the dramatic changes currently under way in the entire region — especially the emergence of autonomous interest groups for political reform — and to relate those changes to developments within the USSR itself. Given the importance and the differences in developments in individual countries, we shall deal briefly with each of the countries in turn — beginning with those with the strongest and most visible recent tradition of reform, Poland and Hungary, and concluding with Romania, which, prior to the revolution of December 1989, was ruled by the most adamantly Stalinist leadership. It is essential to keep in mind that we are observing and attempting to assess a process of change and reform that is in midstream; that the events of 1989 and early 1990, for example, are but part of a process the end of which is not yet visible. Whether stable pluralist, democratic political systems and effectively functioning economies will emerge from the current chaos into which traditional state socialist systems have fallen is also not clear.

Poland

Poland is the society that first and most dramatically moved toward genuine political pluralism, despite the crackdowns and imposition of martial law in 1981. Moreover, Poland's success has, to a substantial degree, served as a stimulus for reform elsewhere in Eastern Europe and the USSR. Autonomous initiatives for reform began long before Solidarity became synonymous with Polish opposition. In the pre-Solidarity years analysts identified three main sources from which Polish society would press reforms on state authority: intellectuals and students, industrial workers, and the Catholic church. While relatively isolated from each other, these interests achieved a degree of convergence during periods of systemic crisis at the top, as in 1968–70.[1] In 1968 students and intellectuals presented demands for greater freedom of expression but remained separated from workers, and in 1970–71 workers struck en masse for economic demands and confronted state suppression without the support of the intellectuals and students.[2] As the economic and social situation worsened throughout the country, the center of gravity of reform shifted from limited circles of intellectuals to broader social strata, where thousands were prepared to engage in public protest. What occurred during this period was the gradual evolution of a social movement that changed its strategy from attempting to influence the system by exerting pressure from within the party to an emphasis on social pressure from outside designed to transform the relationship between state and society.[3]

The workers' strikes of 1970–71 were brought about in part by a decline in real wages and a general failure to maintain living standards. Indeed, some analysts contend that Poland suffered crises of identity, penetration, and participation most severely of all the European socialist countries.[4]

While these crises escalated during the 1970s, numerous organs of direct democracy were formed, such as the workers' councils in Szczecin, which proved troubling to authorities because they could never be brought under complete control. By the mid-1970s a significant number of autonomous civic organizations, such as the Workers' Defense Committee (KOR), came into being because existing official institutions had failed to fulfill their functions and clearly could not meet citizen needs. It was up to new groups to limit the state's decision-making power and to introduce innovation into the social system.[5]

Because of the extensive development of autonomous social groups over the decades, Poland became the laboratory par excellence for observing the relationship between system performance and societal reform initiatives. Scholars have catalogued a bewildering array of autonomous associations derived from pluralist elements in society, such as the three main groups noted above.[6] In the Solidarity period of 1980–81 a full range of societal interests and groups developed a successful coalition strategy of "consolidated pluralism" that mobilized the majority of society against the regime.[7] This effort had the direct impact of diminishing the preeminence of the Polish United Workers' Party (PUWP) as the leading and guiding force in Polish society in the years following the suppression of Solidarity. Subsequent efforts to promote a political dialogue between nonparty interest organizations and PUWP-sponsored associations failed and were made all the worse by steadily deteriorating economic conditions.

Until 1986–87 there was some discernible weakening of opposition efforts; the number of independent activists declined markedly after the lifting of martial law and the issuance of an amnesty for political prisoners. Yet, pluralist ideals and hopes for reforms were at an all-time high among citizens.[8] The veritable explosion of civic activity in 1988–89 was the direct result of a seriously weakened state; disastrous economic problems, including a severe slide in living standards; and an increasingly well-organized and determined civil society, which had not only survived the crackdown of 1980–81 but benefited from the party's resulting tarnished image. In fact, the opposition in the post-1981 period had diversified considerably, now having at least four identifiable elements:[9] The *legitimist activists*, who wanted to continue the Solidarity movement; the *realistic opposition*, who emphasized expanding the sphere of freedom; the *political radicals*, who emphasized winning national sovereignty and building a democratic system; and the *church-oriented opposition*. These categories serve as a rough typology of the hundreds of new groups that emerged in Poland in 1987–1989.[10]

It is scarcely surprising that by January 1989 the PUWP Central

Committee had passed a "pluralism resolution" amidst heated debate and apprehension among officials that the leadership's new strategy of legalizing independent trade unions could prove to be suicidal.[11] Less than a month later Politburo members began deliberating the prospects for a multiparty system, where the PUWP might give up its leading role if ousted by a "legitimate successor."[12] While the regime did not define clearly what type of alternative party would be considered "legitimate," some officials expressed the desire for competing socialist parties to vie for the voters' favor in free elections. Nonetheless, a variety of parties representing different ideological positions either emerged or, in the case of parties that had existed before communism, reestablished themselves. From nationalist-oriented organizations like the Polish Independence party to the resurrected Polish Socialist party, a multiparty spectrum emerged to challenge the PUWP's position. Other, more narrow, autonomous interest organizations joined those already in existence, representing a broad spectrum of views and programs. Environmental groups such as the Polish Ecological party joined existing organizations like Freedom and Peace to advocate environmental reforms. These efforts had a discernible impact on policymaking; in 1988 Freedom and Peace collected over two thousand signatures in Gdansk to protest the building of the first Polish nuclear power station at Zarnowiec, resulting in government officials' reassessing the project's viability.[13]

Another important development in 1989 that spurred reform efforts was the establishment by independent groups of umbrella organizations that could defend them more effectively against the state. Government officials agreed to accept the establishment of separate public groups to deal with economic problems, a tacit admission of the party's failure to respond adequately to the continuing economic impasse.[14] The economic associations would operate alongside the existing semi-private and private enterprises already flourishing in Poland, and they would emphasize the importance of capital investment and market principles. These initiatives, along with many others, including recently concluded negotiations between the regime and Solidarity, were taken by organized citizens and not by local officials, elites, or specialists.

In Poland, more than in any of the other East European countries, the spontaneous growth of independent activity and its gradual politicization were fueled by the failure of a highly centralized system. The programs of autonomous interest groups pushed the country in a pluralist direction with a functioning parliamentary system; a delegitimized communist leadership could offer nothing to stem the growing tide of demands.

In contrast with the situation of the then-hardline regimes of East

Germany and Czechoslovakia, however, Poland's relationship with Gorbachev's USSR was convivial to the extent that the Soviets showed much more understanding of the complexity of the Polish situation. The Jaruzelski leadership was less concerned about the spillover effects of Soviet reforms than with the positive endorsement that such reforms lent to Poland's own efforts.[15] Gorbachev was praised for showing "energy, boldness, and farsightedness" in pursuing reforms and also for taking a realistic position regarding the nature and limits of intra-bloc relations. Until Jaruzelski stepped down from power, however, there were no overt gestures of concern about the prospects for substantial economic and political instability in the immediate future. Moscow remained calm during the roundtable discussions between the Polish government and Solidarity that led to the legalization of the independent labor movement and the electoral reforms of spring 1989.

The June election stood as the most far-reaching manifestation of the reform process in Eastern Europe until the upheavals in the fall of 1989. In terms of formal political power, the reforms were meant to limit the power of the opposition. The elections for the newly established 100-seat senate were entirely free, while only 35 percent of the 460 seats in the Sejm, or lower house, were filled through competitive contests. The results, however, proved a stunning defeat for the ruling Polish United Workers' party. PUWP candidates failed to win a single seat in any contested race. Solidarity candidates took all but one of the seats lost by the PUWP and received an average of 70 percent of the total popular vote. Moreover, only two of thirty-five key PUWP figures who ran unopposed managed to gain the required majority of the votes cast to ensure reelection. Government efforts to limit the impact of the new electoral system failed largely because the voters were able to cross out the names of so many officials on the ballot.[16]

Over the summer much political jockeying occurred before the emergence of a Solidarity-led government in September. In July the issue was the selection of a new president. Only after once withdrawing from the race and pushing the candidacy of Interior Minister General Czeslaw Kiszczak was General Jaruzelski eventually elected president on July 19 by the margin of a single vote. After his election to the presidency, Jaruzelski fulfilled an earlier pledge to resign as head of the PUWP. Though the communists successfully pushed General Kiszczak through parliament to become prime minister, he failed in his efforts to form a grand coalition government; and on August 24 Tadeusz Mazowiecki was elected prime minister. Mazowiecki, a Catholic intellectual with extensive political experience, had played a major role in the creation of Solidarity in 1980. He was editor-in-chief of *Tygodnik Solidarność*, the communist bloc's first fully independent weekly.

After decades of the most intense and tenacious opposition activity in the region, the Poles had broken the political dominance of the Communist party. For the first time since World War II Poland has a non-communist prime minister and a true coalition government — but one faced with imminent economic collapse and problems of generating effective public support for economic reform policies.

In January 1990 the government introduced the first stage of a series of policies aimed at creating a free market economy out of the chaos of a moribund centralized communist economic system. The prices of many basic commodities were increased — in some cases by as much as 400–600 percent, subsidies were eliminated from most goods, and wages in the state sector were frozen after initial adjustments as part of an effort to bring inflation under control. The initial results of the experiment were mixed. While inflation rates began to drop and food and other goods reappeared in the market, hundreds of firms went bankrupt, total production fell and unemployment rates skyrocketed. The long-term impact of the reform program is not yet clear.

Hungary

In Hungary the path toward reform differed from that taken in Poland or elsewhere in the region, complicated by the now-diminished economic prosperity brought about by "Kádárism" in the wake of the 1956 revolution and Soviet military suppression. The "democratic opposition" in Hungary was largely confined to a handful of intellectuals who did not engage in creating or advocating the establishment of rival political parties or other institutional challenges.[17] Recent economic problems led to an evaluation of the need for political reforms to supplant the "secret corporatism" of the Kádár period. While the former party leader spoke of the need for autonomy within a one-party system, some officials argued openly that only Western-type pluralism, with multiple parties, would represent a real improvement.[18]

Barely a decade before, however, analysts generally agreed that the likelihood was remote at best that well-entrenched political elites would suddenly permit average citizens to share the privilege of autonomous decisionmaking in politics and economics.[19] Yet, even then Hungarians such as philosopher György Márkus and sociologist András Hegedűs were openly declaring the necessity of pluralism in a Marxist system. While the government gradually began to tinker with political mechanisms and produced multicandidate elections in 1985, some analysts also began to discuss the serious possibility of real political pluralism. Party officials categorically rejected competitive, Western-style pluralism, using the historical justification that Hungary had evolved as a one-party system and what was needed was recognition of a "plurality of interests."[20] Given that multicandidate systems were already established in Poland and had not resulted in a challenge to party control, it appeared doubtful that the opposition could use the electoral changes to effect a political reversal!

In the early 1980s, spurred by an international climate of tension between the United States and the Soviet Union, a burst of opposition activity occurred in Hungary that focused on peace and disarmament issues. Spearheaded by the Peace Group for Dialogue, a movement involving a handful of autonomous peace groups, this activity challenged the official Peace Council's legitimacy and involved relatively large numbers of citizens in antinuclear activities.[21] Dialogue was forced to disband in 1983 after refusing to merge with the Peace Council; a host of lesser groups either followed Dialogue's example or were absorbed into official institutions.

Until recently this was the pattern of societally initiated reform activity in Hungary. A handful of dissident intellectuals would organize around a specific set of issues and disband relatively soon thereafter. By the mid-1980s, however, concrete social initiatives reappeared from what dissident Gábor Demsky called "suspended animation."[22] Acknowledging that the various groupings in society did not yet know what to demand, he noted the fact that independent groups were undertaking large-scale tasks traditionally the responsibility of official social institutions. These included supporting refugees from neighboring Transylvania, offering legal aid to citizens, and attempting to create some sort of organization dedicated to the protection of workers' and young people's interests. Indeed, as in Poland, the development of "parallel institutions" was unprecedented in response to the inertia and creeping incompetence of official institutions.

Many of these initiatives were resurrected efforts at grassroots citizen influence on policymaking. In 1981 an autonomous environmental group, the Danube Circle, was created in Hungary to articulate public outrage over the proposed diversion of the Danube between Gabcikovo in Slovakia and Nagymaros in Hungary as part of an immense hydroelectric project. The government expressed its own reservations about the project, and its hesitation led to the Danube Circle's collecting some 10,000 signatures on a protest petition by 1986. Facing severe government disapproval for operating outside the official sphere, the group disbanded in 1986, prompting some writers to declare that such citizen activity was doomed to failure, in Hungary and throughout Eastern Europe. By 1988–89, however, the

Danube Circle's activity resumed in cooperation with two other groups, the Danube Foundation and the Nagymaros Committee.[23] The combined effort collected over 100,000 signatures, was endorsed by nineteen members of parliament, and by summer 1989 had forced the government to halt the project.[24]

Despite some harassment, the controversial Federation of Young Democrats (FIDESZ) achieved the status of an officially recognized alternative to the Communist Youth League (KISZ). The group was first declared illegal for advocating a multiparty system and a free market economy, but persistence and an increasingly large nationwide membership eventually guaranteed its new legal status.[25] Moreover, at its first national congress in November 1988 the group joined a newly created umbrella organization, the National Council of Youth Organizations in Hungary, which served as a channel for shared information and a forum for discussion among Hungary's independent youth groups. While the council also included the official group KISZ, it was understood that no one group would have authority over another and relations between the official and independent groups would remain minimal.[26]

Across Hungary some thirty or more new organizations were established with aims ranging from support of *glasnost* to the reestablishment of Western-style democracy. As in Poland, Hungarian civil society found expression in new and old political parties as well as protective umbrella organizations. The Democratic Forum, the Independent Smallholders party and the Free Democrats are but three of the opposition parties that competed with the renamed Hungarian Communist party in the March 1990 elections.[27]

More important from a reform perspective were the Communist party debates surrounding the status of multiple political parties. Although memory of the brief reemergence of pre-war parties in 1956 left officials understandably concerned, by 1989 many admitted that such parties were not categorically forbidden.[28] All of these parties ran candidates in the elections. In the first round of voting the Democratic Forum, Smallholders, and Free Democrats received a combined 57 percent of the votes, while the former Communist party got only 10 percent. In the second round the conservative Democratic Forum won 165 of 386 seats and 43 percent of the vote; the reform Communists won 8.5 percent of the vote and 33 seats. József Antall, the new Hungarian prime minister is committed to reuniting his country politically.

In both Poland and Hungary well-organized, broad-based autonomous organizations now participate in an open political process. In Hungary fully open multiparty elections have already occurred, while in Poland Lech Walesa was elected president in open elections in December 1990.

As we shall see, the situation throughout the rest of the region has been quite different, for political change has been far more convulsive, and gradual development over time has not been possible for well-organized groups that represent political alternatives to the ruling Communist parties.

German Democratic Republic

Analysts long held that of all the East European regimes the German Democratic Republic was most willing and able to withstand opposition political initiatives either from within the party or from society. In the midst of the initial social upheaval and political turmoil of 1989, the aging, hardline Honecker leadership appeared to be in the strongest position to maintain its decision-making hegemony. Yet, as regional events took a course of their own, the Socialist Unity party (SED) was, in a matter of weeks, transformed from the dominant political force in society to a splintered, disintegrating institution facing a massive upsurge of opposition.

From May 1971 until October 1989 the Honecker regime had successfully resisted all attempts at fundamental political change from within, as well as overt pressure from the Gorbachev administration to liberalize. While the scope of the events of 1989 was unprecedented, the coalescence of initiatives for reform was not entirely unpredictable.

After taking power from Walter Ulbricht in 1971, the Honecker leadership was subjected to a variety of social, economic, and political strains, which analysts tended to downplay while emphasizing the "successes" of the GDR's economy. What was unique about the pressures on East Germany was the increased influence exercised by the Federal Republic of Germany as a result of the opening up of travel and the impact of the media. As the detente of the 1970s drew East and West closer economically, the two German states concluded a whole series of agreements, the most important of which was the *Basic Treaty of December 1972.*[29] These agreements meant recognition of the East German state by the Federal Republic, but they also opened up East Germany to influences from the West. The implication for the GDR was increased economic, political, and cultural penetration by its economically more powerful and politically more legitimate neighbor. The majority of East German citizens received both East and West German radio and television programs and have generally been better informed than most of their Eastern bloc neighbors.[30]

For example, the Western media ensured that the GDR had an alternative source of information about the Polish events of 1980–81. As the

PUWP acknowledged the workers' right to strike and to form independent trade unions, as well as to question the principles of democratic centralism, the SED tried to exploit anti-Polish sentiments. Despite this effort, the GDR did experience clashes between young demonstrators and the police, as well as minor strikes and protests in support of Solidarity.[31]

Moreover, already by the mid-1970s the vaunted East German economy was running into problems. Where economic reports for the first half of the decade had showed healthy annual growth rates, dramatic price increases for the energy supplies imported from the USSR began by 1975. The targets for growth in the national economy set in the five-year plan for 1976–80 were not achieved, and living standards failed to rise in line with popular expectations. Analysts noted the potentially troubling implications of the SED's being unable to justify this aspect of the GDR "social contract," whereby the party guaranteed the people a secure existence and rising standard of living in return for political acquiesence.[32]

While the potential for discontent and opposition was fueled by these developments, the SED made good use of its restrictive provisions, such as its ability to restrict freedom of assembly, expression, and the press "in accordance with the basic principles of the constitution." In practice this meant the option of condemning as unconstitutional any individual or group activity of which it disapproved and taking legal action against East German citizens who grouped together to demand that their "constitutional rights" be observed.[33] Elections to the East German parliament, the Volkskammer, were designed to limit the voters' choices to candidates selected by the National Front, which embraced all accepted parties and mass organizations and which accepted the leading role of the SED. Party resolutions were binding on all political groups in the GDR; the presence of party representatives as watchdogs at all levels of the state and mass organizations also helped to ensure that party resolutions were put into practice. While criticism and self-criticism within the party were encouraged officially, they were by and large manipulated to reaffirm the leading role of the Communist party under Honecker.[34]

Against the backdrop of rigid centralization imposed from above and increased influence of the political environment outside the party, a minor wave of extraparty opposition developed in the early 1980s, spearheaded by dissident intellectuals and an unofficial peace movement under the auspices of the Evangelical (Lutheran) church. Criticism of the GDR government by such notable figures as Robert Havermann, Rudolf Bahro, and Stefan Heym drew attention to the confrontation between East German society and a state apparatus that determined what would be produced and how it would be allocated. There was by no means consensus among this opposition; for example, arguments diverged concerning the issue of the Prague Spring of 1968 — did it represent an adequate model for reform, or should it have gone further than it did?[35]

Far more important was the organization by 1982–83 of a network of autonomous peace groups that was the largest in Eastern Europe and capable of turning out large numbers of citizens for events organized independently of the state. The development was in large part stimulated by the presence of a mass disarmament movement in West Germany, and by what was perceived of as the increased militarization of East German society. Under protection of the Evangelical church the peace movement spread throughout the country and engaged in opposition activity in spite of state pressure and coercion. During 1982 and 1983 organized protests, meetings, and petition campaigns became commonplace. In February 1982 the Dresden Peace Forum drew some 5,000 activists to its first demonstration, while other protests spread to Weimar, Potsdam, Leipzig, and Berlin the next year.[36] In 1983 authorities cracked down on the thriving peace community in Jena, deporting most of its members.[37] While some antinuclear activity continued, particularly through the Evangelical church, further repression in 1988 forced many more activists to emigrate.

Scarcely one year later, the GDR underwent the greatest social upheaval in its history, as massive citizen protest led to the dissolution of the SED dictatorship in a matter of weeks — a pattern that was repeated in Bulgaria and Czechoslovakia. The dizzying pace of events took analysts by surprise.[38] Yet the crackdown on dissident groups in 1988 precipitated a steady buildup of social tension, rather than reducing it. In the local elections of May 7, for example, peace activists and human rights groups reemerged to monitor vote counting while organizing protests against the electoral system in Leipzig, which would become the hotbed of the 1989 opposition activity.[39] More significantly, throughout the country a rapid increase in public dissatisfaction was represented by an all-time high in non-voting (17 percent).[40] At the same time more and more petitions were being sent to the Honecker leadership by citizens previously unconnected with opposition activism.[41]

The catalyst for the next phase of the opposition reform movement was the beginning of the mass emigration during the summer of 1989, which further indicated the SED's resistance to both economic and political reform. Despite continued harassment of new opposition groups and party reformists like Dresden party leader Hans Modrow, the opposition began to broaden its appeal and organize a nationwide network. By September an umbrella organization calling itself the New Forum had been established and tried unsuccessfully to obtain recognition as an independent political party.[42]

Throughout October an escalating systemic crisis was aggravated by several key developments: (1) a rapidly growing and increasingly effective opposition network throughout the country, (2) an increased level of social tension as demonstrators and police fought in the streets, and (3) a deteriorating economy made worse by the exodus of an estimated 200,000 people, many of whom were skilled workers. The number and size of the opposition groups swelled to encompass a broad spectrum of society, thus approaching the level of coalescence that occurred in Poland during the late 1960s and early 1970s. By mid-October Honecker had been forced to resign by the Politburo amid rumors of an impending police massacre of citizens. Under the leadership of new party chief Egon Krenz, the emphasis on reform shifted from "when" to "how." The ability of the SED to pacify the restive population depended crucially on how much power Krenz would surrender to genuine political reformers at regional and district levels.

Mass resignations from the SED of both leaders (including Krenz, who was replaced by Gregor Gysi) and rank-and-file members, coupled with the appointment of Hans Modrow to the prime ministership in December, smoothed the way for discussion of real reforms, although they did not halt the defection of the party's membership.[43] What was especially interesting was the level of reform sentiment within the party, as Krenz misjudged the mood of the SED district committees and the rank and file. More troubling to the government was an opinion poll that found that the SED would get only 9 percent of the vote in the free elections promised for spring 1990 — implying that half the SED's 2.2 million members (or ex-members) would vote for another party.[44]

While the embattled coalition government in Berlin faced growing demands for radical reforms in the political sphere (including reunification with the Federal Republic), the format for economic reform began to emerge, including decentralization of decisionmaking, price reform, the restructuring of the huge cooperatives into more competitive smaller enterprises, the welcoming of Western capital and joint ventures, and the introduction of free market measures.[45]

The March 1990 elections resulted in a victory for the conservative Alliance for Germany (composed of the Christian Democrats, the German Social Union, and the Democratic Awakening), which received 49 percent of the votes while the renamed communists received only 16 percent.

In early April a grand coalition of the Alliance for Germany and the Social Democrats was announced, and Christian Democratic leader Lothar de Maizière was selected as the new prime minister. The primary objective of the new government was to negotiate the economic and political reunification of the GDR with West Germany, which occurred in October 1990.

Czechoslovakia

In Eastern Europe's second major hardline state (where also the greatest increase in independent activity was registered in the fall of 1989), the 1968 experience stands as a clear watershed in postwar experiments with economic and political pluralism. In the spring of 1968 there occurred a veritable explosion of mass associations, interest groups, and noncommunist political parties as official organizations disintegrated or divided into new autonomous organizations. "Pluralist socialism" became the byword of the Czechoslovak People's party, the Czech Socialist party, and the National Front, all of which advocated giving citizens "real choice between different political forces."[46]

The general consensus among Communist party intellectuals of the desirability of a limited pluralism confined within the framework of the party's leading position was initially regarded as a better way to achieve democratization than more radical proposals. Radical opinion won out by March 1968, however, as social groups outside the circle of intellectuals exerted greater influence. What had begun as "latent tensions" gradually led to a powerful coalition of social forces interested in extreme change in the "bureaucratic-egalitarian order" and culminated in a radical political outburst.

As in East Germany, however, the impetus for reform in Czechoslovakia in 1968 and 1988 came from the intellectual sector of society. As indicators of economic growth had declined markedly in the years preceding the 1968 crisis, the regime had begun to rely increasingly on the advice of economists both inside and outside the party apparatus.[47] At the same time, the short-lived Dubček regime made every effort to channel and control mass energy, while defending the leading role of the Communist party.[48]

With the Warsaw Pact invasion and the enunciation of the Brezhnev Doctrine, a number of analysts forecast the near total erasure of all vestiges of a pluralist political culture in Czechoslovakia.[49] Moreover, the dominant political-cultural orientation of the great majority of the Czechoslovak people was, as late as 1989, hypothesized as a participatory-subject culture where "ordinary citizens must be obedient to their rulers' demands and must also comply with their instructions."[50] While reformist elements within and outside the party were subject to purges, harassment, and criminal prosecution through the mid-1970s, the nexus of opposition, the intellectual sector, remained active. Given little more than periodic passing attention, their survival and activity proved crucial to the rapid turn of events in November-December 1989 (as in 1967–68).

In the process of shelving the Dubček leadership's economic and politi-

cal reforms, the Gustáv Husák regime throughout the late 1970s and early
1980s was faced with the same economic problems that had first provoked
systematic reexamination of the centralist model: an outdated and inflexible economic structure, declining efficiency of investment, acute tensions
in supplies of raw materials and labor and their inefficient use, an increasingly alarming technological lag, and chronic problems in foreign trade.[51]
The reticence that the leadership showed in addressing the problems of
the economy was paralleled in other areas as well. Czechoslovakia
achieved the dubious honor of being the European country worst hit by
catastrophic environmental problems. As a result of heavy and inefficient
use of cheap brown coal in industry and energy production, by 1983 some
25 percent of all forests were dead or dying, and a third of all watercourses
were too polluted even for industrial use.[52]

In response to this series of systemic crises, the first serious organized
societal initiative, Charter 77, was formed in 1977 by 240 intellectuals. The
dissident group suffered from high rates of member turnover, and its
repeated attempts to organize national opposition networks were largely
unsuccessful. Yet several leading members of Charter 77, such as the playwright Václav Havel, came to play a vital role in the 1989 events.
Throughout the long Husák tenure, this group spawned a wealth of cultural, publication, human rights, peace, and ecological activities.[53] With
regard to peace and environmental issues, the group established ties with
movements in other East European countries during the mid-1980s.[54]

As the aging Husák leadership grew increasingly unable and unwilling
either to address fundamental economic and social problems or to thoroughly suppress the growing opposition, a third source of pressure came
from without, in the form of Mikhail Gorbachev's *glasnost* and *perestroika*
strategies. Even before the crucial Twenty-seventh Soviet Party Congress in
1986, Czechoslovak leaders had expressed their concerns about the turn
of events in Moscow. Presidium leader Vasil Bilák warned of disrupting the
"system of political power of the working people" and reiterated the "correctness" of the 1968 Soviet invasion and the subsequent purge of the
party.[55]

Yet, in an increasingly tense social climate, signs emerged of differences within the leadership concerning the way to move into the
Gorbachev era and deal with their growing internal opposition. Premier
Lubomír Strougal in 1987 praised Gorbachev's "frank and innovative
approach to all issues" and claimed, in contrast with Bilák, that the 1968
reforms had "contained a number of correct and valuable elements."[56]
For his part, Gorbachev reaffirmed the theme that would in 1989 lead to
the public repudiation of the Brezhnev Doctrine and to the assertion
that each East European party should be "responsive to its own people,

and [have] the right to decide in a sovereign manner how each country should develop."[57]

Thus, a situation similar to that of 1967–68 took a significantly different turn, as it became increasingly clear to the Husák leadership, and then to that of his successor, Miloš Jakeš, that it was more or less "on its own" and could not count on direct Soviet support. Taking advantage of this changed climate, new opposition groups (like the Initiative for Social Defense, the Thomas G. Masaryk Association, and an incipient umbrella organization, the Democratic Initiative) joined Charter 77 in pressing for reform.[58] Government policy grew increasingly contradictory; internal Communist party reports in May 1988 praised Charter 77 and other groups for providing a forum for youth, while simultaneously the government cracked down on their meetings and forced the Democratic Initiative to suspend its activities for several months.[59]

Throughout the spring and summer of 1988, however, the situation intensified to the point where, despite the government's periodic hardline tactics, the number of demonstrations, protests, and new groups seeking recognition continued to rise dramatically. To make matters worse from the point of view of the regime, in the wake of several large demonstrations in Prague in October CPSU Politburo member Aleksandr Yakovlev visited the country and lectured Czechoslovak party officials on "the need for a plurality of views."[60] By early 1989 it had become clear that divisions now existed in the leadership over the issue of reform. On January 25 Presidium member Jan Fojtik warned that the public influence of opposition groups was increasing at a rate to which the government could not respond, while reform had lagged substantially.[61]

By November Czechoslovakia was in a new phase of reform, the most extensive since 1968. The impact of developments in Poland in the spring and in the GDR by late summer contributed to the growth of autonomous political activity and the growing demands for reform. Similarly to the Honecker regime, the Jakeš administration proved to be unable to cope with the nationwide opposition and with internal divisions that resulted in a clear lack of direction. In a matter of weeks the opposition's emphasis had shifted from the crackdown on demonstrators in late November, to debating the relative merits of Alexander Dubček and Václav Havel as candidates for the presidency. By early 1990 the long-time dissident Havel had been elected president, while Dubček, the former party leader, was selected as leader of the revitalized parliament.

As had occurred in East Germany, an ideologically rigid regime proved unable in Czechoslovakia to withstand the impact of declining economic and political performance, and rising opposition combined with pressure and lack of support from the Soviet political leadership. Unfortunately, the opposition that had emerged to challenge the dominant role of the Communist party was not as effectively organized as that in Poland, and the rate of introducing economic reforms was much slower. By spring 1990 voices were heard criticizing the government for its indecision.

Bulgaria

While the Western media's attention was riveted on events in Poland, Hungary, the GDR, and Czechoslovakia in the fall of 1989, fundamental and largely unnoticed change was transpiring in Bulgaria. The historical affinity of this Balkan nation for Russia had a major impact on the emergence of political pluralism at the decade's end. The *glasnost* that emanated from the USSR in 1987–88 emphasizing a cautious path to democratization was echoed in the Bulgarian media in 1988–89. While the aging leadership of Todor Zhivkov continued to maintain a tight rein on the domestic political environment, extensive debate quickly developed on freedom of the press, artistic creativity, and the establishment of "parallel associations" in the political arena.[62]

As in the Soviet Union, the Bulgarian leadership's initial lip service to the idea of *glasnost* opened the window for a range of autonomous reform initiatives to flow in from society. An environmental movement emerged to protest the catastrophic pollution of the town of Ruse by a caustic soda works on the Danube. Activists from the Citizens' Committee for the Ecological Defense of Ruse initiated a series of demonstrations and petition campaigns that led to the plant's eventual closing as well as to the expulsion of the activists from the Communist party.[63] Despite the crackdown on the group, this was one of the first times that Bulgarian citizens outside the framework of officialdom had effected a policy decision.

Until Todor Zhivkov's sudden resignation in November 1989 the pattern of autonomous reform initiatives and the regime's response to them differed little from those of the hardline regimes of Czechoslovakia and the GDR. Throughout the fall of 1988 and the spring of 1989 numerous independent groups of several hundred members each surfaced across the country, each with an issue to press on a recalcitrant leadership. One of the first, the Independent Club for the Support of Perestroika and Glasnost, initiated a broad range of proposals addressing living standards, ecology, demographic problems, culture, and science, while openly remaining unofficial to "avoid outside patronage and manipulation."[64]

Authorities responded to the actions of the club in much the same manner that characterized their treatment of other organizations; they harassed, arrested, and expelled activists but stopped short of attempting to eradicate the group. This produced speculation that Bulgaria's leaders were becoming responsive to citizens' feelings.[65] From February through May of 1989, the Zhivkov regime adopted the carrot-and-stick approach of cooptation and crackdown. The government's policy of legal registration for associations was aimed at controlling groups, despite the fact that prominent legal experts pointed out that the existing Bulgarian legal code did not require groups to seek an official registration.[66]

While groups such as the Ruse Committee, the Discussion Club, and the various Green parties were subjected to harassment, intensive persecution was reserved for groups presumed to or claiming to have ties to the country's Turkish minority, such as the Independent Human Rights Association. A national policy of forced assimilation of the large minority evolved into a virtual pogrom, as ethnic Turks were attacked and driven out of the country by the thousands. Ethnic Turks and their few non-Muslim sympathizers initiated a series of hunger strikes and organized large demonstrations, which were met with severe police repression. The "Turkish question" became the focus for the regime's non-negotiable demands vis-à-vis the populace, and organizations pressing for reform in this area were treated far more harshly than their peers whose demands the authorities could more easily accommodate.[67]

By November 1989 a fundamentally new and curious situation had developed, further illustrating the difficulties of East European leaders in coopting autonomous opposition groups. Bulgarian opposition groups, spearheaded by the Discussion Club, launched a series of actions through the fall calling for fundamental political reform. The regime's alarmed and haphazard response revealed clear divisions within the leadership; some Central Committee members and at least one Politburo member became loosely allied with the Discussion Club.[68] This de facto alliance was instrumental in the November 10 ouster of Todor Zhivkov from office following his open reluctance to adopt fundamental changes in the political process.

The resultant palace coup and the housecleaning of the Communist party that followed paved the way for a proliferation of independent associations, trade unions, and political parties by early 1990. While the reformist communist leaders gradually gave way in the face of escalating public demands, they committed a serious political error in mid-January in calling for an end to the anti-Turkish policy — evidence of the negative side of the emergence of political pluralism. Though the reform wing of the Communist party continued to dominate Bulgarian politics and emerged victorious from the spring 1990 elections, it continued to face serious challenges to its authority.

Romania

In Nicolae Ceausescu's Romania the reform process began with a whimper and ended with the loudest explosion in the Eastern bloc since 1956. Yet, even in this most highly centralized East European state, societal opposition managed to survive in the face of heavy persecution. In 1977 the government had been shaken by worker unrest in the Brasov region, which it met with force. The Gorbachev era touched all of Eastern Europe, and in the end not even Romania was immune to the forces that were released. There had been attempts at an organized opposition in 1985, as activists met clandestinely to discuss the possibility of resurrecting the old pre-war political parties.[69] Such activities continued until the December 1989 revolution and were routinely suppressed.

By 1987 a handful of opposition groups had emerged in Romania such as the National Peasant party and the Romanian Association for the Defense of Human Rights. These groups focused on promoting public awareness of and the authorities' compliance with the provisions on human, civil, and political rights contained in Romania's constitution and in the Helsinki Accords.[70] While the groups pledged themselves to nonviolence and to dialogue with the authorities, they also released documents purporting to reveal the "feudalization" of the country under Ceausescu's rule. Resulting crackdowns on such groups in 1987 silenced them for a while, as leaders were arrested, beaten, and fined.

Workers in the Brasov region were the next to press the government for reforms, in 1987 and 1988. In November 1987 they initiated street demonstrations and strikes over cuts in salaries, the continuing decline in living standards, and Ceausescu's policy of razing roughly half of the country's villages.[71] The authorities responded by arresting leaders and moving on the workers with tanks and tear gas. In the summer of 1988 an embryonic independent trade union, the Zarnesti Arms Factory Group, leaked evidence to the West that unrest was again building in this "weakest point in Ceausescu's Kingdom."[72] In June union activists disseminated manifestos in Brasov factories protesting living conditions and were promptly arrested and beaten by Securitate officers. Activists attempting to resurrect another independent trade union, Freedom, met a similar fate in Cluj that summer.[73]

As in Bulgaria, however, proponents of reform were not confined to isolated groups in society, and by the spring of 1989 there were clear signals that the Romanian leadership was not of one mind. At the beginning of March, six former top figures in the Romanian Communist party addressed an open letter to Ceausescu, a scathing indictment of the regime's policies and an alternative platform for the establishment of a "decent social life" in Romania.[74] At the same time more and more party veterans, particularly journalists, came under suspicion for treason, and many were arrested, as divisions within the party became impossible to conceal. Criticism by Romanian intellectuals at home and in exile also increased markedly, as letter after letter reached the West condemning the stifling political atmosphere in the country and as thousands of Romanian citizens, including a growing number of ethnic Romanians, fled into exile.[75]

While opposition grew steadily in the Soviet bloc's last Stalinist stronghold, the regime adopted increasingly harsh means of silencing it. In the second week of December, the "rolling revolution" that had toppled regimes in the GDR, Czechoslovakia, and Bulgaria came to Romania in the form of large-scale demonstrations in the western city of Timosoára. Protests that began after the police removed a popular Hungarian clergyman were met with a bloody reprisal by Securitate forces, leaving several thousand dead. Rather than receding, opposition to the regime escalated and became increasingly violent, with protests, strikes, and demonstrations spreading to the capital and other cities. In his last public appearance before a public rally on December 21, Ceausescu was shouted down by the crowd and forced to flee the Presidential Palace, as the armed forces sided with the demonstrators at the critical moment.

The resultant stunning turn of events left the country in a state of virtual civil war, and regular army units battled Securitate forces in the streets. Ceausescu and his wife Elena were captured, tried in secret, and executed in a matter of hours. The regime that could least accommodate autonomous initiatives for change was brought down most violently by them.

Events since the overthrow of Ceausescu indicate that Romania may well have the greatest difficulty of all of the post-communist states in establishing a stable political system committed to pluralist values. Long-standing ethnic divisions, deep political divisions, the lack of any democratic traditions, virtual economic collapse and ecological devastation present serious challenges to a government leadership that seemingly has not yet committed itself to full political pluralism.

The USSR and the East European Revolutions

Since the Gorbachev reform effort was so very central to the revolutionary changes that have occurred in Eastern Europe, it is important for an understanding of the latter briefly to outline its most prominent contours. It is essential to recall that, when Gorbachev arrived on the scene in 1985, the Soviet Union was already in the throes of a major crisis. In the economic realm Soviet GNP had stagnated — according to key economic advisor Abel Aganbegyan real growth ceased by the mid-1970s. Politically the population gave evidence of increasing levels of political ennui and withdrawal; alcoholism and incompetent medical care resulted in reduced life expectancy, especially among males, and in higher infant mortality rates.[76] Soviet allies in Eastern Europe were suffering from similar problems and had become a growing drain on the Soviet economy, clients in the third world had proven incapable of establishing stable political or economic systems and contributed to the growing "costs of empire" for the Soviet state, the exponential growth of Soviet military capabilities had occurred at the expense of other sectors of the economy, and many of the assumptions that had undergirded Soviet foreign policy during the Brezhnev years had proven to be false.

It was in this environment that Gorbachev proposed dramatic reforms as a means to rejuvenate the Soviet economic and political system. In effect, the initial Gorbachev message can be summarized as follows: The Soviet Union finds itself in an economic and political crisis that undermines its ability to provide basic goods and services to its population and threatens to erode its position as a global power. To deal with this problem revolutionary changes are required within the economy — including decentralization of decisionmaking, the establishment of competition within the system, the emergence of elements of a market economy, and related changes of a comparably revolutionary character within the context of the Soviet economy. Increased efficiency, enhanced quality, and the reduction of the technological gap with the West are among the central objectives of the economic reform.

Such reforms, however, will inevitably confront opposition within the party-state bureaucracy which benefits greatly from the perquisites associated with the present system. To overcome this opposition *glasnost* (or openness) and democratization will create an alliance between the reform-minded leadership and the masses of the population aimed at exposing the corruption, incompetence, and inefficiences of the current system and, thus, contributing to the success of the reform effort. Initially, therefore, *glasnost* and democratization were viewed in rather narrow, instrumental terms as the means to facilitate the introduction of radical economic reforms.

There also existed the realization among many of the reformers that the centralization of political power and the absence of political participation and, thus, political responsibility had been key elements in explaining the failure of the Stalinist system. These attitudes contributed to the view that the entire reform movement also included an important political component that would open access to political decisionmaking to ever broader segments of the population. On the negative side, from their perspective, the reform leadership underestimated the degree to which *glasnost* and democratization would develop a life of their own, as the political agendas of the minority populations — Lithuanians, Armenians, Uzbeks, and others — emerged differently from the agenda of the reformers in Moscow.

Thus, *perestroika*, openness and democratization have been intimately interrelated ever since the beginning of the Gorbachev reform program. Moreover, "new thinking" and new behavior in foreign policy have also been an integral part of the Gorbachev reforms. First, the nature, scope, and cost of domestic reform requires an international environment in which the Soviet leadership is not concerned with a new cold war or arms race and is able to devote more of its attention to the issues associated with reform. Moreover, the costs of Soviet foreign policy must be reduced dramatically, given the expanded investment demands of a successful revitalization of the economy. Since the past commitment of extensive resources to allies and clients in Eastern Europe and the third world have not resulted in politically stable and economically productive states, those commitments must be reconsidered and in many cases reduced. Since the expansion of Soviet military capabilities and the building of bigger and better weapons systems did not result in expanded security, efforts to achieve security through accommodation and assurance strategies toward the West and, thus, to reduce the military burden are also essential.

Soviet policy since 1985 has undergone more than than mere rhetorical change. The dramatic shift in position on a number of key issues concerning nuclear weapons and arms control by the Gorbachev leadership was essential to the agreement to scrap all intermediate-range nuclear weapons in Europe and Asia. The announcement in December 1988 that the USSR would unilaterally reduce its military strength in Central Europe by 500,000 troops and upwards of 10,000 tanks — and the ongoing implementation of the first stage of that withdrawal, accelerated by the demands of the new East European governments — represents yet another shift in Soviet security policy. These moves were apparently meant to accomplish several important objectives. First, they indicated to the West that "new thinking" in the foreign and security policy areas was more than rhetoric, that it presaged a dramatic shift in the way in which the USSR was to deal with the outside world, in particular with the countries of Europe. Secondly, they were meant to encourage the West to enter into a mutual process of arms reduction. A third objective concerned the hope that arms reductions, especially in the conventional area, would eventually bring with them the economic savings required if the domestic program of economic restructuring and reform in the Soviet Union is to succeed.

An important component of Gorbachev's foreign policy initiatives has concerned bilateral relations with the countries of Eastern Europe. Since at least 1987 Gorbachev's response to the growing economic and political problems of the region, as well as to the erosion of unity and cohesion within the socialist community, was to call upon the leaderships of the East European countries to reform their own political and economic systems. Unlike past Soviet leaders, Gorbachev argued that ultimately the decision on reform — as other major decisions — must be made by the East Europeans themselves. He and other Soviet leaders no longer viewed the USSR as the final arbiter of ideological orthodoxy for its East European allies. This new interpretation of socialist internationalism has been verified by Soviet reactions to the revolutionary events of 1989. High-level Soviet officials have stated that the USSR was wrong to intervene militarily in Czechoslovakia in 1968, noncommunist governments in Poland and elsewhere have been accepted as partners within the Warsaw Treaty Organization, and Gorbachev himself virtually renounced past Soviet policies in statements made during his visits to Strasbourg and Helsinki in August and October of 1989. Even the integration of its key East European ally, the German Democratic Republic, into a reunited Germany still in NATO has been accepted.

Initially it appears that Gorbachev hoped that East European communists could reform their economies and their political systems in a manner to make them viable and productive. However, given the failure of East European communists to accomplish this task and the revolutionary changes that have brought noncommunist or coalition governments to power throughout the region, he has accepted the idea of an Eastern Europe comprised of stable, economically efficient, though noncommunist systems as preferable to a continuation of the status quo of the 1980s. The effort to maintain politically illegitimate and economically inefficient regimes in Eastern Europe by force or threat of force has been abandoned in the hope that mutually beneficial relationships can emerge in the future between the Soviet Union and Europe's dominant economic power, Germany, and a revitalized set of "Finland-like" systems in Eastern Europe.

The dramatic changes that have occurred in the USSR, in Eastern Europe, and in East-West relations and which have led to a changing European international security system are the result of both the domestic imperatives of the communist political systems and the cold war environment in which they developed. The cold war, defined in part as the emergence in Europe of a stable security regime that prevented war because of the dangers of escalation to nuclear confrontation, was a necessary condition for the recent revolutionary changes that have occurred in Europe. It created an international environment in which competition was diverted to areas of peripheral concern for both superpowers, though an environment in which ever greater amounts of military capabilities were being created and greater stress placed on domestic economies.

At the same time, however, within both alliance systems domestic political and economic developments ran their own course. In the West extensive political and economic cooperation contributed to an unprecedented expansion of both economic welfare and political participation. In the Soviet Union and Eastern Europe the experiment in applied Marxism-Leninism proved to be a failure. By the 1980s centralized economies could no longer provide adequately for the welfare of their populations (especially when compared with the almost unbridled economic successes of Western states) and were faced with ever greater demands for real political participation. In many respects George Kennan's prediction of the internal non-viability of the Stalinist political-economic model has proven to be accurate.[77]

Conclusions

It is by no means clear in early 1991 where events in Eastern Europe will lead, for the revolutionary transformations discussed above are still in process, and their outcomes are not predetermined.[78] It is most likely that the changes will result in the emergence of political-economic systems that are not homogeneous throughout the region. In the political realm it is conceivable that in some countries stable pluralist political systems will emerge, while in others the response to political fragmentation and semi-anarchy may result in the reimposition of some form of authoritarian political controls. In the economic realm mixed economies combining elements of traditional state socialism with market factors will probably result, but the mix may well differ substantially from country to country. Moreover, the degree to which new regimes will be able to resolve the fundamental economic and ecological problems that they have inherited will probably differ as well and will likely depend on the degree to which they are able to be integrated into the Western economy.[79]

Though it is not possible at this point to predict with any degree of confidence the contours of a post-communist Eastern Europe, one can assert that state socialism as it has existed in the region for more than four decades will not be reinstated; that, except perhaps in the Balkans, local

Communist parties will, at most, play but a supportive role in the political and economic reconstruction of the region; and that the influence of the USSR over the East European states will be at least dramatically reduced.

Several important points emerge from the current analysis. First of all, the revolutionary changes that have occurred in all six of the Soviet-oriented communist states are interconnected and have common roots. Those roots can be found in the fact that throughout the entire region, even in Romania and Czechoslovakia, emerging social groups placed increasingly greater demands for participation on the communist elites who dominated the systems. At the same time the internal contradictions of the Stalinist socioeconomic-political model, with its inflexibility to external demands and its virtual ignoring of the costs of industrial production, reached crisis dimensions in most countries. Authoritarian elites were no longer able to suppress these groups or ignore their demands, with the result that during the last months of 1989 they were displaced.

Not only did the revolutions of 1989 have similar origins, they were also influenced by the dramatic changes in Soviet policy toward the region and by the "demonstration effect" of developments elsewhere in the region. In many ways Gorbachev's repeated statements that East Europeans should determine their own fate and that the Soviet Union would not intervene to undermine the process of long-needed political reform contributed to the radical political changes.[80] This "hands off" approach to the political challenges to the ruling party elites in Eastern Europe — in fact, Gorbachev's open advocacy of political reform in some countries — helped create the environment that permitted, even encouraged, advocates of political change to press their demands more openly. The fact that Polish Solidarity was able successfully to challenge Communist party domination, win an election, and take over political power — all without Soviet intervention — had a powerful influence elsewhere in Eastern Europe.

To a great degree, therefore, the dramatic changes that have occurred throughout Eastern Europe find their basis both in internal factors (economic crises and growing pressures for political participation) and in the external environment (the shifts in declared Soviet policy and the evidence of reformers' success elsewhere, as in Poland).

Despite the similarities in the reform process throughout Eastern Europe, substantial differences exist as well. Perhaps the most important is the degree to which alternative political forces were able to organize prior to the developments of 1989 and, thus, the degree to which they represented a viable political alternative to the communists. In Poland, for example, Solidarity, which has a decade of organizing experiences, has been able — at least thus far — to coalesce to the point where it has formed a government, passed legislation, and implemented policy. Moreover, the Polish communists have virtually disappeared as a viable political force. Yet, in Bulgaria, the communists have yet effectively to give up power, and the opposition has splintered into many competing factions. Thus, differences exist throughout the region concerning both the remaining organized strength of the communists and the ability of the "opposition" to organize effectively and win a working majority in competitive elections.

A related problem, most evident already in Poland, is the reform government's need to rely on the communist bureaucracy to carry out its policy decisions. Will the members of that bureaucracy, long accustomed to the perquisites associated with the Communist party elite, function as a nonpolitical civil service willing to carry out policies diverging strongly from those of the past? And will the new regimes be able to train a new noncommunist civil service?

Yet another issue concerns the patience of populations long repressed and long deprived of material goods in accepting the austerity programs, as in Poland, that will be necessary virtually everywhere in order to turn around moribund economies — assuming, of course, that the new leaderships are able to agree on programs of economic reform, successfully implement them, and then reap positive results?

As argued at the beginning of this essay, events in Eastern Europe since mid-1989 have been revolutionary in nature. In terms of structural changes of the state socialist system, they have already gone far beyond anything envisaged in Gorbachev's reform program for the USSR. Gorbachev has been committed to retaining Communist party viability while expanding political liberties, and to making a state socialist economic system more efficient and more responsive to public needs. The East Europeans, however, have moved far beyond those positions. New governments in Poland and elsewhere are already in the process of dismantling portions of the economic infrastructure of the old centralized system; everywhere throughout the region coalition governments are now in place, party militias used in the past to help enforce party dominance have been dismantled, and open multiparty elections have occurred or are scheduled.

Eastern Europe has entered a new era, the contours of which are by no means clear. Though other factors have been important, as we have attempted to document, key to the developments leading to the revolutionary changes that have already occurred and will continue to develop has been the emergence of autonomous groups within the framework of centralized and authoritarian political systems. These groups have challenged the ruling communist elites and forced the latter, in varying degrees to this point, to respond to their political demands and to share political power.

Notes

1. Jacques Rupnik, "Dissent in Poland, 1968–78: The End of Revisionism and the Rebirth of Civil Society," in Rudolf Tókés, ed., *Opposition in Eastern Europe* (Baltimore: Johns Hopkins Press, 1979), p. 60.

2. Ibid.

3. David Ost, "Towards a Neocorporatist Solution in Eastern Europe," *Eastern European Politics and Society* 3 (1989), p. 164.

4. Andrzej Korbonski, "Nationalism and Pluralism and the Process of Political Development in Eastern Europe," *International Political Science Review* 10 (1989), pp. 254–59.

5. See Peter Raina, *Independent Social Movements in Poland* (London: Orbis Books, 1989), pp. 13–21.

6. See Maria Halamska, "Peasant Movements in Poland, 1980-81: State Socialist Economy and the Mobilization of Individual Farmers"; Barbara Wejnert, "Student Movements in Poland, 1980–81"; and Pawel Kreczynski and Krzysztof Nowaki, "The Solidarity Movement in Relation to Society and the State: Communication as an Issue of Social Movements," all in *Research in Social Movements, Conflicts and Change,* vol. 10 (Greenwich, CN: JAI Press, 1988).

7. For a theoretically based discussion of the emergence of pluralism in European communist systems see Alexander C. Pacek, "Changing Political Processes in Soviet-Type Systems," *Crossroads: An International Socio-Political Journal* 28 (1989), pp. 75–91.

8. The survey "Studenci Warszawy 1983" documents these views. It was administered in the first half of 1983 with a sample of 650 students from Warsaw University and the Warsaw Polytechnic. Cited in Maurice D. Simon, "Citizenship in a New Polish Context: Prospects for Stability in the Post-1981 Period," in Charles J. Bukowski and Mark A. Chichock, eds., *Prospects for Change in Socialist Systems: Challenges and Responses* (New York: Praeger, 1987), pp. 87–94.

9. A. Smolar and P. Kende, *The Role of Opposition: The Role of Opposition Groups on the Eve of Democratization in Poland and Hungary, 1987–1988* (Munich: "PROJEKT," 1989), pp. 11–34.

10. Jiri Pehe, "Independent Movements in Eastern Europe," *Radio Free Europe Research,* RAD Background Report (hereafter *RFER,* RAD BR) /228, 17 November 1988, pp. 1–21.

11. J.B. de Weydenthal, "PUWP Accepts the Prospect of Legalizing Solidarity," *RFER,* Polish Situation Report (hereafter SR) /2, 20 January 1989, pp. 3–6.

12. Roman Stefanowski, "Poland's Economic Results in 1988," *RFER,* Polish SR/4, 3 March 1989, pp. 33–35.

13. Tony Judt, "The Dilemma of Dissidence: The Politics of Opposition in East Central Europe," *Eastern European Politics and Societies* 2 (1988), p. 210.

14. Louisa Vinton, "Is Dialogue More Likely after the Strikes?," *RFER,* Polish SR/9, 7 June 1988, pp. 3–8.

15. Karen Dawisha, *Eastern Europe, Gorbachev and Reform: The Great Challenge* (Cambridge-New York: Cambridge University Press, 1988), p. 167.

16. Vladimir V. Kusin, "Voting Communism Out of Office Polish Style," *RFER,* RAD BR/108, 19 June 1989, pp. 1–5.

17. Ivan Volgyes, *Politics in Eastern Europe* (Chicago: Dorsey Press, 1986), pp. 197–207.

18. Bennet Kovrig, "Fire and Water: Political Reform in Eastern Europe," in Nicholas W.

Kittrie and Ivan Volgyes, eds., *The Uncertain Future: Gorbachev's East Europe* (New York: Paragon House, 1988), p. 26.

19. Rudolf Tókés, "Human Rights and Political Change in Eastern Europe," in Tókés, *Opposition in Eastern Europe*, p. 23.

20. Barnabus Racz, "Socialist Democracy Revisited: The Case of Hungary," in Bukowski and Cichock, *Prospects for Change in Socialist Systems*, pp.66–70.

21. Ferenc Kőszegi and E.P. Thompson, *END Special Report: The New Hungarian Peace Movement* (London: Merlin Press LTS and END, 1983).

22. Gábor Demsky, "Initiatives for Hungary," *East European Reporter*, Autumn 1988, pp. 49–51.

23. Edit Kery, "A Tizenkilencek," *Hitel* 4 (February 1989).

24. Vladimir Kusin, "Gabcikov-Nagymaros: The Politics of a Project," *RFER*, RAD BR/206, 24 November 1989, pp. 1–6.

25. Judith Pataki, "New Umbrella Organization for Youth," *RFER*, Hungarian SR/19, 5 December 1988, pp. 11–14.

26 Béla Liptek, "Ujabb Fejlemények a Duna Védelmében," *Magyar Nemzet*, 21 November 1988; Edith Markos, "Independent Youth Organization Holds National Congress," *RFER*, Hungarian SR/19, 5 December 1988, pp. 15–19.

27. Jiri Pehe, "Independent Civil Activity in Eastern Europe," *RFER*, RAD BR/1, 4 January 1989, pp. 1–11; Zoltán D. Bárány, "Hungary's Independent Political Groups and Parties," *RFER*, RAD BR/168, 12 September 1989, pp. 1–11; Edith Oltay, "Constitutional Amendments Strengthen Civil Rights, Pave Way for Multiparty System," *RFER*, Hungarian SR/17, 30 November 1989, pp. 3–7.

28. Judith Pataki, "The Rebirth of Political Parties," *RFER*, Hungarian SR/1, 12 January 1989, pp. 3–8.

29. Roger Woods, *Opposition in the GDR under Honecker, 1971–1985* (London: Macmillan Press, 1986), p.8.

30. Ibid., pp. 10–11.

31. Ibid., p. 14.

32. Martin McCauley, *The GDR Since 1945* (London: Macmillan Press, 1983), pp 3–20.

33. Woods, *Opposition in the GDR*, p. 3.

34. Ibid., p. 6.

35. Ibid., p. 9.

36. *From Below: Independent Peace and Environmental Movements in Eastern Europe and the USSR* (New York: Helsinki Watch Committee, 1987), p. 30.

37. Ibid., p. 31.

38. For example, Andrzej Korbonski has written recently that "the process of East German nation-building has been relatively successful ...resulting in the emergence of a significant degree of loyalty and commitment on the part of citizens" and that the regime had been "successful in its socialization efforts." Korbonski, "Nationalism and Pluralism," *International Political Science Review* 10 (1989), pp. 251, 262.

39. Reported in *Eastern European Newsletter* 3, no. 10 (1989).

40. Ibid.

41. "Calls for Democratization in the GDR," *East European Reporter* 3, no. 4 (1989), pp. 29–31.

42. See Serge Schmemann, "East German Opposition Party Forms," *New York Times* (national edition; hereafter *NYT*), 20 September 1989, p. 3; Barbara Donovan, "Opposition in the GDR Grows," *RFER*, RAD BR/180, 29 September 1989, pp. 1–5; and *Soviet/East European Reporter* 8, no. 1 (1989), pp. 1–2.

43. Barbara Donovan, "East German Politburo and Central Committee Resign," *RFER*, RAD BR/216, 6 December 1989, pp. 1–5.

44. "GDR: Apostasy," *Eastern European Newsletter* 3, no. 23 (1989).

45. Ibid.
46. H. Gordon Skilling, *Czechoslovakia's Interrupted Revolution* (Princeton: Princeton University Press, 1976), pp. 233, 357.
47. While major economic initiatives such as Ota Šik's "Draft Principles" and political reforms such as Alexander Dubček's "Action Program" were developed within the party framework, the party leadership solicited advice from specialists outside the CCP. See Benjamin Page, *The Czechoslovak Reform Movement, 1963–1968: A Study in the Theory of Socialism* (Amsterdam: B.R. Bruner B.U., 1973).
48. Judy Batt, *Economic Reform and Political Change in Eastern Europe: A Comparison of the Czechoslovak and Hungarian Experiences* (London: Macmillan Press, 1986), pp. 171–206.
49. Ota Šik, *The Communist Power System* (New York: Praeger Press, 1984); H. Gordon Skilling, "Czechoslovak Political Culture: Pluralism in an International Context," in Archie Brown, ed., *Political Culture in Communist States* (New York: M.E. Sharpe, 1984), p. 17.
50. Korbonski, "Nationalism and Pluralism," p. 256.
51. Batt, *Economic Reform and Political Change*, p. 231.
52. Judt, "The Dilemma of Dissidence," p. 206.
53. *From Below*, p. 5.
54. Ibid., pp. 11, 19.
55. Dawisha, *Eastern Europe, Gorbachev and Reform*, p. 167.
56. Ibid., p. 169.
57. Ibid., p. 170.
58. "New Groups Spring Up," *East European Reporter*, Autumn 1988, pp. 25–26.
59. Peter Martin, "On the Eve of Mitterrand's Visit," *RFER*, Czechoslovak SR/21, 9 December 1988, pp. 5–6.
60. Peter Martin, "CPSU CC Member Aleksandr Yakovlev in Czechoslovakia," *RFER*, Czechoslovak SR/20, 18 November 1988, pp. 5–7.
61. Vladimir Kusin, "The Leadership Taken Aback by the Ground Swell of Opposition," *RFER*, Czechoslovak SR/2, 26 January 1989, pp. 9–10.
62. Kolyo Kolev, "Glasnost for All," *NYT*, 27 September 1988, pp. 34–35.
63. "Bulgarian Crackdown," *Eastern Europe Newsletter* 2, no. 22 (1988), pp. 6–7.
64. Stephen Ashley, "Intellectuals Form an Independent Club for the Support of *Perestroika* and *Glasnost'*," *RFER*, Bulgarian SR/12, 20 December 1988, pp. 11–13.
65. "The Sofia Slide," *Eastern Europe Newsletter* 3, no. 1 (1989), pp. 3–7.
66. Stephen Ashley, "More Independent Groups Emerge," *RFER*, Bulgarian SR/2, 9 March 1989, pp. 15–19.
67. "Bulgaria: The Opposition and the Turks," *Eastern Europe Newsletter* 3, no. 19 (1989), pp. 3–4; "Balkan Bust-Up," *Eastern Europe Newsletter* 3, no. 11 (1989), pp. 1–2; Stephen Ashley, "A Political Trial in Varna," *RFER*, Bulgarian SR/8, 1 September 1989, pp. 25–28.
68. "Bulgaria: Towards the End," *Eastern Europe Newsletter* 3, no. 22 (1989), p. 3–4.
69. Vladimir Socor, "Are the Old Political Parties Stirring in Romania?" *RFER*, RAD BR/69, 22 July 1985, pp. 6–10.
70. Vladimir Socor, "National Peasant Group Silenced after Human Rights Initiative," *RFER*, Romanian SR/1, 6 February 1987, pp. 23–25.
71. *East European Reporter* 3, no. 2 (1989).
72. Vladimir Tismaneanu, "Bulldozer Socialism," *East European Reporter* 3, no. 4 (1989), pp. 21–25.
73. Ibid.
74. Ibid.
75. Crisula Stefanescu, "Human Rights Activist Doina Corena Complains about the Position of the Romanian Intellectual," *RFER*, Romanian SR/8, 8 November 1989, pp. 13–15;

Crisula Stefanescu, "Exiled Literary Critic Mircea Iorgulescu Speaks Out," *RFER*, Romanian SR/8, 8 November 1989, pp. 23–27.

76. This discussion draws from a number of sources. Especially important are Mikhail Gorbachev, *Perestroika, New Thinking for Our Country and the World* (New York: Harper & Row, Publishers, 1987); Abel Aganbegyan, *The Economic Challenge of Perestroika* (Bloomington/Indianapolis: Indiana University Press, 1988); Tat'iana I. Zaslavskaia, *A Voice of Reform: Essays by Tat'iana I. Zaslavskaia,* (Armonk, NY/ London: M.E. Sharpe, 1989); Ed A. Hewett, *Reforming the Soviet Economy: Equality versus Efficiency* (Washington, DC: The Brookings Institution, 1988).

77. Kennan's 1947 "Mr. X" article on containment is reprinted in Charles Gati, ed., *Caging the Bear: Containment and the Cold War* (Indianapolis/ New York: Bobbs-Merrill, 1974).

78. For a perceptive article that focuses on the problems of reestablishing stability see Serge Schmemann, "East Europe's Next Test: To Survive Democracy," *NYT*, 21 January 1990, pp. 4–1.

79. Vlad Sobell, "Beyond Communist Economics: Postcommunist Transition in Eastern Europe," *RFER*, RAD BR/224, 22 December 1989, pp. 1–8.

80. For example, during his address to the Council of Europe parliamentary assembly in Strasbourg on July 6, 1989, he said, "Social and political orders in one country or another have changed in the past and may change in the future. But this is exclusively the affair of the people of that country and is their choice. Any interference in the domestic affairs and any attempts to restrict the sovereignty of states — friends, allies, and others — are inadmissable." *Pravda*, 7 July 1989. In October, during a visit to Helsinki, he repeated this argument and set up Soviet-Finnish relations as a model for "relations between a big country and a small country, a model of relations between states with different social systems, a model of relations between neighbors." *NYT*, 26 October 1989, p. 7. See, also, Vladimir V. Kusin, "Mikhail Gorbachev's Evolving Attitude to Eastern Europe," *RFER*, RAD BR/128, 20 July 1989, pp. 1–12.

9. HUNGARY:
REFORM AND TRANSITION

Paul Marer

This essay has a threefold purpose. One is to summarize the successes and failures of Hungary's reform experience (1963-1989), which until recently was considered pioneering in the socialist world. Another purpose is to indicate the complexities of the systemic transformation that is now getting under way and can succeed — say, by the year 2000 — only if Hungary's decision makers choose the right course and if the external environment is supportive. The essay concludes with a few observations on Western policies that could promote the difficult transition — as much in the interest of the West as in that of Eastern Europe.

Past Reform: An Evaluation

Despite a generation of reforms, at the turn of this decade Hungary finds itself on the brink of an economic and political crisis. Why is it that even though the New Economic Mechanism (NEM) was introduced in Hungary more than two decades ago, the country is still in such a precarious economic situation?

Parts of this chapter are based on the author's two non-copyrighted essays that appeared in the 1989 Joint Economic Committee, U.S. Congress Compendium on Eastern Europe.

Much of Hungary's past reform is associated with the name of Janos Kadar, the communist leader who ruled the country for thirty-two years, from November 1956 until May 1988.

Kadar and his group of influentials had two fundamental and unchanging objectives: to maintain their monopoly on political power and to build and consolidate a socialist economic system.

Monopoly of Political Power

Although Kadar made significant changes in the *strategy* of exercising political power, power remained firmly the monopoly of the party or, more accurately, those self-selected to exercise it. The goals and tasks of state organizations were defined outside the organization; their interests were in carrying them out. Power flowed from top to bottom. Those who wanted it had to gain support from above rather than mobilize a constituency from below. In this respect, Hungary remained a traditional communist country.

Socialist Economic System

In a (pre-Gorbachev) Soviet-type economy, the socialist economic system is defined by the following subgoals of its influentials: (1) predominantly socialist ownership of the means of production, (2) full employment, (3) a quasi-welfare state, (4) elimination of extreme disparities in income and wealth, and (5) consumer price stability.

1. SOCIALIST OWNERSHIP. The authorities view ownership hierarchically: state ownership is preferred over cooperative ownership, which in turn is superior to private property. Private enterprise is tolerated as a transitory concession, prompted by economic necessity. Under Kadar, the hierarchy of ownership was maintained. More accurately, sometime during the 1960s large cooperatives were declared to be of equal rank with state ownership. But "socialist" property was consistently considered superior to private property. Although in 1957, in 1968, and again in 1981, the scope of second-economy activities was expanded, no constitutional protection was granted to private ownership. Ambivalent and frequently changing stop-and-go policies were pursued toward the sector, and the preferential allocation of capital, inputs, and subsidies to state-owned firms and large cooperatives continued. Thus, this objective of a CPE was not really altered. This created hardships and uncertainties for private activities, which limited greatly their scope and effectiveness and gave rise to a whole set of new and complex problems, as will be indicated.

Furthermore, the predominance of socialist ownership prevented the establishment of markets for factors of production, especially for capital. That, in turn, impaired greatly the efficient operation of the economic system.

2. FULL EMPLOYMENT. The preservation of full employment is both a short-term and a long-term goal in a Soviet-type model, for ideological as well as political reasons. It is not the goal itself — which after all is a worthwhile objective of political leaders in any country — that is problematic, but the way it is interpreted in practice. In the interest of full employment, the authorities allow labor to be hoarded by enterprises and provide that practically all jobs become permanent entitlements to their holders, largely irrespective of need or the individual's performance. This, of course, limits structural change and weakens labor discipline. The preservation of this kind of full employment remained a basic objective under Kadar. Thus, in this respect, too, Hungary remained a Soviet-type economy.

3. QUASI-WELFARE STATE. Soviet-type systems may be called quasi-welfare states because access to most of the benefits the state provides (health care, housing, social security, subsidized basic foods and services) is tied to employment, not to country of residence or citizenship. During Kadar's tenure, these benefits were nominally maintained even though the rapid deterioration of the medical, social, educational, and cultural infrastructure during the last decade suggests that making good on this aspect of socialism had become in recent years a relatively low priority.

4. OVERCOMING EXTREME INCOME AND WEALTH INEQUALITIES. Contrary to impressions, an egalitarian distribution of income and wealth is neither a basic objective nor a practice in a CPE model. Rather, the goal is to eliminate extreme inequalities as well as incomes based on returns on property and entrepreneurship. However, earnings differentials among workers and employees (but not between them and the *nomenklatura*) are kept small, not as a matter of principle but arising out of the logic of the system and from social pressures. The systemic reforms introduced under Kadar were associated with an increase in the inequalities of income and wealth. But much of it was due not to marketization per se, but to the glaring imperfections in the market mechanism (taking the form, for example, of niche monopolies for a significant number of participants in the second economy, who thereby reaped large, unearned incomes). The authorities' response has been to periodically clamp down on all private activities rather than to strengthen market forces. Thus, in this area, too, the goals and behavior of the authorities had much in common with those in a traditional system.

5. Consumer Price Stability. This objective was pursued in Hungary vigorously until 1979, that is, even after the introduction of the NEM. Its main instrument was administered price determination or rules enterprises were to follow that achieved the same thing. This made it all the more difficult to adjust relative prices to scarcities, to allow market forces to operate, and to let enterprise profits serve as true indicators of their performance. That, in turn, contributed to the maintenance of paternalistic relations between enterprises and the authorities. After 1979, the authorities in Hungary were compelled to give up price stability, for the time being, in order to hold down domestic consumption via inflation and thereby improve the balance of payments. As a byproduct, relative prices did improve, but the practice of cost-plus pricing continued.

Strategies

Hungary developed strategies to deal with (1) exercising political power, (2) the standard of living, (3) resource mobilization, (4) resource allocation, (5) foreign economic relations with the CMEA, (6) foreign economic relations with the West, (7) foreign borrowing and debt management, and (8) economic reform design and implementation.

1. Exercising Political Power. Several years after the ruthless suppression of the revolution of 1956, Kadar changed his strategy of exercising political power. After 1963 he instituted, gradually, a set of policies often referred to in the West as political liberalization (but which would be more accurately called enlightened absolutism) that increased the personal security of the citizenry and made life in Hungary much more tolerable than in any other STE, with the possible exception of Poland. This strategy (together with that regarding the standard of living) was, in Kadar's judgment, the best way to ensure that the events of 1956 would not be repeated.

Kadar in effect told the Hungarian people: "The Soviet Union and its basic policies are here to stay. Cooperate with me by not challenging the political system, and I'll make life as tolerable for you as it can possibly be under our geopolitical circumstances." At the same time, Kadar said to the Soviet leaders: "Hungarians are unhappy with your rule, as you saw in 1956. If you give me a free hand in domestic affairs, I can calm this explosive situation, and my management will thus be to your advantage."

Kadar's great historical merit was his skill in designing and managing this grand compromise. But its successful implementation ultimately rested on two pillars: steady improvements in the standard of living and the

Brezhnev Doctrine. The combination of a carrot and a stick made the Hungarian people willing to tolerate a situation that, fundamentally, was not acceptable to them. Once the two pillars collapsed, more or less simultaneously in the late 1980s, so also did the great Kadar compromise and the regime's stability.

2. STANDARD OF LIVING. Kadar gave high priority to steady improvements in the citizenry's material well-being. When this could no longer be assured from domestic resources (after 1972), Kadar resorted to extensive borrowing from foreign sources to maintain the expansion of both consumption and investment. After 1980 this strategy could no longer be implemented, owing to the great inefficiencies of Hungary's economy and the huge debt-service burden. That, in turn, gradually eroded the implicit compromise between the regime and the population (the social contract, as it is often called), helping to undermine political stability.

3. RESOURCE MOBILIZATION. A hallmark of a CPE is that resource mobilization is forced and highly centralized. By and large this continued after the introduction of the NEM, but with one (not very important) difference: Whereas before the NEM was introduced, resources were mobilized through mandatory directives and campaigns, after the NEM was put in place, resources were mobilized by manipulating a variety of "regulators." During the first half of the 1980s, taxes and other levies still centralized, on average, more than 80 percent of enterprise incomes and about 60 percent of GNP. Thus, there does not seem to be a fundamental difference in this area between Kadar's Hungary and the more traditional CPEs.

4. RESOURCE USE. This strategy refers to decisions on investments and to the size and purposes of state budget expenditures. The NEM envisioned giving enterprises substantial autonomy only regarding replacement investment plus "small" new investment, and retaining for the center the strategic decisions on expansion. Even when enterprises could, formally, initiate a project, since they were left with meager resources after taxation and were also limited as to the purposes for which after-tax incomes could be spent, they had to rely on the authorities for subsidies and imports, on the monobank for credits, and on the state budget for grants. Investment projects of significance were determined by the preferences of top policy makers and by the interests of powerful lobbies, not by market forces. Their revealed preferences show that the strategy of investment did not depart very far from those of the more traditional CPEs: basic and heavy industries (coal, steel, petrochemicals), selected branches of manufactur-

ing, projects to increase exports to the CMEA or to replace convertible imports, and projects that were massive. The revealed non-preferences included infrastructure, services, light industry, projects to increase exports to the West (except for periodic campaigns), environmental protection, and projects in the second economy.

5. FOREIGN ECONOMIC RELATIONS WITH THE CMEA. The foreign economic strategy of a typical East European country after about 1950 was to maximize the growth of imports of energy, basic materials, and intermediate products ("hard goods") and to pay for them by shipping (mostly or increasingly) "soft" manufactured products. Each East European country could, of course, realize such a strategy only vis-à-vis the USSR. The strategy's rationale was that it facilitated rapid economic growth, provided economies of scale and full employment, and made possible the production of intermediates that were nonexpendable hard-currency earners. However, the long-term consequence of pursuing such a strategy was to build, expand, and maintain an industrial structure not in accordance with comparative advantage. It made the East European economies extremely vulnerable to Soviet ability and willingness to continue this pattern of trade and contributed to continued loss of export-competitiveness on the world market. In all these respects, Hungary did not appear to have pursued a strategy fundamentally different from those of the other, less reform-minded countries of Eastern Europe.

6. FOREIGN ECONOMIC RELATIONS WITH THE WEST. A typical CPE foreign economic strategy vis-à-vis the West is one of extreme inward orientation: Incentives are biased in favor of production for the domestic or CMEA market and against both export and import trade with the world market. If the purpose of convertible imports — and this is where strategy comes into play — is (1) to purchase technology and inputs to produce exports to CMEA, where payment is not in convertible currency; (2) to alleviate bottlenecks created by overambitious investment drives, poor investment projects, planning mistakes, and inefficiencies at the micro level; and (3) to sustain, with the help of foreign loans, domestic absorption above the level of production, then the resulting increase in convertible imports cannot be taken as evidence of "openness." By contrast, if the strategy of imports from the West is to lower the cost of production and to generate competition, then one can speak of an economy opening up to foreign markets. On the export side, if too much of the wrong kinds of imports, plus debt-service, is paid for by exports that are generated with large subsidies (much greater than what is needed to offset the protection of inputs) and with short-term export incentives that undermine the sustained expansion of exports, then such trade, too, does not evidence "openness."

Hungary's strategy was essentially that just indicated, and it had two main consequences. One, paradoxically, was a very substantial increase in dependence on the West for essential imports (there were also other contributing causes), making the economy highly vulnerable to import-supply disruptions. The other consequence is that a significant part of Hungary's trade is not in accordance with the country's long-term comparative advantage. Therefore, its gains from trade have remained much smaller than the volume and relative importance of exports and imports in its economy would suggest. One modestly significant difference between Hungary and the other East European countries: It was the first to liberalize — half-heartedly, to be sure — joint ventures with Western partners. But through the Kadar years, the number of joint ventures and the total inflow of capital and export earnings linked with them remained modest.

7. FOREIGN BORROWING AND DEBT MANAGEMENT. During the last two decades, Hungary's debts to the West increased rapidly not because of a strategic decision to tap the long-term inflow of foreign resources for development (as Poland and Romania did during the 1970s), but to finance time and time again the unplanned excess of imports and shortfalls in exports. But Hungary did make a strategic decision in the late 1970s not to reschedule repayment of loans. This was a factor in the austerity program that has now been under way for about a decade. In the 1970s, Kadar borrowed to raise the standard of living, to pay for the import costs of misguided investments, and to buffer the country from the effects of a large deterioration in its terms of trade. In the 1980s, Kadar borrowed to refinance the payment of principal and a portion of the interest on the foreign debt. Since there is no CPE strategy on foreign borrowing and debt management, the analogy here is best made with countries, not necessarily CPEs, where the authorities and foreign lenders bear joint responsibility for taking and providing excessive amounts of credits.

8. ECONOMIC REFORM. Strategic issues on reform involve decisions on when to initiate it, what kind of reform should be introduced, whether to put it in place experimentally or broadly, and how to sequence its implementation.

As background for discussing the kinds of reforms Kadar supported, let us divide the economy into two sectors: (1) state firms and large cooperatives (the first economy) and (2) private and semi-private firms and activities (the second economy). The two sectors have different relationships with the authorities. Reform strategy during the Kadar era can be divided into four periods: 1956-64, 1965-72, 1973-78, and 1979-88.

1956-64: Immediately after Kadar's ascendancy in 1956, a reform commission prepared a blueprint that was very close to that of the NEM of

1968, but the reform was not introduced. Instead, a series of politically motivated, ad hoc concessions were made to the second economy, which turned out to be significant building blocks for subsequent reforms.

1965-72: Prompted by growing tensions in the first economy and by the success of reforms in the second economy, the NEM was introduced to improve the first economy. Central planning was retained, but mandatory plan targets to enterprises and central resource allocation were replaced by financial and administrative regulators, that is, by indirect planning. The NEM did not aim to enlarge the second economy, but the combination of allowing workers to change jobs and giving greater autonomy to cooperatives actually brought about that result. Agricultural and retail trade cooperatives established subsidiaries in industry and construction. Those ventures became the first important forms of semiprivate activity, characterized by strong profit orientation and de facto independence from the authorities. Because many aspects of the NEM were introduced simultaneously, it is called a comprehensive reform. This is not a fully accurate term because a great deal of the economy was not touched (such as economic institutions and the political superstructure). Nevertheless, on balance, the reforms implemented through the NEM were sufficiently wide ranging, in terms of changes in the economic system, to warrant the conclusion that it transformed Hungary from a Soviet-type economy into a modified CPE.

1973-78: The reform was "frozen" for about six years because of a domestic backlash by union leaders and managers of powerful enterprises, antireform trends in the USSR, and efforts to protect Hungary from the adverse impacts of the world energy crisis.

1979-88: Increasingly acute tensions, especially in the convertible balance of payments, prompted Kadar once again to turn to reform. But the suggestion of economists to create a real market mechanism was rejected. Instead, a series of partial reforms was implemented over a decade, in both the first and the second economies (summarized below). However, owing to the lack of a clear concept of what model was desired and the many constraints imposed by the simultaneous pursuit of a CPE's fundamental objectives as well as strategies that were enumerated, the reform steps were full of contradictions.

The System: Institutions and Instruments

A great deal has been written about systemic reforms in Hungary, so this section can be brief.

POLITICAL SYSTEM. There was no significant change in the political system.

The fact that many actions and activities were permitted, not as constitutionally guaranteed rights but as an aspect of exercising political power (for example, publishing articles critical of some aspects of the regime or its policies, travel to the West, tolerance of second-economy activities) brought about an improvement in the quality of life. But, at the same time, such privileges became a corrupting influence in society. This was so because many of those who enjoyed its benefits became regime supporters to protect their "privileges." Just like many activities in the second economy (that is, the privileged money-making opportunities through bribery, monopoly, access to information, connections), it created supporters of the prevailing undemocratic political and corrupt economic arrangements.

ECONOMIC SYSTEM. The most important reform measures were the following:
1. Reducing the scope and rigidity of the central plan.
2. Changing the plan instruments: plan directives and material allocation through the system of material balances were replaced with indirect regulators.
3. Increasing, in a limited way, the autonomy of enterprises (for certain categories more than for others), in most cases creating dual dependence for them: vertically on the authorities and horizontally on suppliers and customers. This established (in Tamás Bauer's phrase) an economy that was neither fully centrally planned nor anywhere near fully a market system.
4. Enlarging the second economy, but in a way that simultaneously promoted and constrained it. On the one hand, the austerity program in place since 1979 put great pressure on the work force to have two jobs (one in the first economy, for the sake of security and its entitlements; and one in the second economy, for money, and in some cases for creative satisfaction). It also provided opportunities, selectively, to engage in the second economy (selectively, because one had to have the right marketable skills or access to a plot of land). But, at the same time, the expansion of the second economy contravened many other objectives (such as social ownership of the means of production, price stability, successful competition for the first economy's most productive labor). For this reason, actions affecting the second economy were ambivalent and of Rube Goldbergian complexity, with the design changing frequently as the authorities attempted to reconcile so many contradictory objectives. As a consequence, the efficiency of the second economy has remained low and the cost to its participants high. About half of the work force has had to hold two jobs, so that

Hungarians, on average, are reported to work longer hours than any other nation's workers, leading to stress and to a significant deterioration in health and demographic indicators. The relationship between the first and second economies was full of bureaucratic irrationalities (more than in agriculture). This has contributed greatly to the corruption that has mushroomed during the last decade. But in spite of these negatives, reforms in the second economy were sufficiently important to generate all of the economy's modest growth in the 1980s.

5. Creating, since 1979, some of the institutional preconditions of a market system. Specifically, the authorities began to break up some of the large trusts in production and distribution and introduced legal provisions for establishing subsidiaries and new ventures (1979); combined three industrial-sector ministries into a single ministry, putting it in charge of industrial policy (1980); decentralized more and more of foreign trade decisionmaking (since 1980); eased and then eliminated production profile restrictions (1982-85); introduced a system of tenders for managerial positions (1983); introduced the right of enterprises to issue bonds (1983) and established a "stock market," where the bonds could be traded for an hour or so once a week; set up enterprise councils to elect and "supervise" the director (1985); enacted a (weak) bankruptcy law (1986); and created a two-tier banking system, without, however, all the conditions that would make it possible for commercial banks to be largely profit driven (1987).

Reforms and Economic Performance

While one should not minimize the importance of the many reform steps taken between 1979 and 1988, they did create an exaggerated impression in the West of what was taking place.

The importance of the institutional changes made between 1979 and 1988 for the economy's performance lay not mainly in their improvement of contemporary performance but in their potential. That is, these measures signaled the direction in which Hungary appeared to be moving and held out the hope that the fundamental problems would also be tackled.

The fundamental and mutually reinforcing problems that remained were these: Ill-defined ownership, no market for the factors of production, weak financial discipline in enterprises and in the state budget, no clear criteria for investment decisions other than the interests of the lobbies (partly a consequence of the ill-defined ownership structure), heavy taxation, and an incredibly complex and continually changing system of administrative and financial regulation that has tried, unsuccessfully, to reconcile a series of incompatible objectives, strategies, and system features.

None of the reforms introduced in the Kadar era had solved the fundamental question of ownership. As of 1988, the reforms had not yet succeeded in permitting an individual or an institution to have full property rights, that is, with full responsibility for and the right to appropriate the returns on productive assets. Regulation has often remained enterprise-specific in order to achieve economic and social objectives, such as domestic supply, exports, employment, and price stability.

These unsolved problems in large part explain the Hungarian economy's unsatisfactory performance. They were compounded by a number of major mistakes in economic policy. The most significant policy mistake was allowing foreign credits to rise much too rapidly.

At the same time, however, the reforms did yield significant results, especially in agriculture and in the second economy. Living standards improved considerably in the 1960s and early 1970s (thereafter the improvement was based on foreign credits). Hungary was able to move away from the classical shortage economy. The supply, assortment, and quality of food and many other consumer and industrial products became significantly better than those in most other CPEs. Queuing in retail stores was eliminated (but continued for a segment of the housing market, cars, and major repairs). For tourist purposes within the CMEA, the forint became practically a convertible currency.

Many of these improvements are not captured readily in standard economic statistics, such as the growth rate. Also, Hungary's economic statistics are considered by experts to be much more reliable, much less subject to exaggerations and distortions, than those of a number of East European countries against which its performance is often compared.

Transition after Kadar

Janos Kadar died in July 1989, a year after he was replaced in office. It was the intention of his successors to continue Kadar's policy of geopolitical balancing and domestic compromise. However, the new leaders did not realize that the two pillars supporting Kadar's policies — the Brezhnev Doctrine and steady improvements in the standard of living — had crumbled in the meantime.

By 1988, Gorbachev and his influential advisers in effect had repudiated the Brezhnev Doctrine and did so more explicitly the following year. From this, Hungary's leaders could infer that they were on their own and should not count on Soviet troop support under any circumstances. The repudiation of the Brezhnev Doctrine made it possible for Hungary's politically attuned population to express long-suppressed views and desires. The other pillar of the Kadar policy, steady improvements in the standard of living, could not be continued for the reasons already mentioned. There were no other reserves, under the prevailing model of the political economy, to tap.

Given the extremely high dependence of the Hungarian economy on imports from the West and the distaste of Hungary's military leaders for using troops against their own people, the communist leaders concluded that the best course was to make whatever domestic political concessions were sufficient to keep the lid on, given the potentially explosive situation in the country.

Many of the political liberalization measures introduced or accepted by the party during 1988-89 and early 1990 were intended as lightning rods for the pent-up tensions of the population, such as taking down the barbed-wire fortifications on the border with Austria; allowing unlimited travel to that neighboring country; giving Hungarians the right to have a valid global passport; permitting substantial press freedoms; revising the party's previous condemnation of the events of 1956; reinterring Imre Nagy who, as the communist prime minister during the revolution of 1956, was subsequently tried, executed, and secretly buried in a forest; and — the ultimate concession — agreeing to free elections.

To have even a modest chance to share political power with the emergent noncommunist parties, the Hungarian Socialist Workers (Communist) party disbanded in the fall of 1989. The dominant reform wing reconstituted itself as the Socialist party, embracing a social democratic platform similar to those of the Western European socialist parties. Along with most of the nearly dozen political parties that were formed during 1989, this Socialist party, too, offered a platform committed to political democracy and to a major role in the economy for market forces.

The two-stage elections that were held in March and April 1990 gave about 40 percent of the vote to the Democratic Forum. The Forum has several wings. Perhaps the strongest is the group espousing nationalist-populist policies. Another strong group — represented by the party's leader, Jozsef Antall, who subsequently became prime minister — is right of center, professing to be similar to the Christian Democrats in Germany. The third group is made up of former communists, who wish the party to maintain certain socialist ideas, although this is not the label they use nowadays. The Forum won the election by standing for a market-oriented change but promising to make the transition smoothly, cushioning the shocks, making the pace deliberate rather than hasty. The second-strongest party, with about 25 percent of the vote, is the Free Democrats. Although it, too, has wings, its leaders stood for a sharp break with the past and a quick transition, telling the electorate that the transition will be painful. The third-strongest party, with about 17 percent of the vote, is the Smallholders, with strength mainly in the rural areas, which ran on the platform of returning agricultural land to their former owners. Less than 10 percent each was obtained, respectively, by the Socialist (former Communist) party, the Christian Democrats, the Social Democrats, and FIDESZ (an idealistic group of mostly young people).

The Democratic Forum formed a coalition government, entering into partnership with the Smallholders and the Christian Democrats; the other parties became the opposition in the new National Assembly. In addition to the huge problems of dealing with the many unenviable legacies, the prime minister has his hands full trying to control his own party and to come up with workable compromises with his coalition partners.

Future Transformation:
Problems and Prospects

Hungary's reforms, implemented by the communist governments that ruled until April 1990, were not successful because political constraints forced compromises and inconsistencies that, in the end, stood in the way of attacking the economy's fundamental problems. Would it be correct, therefore, to conclude that now that the external and domestic political constraints have all but disappeared, Hungary's economic transition will proceed smoothly and with good prospects of success?

One lesson that scholars of socialist systems have learned in recent years is to avoid strong predictions. Nevertheless, it behooves us to point out the immense political, social, and economic difficulties in the path of successful transformation. The reason for being sober about prospects is the immense burden of the legacies and difficult dilemmas that Hungary's new, democratically elected government, and the population, have to contend with.

Hungary's constitutional state and political pluralism were destroyed by the communists during 1948-50. The rebuilding process was well under way by the summer of 1990, a few months after the free elections in March-April 1990.

But Hungary's new government and its democratic institutions are very fragile, not only because political life was disrupted for forty years or because of the present and often acrimonious feud between the parties that are reaching for power. There are also more fundamental reasons.

One is that coalition governments, especially those composed of more than two parties, are inherently unstable. Hungary is in the midst of an economic crisis whose resolution is uncertain, owing to a series of mutually reinforcing vicious circles (discussed below). Moreover, Hungary is overhauling its entire economic, social, and political system, which certainly will disrupt existing institutions, business networks, and social ties without being able to replace them quickly with smoothly functioning new institutions and relations. The costs of transformation will be paid immediately while many of its benefits will appear only later.

A still further reason that the new government is fragile is that many of Hungary's best brains are leaving the administration. Some are being pushed out by the worry that they will be held accountable for the mistakes of the communist leaders or will simply be sacked by the new rulers. Others are being pulled by the lucrative opportunities that are opening up for the best and the brightest in the rapidly expanding private sector.

Another problem is the disappointment felt by segments of the public in representative government, even before the institutions of such government have emerged from the present still-embryonic multiparty system. A growing number of people in Hungary are complaining about the multitude of political parties as well as about their tendencies to squabble over seeming irrelevancies rather than addressing the country's economic and social problems.

The economic potential of the transformation that is getting under way is very large. Whether, when, and to what extent this potential will be realized depends on the ability of the Hungarians to skillfully manage the political, social, and economic dilemmas they are facing.

The biggest short- and medium-term danger in Hungary is no longer that the Soviet Union will intervene in the country's internal affairs. Even if Gorbachev is replaced or changes course, leaders of the Soviet Union will have to deal with too many domestic crises to have much energy and resources left for determining East Europe's economic and political future.

Rather, the concern is that there will be great pressures and temptations for the new govenment to have a short-term horizon, to agree to unworkable compromises, or to follow populist policies — for example, to impose price controls, to soak the rich, and to blame foreign lenders and investors for economic problems.

Weighing against a pessimistic scenario, however, is the popular rejection in Hungary of the experience under both right-wing (1944) and left-wing dictatorships (1949-88), the emergence of democratic politics in the neighboring East European countries, the positive example of democratic market economies in Western Europe, and the economic and political leverage that Western and Asian democracies do have — if they are willing to use it — in influencing political and economic developments in Hungary and in the other countries of Eastern Europe.

Hungary today faces momentous economic dilemmas — some of them vicious circles. The new government has to tackle them all more or less simultaneously.

The Foreign Debt Burden

Hungary has a $21 billion convertible-currency debt (40 to 100% of GDP, depending on how GDP, valued in domestic currency, is converted to dollars). The debt-service ratio for the next several years is projected to be around 50 percent of convertible-currency merchandise exports. Stopping the further growth of Hungary's debt requires a trade surplus equivalent to 3 to 4 percent of GDP for several years. Unless the growth of Hungary's nearly stagnant economy can be accelerated quickly and exports increased substantially and in a sustained manner, the social-political costs of holding domestic absorption (consumption plus investment, plus net government expenditures) 2 to 4 percent below domestic production do not appear to be politically manageable. This is especially so in view of the fact that Hungary has been in a growth recession nearly continuously for a decade.

Until now, Hungary has avoided rescheduling, for which it was rewarded by continued access to foreign credits. But Hungary's major lenders now appear to be approaching their country limits for Hungary, unless unmistakable new signs appear soon that the new government is able to jumpstart the economy's growth and achieve a sustained expansion of convertible-currency exports.

Negotiating debt relief would be neither advisable nor simple. This is because Hungary owes much of its foreign debt to commercial banks and to bondholders rather than to foreign governments and international organizations. Debt rescheduling would not be in accord with IMF programs and would undermine the creditworthiness Hungary has fought so hard to maintain.

Inflationary Pressures

Inflation is already at 30 percent per annum and is accelerating. Many of the economic policy and systemic reform measures that are required at this stage in the transformation are likely to be inflationary, such as the following:

- Freeing more prices to be market determined will fuel price rises because Hungary is still a shortage economy, because industrial structure is so highly concentrated that many if not most firms have monopoly power, and because the balance of payments does not permit the economy to be opened up quickly to import competition.

- Owing to years of deficit financing, the Hungarian national debt is the equivalent of 65 percent of GDP, one of the highest in Europe. Stabilization requires that the deficits be brought under control and that subsidies be cut severely. But significant reduction of subsidies will push up prices or (if price rises are not allowed) cause large unemployment. Taxes on business and personal incomes are already high, so it is unlikely that they could be raised.

- Exchange rates are much lower (fewer forints per dollar) than what would be required for equilibrium in the balance of payments. But because the economy is inflexible, because Hungary is unable as yet to produce many goods and services that can be sold on the world market at competitive prices, and because of Western discrimination, bringing the exchange rate much nearer to equilibrium level would require a substantial depreciation. In Hungary's heavily import-dependent economy, this would increase prices substantially.

- The population fears — correctly, it seems — that the rate of inflation will continue to accelerate. Consequently, people are "escaping" into foreign currencies and other nonproductive assets, rather than saving and productively investing.

East-Bloc Trading

Hungary's trade and payments relations with its East-bloc partners are poor and likely to deteriorate further.

Hungary is unable to obtain from its CMEA partners the kinds of goods and services that its enterprises and consumers want. Much of the high-quality goods produced in the CMEA countries is exported to the West and not to other member nations, to pay for imports and for debt service. Moreover, the USSR's ability to continue to sell to Hungary acceptable-quality energy, raw materials, and intermediates is rapidly declining. The Soviet Union, on the verge of severe economic and political disruption itself, appears to have no choice but to effect sudden and drastic cuts in its export obligations to Eastern Europe. Since in the short run Hungary does not have the ability to reorient to the West all of its exports to the CMEA countries, it is also constrained from reorienting its imports, much of which is needed for capacity utilization and thus the maintenance of employment.

Another problem is the huge trade and current-account surplus that Hungary has been running in recent years with the CMEA countries — mainly the USSR — about $1 billion in 1989 alone. A combination of factors explains this:

- Decline in Hungary's imports from the CMEA (caused by supply, not demand, factors)

- Hungary's improved terms of trade

- The strong bargaining power of large Hungarian enterprises vis-à-vis their own authorities (Since export plans were approved earlier and represent obligations of the state, enterprises argue that forbidding them to export would not only be unfair but would also cause large unemployment.)

Hungary's large surplus is not convertible into hard currency. On the contrary, diverting supplies and inputs from the domestic and export markets adds to Hungary's inflation and balance-of-payments woes. This is why, early in 1990, Hungary's government imposed severe administrative restrictions on Hungarian exporters to the CMEA. This forced many to seek new markets in the West, often through joint ventures, and it is also causing growing bankruptcies and unemployment.

There is an even more fundamental problem, mentioned earlier: Enterprises have prospered by marketing their manufactures on the relatively "soft" CMEA market. But the more they have succeeded there, the more they have undermined their ability to compete on the world market, for the obvious reasons.

In 1989, the Hungarian government made a proposal to the Soviet Union to move the pricing and settlement of Hungarian-Soviet trade fully onto a convertible-currency basis. In June 1990 the Soviet Union accepted this; in fact, it now insists on a similar arrangement with each of the East European countries, as of January 1, 1991. But in the short run, this will have a substantial negative impact on Hungary's hard-currency payments.

In the medium and long run, however, important benefits will accrue to Hungary. Hungarian firms will have to compete with Western firms for a share of the Soviet market, will be under pressure to upgrade their products and to learn how to produce for the market. Equally important, the new arrangement will cut the umbilical cord that ties Hungarian firms to the authorities in their own country, with whom they have learned to bargain for all kinds of support and subsidies. Therefore, in time, the proposed new arrangements should improve the balance of payments. But how long will this take, and what might happen during the transition?

Can Efficiency Be Improved Quickly?

In the years preceding World War II, Hungary's average standard of living and productivity were approximately two-thirds those of Austria and perhaps half those of the most developed countries in Western Europe. Today, after four decades of the economy's being centrally directed, Hungary's relative position vis-à-vis Western Europe is significantly weaker. The basic problem is that the level of productive efficiency is almost uniformly low. The problem has many interrelated causes:

- Most firms in the "socialist" sector (the still essentially state-owned producers and large cooperatives) employ an excess of labor.

- Much of the capital equipment is outdated. Generally, the technology employed upstream and downstream in the production process is uneven and not well matched, impeding effective quality-control procedures.

- In agriculture — a sector where significant successes have been registered as a consequence of the reforms introduced since the mid-1960s — yields per acre are good, but efficiency is a problem. State and large cooperative farms employ much too much capital and are saddled with structures and technologies that are excessively capital- and energy-intensive. By contrast, private producers have insufficient access to the appropriate technology, so their mode of production is much too labor-intensive.

- Poor management is a pervasive problem in all sectors of the economy. The most fundamental reasons are insufficient competition and, in the socialist sector, the fact that no one has been able to effectively exercise many of the basic ownership functions.

There are great possibilities for improving the efficiency of production, provided that the constraints enumerated can be tackled successfully and more or less simultaneously.

Foreign Capital

The parliament of Hungary has promulgated an Act on Foreign Investment, which came into force on January 1, 1989. The legislation permits the establishment of Hungarian companies with foreign participation, foreign participation in existing Hungarian firms, and the setting up of wholly foreign-owned firms. To be sure, considerable legal, regulatory, and "business environmental" obstacles have to be overcome before foreign capital can be attracted on a large scale.

One of the main legal obstacles is that it is not entirely clear who in Hungary has the right to sell assets, including stocks in existing enterprises, and also what is to happen to the proceeds. It is also unclear on what basis the value of assets offered for sale is to be determined (given that, in most cases, there has been no competitive bidding).

These uncertainties have given rise, if not to corruption, to the perception of the general public (based on newspaper reports) that some of the privatization and sale of state property has been not fully at "arm's length," that it served more the interests of the managers who negotiated such deals, than those of the state, the owner.

Parliament is considering a new law that would centralize in the hands of the state the preparation and conduct of domestic privatization as well as that of large foreign investments. The new law may impose certain restrictions and may also make foreign investment more bureaucratic. Hopefully, it will also address some of the problems mentioned. In any event, although Hungary has clearly been marching toward liberalizing foreign investment, substantial economic, political, and legal uncertainties remain even after the new government has taken over.

Ownership

Who are the owners of Hungarian firms? During 1985-86, for the majority of state-owned firms, ownership was transferred to enterprise councils (50 percent appointed by management and 50 percent elected by the workers and employees). The intention was to take ownership away from the state so as to reduce state tutelage over the firms. Since at the time the political situation did not permit large-scale private ownership, a second-best solution was to establish enterprise councils. The solution did not result in substantial improvement in performance. One reason is that workers are much more concerned with such short-term issues as wage increases and employment security than with the long-term profitability of their business units.

Prospects

The medium-term future of Hungary hinges on the ability of the new government to move decisively in transforming Hungary's economy into a predominantly market-driven system while at the same time maintaining political stability and social peace. The new government is fragile and faces dissatisfaction arising from the country's decade-long austerity, accelerating inflation, fears for job security, and threats to vested interests.

All this may lead to explosions of social protest, strikes, hunger marches, and possibly even social disorder. In the absence of strong social organizations (like trade unions, chambers of commerce, professional bodies), which could control their own constituencies, the new government will have few partners to cooperate with. At the same time, the government will realize that unless radical transformation is attempted, the country will surely sink further economically and social tensions eventually will also become unmanageable. With radical transformation, the chances of success in the long run are enhanced considerably, but tensions in the short run will be greater.

Western Policy

Developments in Hungary, as elsewhere in Central and Eastern Europe, are fundamentally driven by internal forces. At the same time, both Soviet and Western policies are important. The interest of the West lies in seeing that Hungary moves, with all deliberate speed, toward becoming a democratic and market-oriented country in which human rights are respected and international obligations observed.

The successful integration of Central and East European reforming countries into the international economy is in the vital interest of the West. First and foremost, integration will prevent undesirable outcomes, such as emigrants flooding into Western Europe through the now practically open borders. Even more undesirable would be a negative "demonstration effect" in the Soviet Union and China, where conservative forces would be strengthened if even in Hungary the attempted transformation could not succeed within a reasonable time frame. What can the West do? The immediate task is to help (if requested) with the design and implementation of the extremely difficult problem of transition from a modified CPE to a more open, pluralistic, and market-driven system. The problem of transition is intellectual, financial, and political.

The intellectual task is to help design, with sufficient sensitivity to the local environment, a transition program: what needs to be done, why, how, and in what sequence?

The financial dimension is also important, and it is particularly tricky: How to ensure that the huge foreign debt will not place an unmanageable burden on the government during the especially difficult early years of the transition. At the same time, any debt relief or new credits that may be granted must be used productively and for the right purposes, rather than for postponing the changes that are needed, or simply piling more debt on an already high debt mountain. Therefore, the financial aspects of the problem, too, are in part design issues.

The political aspect is again difficult but important: How can the forces of democracy, tolerance, and professionalism be strengthened over the ascending forces of demagogy?

10. REFORM IN POLAND

Andrzej Korbonski

Introduction

Before launching into a discussion of reforms in Poland, it may be useful to dispose of some definitional issues. Let me begin by choosing a definition of reform that would provide us with a convenient yardstick for comparison and analysis. Interestingly enough — and perhaps not surprisingly — an American dictionary offers several definitions of reforms: one in terms of adjusting past policies, another emphasizing the notion of "improvement," and still another combining the previous two.[1] Personally, I am opposed to a definition that sees a reform as necessarily an improvement: After all, not every reform represents an improvement over the past: the post-1948 Stalinization of Eastern Europe was obviously a reform of the previous system, but it was hardly an improvement. Hence, in the analysis that follows I shall treat reform as an attempt to change past policies that in the eyes of the decision makers required an adjustment for one reason or another.

The second issue that needs clarification is the scope of the reforms — the breadth and depth of the adjustments. The record shows that, until most recently, scholarly attention in the West has been focused primarily on economic rather than on political reforms. The explanation of this emphasis is most likely the fact that throughout most of the past thirty years or so, most of the countries in Eastern Europe attempted to introduce some changes in their economies while being most reluctant to tamper with their political systems. There were, of course, significant exceptions such as Czechoslovakia in 1968; but by and large it was not until the second half of the present decade that we began to witness radical changes in the political systems of Hungary and Poland, not to mention the Soviet Union.

The analysis that follows will consider both political and economic reforms in the belief that they reinforce each other and that, for example, treating economic reforms as occurring in a political vacuum would give us a highly distorted and incomplete picture of the actual situation.[2] The same is true with regard to political reforms: by now there is considerable agreement that most political reforms in the communist camp have been induced by popular dissatisfaction caused by a deterioration in economic conditions.

The third issue concerns the time dimension of our analysis, which covers the eight-year period 1981–1989. This particular interval, from the imposition of martial law on December 13, 1981, to the swearing-in of the first noncommunist government of Poland in forty-five years on September 13, 1989, also witnessed a most fascinating process of reforming the political and economic system in Poland. To be sure, the changes in the 1980s represented a logical continuation of the process of reforms that began in Poland in the mid-1950s, but the earlier reforms will be mentioned only briefly.

Finally, there is the question of choosing the best method of analyzing the process of reform. As indicated at the outset, my own preference is to view reforms broadly, as part and parcel of the process of sociopolitical and economic change. Specifically, I see reform as an integral component of the process of democratization that has been taking place in some East European countries, including Poland, in the past few years.

The problem of democratization of nondemocratic societies has occupied the attention of political scientists for a long time, and much has been written about what conditions make democracy possible and what conditions enable it to survive.[3] In the 1970s, scholarly interest in this particular question was stimulated by the demise of authoritarian, nondemocratic regimes in Greece, Portugal, and Spain, all of which succeeded in establishing democratic polities. In addition, some attempts at democratizing bureaucratic-authoritarian rule in several Latin American countries have also attracted the attention of political scientists in the United States interested in the process of transition to democracy in the region.[4]

In contrast, the issue of democratization of communist states in Eastern Europe has been largely ignored by Western scholars, who apparently considered the topic intellectually unrewarding and uninteresting. Part of the reason for the neglect has been the lingering belief that, despite some changes, the traditional totalitarian model retained its validity, meaning that communist societies were not likely to change drastically in the foreseeable future.

To be sure, the events in Hungary and Poland in 1956 persuaded some experts that the Soviet monolith was beginning to show deep fissures and that communist political systems could change and even liberalize. As a result, in the late 1950s efforts were made to explain the differing reactions of individual East European countries to the de-Stalinization campaign decreed by Moscow, emphasizing such key factors as the magnitude of internal socioeconomic crisis, the degree of alienation of the working class and the intelligentsia from the regime, and the availability of alternative leadership.[5]

The developments in Eastern Europe in the 1960s, culminating in the Prague Spring of 1968, generated a new surge of interest in the process of liberalization in communist societies. The most comprehensive definition of the process of change away from the totalitarian model in a direction of a more liberal system was said to include the following:[6]

1. Changes in the structure of the political system, generally away from a one-party system with an autonomous dictator to one with collective leadership
2. Changes in the reliance on terror to elicit elite-approved social behavior, generally from a high reliance on terror to a moderate or even low reliance
3. Changes in the structure of the economic system, generally from a centralized economy to a decentralized, market-oriented socialist economy

While this definition appeared unambiguous and noncontroversial, it did not tell us much about the actual process of democratization. In order to throw some light on the various stages of that process, an attempt was made to define a "liberalization paradigm" with liberalization or democratization viewed as an outcome of changes occurring in a number of key political, social, and economic variables, which also determined the direction and depth of the process of change.[7]

Following this flurry of interest, scholarly concern with democratization of communist societies declined sharply in the 1970s, for reasons that are difficult to fathom. Scholarly attention during that period seemed to have been focused mostly on such issues as European security, economic reforms, Eurocommunism, and political dissent, without attempting to link them with the broader problem of transition to democracy. It was the events in Poland in 1980–1981 that once again aroused interest in the process of liberalization of communist rule.

The Dynamics of Reform

The question of how a communist East European country such as Poland could transform itself into a liberalized and ultimately a democratized polity is the focus of our discussion. However, before suggesting an approach that would more systematically explain the process of democratic reform, some observations are in order.

To begin with, while there is considerable consensus that communist regimes can and do change, there is still some disagreement regarding the character of that change, as between "liberalization" and "democratization."[8] The former is viewed by some as simply a synonym for de-Stalinization: the essentials of the communist system remain essentially unchanged, the impulse for the reforms comes from above, the stimulus is usually from the outside, and the whole process meets with relatively moderate resistance from within the system. In contrast, "democratization" is a much rarer phenomenon, characterized by far more drastic political and institutional changes, by strong pressure from below, and by a much greater resistance from the system. This is not the place to deal with the controversy. It may be argued that making a sharp distinction between these two concepts is neither convincing nor useful, and that in Eastern Europe for the past thirty years we have witnessed a synthesis of the two phenomena rather than two separate processes. What matters here is the ultimate goal or target of these processes — which is a "liberalized" or "democratized" system. For the purpose of the discussion, I shall define the latter to be a system containing a measure of pluralism, a degree of political and economic decentralization, and freedom of expression by the system's participants.[9]

Although the above definition of a "liberalized" or "democratized" system may not be conceptually watertight, it has several advantages, one of which is its neutrality in the geographic and systemic sense. Its major disadvantage lies in the difficulty of measuring the degree or weight of the three major components. In other words, how does one measure pluralism and freedom of expression? There is no satisfactory answer to this question, and ultimately we are forced to rely on intuition and informed guessing, pending availability of additional empirical data.

What I call the "paradigm of reform-making" in Poland in 1981–1989, which I consider a key aspect of the process of transition from the traditional communist system to a democratized polity, consists of eleven variables, grouped as follows:[10]

I. Background conditions
  1. Economic difficulties
  2. Divisions within the party
  3. Alienation of intellectuals and youth
  4. Political reforms
II. Changeover conditions
  5. Changes in the party
  6. Changes in the government
  7. Changes in the economy
III. Democratization conditions
  8. Emergence of pluralism
  9. Freedom of expression
  10. Economic reforms
  11. Tolerance by other communist countries

The first four variables, grouped together under the heading of "background conditions," are thought to be responsible for setting the stage for the process of liberal reform. The intermediate stage of "changeover conditions" lists changes and reforms in the key components of the polity and the economy, which caused the appearance of the third stage in the process, the "democratization conditions." The individual variables are in most cases aggregates that will be disaggregated and discussed in greater detail below.

Each variable and subvariable is assigned a rank of "high," "mixed," and "low," and similar values are assigned to each of the three major categories. Finally, an overall judgment will be made with regard to the question under discussion — the chances of reform in Poland in the 1980s resulting in creation of a lasting and successful democratized state. The results are shown in table 1.

One final clarification is in order, and it concerns the time dimension of each category of conditions. It is obvious that the longer the time span, the larger the number of conditions one is likely to find changing. Rather arbitrarily, I decided to limit "background conditions" to the period 1981–1986, or from the imposition of martial law in December 1981 to the announcement of a far-ranging amnesty in September 1986. The "changeover conditions" span the three-year period from 1986 to 1988, from the 1986 amnesty to the announcement of roundtable negotiations between the government and the opposition in September 1988. The "democratization conditions" will cover the one-year period 1988–1989, between the roundtable announcement and the formal parliamentary approval of the Mazowiecki cabinet in September 1989.

TABLE 1

Democratization Paradigm: Poland, 1981–1989

I. Background conditions: 1981–1986

1.	Economic difficulties	high
2.	Divisions within the Communist party	mixed
3.	Alienation of intellectuals and youth	high
4.	Political reforms	mixed
	TOTAL JUDGMENT	mixed-high

II. Changeover conditions: 1986–1988

5.	Changes in the Communist party	mixed-low
	a. First secretary	low
	b. Politburo	mixed
	c. Central Committee	mixed
	d. Lower party organs	low
6.	Changes in the government	mixed
	a. Head of State	low
	b. Council of Ministers	high
	c. Armed Forces command	low
	d. Parliament (Sejm)	mixed
7.	Changes in the economy	high
	TOTAL JUDGMENT	mixed-high

III. Democratization conditions: 1988–1989

8.	Emergence of pluralism	high
	a. Political parties	high
	b. Political clubs	high
	c. Labor unions	high
	d. Youth organizations	high
9.	Freedom of expression	high
10.	Economic reforms	high
11.	Tolerance by other communist countries	high
	TOTAL JUDGMENT	high
	Probability of a lasting democratized system	high

Changes and Reforms: 1981–1989

I. Background Conditions

1. ECONOMIC DIFFICULTIES: The striking deterioration in Poland's economic situation in the wake of martial law imposed in December 1981 has been extensively documented and discussed in the literature, and there is no need to go over it again. It suffices to say that probably the most shocking element was the steep decline in the country's gross national product, due primarily to the fall in industrial production. Despite rather impressive performance of the agricultural sector, which showed a steady growth throughout the period, there was a striking reduction in the living standard and household consumption, pushing them back to the levels of the 1970s. Poland's hard-currency debt kept increasing, mostly because of the country's inability to keep up with interest payments. The United States-led Western embargo on credits and other restrictions on trade made the situation worse. The government tried to deal with it partly through drastic price reforms intended to reduce inflationary pressure, and partly through the announcement of an economic reform modeled after that in Hungary, but both measures proved ineffective. By the middle of the 1980s, the overall economic situation appeared worse than ever.

2. DIVISIONS WITHIN THE PARTY: The imposition of martial law actually defused much of the intraparty conflict that was so visible in 1980–81. Although there may have been some resentment of General Wojciech Jaruzelski's being the top leader in addition to his holding the premiership and being in command of the military, the party's *apparat* and its rank and file realized only too well that but for martial law and Jaruzelski's apparent refusal to negotiate with both the Catholic church and Solidarity, their situation in the post-1981 period would have been much worse.

   Thus, although the party appeared united on the surface, the old differences between the hard- and softliners appeared as wide as ever. The former group was rather closely identified with Moscow, and as long as Brezhnev was alive, they could not be touched. With the changeover in the Kremlin, the traditional links also began to change. Neither Andropov nor Chernenko apparently raised serious objections to Jaruzelski's purge of the hardliners following the assassination of the Reverend Jerzy Popieluszko. The Tenth Party Congress in June 1986, attended by Mikhail Gorbachev, witnessed a major reshuffle in both the Politburo and the Central Committee and seemed to provide a good testimony to

Jaruzelski's ability to control the party. That this was a false impression became obvious less than two years later, when several Politburo and Central Committee members viewed as loyal and reliable strongly opposed opening a dialogue between the party and the opposition. For the time being, however, in the mid-1980s the party appeared less divided than in the previous ten years.

3. ALIENATION OF INTELLECTUALS AND YOUTH: Alienation of intellectuals and youth has been a feature of the Polish political and cultural scene since the mid-1950s, and over the years it has escalated rather than declined. Even before the creation of Solidarity in August 1980, the intellectuals were in the forefront of anti-regime activities, first as the moving spirits behind the Worker's Defense Committee (KOR), formed in 1976, and then together with the students as creators of the so-called "Flying University" in 1977–1978. Not surprisingly, many of the leading intellectuals acted as advisers to Solidarity in the critical negotiations in the summer of 1980, and many of them remained within the workers' movement as advisers, editors, or spokesmen.[11] Again, not surprisingly, most of them were arrested on December 13, 1981, and were kept interned for a rather long time.

As part of a comprehensive housecleaning, the military junta ordered a dissolution of various associations representing intellectuals and students and tried, without much success, to bring back the system of the discredited "transmission belts." Following their release from internment camps, the intellectuals as a rule continued their resistance either by involvement in the so-called "second circulations" of illegally published books and articles or by maintaining informal circles of writers and artists opposed to the Jaruzelski regime. Several of them were ultimately rearrested, and most of them suffered a good deal of discrimination of various kinds. As a result, the alienation of these two key groups in the mid-1980s was higher than ever.

4. POLITICAL REFORMS: The early hopes of the government's resuming the triangular dialogue among itself, the church, and Solidarity came to nothing during 1982, but it also became clear that the Jaruzelski regime right from the start was trying to restore some sense of political normalcy, without compromising, at least initially, its own tough stance. Among the most important steps in the process of restoring a semblance of political relaxation were the suspension and then the abolition of martial law; a continuing flirtation with the church; the drastic purge of the security apparatus in 1984; and the talk about reforms of the electoral system, including the possibility of a popular referendum, the first one since 1946. The far-

reaching amnesty resulted in a release of some of the best-known opposition leaders, whom everyone had expected to be tried soon and sentenced to long prison terms. It was the most surprising event and testified to Jaruzelski's eagerness to resume some kind of dialogue with the opposition. There were two possible reasons for the softening of the regime's stance: one, the continuing strength of the opposition, characterized, for example, by regular demonstrations by workers and students; and, two, support given to Jaruzelski by Mikhail Gorbachev, who not only attended the Tenth Party Congress but also went out of his way to endorse Jaruzelski's policies, including, most importantly, the purging of the secret police and the appointment of General Czeslaw Kiszczak, a close confidant of Jaruzelski's, as minister of the interior. He replaced another general, Jerzy Milewski, who was generally identified as Moscow's man in Warsaw.

Looking back at the situation in Poland toward the end of 1986, it was a snowballing crisis. It became apparent that neither the imposition of martial law nor its ultimate lifting had succeeded in establishing even a modicum of political or economic stability. With the possible exception of agriculture, the economy continued deteriorating, and the proclaimed economic reform made hardly any headway. While the government managed to achieve some successes in removing some of the worst hardliners, it could not summon up enough political will to initiate a serious dialogue with the opposition. Still, it appeared that negotiations were only a matter of time and that the beginning of a second stage in the democratization process was around the corner.

II. Changeover Conditions

5. CHANGES IN THE PARTY: The two-year period 1986–1988 produced relatively few changes at the top of the party hierarchy. The Politburo and the Central Committee elected at the Tenth Party Congress in June 1986 appeared at least initially to be "safe" and loyal to General Jaruzelski, who was responsible for choosing most of them. One of the most interesting aspects of his choice was a rather obvious attempt to increase the number of workers on the Central Committee at the expense of the bureaucrats and intelligentsia. The workers, needless to say, were members of the low-echelon *nomenklatura* and occupied the positions of party secretaries in mining and heavy industry, which together with other smokestack industries were increasingly mentioned as most likely to be closed down.

Thus, by and large, in contrast to the Politburo, the Central Committee appeared conservative and unenthusiastic about Jaruzelski's overtures to the opposition. Within the Politburo, the general could rely on several loyal supporters who apparently shared his vision of a reconciled and stable Poland. They included the two generals — Florian Siwicki, the minister of defense, and Kiszczak, the recently appointed minister of the interior — some veterans such as Kazimierz Barcikowski, the perennial troubleshooter; Jozef Czyrek, often viewed as number two in the Politburo; and Stanislaw Ciosek, an up-and-coming politician whose task it was to maintain good relations with the workers, including members of Solidarity. The situation in the regions remained essentially unchanged. The local *nomenklatura* had not yet been affected by the changes at the very top although there was growing evidence of some apprehension on the part of the regional secretaries, who realized that popular dissatisfaction with the economy was increasing and who feared a repetition of the events of the summer of 1980. That such fears were well founded was amply demonstrated by two waves of strikes, in Silesia and the Baltic Coast — the former in the spring and the latter in late summer of 1988. In both cases the impact of the strikes was unexpectedly powerful, especially considering that neither of them showed signs of spilling over and becoming a general strike affecting the entire country. The reason was that from the beginning the local party officials had proved unable to negotiate with the strikers, and ultimately the government had to call upon Lech Walesa, the supposedly discredited and forgotten leader of Solidarity, to help restore law and order. Moreover, it became clear that the strikers of 1988 were much tougher to deal with than the workers of 1980, and even Walesa had considerable difficulty persuading them to return to work. Thus, it may be said that, despite an absence of significant change in the regional party personnel, the party was clearly losing control of the country at large.

6. CHANGES IN THE GOVERNMENT: Insofar as the government proper was concerned, General Jaruzelski continued as head of state, holding onto his chairmanship of the Council of State. The period 1986–1988 witnessed two major changes that affected Jaruzelski personally and that most likely enhanced his stature. One of them was his success in breaking out of the international isolation in which Poland found itself in the wake of martial law. For several years after that, Jaruzelski himself was generally viewed as a villain and a pariah on the international scene, especially in the United States. All this began to change, and in the second half of the 1980s Jaruzelski once again began to meet foreign leaders and dignitaries, suggesting that the period of ostracism was coming to an end. At the same time, it was becoming obvious that he was also developing a close relationship with Gorbachev and that he was assuming once again a leading position in the Warsaw alliance, which he had appeared to lose to Erich Honecker at the beginning of the decade. Domestically, Jaruzelski continued sending conciliatory signals to not only the opposition but also the

population at large. In 1987 he created a Consultative Council composed of leading intellectuals, most of them outside the party, which was intended to advise him on various issues. He continued developing warm relations with the church and in 1988 paid an official visit to the Vatican. There was little doubt that both his domestic and international stature rose dramatically in the previous few years.

While Jaruzelski was gaining popularity, the prime minister, Zbigniew Messner, and his council of ministers were losing theirs. Here the principal reason was the progressive deterioration of economic conditions and the inability of the government to stop the decay. On top of that, the regime's failure to settle the spring and fall strikes added to the discomfiture of the government, which was finally forced to resign in October 1988. Although it is hard to offer a single reason for the government's fall, the economic crisis was clearly the principal cause. Moreover, by August it had already become obvious that the prime minister simply could not speak a common language with Walesa and the opposition. The government's side in the developing dialogue with the workers was taken over by Kiszczak, the interior minister, who was also the first government and party leader to suggest the possibility of roundtable negotiations with the opposition.

Soon after a new government was formed under the leadership of another of Jaruzelski's close friends, Mieczyslaw Rakowski, who managed to overcome Soviet suspicion and get himself elected to the Politburo. Rakowski took his time in selecting the ministers, and he tried, for the first time in Poland's postwar history, to recruit well-known opposition leaders to his cabinet — alas, without success. Still, the new government included some new and interesting ministers, and there was some hope that it would be more successful than its predecessors in doing something for the economy.

The new cabinet made no changes in the Ministries of Defense and Interior. This suggested that both Generals Kiszczak and Siwicki were in favor of the policy of bridge-building, clearly pushed by Jaruzelski. As mentioned above, Kiszczak became the architect of the roundtable negotiations, and Siwicki, as well as the rest of Poland's high military command, showed not the slightest disagreement with the policy. The Polish secret police, thoroughly purged after the Popieluszko killing, appeared faithful and loyal to Kiszczak; and the same was true for the armed forces, where Jaruzelski remained as popular as ever. All this meant that a reimposition of the martial law of 1981 in the late 1980s was less and less likely.

The final institution that deserves some attention is the national assembly, or Sejm. To no one's surprise, the Sejm also began to change rather dramatically in the second half of the decade. It may be said that during the early eighties, the Sejm behaved largely in its traditional manner, as a rubber-stamping institution, and the contrast between the changes in the country as a whole and the passivity of the constitutionally highest decision-making body was striking. The assembly obediently continued to pass restrictive legislation ordered by the government, which progressively curtailed civil rights and in some cases appeared openly to violate the constitution. Nothing in the Sejm's behavior suggested the dramatic changes that were to transform it into the truly dynamic parliament of 1989.

7. CHANGES IN THE ECONOMY: The only thing that can be said about the economic situation was that it showed no improvement between 1986 and 1988. Neither the economic reforms supposedly being introduced since 1982 nor various ad hoc income and price policies applied by the Messner government seemed to help in slowing down inflation and reversing the decline in industrial production. The government was simply too weak to implement tough and consistent deflationary measures, preferring instead to print money and grant indiscriminate across-the-board pay raises to workers who were becoming increasingly militant. Although the previously mentioned strikes were mostly led by supporters of Solidarity, the workers belonging to the official labor unions were also getting restless.

It was clear that unless some drastic measures were taken soon, the country might well face another series of angry explosions and confrontations in the coming winter. The government's proposal to start roundtable negotiations with the opposition must be seen in this light.

III. Democratization conditions

8. EMERGENCE OF PLURALISM: Although the initial proposal for government-opposition talks was made in September 1988, for a while it appeared as if the communist regime might disavow its offer. Even after the television debate between Walesa and the leader of the official unions, Alfred Miodowicz, in November, ending in a striking victory for the head of Solidarity, the Rakowski government still hesitated to follow up on the talks.

The government's reluctance was most likely due to the growing resistance to the talks on the part of significant segments of the Communist party, which viewed the planned discussions as a major threat to its own survival and began to accuse Jaruzelski, still the party's first secretary, of outright betrayal and selling out. At the two-part Tenth Central Committee Plenum in December 1988-January 1989, Jaruzelski and some of his closest collaborators put all their prestige on the line and had to threaten to resign in order to have the roundtable talks approved.

Once again it was a Pyrrhic victory for the party. Jaruzelski won the day, but the price he had to pay was high. It amounted to a de facto split in the party, which deepened in the aftermath of the talks and especially in the wake of the June 1989 parliamentary elections. As a result of these elections, the party remained sharply divided into three parts: the hardline faction, supported by regional and local party *apparatchiki,* some of whom are still on the Central Committee; the reformist wing, led by young Central Committee secretaries coopted after the June 1989 elections; and the center, headed by the new first secretary, Rakowski, who exchanged his premiership for the leadership of the party in July 1989. These divisions continued until the next party congress, which, originally scheduled for 1991, met on January 27–29, 1990. At the congress, the existing party was dissolved and two new parties created, with the claim that this move showed adherence to social democratic principles.

The two satellite parties, the United Peasant party and the Democratic party, which had served as faithful and loyal transmission belts for the Communist party for at least four decades, experienced considerably less turmoil than their master and certainly showed no great desire to break out of the electoral alliance with the Communists agreed upon at the roundtable talks. It was only after the Communist debacle in the June 1989 elections that the leaders of the two parties decided to abandon their patrons and negotiate with the victorious Solidarity in order to divide the spoils and allocate cabinet seats.

Although Solidarity still saw itself as a labor movement rather than a political party, during the roundtable discussions and later, in the course of the pre-election campaign, it had little choice but to assume the standard trappings of a party competing for electoral votes. To be sure, its political wing chose to call itself a "citizens' club," but in this case it was clearly a misnomer. Also, after the elections, in the course of the prolonged negotiations on the composition of the government, Solidarity leaders behaved as members of a political party and not as members of a political club.

Thus by mid-1989 it was obvious that political pluralism had arrived in Poland with a vengeance. In addition to the three political parties discussed above, the spring and summer of 1989 saw a proliferation of political clubs and associations of various hues, which mushroomed following the Sejm's passage of a new law on associations.[12] The rapid growth in the number of associations was followed by another fascinating phenomenon — the return to the political scene of parties banned at the beginning of the communist takeover, such as the National Democratic party and the Labor party, not to mention others outlawed somewhat later, such as the Polish Peasant party. The competition among the political parties and clubs was paralleled by even fiercer competition between Solidarity and the official unions. This particular struggle began escalating in the mid-1980s, when Solidarity was still outlawed and the official unions tried not only to recruit many Solidarity members but also to preempt many Solidarity policies.

While the government-sponsored unions scored some successes, the previously mentioned television debate and a rather embarrassing debacle suffered by the leader of the official unions showed conclusively that Walesa and Solidarity had lost little of their appeal. The official unions tried to sabotage the roundtable negotiations and also threatened to disrupt the election campaign, but ultimately their efforts came to nothing.

Among the youth organizations, the most notorious proved to be the Independent Student Union (NZS), which was banned by the government after martial law, as were many professional organizations such as the writers' and journalists' associations. However, while the latter were ultimately legalized in early 1989, the Student Union was not, and that in itself threatened to destabilize the political situation. However, the Union was finally made legal following the swearing-in of the noncommunist government in September 1989.

The record shows that the Catholic church remained influential in 1988–1989, although it attempted to maintain a rather low profile during the roundtable talks and election campaign. The record shows that between the Gdansk accords of August 1980 and the imposition of martial law in December 1981, the attitude of the church toward Solidarity remained rather cool, which could be explained by the fact that the episcopate was gradually becoming envious of the movement's pre-empting the leadership of the anticommunist opposition, until then monopolized by the church.

It may be further argued that the period following the imposition of martial law reflected an extremely cautious policy on the part of the church. During that time Primate Jozef Glemp, the leader of the Polish church, did everything possible not to antagonize the Jaruzelski regime. While the primate was helpful in arranging the second visit of Pope John Paul II to Poland in 1983, it is clear that the visit was not a resounding success, especially when compared to the pontiff's visit in 1979; and its main accomplishment was a papal semi-legitimization of the Jaruzelski government. In light of the above, it is not surprising that there developed a major split within the church, between the higher and the lower clergy. One may speculate that because of all this, the decision was taken in the mid-1980s to reduce the church's role in Polish domestic politics. The most recent event affecting the church was the 1989 reestablishment of diplomatic relations between Warsaw and the Holy See, which were broken off in 1945.

To sum up, in the second half of 1989 Poland appeared for all practical purposes to be a free, pluralistic polity, with political parties, political clubs and associations, labor unions, and student associations competing with each other for support and membership. Although the 1989 electoral law still gave a major advantage to the Communist party, that advantage was seriously compromised by the behavior of the Communist allies, who simply switched allegiance and began to support Solidarity.[13] There was growing talk about speeding up the next parliamentary elections, which were to be completely free.

9. FREEDOM OF EXPRESSION: Some major cracks in the seemingly impenetrable facade of censorship were first achieved in 1981 as a result of pressure exerted by Solidarity. During most of the eighties, the censors behaved selectively, allowing ever greater freedom to different mass media. As a result, on the eve of the momentous changes in 1988-1989, censorship de facto disappeared in the cases of books and periodicals, and its use with respect to daily newspapers and some weeklies became even more selective than in the past, which meant that especially the dailies became essentially free.

The growth of the so-called "second circulation" *(drugi obieg)* continued unabated, and it was only a matter of time for the distinction between the legal and semi- or illegal publication sectors to disappear completely.

10. ECONOMIC REFORMS: As economic conditions continued deteriorating from 1988 into 1989, ways of improving the economy formed one of the most important topics of the roundtable negotiations. An agreement hammered out between the Communist party and the opposition called for several drastic measures intended, above all, to reduce inflation and stabilize the economy. They included the introduction of so-called "indexing," an escalator clause calling for 80 percent compensation for price increases, hoping this way to slow down the inflationary spiral and eventually bring it under control. Other decisions included lifting of food rationing, removal of price controls, marketization of food sales, and gradual privatization. Obviously, after years if not decades of indecision, the leaders of all political parties and labor unions agreed that extraordinary measures were needed to restore some semblance of normalcy to the Polish economy. Moreover, if Poland were to get badly needed economic aid from the West, it had to demonstrate its serious commitment to renovating the entire economic system. Judging from government decisions made in the second half of October, the program of reforms is on the right track.

By now there is clear consensus that the economic reform introduced in Poland on January 1, 1990, represents by far the most drastic attempt to overhaul a Soviet-type economy and to introduce a competitive free-market economic system. At the time of this writing (March 1990) it is still too early to say anything concrete about the reform's success or failure, but preliminary results suggest that for the first time in the long history of Polish economic reforms (going back to 1958), the strong medicine applied to the ailing economy seems to work, inspiring some optimism among both Eastern and Western observers.[14]

11. TOLERANCE BY OTHER COMMUNIST COUNTRIES: Needless to say, the attitude of other communist countries to the process of democratic reforms has been of great importance for the success or failure of these reforms. The record has shown very clearly that at least until the mid-1980s, the Soviet Union and Poland's immediate neighbors — Czechoslovakia and East Germany — watched the developments in Poland with considerable suspicion. Although the imposition of martial law in 1981 seemed to alleviate most of their concern, it can be argued that it was not until the arrival of Gorbachev on the Soviet scene and his own initiation of reform policies that the Polish reforms acquired some legitimacy in the Warsaw alliance. In the second half of the decade, the Warsaw Pact became divided between the reformist countries — the USSR, Hungary, and Poland — and the conservative, anti-reform states — Bulgaria, Czechoslovakia, East Germany, and Romania. Obviously, having the support of Gorbachev helped Jaruzelski in his own policy of reforms, which included reaching an accommodation with the political opposition.

Similarly, the Soviet endorsement of Polish democratic reforms, including the formation of the noncommunist government of Prime Minister Tadeusz Mazowiecki, largely disarmed the hardline East European critics, led by Nicolae Ceausescu, who, according to recently released information, at one point advocated the invasion of Poland by Warsaw Pact troops in order to stop the process of democratization.[15]

Conclusion

The question to be asked at this stage concerns the probability of the various democratic reforms' resulting in the creation of a lasting democratic political system in Poland. As was discussed above, 1981–1989 was not the only period in Polish postwar history in which an attempt was made to introduce liberal or democratic reforms. Similar efforts were undertaken in 1953–1956, 1968–1971, and 1976–1981; and, as shown elsewhere, they met with failure rather than success.[16]

Comparing the character and intensity of the various changes and reforms in 1981-1989 with those that took place in the past, it becomes clear that in contrast with those of the fifties, sixties, and seventies, the chances of success were much brighter for the most recent reforms. The preceding discussion has tried to explain the reasons for the optimism, and the results of the analysis are shown in table 1.

There is little doubt that despite the favorable prediction discussed above, the ultimate resolution of the Polish crisis depends greatly, if not totally, on the success or failure of the drastic economic experiment introduced in the country at the beginning of 1990. As suggested earlier, the initial signs are positive in both the economic and political spheres: the various economic indicators show clear progress, and popular support for the Solidarity government continues unabated, despite harsh economic measures. A major factor in economic reforms is, of course, the attitude of the West; and here, too, both the United States and Western Europe have proven highly supportive in economic and political terms. The question, "Is Poland out of the crisis?" cannot be answered with total confidence, but the preliminary evidence appears most encouraging. Another factor of crucial importance for the future of Poland is the role of individual leaders in the process of reform. The history of the past forty years has shown rather conclusively that Poland has poor luck with its political leaders, who often begin their rule on a wave of popular support that they soon squander for one reason or another. Wladyslaw Gomulka in October 1956 was probably the only truly legitimate ruler in communist Poland, yet fourteen years later he was universally hated and finally ousted ignominiously from his post. Although Edward Gierek never achieved Gomulka's original stature, for a few years he generated considerable support in his efforts to improve the country's economic well being. He also ended up discredited and humiliated. Wojciech Jaruzelski, perhaps more than anyone else, seemed destined to break the vicious circle and become accepted as the country's second legitimate leader after Gomulka. But in his case, the decision to impose martial law destroyed his chances.

From a perspective of eight years, the martial-law decision looks different than it did in 1981. However, much more significant is the fact that Jaruzelski, who was generally hated following martial law, somehow refused to give in and gradually managed to build a base of support — so effectively that beginning in 1986 he was able to embark on a policy of liberal reforms that brought the country to the situation of mid-1989 and its noncommunist government — something unthinkable only a short while earlier. By hindsight it is clear that, although the victory of democracy had many fathers, Jaruzelski played an absolutely key role in the process, a role perhaps not fully appreciated and awaiting a separate analysis. The fact remains that throughout most of the period under discussion, Jaruzelski was in the position to do considerable harm and even to stop the democratic process altogether, just as he had not hesitated to impose martial law when he felt that the country was threatened with civil war. The fact that he allowed the process of democratization to proceed unimpeded is a testimony to his own sense of leadership and responsibility for Poland's democratic future. The other key actor on the Polish scene in the 1980s was, of course, Lech Walesa, most likely the most charismatic leader in recent Polish history. Just as no one really expected General Jaruzelski to become an acknowledged leader in the process of democratic reform, no one believed that Walesa, the highly visible and popular leader of Solidarity during 1980–1981, would ever be able to make a political come-back following years of living in obscurity and being subjected to consider-able criticism by his erstwhile supporters. The fact that he was able to over-come various obstacles and hindrances and assume a leading role in the negotiations that began in 1988 speaks for itself; and, as in the case of Jaruzelski, it provides a telling testimony to Walesa's extraordinary leader-ship qualities and genuine charisma.

Thus, to conclude, for the first time in its modern history, Poland has had the rare good fortune to produce two leaders who for once did not bend and surrender to adversity but were willing to take considerable risks in order to lead the country out of the crisis that threatened its very exis-tence. Although the ultimate victory is not yet in sight, both men will go down in history as the major architects of democratic reform, without which Poland could not even dream of rejoining Europe and resuming normal existence.

Notes

1. *Webster's New Collegiate Dictionary* (Springfield, MA: G. & C. Merriam Company, 1974), p. 971.

2. Andrzej Korbonski, "The Politics of Economic Reforms in Eastern Europe: The Last Thirty Years," *Soviet Studies* 41, no. 1 (January 1989), pp. 1–19.

3. See, for example, Dankwart A. Rustow, "Transitions to Democracy," *Comparative Politics* 2, no. 3 (April 1970), pp. 337–63.

4. Philippe C. Schmitter, "Speculations about the Prospective Demise of Authoritarian Regimes and Its Possible Consequences," Latin American Program, The Wilson Center, *Working Paper* No. 60, 1981; and Kevin J. Middlebrook, "Prospects for Democracy: Regime Transformation and Transitions from Authoritarian Rule," ibid., *Working Paper* No. 62, 1981.

5. Zbigniew Brzezinski, *The Soviet Bloc*, rev. ed. (Cambridge, MA: Harvard University Press, 1967), pp. 205–6.

6. Chalmers Johnson, "Comparing Communist Nations," in Chalmers Johnson, ed., *Change in Communist Systems* (Stanford, CA: Stanford University Press, 1970), p. 3.

7. Andrzej Korbonski, "Comparing Liberalization Processes in Eastern Europe: A Preliminary Analysis," *Comparative Politics* 4, no. 2 (January 1972), pp. 231–49, and "Liberalization Processes," in Carmelo Masa-Lago and Carl Beck, eds., *Comparative Socialist Systems* (Pittsburgh: University of Pittsburgh Center for International Studies, 1975), pp. 192–214.

8. Guillermo O'Donnell and Philippe C. Schmitter, *Transitions from Authoritarian Rule* (Baltimore and London: The Johns Hopkins University Press, 1986), pp. 7–11; and Adam Przeworski, "Some Problems in the Study of the Transition to Democracy," in Guillermo

O'Donnell, Philippe C. Schmitter, and Laurence Whitehead, eds., *Transitions from Authoritarian Rule: Comparative Perspectives* (Baltimore and London: The Johns Hopkins University Press, 1986), pp. 53–58.

9. Korbonski, "Liberalization Processes," p. 194.

10. Korbonski, "Transition to Democracy in Eastern Europe," paper presented at the U.S. State Department Conference on "Democratization in Communist Countries," Washington, D.C., 18–19 October 1982.

11. For an interesting discussion of the role of the intellectuals in the East European ferment, see Timothy Garton Ash, "Eastern Europe: The Year of Truth," *New York Review of Books*, no. 2, 15 February 1990.

12. For a listing of various clubs and associations, see "Opozycja w Polsce," *Reporter* (Warsaw), Spring 1989.

13. .The new electoral law, approved as part of the roundtable agreement in early April 1989, called for 65 percent of the seats in the lower house (Sejm) to be allocated to the Communist party and its allies and 35 percent to the opposition. The 100 seats in the resurrected upper chamber (Senat), were to be contested without prior restrictions. In the wake of the June 1989 elections, in which the opposition won 99 seats in the Senat and all 35 percent of the seats in the Sejm, the United Peasant party and the Democratic party, which together controlled 22 percent of seats in the lower house and which until then were traditionally allied with the Communists, switched their allegiance and joined the opposition in electing the first noncommunist government of Poland since 1945.

14. John Kifner, "Poland's Chances to a Free Market Show Early Gains," *New York Times*, 3 March 1990.

15. Flora Lewis, "Good/Bad News," *New York Times*, 11 October 1989.

16. Korbonski, "Liberalization processes," passim.

17. For a somewhat different view, see Grzegorz Ekiert, "Democratization Processes in East Central Europe: A Theoretical Reconsideration," unpublished paper, Harvard University, October 1989.

11. REFORM IN YUGOSLAVIA

Lenard J. Cohen

Yugoslavia on the Brink:
From Socialist Reform to Post-Socialism

Reform has been the quintessential feature of Yugoslav socialism. Initially fashioned as a makeshift alternative to Soviet-type socialism in the wake of the Tito-Stalin split, Yugoslavia's regime-sponsored reforms gradually acquired stature as a distinct model of Marxist development. The notion of workers' self-management — originating with the slogan "factories to the workers," and later recast as a more participatory form of "self-managed socialism" — has served as the conceptual basis and label for the Yugoslav reform model. During the 1950s and 1960s, efforts by the Belgrade regime to construct a less bureaucratized and more democratic variant of socialism won widespread praise both within and outside Eastern Europe. By early 1973 Edward Kardelj, the principal architect of most major Tito-era reforms, could proudly assert that "self-management had not only demonstrated its economic effectiveness," but also allowed Yugoslavia to "solve democratically most of the contradictions and conflicts that cropped up in society."[1]

Only fifteen years later, confronted by a deep systemic crisis, top Yugoslav leaders regretfully conceded that their country lacked the "elementary rules of behavior in conflict situations which the crisis imposes,"[2] and that "priority efforts" must be directed at "raising Yugoslavia's low credibility in the world.[3] How did Yugoslavia plunge from its position as a positive model to an essentially negative case of socialist reform, and what measures for recovery have been advanced by the country's ethnically and regionally segmented elite? After briefly reviewing the general course of reform during the Tito era, this analysis will focus on the features and prospects of the major reform strategies under debate in Yugoslav elite circles at the beginning of the 1990s.

Perestroika's Progenitor:
The Reformist Legacy of the Tito Era

The reform strategy adopted by Tito and his colleagues not long after their 1948 excommunication by Moscow provided the Yugoslav regime with fresh ideological legitimacy and also positioned it as the front-runner in the restructuring of East European socialism. Considering the internal context of the early Yugoslav reforms — an economically weak and politically isolated state still burdened with post-war reconstruction — the achievements of the Belgrade regime are quite impressive. For example, by the time the Czechoslovak communist reformers and Alexander Dubcek articulated their restructuring agenda in the mid-1960s — twenty years before Gorbachev — the Yugoslav communists had already accumulated a rather remarkable record of socialist experimentation: reduction in the size and responsibility of the central party and state bureaucracies; multicandidate electoral races and a more active legislative system; novel structures for citizen participation in enterprises and local communities; a foundation for market socialism and mixed forms of property ownership. The communist party organization — renamed the League of Yugoslav Communists (LCY) in 1952 — retained its monopoly over general ideological "guidance" and recruitment of personnel, but its detailed management of all societal activities was abandoned, as was the intimate party-state linkage typical of other communist regimes.

Yugoslavia's impressive economic growth and the country's political consolidation as an independent state seemed to confirm self-management's vitality as an alternative to "orthodox" state socialism. The momentum of reform was neither constant nor without strong political opposition, but despite various obstacles (and Tito's rather equivocal support for self-management's pluralist facets), Yugoslavia stood out as a bastion of "liberal communism."[4] The 1966 purge of the secret police, the reorganization of the party on a more decentralized basis in 1967, constitutional amendments (1968-1971) devolving more authority to the republics and provinces, all strengthened the reputation of Tito's regime as the cutting-edge of East European reformism. Thus, despite Tito's "surgical" use of central political and military power to stifle intellectual dissent and resurgent nationalism in the early 1970s, foreign observers continued to laud the participatory and pluralistic structural novelties of Yugoslav socialism, as well as Belgrade's nonaligned foreign policy.

Less discussed by observers, however, were trends that seriously undercut the momentum of political and economic reform during the 1970s. Fearing that the unchecked centrifugal tendencies of marketization and political pluralism might restore capitalism and also eliminate the party's leading role, political conservatives around Tito successfully diverted reform initiatives into essentially formalistic schemes for the extension of self-management rights (for example, the much-touted concept of "associated labor"), while informally maintaining various conventional modes of statist economic operation and hegemonic party control. As one prominent Yugoslav political scientist recently observed, "The conception of associated labor and the curtailment of market principles in the 1970s served more for the strengthening of the political bureaucracy's power, even more than before the economic reform [1965] when Yugoslavia was centrally organized."[5] "Self-management theory," as another critical Yugoslav sociologist puts it, "was one great utopia, which was really needed as an alibi for the absence of political democracy."[6]

The adoption of a new constitution in 1974, formally advancing the role of "associated labor" and self-management through a rather novel system of "delegational representation," and the enhanced devolution of power to regional and local authorities, was heralded domestically and abroad as evidence of Yugoslavia's ongoing commitment to socialist reform. The League of Communists continued to exercise single-party hegemony in the political system, but Kardelj's 1977 theoretical outline for a "pluralism of self-management interests" promised more space for contending ideas, provided that such views were not "anti-socialist." Tito's elaboration of a mechanism for the frequent rotation of officials heading the regionally balanced "collective" state and party leadership bodies, also appeared to extend the Yugoslav pursuit of inter-ethnic concord and "debureaucratized" governance. Moreover, defects of the regime such as party domination of managerial recruitment, the expanded size and influence of the administrative apparatus, the oligarchic power distribution in Yugoslav enterprises, and growing inter-ethnic tensions were candidly discussed by the country's lively media and research scholars.[7] Compared to the geriatric leadership and conservatism of other East European regimes at the time, Yugoslavia was a relatively open society that seemed destined for a better future. Indeed, the successful assumption of power by Tito's heirs in 1980 seemed to confirm the value of the novel institutional legacy bequeathed by the regime's founder. Unfortunately, a challenge far more difficult than the institutionalization of leadership succession would soon threaten the stability and survival of socialist Yugoslavia.

Crisis and Reform in the 1980s: Salvaging Self-Managed Socialism

The symptoms of the economic and political crisis that befell Yugoslavia in the early 1980s are well known. By 1989, the country was afflicted by sky-rocketing inflation, high unemployment, a huge foreign debt, and serious food shortages. According to official figures, salaries in the country dropped by 24 percent in 1988, and living conditions plunged to the level of the mid-1960s. Despite the plethora of institutional channels for citizen self-management established by the Tito-era reforms, strikes and mass public demonstrations became the preferred mode of participation for groups expressing strong dissatisfaction with the country's economic and political management. During 1988, an estimated four million Yugoslavs took part in protest demonstrations. Unpopular government-sponsored controls proved unable to resolve the economic crisis, and at the end of December 1988, Prime Minister Branko Mikulić and his cabinet, the Federal Executive Council, resigned from office.

Throughout Yugoslavia, but especially among the Serbs and Albanians, economic discontent became closely intermingled with ethno-regional nationalism during the late 1980s. The Serbs (and their close ethnic cousins, the Montenegrins) were particularly outraged at the serious problems faced by their brethren in the predominantly Albanian province of Kosovo, a region that has been a particularly volatile zone of inter-nationality conflict since the late 1960s. Ethnic violence in Kosovo intensified in early 1989, when Albanians protested the adoption of new constitutional measures placing the province more firmly under the control of Serbian authorities in Belgrade. The continued deterioration of ethnic relations in Kosovo, along with other sectors of serious inter-nationality discord, resulted in growing division among the ethno-regional segments of the Yugoslav political elite. Such divisions were in part exacerbated by individual communist leaders — most notably in Serbia and Slovenia — who saw an opportunity to garner political support through the mobilization of their respective ethnic and regional communities.

Yugoslavia's economic and political deterioration during the 1980s spawned a cottage industry of commentators offering reasons for the country's crisis and suggesting various measures to put things right — specialists in what some Yugoslav political activists facetiously termed the field of "crisisology." More importantly, the crisis resulted in a major replacement of top personnel within the country's discredited political elite. The generally younger and technically specialized group of political leaders who emerged at the end of the 1980s naturally became preoccupied with developing fresh reform strategies to repair Yugoslavia's economy and renew the legitimacy of the regime. For purposes of discussion here, the complex Yugoslav debate about the problems and future of self-managed socialism can be clustered around the three major contending "reform options": (1) THE SERBIAN STRATEGY, inspired by the leadership of Slobodan Milošević, who is presently serving as president of the republic of Serbia; (2) THE SLOVENIAN STRATEGY, representing the views expressed by the republican state and party leadership in Slovenia; and (3) THE FEDERAL GOVERNMENT'S STRATEGY, associated with the program of Ante Marković, who currently heads the Federal Executive Council (FEC), Yugoslavia's cabinet. While a wide spectrum of commentary regarding crisis management and reform could be found in Yugoslavia during the late 1980s, the three major reform strategies discussed below are the ones which generated the most attention and controversy in the country's political debate.

The Serbian Strategy: Populism and Federal Power

NATIONALISM AS AN ELITE RESOURCE. Throughout Yugoslav communist history some party leaders have regarded inter-ethnic rivalry more as an opportunity than a danger. In the late 1960s and early 1970s, for example, several leading Croatian party leaders tapped the nationalism that was sweeping their republic in order to build a base of popular support. A similar development occurred in the province of Kosovo between 1968 and 1981, when the regime's unprecedented tolerance for ethno-regional autonomy in that area allowed local Albanian leaders to politically mobilize the long-suppressed aspirations of their ethnic group.

The most successful Yugoslav communist functionary to exploit ethnic nationalism as a political tool in recent years has been Serbia's Slobodan Milošević.[8] As head of party organizations in Serbia — first in Belgrade (1984-1986) and then for the entire republic (1986-1989) — Milošević associated himself with growing Serbian outrage about both the Kosovo issue and economic conditions in the country. Deftly engineering the removal of regional Serbian political and media leaders considered "soft"

on the issue of Albanian nationalism, Milošević called for new constitutional provisions reasserting the control of Serbian republican authorities
over the autonomous provinces of Kosovo and Vojvodina (the latter,
although predominantly Serbian in ethnic composition, has tended to
protest the hegemony of officials in Belgrade). In effect, Milošević exploit-
ed a backlash of Serbian nationalism in order to build a cross-regional
alliance of ethnic Serbs unprecedented in Yugoslavia since the formation
of Tito's World War II Partisan movement. When mass protest demonstrations by Serbs and Montenegrins erupted in Kosovo, Serbia, Vojvodina,
and Montenegro in 1987 and 1988, "Slobo" Milošević emerged as a hero
to the crowds. By November 1988, when Milošević addressed a Belgrade
rally estimated at between 800,000 and 1.3 million Serbs, it was apparent
that he enjoyed more popular support (albeit regionally concentrated)
than any other Yugoslav political leader since Tito and that he had transformed the character of Yugoslav political life.

While the Albanian issue and economic problems were certainly important catalysts for the recent explosion of Serbian nationalism, the
Milošević phenomenon is also related to the Serbs' more general and
long-standing dissatisfaction with the course of Yugoslav political development. For example, many Serbs viewed the regime's decentralizing policies and constitutional initiatives as having seriously weakened the influence of both their republic and their ethnic group in the Yugoslav federation. The 1974 constitutional arrangements providing parity representation for each of the six republics in the Yugoslav federation also gave
Serbia's two autonomous provinces a voice in federal decisionmaking,
thereby reducing Serbia to one player in an eight-sided political game. As
the core nationality in the 1918 creation of the original Yugoslav state, the
nationality that predominated in the ranks of the wartime communist
movement, and the largest ethnic group in the country, the members of
Milošević's ethnic constituency feel that their interests are insufficiently
recognized under the 1974 constitution, and that they have legitimate
grounds for expressing their strong dissatisfaction.[9]

The pluralizing tendencies of Yugoslavia's "confederal" constitutional
system, which formally diminished Serbia's influence in Yugoslav political
life, have also been blamed for the country's recent economic difficulties.
From the Serbian vantage point, constitutional provisions requiring the
representation and "harmonizing" of the country's many ethnic and
regional interests — including the accommodation of small, but ethnically
aggressive nationalities such as the Albanians — prevented the central
government from decisively responding to the economic crisis. As
Milošević told one interviewer with regard to decisionmaking under Tito's
1974 constitution, "Even before his death the system didn't function, Tito

functioned. After his death, nothing has functioned, and nobody has been able to reach agreement on anything."[10]

Many Serbs also believe that the regime's Titoist precepts regarding constant elite rotation, and also the use of "ethnic arithmetic" in elite selection, have prevented the recruitment of a technically qualified and influential team of central officials. According to Milošević, the system limiting the tenure of high officials to one-year terms destroyed a feeling of responsibility on the part of decisionmakers, resulted in administrative errors, and prevented long-term policy implementation.[11] Milošević's emphasis on an "anti-bureaucratic revolution" appeals to many Serbs who feel that "rotating" federal politicians and senior administrators are able to enrich themselves and evade accountability by means of short-term service in various public positions. While certainly benefiting from deeprooted facets of Serbian political culture favoring strong, heroic leadership in times of crisis — such as the notion of the tribal chieftain or ethnic savior required to employ the policy of the "hard hand" — Milošević's support within Serbian specialist, intellectual, and political elite circles is based on a more complex admixture of ethnic and nonethnic ingredients.[12] For example, many Serbian intellectuals and dissidents (including Milovan Djilas) who harbor serious reservations about Milošević's demagogic methods and also his failure to enthusiastically embrace political pluralism are still attracted by his commitment to "Serbian rights" and his vocal disdain for elite mismanagement and bureaucratic corruption. Indeed, the essence of the Milošević phenomenon among Serbs might be conceptualized as *ethno-technocratic populism*, that is, a simultaneous appeal to both mass ethnic sentiments and the widespread conviction that professional economic competence, efficiency, and honesty should be the major considerations determining elite appointment.

THE REFORMS OF THE "MILOŠEVIĆ COMMISSION." Troubled by criticism tha his views are "anti-reformist" and vague, Milošević has sought the assis tance of prominent Serbian economic and political specialists in formulat ing a coherent reform program. One group of experts, personally headec by Milošević, is constituted as a Commission of the Presidency of the Republic of Serbia: "The Commission for Questions of Social Reform (originally "Economic Reform"). An associated subgroup of experts func tions under the aegis of the commission as a "Group of the Presidency o the Republic of Serbia for Reform of the Political System."

The Milošević Commission, as it has come to be known in Yugoslavia first presented a broad outline for economic recovery in May 1988 Premised on the notion of "socialism as a wealthy society," the Miloševi strategy envisions market-oriented reforms in which the "world market and world competition represents the strongest generator of economic operation."[13] A way out of the economic crisis is sought through the stimulation of investments and production in enterprises, introduction of new programs and technologies, stepped-up development of the small-scale economy, and foreign investments. Milošević has urged Yugoslavs to overcome their "unfounded, irrational and...primitive fear of exploitation" by foreign capital. He adds that such prejudices about foreign capital investment have been spread by the bureaucracy, "which itself is on the lowest level of education and cultured existence," and which frequently has made wrong investment decisions regarding foreign loans "on the basis of personal criteria of the top leaders and not on the basis of economic criteria."[14]

In principle, the Milošević reform strategy criticizes the state's role as a regulator of economic development, and particularly measures such as government direction of the banking system. Greater federal governmental authority is encouraged, however, in areas of monetary, financial, and taxation policy, as well as in foreign economic relations. Up to now, according to Milošević supporters, there has been a dearth of state power where it was required and an excess of intervention where it was unnecessary. Stressing the importance of a "united" or "integrated" Yugoslav market, the Milošević reformers blame the existing crisis on constitutional provisions and laws permitting the emergence of "autarkic republican economies." In this view, decisive action by the federal government must no longer be subordinated to the imperative of seeking unanimous agreement from all of the country's regions, the so-called "economy of accord-reaching" or the "consensus economy." According to Milošević, the creation of a united market is a "condition for Yugoslavia's existence" and "cannot be called statism or centralism."

> Yugoslavia is turning into a loose confederation, and with regard to its economic aspects, an increasingly poor hunting reservation in which the less developed are the objects of exploitation by the more highly developed....Yugoslavia must be a unified economic area where identical system-related solutions exist and where products and services, money and capital, people and knowledge move freely....And the state is doing this in all, even the most liberal market economies.[15]

The Milošević plan for economic reform suggests the stimulation and streamlining of the existing system of self-management, not its elimination. Applying the same exhortation/mobilization tactics to the economy that were so successful in rallying ethnic indignation among the Serbs, Milošević hopes to motivate self-managers in Yugoslav enterprises to work harder, curtail bureaucracy, and recommit themselves to the regime. Enterprise "collectives must function on economic principles,...strive to create profits and constantly struggle for their share and place in the market."[16] The urgency is to remove the bureaucratic "blockages" and waste in the enterprises that are allegedly responsible for previous failures. As one prominent member of the Milošević Commission put it, "One of Yugoslavia's paradoxes is that all reorganization in the name of debureaucratization, has had the result of strengthening the administrative apparatus, and with that increasing social costs and parasitism." The problem, he adds, is not to eliminate all state functions, but to change "the mentality and style of administrative work."[17]

While Milošević promotes a "mixed economy" and a "pluralism of property ownership," his reform program stresses that the "social ownership" sector or "public means of production," rather than the private sector, should be predominant. Real equality between the social and private ownership sectors is impossible for Milošević.

> That would be the same as to demand that a society be socialist and capitalist in the same measure, or that one room be simultaneously hot and cold....That would threaten the interests of the working class and bring the question of socialism into question.... Private property is not incompatible with socialism ...but the chief, fundamental form of property in socialism remains social property....Private property is secondary and can develop up to specified limits.[18]

Thus, Milošević has concentrated his reform efforts on the public sector, which formally generates approximately 85 percent of national income in Yugoslavia, rather than on the private sector, where some observers feel that more than 50 percent of the country's potential for economic growth actually lies.[19] While social property is described as the "most developed and dominant form of ownership" in their reform proposals, members of the Milošević Commission nevertheless emphasize that all forms of property need to receive equal legal treatment and that the private sector must be equitably represented in the political system.[20]

In July 1989, the Milošević Commission announced a comprehensive proposal for the political reorganization of Yugoslavia. Reemphasizing Milošević's commitment to a "modern democratic and efficacious federation," the proposal recommends that decisionmaking in the Federal Assembly according to the principle of inter-regional unanimity be limited to only the "narrowest circle" of constitutional questions, while most voting should follow the principle of "qualified majorities" (51 percent, two-thirds, etc.). Decisionmaking along such lines will allegedly promote a federation capable of "actively influencing economic development" and regulating the economy in order to "express and defend general societal interests."[21]

The Milošević reform proposal also calls for a political system that

would guarantee civil liberties, freedom of political expression, democratic control over the work of state organs, the responsiblity of all public officials, and an independent judiciary. The notion of political pluralism was
endorsed in terms of the "democratic expression of different social interests, ideas, and values," as well as "freedom of association" and ending the
League of Communists' monopoly over personnel recruitment and the
state. The organization of citizens in various leagues, alliances, and other
associations is, however, expected to take place under the umbrella of the
Socialist Alliance (the broad-based former national front organization,
which includes both party members and non-members) and the legislative
system, that is, "organized in harmony with the social or interest structures
of our society."

Recognizing that "socialism is in a transition period of its development," the proposal considers the possibility that other forms of "pluralistic political organization" may emerge, provided "they are created on a
democratic and socialist basis and within the Yugoslav frameworks." Multiparty pluralism is neither specifically ruled out nor encouraged in the
political reform outline presented by the Milošević Commission. Thus, the
precise parameters of political pluralism are very indefinite, and the
meaning of a phrase such as "within Yugoslav frameworks" is left unclear.
When the head of the Milošević Commission's "Group" for political
reform was asked whether the draft proposals envisioned the legalization
of opposition parties in Yugoslavia, he conceded that full political pluralism was still not envisioned.

> Logic doesn't exclude the possiblity that tomorrow there would be
> eight communist parties and socialist parties, but not parties whose pro-
> grams advocate the reprivatization of social wealth, a return to capital-
> ism. Here is that barrier.[22]

The Slovenian Strategy:
"Asymmetric Federalism" and Competitive Pluralism

The Slovene reform option as a facet of current Yugoslav political debate
has developed partly in reaction to the Milošević phenomenon but also
reflects internal developments within Slovenia that preceded the rise of
the new Serbian leader. Briefly, while Tito's mechanisms for balancing
regional representation in Yugoslavia's collective leadership structure
allowed Slovenia to enjoy considerable influence in federal political life,
many Slovenes have felt that their economically productive republic (in
1986 providing 18 percent of total GNP and 23 percent of total exports)
was paying an unnecessarily high price for the operation of the federation. Particularly irksome to Slovenes is the fact that each year their repub-

lic, with about 8 percent of Yugoslavia's population, contributes over 25 percent of the total federal budget and between 17 and 19 percent of the Federal Fund for Underdeveloped Regions. Slovenian public and elite opinion has been disturbed that massive federal funds transferred to the less advantaged regions of the country are used for financing bloated bureaucratic structures and economically unprofitable investments.

Federal defense expenditures also have seemed excessive to many Slovenes, particularly since the country is not facing any imminent military threats, and also because citizens of that republic play an extremely small role in the leadership of the armed forces. Such grievances became an important element of the growing political ferment among students and Slovene intellectuals during the first part of the 1980s.[23] The most outspoken voice of Slovenian dissent has been the Socialist Youth Alliance journal *Mladina*, whose iconoclastic criticism of the Yugoslav armed forces and support for the Albanian cause in Kosovo engendered fierce criticism from party conservatives, especially in Serbia and southern Yugoslavia. By early 1989, however, Slovenia's burgeoning political diversity went well beyond the *Mladina* editorial board, and was expressed in over one hundred grass-roots organizations and ten independent political groups.

The reformist mindset of Slovenia's communist state and party leaders has reflected the explosion of political pluralism and regional self-confidence. Although constituting a unique reform orientation, up to early 1990 the Slovene communist position with regard to general economic changes and Yugoslavia's basic cohesion along present territorial lines did not differ much from the views of other Yugoslav political leaders, including the Milošević team. As Slovenia's State President Janez Stanovnik remarked at a 1988 press conference in Washington, D.C., where he was otherwise highly critical of the Serbian political leadership, "There are no significant differences when it comes to the economy. The views of Mr. Milošević with whom I politically disagree on political issues do not differ from mine in economic matters. He is just as liberal as I am when it comes to economic matters."[24] The same point was made by the head of the Milošević Commission's Group for political reform in mid-1989:

> We all more or less agree that Yugoslavia needs to be a socialist, democratic, federal state, of equal nationalities, based upon the predominance of social property, on respect for the rights and freedoms of people, to be a legal state...but the essential difference, for example, with Slovenia, is in the domain of the state structure...and the way it functions.[25]

INSTITUTIONALIZING TERRITORIAL RIGHTS. In terms of Yugoslavia's political architecture, the Slovene communist leadership has been generally supportive of the federal organization and principles elaborated in the 1974

Constitution, that is, the model of parity regional representation and "consensus" decisionmaking that is anathema to the Serbian leadership. Thus, Slovene leaders have agreed that federal authorities must be adequately empowered to deal with major issues of economic policy. In their opinion, however, such policy cannot be established by a principle of majority voting (*majorazacije*), or what the Slovenes interpret as "outvoting" due to the Serbian demographic predominance in the federation. In the Slovene view, the requirement for unanimity of republican positions in federal decisionmaking is a safeguard against the potential subordination of the smaller republics and ethnic groups by the majority. Slovenian writers point out that while Milošević endorses the principle of "one man, one vote" for voting in federal-level institutions, the Serbs would never permit such a principle to determine political decisionmaking in Kosovo, where Albanians are numerically dominant.[26]

The Slovene view of constitutional reform was advanced most forcefully in mid-1989 by Milan Kucan, the head of the League of Communists in Slovenia until the end of that year and his republic's most prominent anti-Milošević spokesman.

> Can the imposition of majority decisionmaking in a multinational community by those who are the most numerous be anything else but the violation of the principle of the equality of nations, the negation of its sovereignty and therefore the right to autonomous decisionmaking?...We will only live in such a Yugoslavia in which sovereignty is ensured, as the permanent and inalienable right to self-orientation of all the nations...where we will regulate common issues in a federal state according to the principle of agreement.[27]

The preference of the Slovene communists has been the principle of "one unit, one vote" in federal decisionmaking with regard to the country's most important economic and political issues, a view that Serbian leaders have denounced as a denial of democratic fair play. As the secretary of the Serbian party's ideological commission suggested in response to Kucan's June 17 speech, "In the name of which democratic principles is the Slovene leadership demanding that one Slovene is equal to five Serbs, or three Croats?"[28] The Slovene rejoinder to this criticism is that although the concept of "one man, one vote" may historically reflect progressive, democratic principles, "Serbian political thought has stopped at this Jacobin maxim," and that any mode of representation and decisionmaking based on Serbian numerical strength in Yugoslavia denies the equality of nationalities.[29]

The Slovenian communist leadership has not only stubbornly adhered to the idea of a federation operating on the basis of unanimity and equally weighted units, but has further enraged the Serbian leadership by endorsing the idea of a so-called "asymmetric federation." As elaborated by Slovene political and constitutional theorists, the notion of federal asymmetry refers to an arrangement whereby each republic would be permitted wide-ranging autonomy in selected spheres of activity such as economic development, education, linguistic and cultural matters, while other domains such as defense and foreign policy would remain the responsibility of a federal government functioning on the basis of inter-regional agreement. As one Slovene writer points out, the "asymmetric federation" is a relatively new "intermediate form" of organization that lies between a federation and a confederation.[30] The Milošević leadership views the Slovene idea of federal asymmetry as a way to further the already "confederalist" or centrifugal aspects promoted by the 1974 Constitution, and thus a prescription for a "feeble federation" presaging the disintegration of socialist Yugoslavia.[31]

Slovenian politicians claim that an "asymmetric federation" will facilitate general inter-regional agreements by avoiding insistence on "standard solutions where they are not necessarily needed."[32] Indeed, anxious to forestall the possibility that Belgrade decisionmakers may one day wish to impose "standard solutions" on their republic, the Slovene Assembly adopted provisions during 1989 that required its agreement before federal authorities can intervene in Slovenian affairs as a result of an allegedly "emergency" situation within the republic. The president of the Slovenian Assembly conceded that this step was taken in light of the federal presidency's declaration of emergency measures for Kosovo in late February 1989. No one had to ask the Kosovo Assembly for permission, the Slovene official asserted, because the Kosovo constitution was silent on the matter of a provincial role in such a situation.[33] Although Slovenia's adoption of the new constitutional provision on state emergencies and an equally controversial amendment giving the republic the formal right to secede from Yugoslavia were declared to be unconstitutional by the country's collective state presidency, the Slovenian assembly proceded to promulgate the measures at the end of September 1989. The amendments immediately triggered negative commentaries by Serbian observers, who claimed that the Slovene elite had launched a "torpedo directed at the bow of Yugoslavia" and were interested in Slovenia becoming a "small Switzerland."[34] Mass protest demonstrations by Serbs and Montenegrins also took place, where demands were made for the removal of the Slovene communist leadership.

PLURALISM WITHOUT A VANGUARD. Slovenian views concerning political pluralism have been especially offensive to Milošević and the Serbs. For example, during 1989 Slovene communists amended their organizational statutes, dropping any reference to their party's "leading role." Claiming

that one-party monopoly is more dangerous to democracy than the proliferation of nonsocialist groups in their republic, top Slovenian officials
insisted that the League of Communists must now compete "equally with
other subjects" if it wishes to assume a paramount ideological position in
society: "In short it [the League] must seek confirmation through its
work."[35] Slovene communists have also been critical of the way their party
organization operates on the countrywide level, and particularly of central
party procedures permitting decisionmaking by majority voting. Thus, the
Slovene communist leaders opposed the convening of an "extraordinary"
Fourteenth Party Congress in January 1990, fearing that such a convoca-
tion would prove detrimental to the relatively autonomous position they
had gradually carved out for themselves. When, during preparations for
the congress, it was announced that voting at the meeting would be conducted on the basis of one vote per delegate rather than by equally
weighted regional delegations, Slovene officials objected that such methods would give a decisive advantage to Serbia and its allies.

In an unprecedented statement on June 20, 1989, Slovene party leaders
warned that if their views were overridden by a system of majority decisionmaking at the extraordinary congress, they would hold their own
congress and "decide either for a unilateral cancellation of democratic
centralism or for the complete organizational independence of the
League of Communists of Slovenia."[36] The Slovene communist threat concerning potential regional party independence was made only after their
unsuccessful efforts to engage Milošević and the Serbian leadership in
negotiations regarding the League's inter-regional problems. Milošević
refused such entreaties for bilateral party discussions, and rebuked the
Slovene leadership for "the most vile stab in the back of Serbia" over the
Kosovo issue.[37]

Serbian communist leaders were also angered by the tolerant attitude
adopted by leading Slovenian politicians toward the spate of independent
party-like political organizations which emerged within Slovenia at the
end of the 1980s.[38] For example, Slovene communist leader Kucan
described such pluralism as "not a danger, but a new chance for the country," although he indicated his personal preference for a nonparty form of
pluralism.[39] While they did not initially endorse a multiparty political system, the interpretation of political pluralism by the Slovene communists
went well beyond the Milošević Commission's much narrower notion of a
"political pluralism on socialist foundations." Indeed, the constitutional
amendments adopted during 1989 in Slovenia offered wide scope for
independent socialist and nonsocialist political organizations to compete
with the communists in the nomination of candidates to run for election
to legislative assemblies.

Throughout 1989, Serbia's leaders and other opponents of such full-blown pluralism warned that tolerance for a multiparty or multigroup system on the regional level, and subsequently in countrywide political life, would reintroduce the fractious pre-World War II squabbling among ethnically and religiously based parties. Moreover, other Serbian political analysts argued that the experience of many developing countries demonstrated that having several political parties offered no guarantee of economic development, democracy, or a solution to the type of crisis presently faced by Yugoslavia. Behind such concerns about the formation of new parties is, of course, the fear that pluralist developments in Slovenia and elsewhere in the country, including Serbia, would inevitably lead to the strengthening of antisocialist forces and thereby undermine the present regime.[40] For example, Macedonian party leader Vasil Tuperkovski, a Milošević ally, pointed out that "the party must rid itself of the monopoly of power, but in such a way that it does not lose its vanguard position and find itself on the margins of social processes."[41] Meanwhile, members of independent noncommunist groups in Slovenia claimed that the notion of a nonparty pluralism, frequently advanced in the Milošević camp as well by other cautious communist leaders, constituted an absurd idea so long as the League of Communists existed as a formidable party structure.[42]

Relations between Serbia and Slovenia seriously deteriorated in November 1989 following a decision by the government in Ljubljana to prevent entry into their republic of Serbs who wished to stage a December 1 protest demonstration. The Serbian communist leadership responded by announcing the termination of all government and business links with Slovenia. The threat to interrupt trading ties between the two republics was supported by 130 enterprises in Serbia, and would, if implemented, have serious economic implications for the country. One Croatian sociologist suggested that the Serbian action meant the collapse of a unified market by breaking the country into two spheres of influence, Slovenia and Serbia, and that "Yugoslavia has effectively been abolished as a state."[43] Whether the Slovenian-Serbian rift actually presaged the eventual disintegration of the Yugoslav state, or whether a compromise strategy would be found to maintain the country's cohesion, was a very open question at the beginning of 1990.

The Federal Government's Strategy: Marketization as a "New Type of Socialism"

The contrasting reform strategies of the Serbian and Slovenian communist leaderships discussed above are essentially both regionally based proposals that have not received countrywide endorsement or application.

While Slovene and Serbian political leaders have engaged in lively intra-party polemics about their respective reform theses, the difficult task of actually elaborating and implementing a cross-regional or "Yugoslav" reform program has been the responsibility of the federal government headed since March 1989 by Ante Marković. Marković is sixty-five years old, a Croat from Bosnia-Hercegovina who was trained as an electrical engineer and has spent most of his career in the economic management of one of Yugoslavia's largest manufacturing enterprises. His two previous jobs involved leadership posts in the Croatian government bureaucracy, where he gained a reputation as a serious political technocrat committed to market reform.

In terms of broad economic goals, Marković's general program has many similarities to the Serbian and Slovene recommendations, such as the enhanced implementation of a market-oriented economy. Calling for a "completely new type of socialism" to solve Yugoslavia's crisis, Marković expressed his belief that "the open market economy to be the ultimate achievement of mankind for which no alternative has yet been found."[44] Untainted by earlier official failures to deal with the economic crisis, Marković began work on his "new socialism" by fleshing out a sweeping package of constitutional reforms adopted near the conclusion of the paralyzed former government.

In November 1988, for example, the Yugoslav Federal Assembly promulgated thirty-nine amendments to the Constitution as a basis for comprehensive economic and political reform. Most of the amendments involved deregulation of the economy to permit the implementation of free market principles and a pro-growth economic policy. The constitutional changes and the initial policy measures adopted by Marković included the elimination of most property limitations (with the exception of landholdings, which are limited to thirty hectares); the reduction of state interference in the banking system; provision for unfettered competition among the social, private, and cooperative spheres of property ownership; liberalized rules for foreign ownership and joint ventures; preparations for the establishment of a money and securities market; and the encouragement of free initiative and profit motivation throughout the economy. Speaking to a German business group in June 1989, Yugoslavia's foreign trade minister claimed that the Marković government's new strategy constituted the "most revolutionary reforms since World War II," and that it was a lack of courage by earlier governments to fundamentally change the system that had contributed to the current crisis. "Capital," said the minister, "must be protected and profit possible."[45]

In order to expedite economic change, the FEC took a number of modest steps toward political reform during 1989. For example, it was decided that federal regulations could be adopted without complete unanimity among the republics and provinces and that the "inter-republican committees," used for the protracted and often impossible task of developing cross-regional unanimity on federal policies, would be dissolved. The balanced representation of republic and provincial personnel continues to be important in the selection of FEC members, but ethnic affiliation was dropped as a major criterion in personnel recruitment. In a move to eliminate the "excessive normativism" plaguing the economy, enterprises are now able to regulate their internal and industrywide operations without the adoption of numerous "self-management" acts, agreements, and compacts.

As part of his pledge to streamline the administration and create a "modern state suited to a market economy," Marković also formed a smaller cabinet (down from twenty-nine to nineteen members) including several younger and highly qualified officials. The two FEC vice-presidents serving under Marković — Aleksandar Mitrović, a fifty-six-year-old Serb educated as an engineer, and Zivko Pregl, a forty-two-year-old Slovene trained in economics — have considerable experience in economic management and administration. Plans were also announced to cut the size of the federal bureaucracy from about 14,000 to 10,000 employees, although the government announced it would hire between 500 and 700 "new experts and professionals."

Beginning his work as prime minister, Marković cautioned that full implementation of his reform program would take at least five years. Moreover, while political reform constitutes an important component of his "new socialism," primary attention during 1989 focused on the country's pressing economic difficulties. In view of the serious regional divisions in the party elite regarding political reform, the central government seemed to have little choice. In an unusually candid interview concerning the policies of the FEC,[46] Vice-President Pregl stressed that although the current crisis cannot be overcome without "profound changes in the political system," economic reform must take priority "because we agree much more on the country's economic matters than on how to harmonize political developments." In contrast to Milošević and his supporters — who usually blame the Yugoslav crisis and reform failures on institutional flaws in the method of decisionmaking or deliberate sabotage by a conservative and corrupt bureaucracy — Pregl argued that the government's main problem is finding competent personnel who understand market-type economic relations. Charges by Milošević that the federal government lacks sufficient power to override parochial republican and provincial interests were downplayed by Pregl: "We do not intend to haggle with anybody about anybody's interests. Our concept is clear — the market! The concept can break these state obstacles in Yugoslavia."[47]

A key political ally for the Marković government team, at least in the shortrun, is Yugoslavia's current (May 1989–May 1990) state president, Janez Drnovšek. At thirty-nine, Drnovšek is Yugoslavia's youngest state president thus far; he has a doctorate in economics and is a specialist in international finance (his Ph.D. thesis was on the IMF and Yugoslavia). Unlike his predecessors, who were chosen by regional party machines, Drnovšek was elected to the collective state presidency in April 1989 by a large popular mandate in his native Slovenia (the first republic to use direct elections to fill such a post).

Drnovšek is a staunch supporter of a market-oriented economy and the policies endorsed by Marković. In his Slovenian election campaign, for example, Drnovšek promoted the idea of making Yugoslavia's currency fully convertible in the next five years and suggested that a similar time-frame be proposed to the European Free Trade Association and the European Council as an adjustment period for closer Yugoslav association with the European economy. Drnovšek has also proposed that the state presidency should ease inter-regional and inter-ethnic differences so that "extremist politicians will lose ground for the further straining of conflicts."[48] He shares the view of the Marković government that the political crisis has largely been caused by economic difficulties and that when the size of the "social product" available for distribution increases, "mutual political tensions will lessen."[49] Drnovšek's support for the government is especially important because of the presidency's authority to intervene in the operation of federal decisionmaking when difficulties arise (such as, regional protests and stalemates in the Federal Assembly.).[50]

One of the most serious problems faced by the Marković government has been how to control runaway inflation. Initially, Marković opted to take a gradual approach to the problem of inflation, concentrating on measures to revive production, alleviate tax burdens on the economy, reduce the federal budget, restrict the amount of money in circulation through borrowing limitations on federal authorities, encourage investment by greater participation of foreign and private capital, and liberalize imports and prices. Utilizing such measures, Marković envisioned a decline in the inflation rate beginning in the fall of 1990 at the earliest. Debt repayment has also been viewed as an important anti-inflationary measure. Future investments must be implemented through carefully conceived joint ventures, because, as Marković argued, "the mistake in the past does not lie in the fact we have borrowed, but in the way we have used these funds."[51] Throughout most of 1989 the Marković government "categorically" rejected an anti-inflation policy based upon price or wage freezes, the method unsuccessfully employed by the former government of Branko Mikulić.[52] "Inflation," FEC Vice-President Pregl stressed, "can be partially stopped through a freeze but we are certain that this is not the right way to do it...We do not treat inflation as a special problem. This was done in the past and we have tonnes of paper with various anti-inflation titles. The effects of this are well-known."[53]

The difficulties inherent in Marković's long-term "systemic solution" to revive the Yugoslav economy, and especially the postponement of immediate relief from the country's current hyperinflation, naturally provided grist for the mills of those forces unsympathetic to the central government. Pleading for quick adoption of his market reform package at the end of June 1989, Marković conceded that "time is our big enemy, if not the biggest enemy we need to confront in the next period."[54] Although he expressed satisfaction that "100 percent unity" existed in the FEC and that none of its members had advanced views on regional or ethnic grounds, Marković's initial honeymoon with Milošević and the Serbian leadership ended after only a few months. In Serbia, a *Borba* journalist quipped in June 1989, Marković is "on the list of those whose replacement has not yet been sought, but for whom 'closed season' no longer applies."[55] Marković's claims about the potential of his reform strategy and its initial achievements have been ridiculed by Serbian leaders as excessively optimistic. One Serbian deputy in the Federal Assembly even suggested that the central government's failure to employ "shock therapy" against inflation — that is, a freeze on prices and income — derives from a desire by some members of the federal government to turn the Serbian people against their leaders. Even the pro-Milošević *Borba* repudiated such extreme views, observing that "there have been all kinds of conspiracies in world history, but a conspiracy using inflation has never been recorded."[56]

By mid-1989 it was clear that the Milošević forces had decided to actively oppose the strategy of the federal government. While Milošević and his Serbian "Reform Commission" were publicly on record supporting the central government's non-freeze policy (controlled prices undervalue Serbian exports of food and electricity to other parts of the country), they nevertheless tried to channel popular dissatisfaction with high inflation away from themselves and toward the Marković government. Marković urged the regime to endure the short-term popular dissatisfaction caused by the unemployment and inflation that are accompanying his market reforms. The Milošević forces, meanwhile, appealed to those Yugoslavs, and particularly Serbs, dissatisfied with the continued fall in the standard of living. For Milošević and his supporters, marketization is deemed important, but paramount emphasis is placed on the political reorganization of the federal structure as a means of eliminating the "absolute domination of partial interests" (such as Slovenia and Kosovo), which allegedly obstruct both the influence of the central government and the interests of the country's Serbian majority.

Badly in need of support for his reforms, Marković had the unenviable task of charting a middle course between the strong centralizing pressure encouraged by populist mobilization in Serbia, and the pluralistic pressure for regional autonomy promoted in Slovenia. At the end of July 1989, at a two-day session of the party Central Committee called to discuss worsening inter-ethnic relations, Marković complained that most reform efforts of the federal government had "either been stopped or slowed down" by regional officials, and he raised the issue of whether Yugoslav political leaders genuinely desired a "new system."[57] Failure to implement the federal government's program has been a major factor undermining comprehensive reform in Yugoslavia, as clearly explained by one of the frustrated vice-presidents in the Marković cabinet:

> Things that the Assembly adopted are not being done. Republics and provinces should have reduced their budgets and…established their deficits. This was not done. These deficits are one of the main causes of our inflation: they amount to more than our entire annual social product….We reach agreements and then spend however much we want….This works according to the system whereby I grab something today and someone else does the same tomorrow, and the inflationary spiral continues. There is no end to this…Inflation demolishes everything, it destroys the economic system, creates bad blood, divides people, and even threatens the political system.[58]

By the fall of 1989, Marković, though visibly frustrated, remained committed to his reform strategy and denied reports his government planned to resign. Visiting the United States in October to obtain financial assistance for Yugoslavia, Marković claimed that opponents of his program were concerned that state property had become "threatened" by the planned economic liberalization of the country, and he expected "an intensification of the conflict between ideology and reforms."[59] In December, Marković accelerated his economic reform program with new measures to fight inflation, including a six-month wage freeze (a policy previously rejected by his cabinet), tight monetary and budget controls, the creation of a convertible dinar, and an end to state subsidies for money-losing companies. The Serbian leadership completely rejected the Marković package, and large mass demonstrations were held throughout Serbia protesting the federal government's threatened austerity measures. Despite Serbian and Montenegrin opposition, however, the new Marković proposals had sufficient support from the other republics to permit their parliamentary adoption as "urgent measures" (requiring only a two-thirds vote rather than unanimity of all the republics).

Conclusion:
Survival or Separation in the 1990s?

> The end has come for authoritarian socialism.... Yugoslavia is undergoing changes and it is time for wholesale and radical social reform.
> *(Draft document for the 14th Extraordinary Congress of the LCY, distributed December 1989)*

> The draft declaration sounds good...but resembles past times and congresses when good documents were passed with optimism...which were never carried out. The question is, can we, after 45 years escape from purgatory in these three days [of the Congress].
> *(Statement by delegate at the 14th Congress, January 20, 1990)*

Yugoslavia's reform debate during 1989 and 1990 represented the continuation of a controversy about marketization, property ownership, political pluralism, and inter-regional power distribution that ensued after the regime's break with Moscow in 1948. Indeed, the issues of constitutional organization, decentralization, and federalism have bedeviled Yugoslav elites since the formation of the country after World War I. During 1989-90, just as in 1939-40 (following the pre-communist regime's two troubled decades), Yugoslavia's segmented elite urgently sought a compromise between central power and regional interests as a means of forestalling further economic and political decline. Unlike the circumstances fifty years earlier, however, when cautious regime reform was shattered by external forces, at the end of the 1980s it was Yugoslavia's deep internal divisions that were obstructing the adoption of countrywide reform initiatives.

Although the sweeping program of economic reforms promoted by Prime Minister Marković throughout 1989 and early 1990 have enjoyed considerable cross-regional support, the political challenges to the central government in areas such as Serbia, Montenegro, Kosovo, and Slovenia, together with mounting popular protests against hyperinflation, have made it very difficult to implement federal policy in a thorough and orderly manner. Of course, Marković and the federal government have not been without resources and allies in the struggle of reform philosophies. Thus the prime minister had the strong support of the military, the federal party apparatus, much of the federal legislature, important regional allies such as the Croatian government and party officials, and those foreign countries and international organizations sympathetic to Yugoslavia's survival. Even such assets, however, may not be sufficient to ensure the implementation of the comprehensive reform program announced by the FEC, particularly in the context of a crisis that regularly engenders new episodes of ethno-political and economic conflict.

Should Marković proceed with plans to close down unprofitable state companies — causing huge layoffs among the estimated 30 percent of the 6.8 million Yugoslavs now holding jobs in public enterprises operating at a loss — he may be unable to survive the probable backlash of resentment. From September to December 1989, for example, thousands of Serbian workers, already practiced at mass protests over ethnic and economic grievances, demonstrated against the federal government's failure to halt inflation. Moreover, while the Milošević leadership has strenuously endeavored to deflect Serbian dissatisfaction onto Marković and the federal government, the "mobilization" of popular protest may have opened a Pandora's box that even Milošević may no longer be able to control. Meanwhile, the inability or disinclination of federal authorities to forcibly halt the Slovene communist efforts to broaden both their republic's authority and the boundaries of political pluralism invites suspicion within conservative political and military circles — inside and outside Serbia — that Marković and state President Drnvošek are endangering the survival of both the country and socialism. The initial success and popularity of Marković's early 1990 initiatives to check inflation took some of the steam out of Milošević's criticism of the federal government's economic program. The Serbian leader, however, continued to hammer away at the government over the question of Kosovo and the political organization of the country.

The main barrier to successful crisis management and reform by the Yugoslav communist regime at the outset of the 1990s was a lack of trust and cooperation among the members of the regionally divided political elite. Without such trust, and given the mobilization of ethno-regional constituencies around popular regional spokesmen in Serbia and Slovenia (and illegal movements in Kosovo), the prognosis for the federal government's comprehensive plan of marketization and gradual democratization remained rather poor. Political dialogue and party factionalism in Yugoslavia have always been characterized by hyperbole, personal attacks, and sharp polemics, but by 1990 the pattern of intra-elite mistrust had acquired more serious significance owing to the deep economic crisis, the sharply divergent strategies for political reform, and the absence of a respected or powerful pan-ethnic authority figure to end stalemates and push through difficult decisions. Recognizing the depth of ethnic and inter-regional elite conflicts, the federal government chose to slow down or sidetrack macropolitical reorganization and concentrated instead on economic renovation. In doing so, however, the danger existed that the economic reforms would be allowed to falter — as had happened so many times before in Yugoslav political history — due to the resistance of entrenched regional political bureaucracies. The problem was not the absence of elite political will to undertake major reforms, but the federal authorities' insufficient cross-regional legitimacy to implement changes on a countrywide basis.

By early 1990, the potential dissolution of the presently configured Yugoslav state had become a real possibility. The catalyst for such dissolution potentially arose from a constitutionally framed secessionist thrust by Slovene political elites[60] — perhaps following the election of a noncommunist Slovene government — or from a possible violent Albanian mass uprising centered in the province of Kosovo.[61] On its own, Albanian secessionism appeared unlikely to provoke Yugoslavia's disintegration, but both Slovenian and Croatian elites seemed unenthusiastic about participating in a future Serbian-promoted regime crackdown against the protracted and proliferating pattern of Albanian protest.

The possibility that resurgent Croatian nationalism might lead to pressure for regional secession was also becoming a more serious consideration. Up to early 1990 the Croatian elite, while sympathizing with Slovene reform proposals, nevertheless steered clear of a major clash with either Milošević or the federal authorities. Croatian moderation could be largely attributed to the republic's residual trauma from Belgrade's suppression of the Croatian mass movement in the early 1970s. By early 1990, however, as the legitimacy of the Croatian League of Communists was rapidly evaporating and noncommunist political organizations began to attract a mass following in the republic, Croatian regional and ethnic self-assertiveness dramatically increased.[62]

Watching the collapse of Communist party political hegemony in one East European state after another during the fall of 1989, all segments of the Yugoslav communist political elite hastened to elaborate a fresh concept of political pluralism that could somehow preserve their own influence, satisfy their deeply discontented and highly volatile mass constituencies, and possibly also maintain the unity of the country. In December, the Croatian party leadership admitted that it had been slow in recognizing "the historic exhaustion of the single-party system" and called for the establishment of a multiparty system in the country. Such recognition followed a petition signed by approximately 25,000 Croatian citizens urging the legalization of different political parties and the holding of free elections.[63] The Croatian move was followed shortly by the publication of a new draft platform of the federal party organization calling for competitive elections and an end to a monopoly by the League of Communists. "We are changing all of this now," the draft declaration stated, "in order that tomorrow it will not be too late for socialism in Yugoslavia."[64] Meanwhile, at the end of December the Slovene League of Communists, which had pioneered the call for greater pluralism, announced that it would "strive for the creation of a multi-party system," and that all communist party organizations in state enterprises and government institutions would be dissolved.[65] As the shockwaves of exploding pluralism reached Serbia from northwestern Europe and Yugoslavia, even the Milošević-guided political leadership in Belgrade was finally forced to endorse the idea of multiparty pluralism, albeit heavily laced with restrictions against "anti-socialist" political formations.[66]

Although the "virus of pluralism" sweeping East Europe had finally convinced most Yugoslav communist leaders that single-party rule was no longer tenable, their delinquent embrace of democratic pluralism proved unable to prevent the organizational fragmentation of the League of Communists. The feud between Serbian and Slovenian communist officials regarding the correct model of reform and the appropriate interpretation of pluralism reached a climax at the Fourteenth Extraordinary Congress of the League of Communists held at the end of January 1990. What many party members had hoped would be a meeting to transform the League of Communists into a nonauthoritarian modern party, instead turned into a bitter struggle between Slovene and Serbian communists. The Slovenes advocated the reorganization of the League into a union of "independent and free republican communist parties" — a "League of Leagues" — while the supporters of Serbia's Milošević charged that those seeking further decentralization of the League were essentially calling for a "war among Yugoslav communists...and a war among Yugoslav nations." The entire Slovene delegation dramatically stormed out of the congress hall when it failed to obtain a congress majority in support of a previously negotiated reform platform that called for the enhanced autonomy of the country's republics, an end to laws allowing the prosecution of political opponents, and greater cooperation with Western Europe. Milošević urged the congress to proceed with its work and elect a new leadership, but the Croatian delegation refused to continue without the participation of the Slovenes, causing the abrupt suspension of the meeting a day ahead of its official schedule. "We left because this [League] is not an organization that can be responsible for social reform in this country," remarked Slovene communist leader Milan Kučan. "When we left, the party ceased to exist."[67] Meanwhile, spokesmen for Prime Minister Marković indicated that the conflict in the League of Communists would have no bearing on the federal government's decision to soon delete all references to the League's "leading role" from the constitution and to completely democratize the electoral system. Alluding to the fact that the League of

Communists had approximately two million members, Vice-President of the FEC Zivko Pregl remarked that the government would not allow the fate of the country to be "decided in quarrels among people representing 10 percent of the population."[68]

As the ruling League of Communists fractured and tottered in a context of ethnic quarreling and continued economic crisis, it was natural that the role of the country's military establishment should become a more important dimension of Yugoslav political stability. Initially, the Yugoslav military expressed some support for the official endorsement of pluralism by the federal government and the League of Communists. One military officer, for example, suggested that the army "would not stand in the way of the country's democratic development," and that it would "adjust itself to the changes in society."[69] As ethnic violence in Kosovo mounted during the first months of 1990, however, military intervention in the ongoing Yugoslav crisis remained a very real, if still extreme, possibility. Thus, while publicly affirming their "ideological and action-oriented unity," some members of the Yugoslav military establishment are undoubtedly troubled, cross-pressured, and divided by the overall breakdown of unity in the political elite. For example, the pro-Milošević Belgrade weekly *Nediljne Informativne Novine* (NIN) reported "whispered" commentaries that recent retirements from the military elite ordered by the collective state presidency stemmed from the "nearness" of certain high-ranking officers to "'Serbian viewpoints' on the diagnosis and the way of curing the crisis."[70]

If direct military intervention in political affairs did occur, it would likely be engineered by pro-Serbian military and bureaucrats at the federal level, supported by regional elites within Serbia and the other southeastern republics.[71] The pretext for military interference might be triggered by the central government's inability to restore order following intensification of the already serious anti-state dissidence among the Albanian population, or by a major outbreak of inter-ethnic violence in some other section of the country. Indeed, the explosive co-mingling of economic and ethnic discontent has transformed many multinational areas of Yugoslavia, such as Croatia and Bosnia, into powderkegs that could seriously threaten regime stability. The real possibility of Slovene or Croatian secession following a future noncommunist electoral victory in either of those two republics might also provoke military interference in the political system.[72] While direct military intervention in political affairs cannot be entirely ruled out, it seems unlikely to occur barring a sharp increase in ethnic violence or a disorderly regional secessionist initiative seeking not only regional self-determination but also threatening the territorial boundaries of neigboring regions. Thus, even conservative and antipluralist military officers are well aware that military involvement in politics is a very high-risk enterprise, which would undoubtedly provoke a violent and potentially unmanageable backlash. Moreover, in the aftermath of direct military intervention the new armed bureaucrats would be faced with the same daunting economic and political challenges that have plagued recent political elites.

The most unlikely scenario for Yugoslavia's future development is a continuation of the chronic pattern of "permanent reform" and "permanent crisis" seen throughout the 1980s. Yugoslav ingenuity may result in yet another patchwork constitutional compromise among central and regional elites, but such a course is unlikely to produce economic recovery or restore the communist regime's seriously eroded legitimacy. Inter-elite squabbling and economic stagnation similar to the pattern experienced over the last decade may continue for a short time, but the present regime's failures and internal fissures suggest the likelihood of a more far-reaching transformation in the early 1990s, such as a transition to post-communist rule, territorial fragmentation, or some form of military intervention. In this respect, the election of April 1990, which will certainly result in a strong showing by noncommunist political forces (especially in the northwestern parts of the country), promises to be a major watershed in Yugoslav political history. In the second part of April 1990, noncommunist coalitions advocating greater autonomy, and possibly eventual independence for their regions, won impressive majorities in Slovenian and Croatian legislative elections. In a separate direct election for the presidency of Slovenia, reform communist official Milan Kučan campaigning under his party's new label — the Party of Democratic Renewal — won a substantial victory (approximately 59 percent of the vote), but both in Slovenia and neighboring Croatia, noncommunist political forces had become the decisive actors in regional affairs.[73]

For reformist forces elsewhere in Eastern Europe, Yugoslavia has lost its innovative luster and become a negative model illustrating the pitfalls of reformism in a one-party Marxist state. Soviet observers, for example, credit Yugoslavia with having achieved "amazing" economic progress in earlier decades, especially success in producing high-quality export goods. Yugoslav *perestroika* is also praised for promoting citizen and group incorporation into the political system, and for the "open frontiers" policy that allowed Yugoslav workers to acquire new skills and foreign currency while simultaneously validating the regime's commitment to human rights in the area of "freedom of movement."[74] More important for Soviet commentators, however, is the downside of the Yugoslav experiment, and particularly the serious socioeconomic threats posed by economic failures such as inflation and regionally unbalanced growth. Like many Yugoslavs, most

Soviet writers also view excessive decentralization as having sparked nationalist unrest and sapped the central government's authority. As a leading Soviet specialist on Eastern Europe recently remarked, the Yugoslav experience contains a warning "not against the market and commodity-monetary levers, enterprises, or competition...the warning is in something different: the inconsistency of reforms, the lack of political change, the misguided decentralization. It was carried out in such a way that it entailed a disintegration of the national market and weakened control over external relations and the country's debt."[75]

For the prudent *perestroika* elite struggling to transform the USSR, the dangers of the Yugoslav model now outweigh its positive features. Meanwhile, for the noncommunist forces recently ascendant in East-Central Europe — who are currently preoccupied with the issues of genuine party pluralism, free trade unionism, and the establishment of market economies — Yugoslavia's reform experience is historically interesting but anachronistic. At the beginning of the 1990s, Yugoslavia appeared unlikely to regain its previous distinction as one of the most innovative regimes in Eastern Europe without the radical transformation of its political system. Paradoxically, owing to the dismal record of regime reform in the 1980s, that very process of political transformation seemed likely to foreshadow the elimination of communist rule in Yugoslavia and quite possibly to destroy the territorial cohesion of the existing state. Following the election of April 1990, the mantle of power in Yugoslavia will almost certainly be assumed by new political forces untainted by yesterday's futile reformist debates and organizational-political loyalties.

Notes

1. "Self Management - A Law Governing the Development of Socialism," *Socialist Thought and Practice* 51 (March-April 1973), p. 28.

2. Stipe Suvar (while serving as president of the Presidium of the Yugoslav League of Communists). *Foreign Broadcast Information Bulletin — Eastern Europe* (hereafter *FBIS-EEU*), *89-021*, February 1989, p. 70.

3. "Statement by Ante Marković in the Assembly of the SFRY on the Occasion of His Election to the Office of President of the Federal Executive Council," *Yugoslav Survey*, 30, no. 1 (1989), p. 54. By 1987 it was estimated that Yugoslavia had dropped to a lower level of development than in 1950, with only Poland, Turkey, and Albania trailing behind it. Zoran Pjanić, "Trends in the Reform of the Economic System," *Socialist Thought and Practice*, 29, nos. 1-2 (1989), pp. 5-20.

4. Astute Yugoslav critics at the time noted that the regime's penchant for constant institutional reform created a certain sense of elite self-deception (a situation that also pertained to foreign analysts of Yugoslavia): "Anybody acting within an institutional activity was able to notice only the reforms substantializing into institutional reality and never perceived how the rest of social reality was stagnating." *Praxis (International Edition)*, no. 2 (1967), p. 206. A good summary of the strengths and weaknesses of Yugoslav reform in

its initial stages is Mihailo Marković, "Self-Governing Political System and De-Alienation in Yugoslavia (1950-1965)," *Praxis* 6, no. 2 (July 1986), pp. 159-74.

5. Dušan Bilandžić, "Velika Reforma ili Propast," *Danas* 1, September 1989, p. 16. The same author has surveyed the continuation of such problems during the first five years of the post-Tito era. *Jugoslavija posle Tita* (Zagreb: Globus, 1986).

6. Professor Josip Zupanov, cited in Milan Jajčinović, "Socijalizam je nešto drugo," *Danas*, 18 July 1989, p. 27. By 1989, although many Western enthusiasts continued to extol the achievement of Yugoslav self-management, participant-observers of the experiment candidly admitted that it "has in practice been shown to be uneconomical, socially unproductive and to a great extent unsuccessful." *FBIS-EEU-89-198*, 16 October 1989, p. 74. For the contribution of the self-management system to the Yugoslav crisis of the 1980s see Svetozar Pejovich, "A Property-Rights Analysis of the Yugoslav Miracle," *Annals* 507 (January 1990), pp. 123-32.

7. These problems are discussed more fully in Lenard J. Cohen, *The Socialist Pyramid: Elites and Power in Yugoslavia* (Oakville, Ontario: Mosaic Press, 1989).

8. Slobodan Milošević is literally a "child of the revolution." He was born on August 29, 1941, two months after the Yugoslav Communist party began its wartime guerrilla struggle. Thus, Milošević was only seven at the time of the Tito-Stalin rift and just ten when "workers' self-management" became the regime's ideological platform. It may be significant that the most formative stage of Milošević's education and career development, from 1961 to 1986, coincides with the burgeoning of ethnic conflict in Yugoslav political life.

    The son of a Serbian Orthodox clergyman of Montenegrin origin, Milošević received a law degree from Belgrade University before enbarking on a managerial career in manufacturing and banking. After rising to become the president of a major Belgrade bank, Milošević entered urban politics in the early 1980s and in 1986 was selected to head the Serbian republic's party organization. In 1989 he was elected state president of Serbia.

    Milošević's wife, Mirjana Marković-Milošević, is an active Serbian political figure and a close ally of her husband. In October 1989 she was elected to the Presidium of the influential City Conference of the Belgrade League of Communists.

9. Milošević continuously emphasizes that Serbs should not have a guilty conscience about Serbian nationalism during the pre-communist era, and should not be self-conscious about striving for their ethnic rights and a strong unified Yugoslav state today. Milošević's collected speeches are in *Godine Raspleta* (Belgrade: Beogradski Idavaćko-Grafićki Zavod, 1989), see especially pp. 35-38, 220-21.

10. *Le Monde*, 12 July 1989, p. 6. Milošević claims that the 1974 Constitution was one of Tito's late initiatives and that "he was unable to imagine the extent to which such a system would destroy the country." For recent Yugoslav analytical studies highly critical of the 1974 Constitution's impact on economic life, see Marjan Korosić, *Jugoslovenska kriza* (Zagreb: Naprijed, 1989), and Stanko Radmilović, *Ekonomska kriza i društvena reforma* (Belgrade: Beogradski Izdavačko-Grafički Zavod, 1989).

11. *Le Monde*, 12 July 1989, p. 6.

12. Milošević's success is closely related to his skill in political communication. As a Slovene journalist observed,

    He's not exactly a born speaker; his delivery is somewhat rapid and it is obvious that he is more accustomed to reading his speeches than to ad-lib. However, what he reads is something new in Yugoslav political practice. Milošević has simply "stepped out" of the bounds of the iron political jargon of our politicians, a jargon that has continued to assert and petrify itself for decades. His speeches include no long and involved sentences whose meaning is grasped by the audience only after it has worked its way through five or six subordinate clauses. In his speeches there is none of that compulsive theorizing that appears in every speech — even on the most banal occasions....His speeches are delivered in short and simple sentences that are filled with metaphors, comparisons, and slogans that are easily understood by everyone and therefore can quickly turn into "folk sayings." *FBIS-EEU-88-208*, 28 October 1988, p. 64.

13. *FBIS-EEU-88-225*, 22 November 1988, p. 39.

14. Ibid., p. 40.

15. Ibid., p. 42.

16. Ibid., p. 39.

17. Professor Kosta Mihailović, cited in *Nedeljne Informativne Novine* (hereafter *NIN*) 1946 (17 April 1988), p. 16.

18. *NIN* 1657 (3 July 1988), pp. 14-15.

19. Ivo Jakovljević, "Miloševićeva šansa," *Danas* 8, no. 391 (1989), p. 21.

20. Oskar Kovač, "Sve svojine su ravnopravne," *NIN* 2013 (30 July 1989), pp. 16-17.

21. Slobodan Vučetić, "Pravna država slobodnih ljudi," *NIN*, ibid., pp. 10-15 (all quotes in this and the next two paragraphs are from this source). Vučetić later reiterated his endorsement of a "pluralism of political organizations" under the condition that they are "generally viewed as being based upon socialist and Yugoslav options." He added that in his opinion a multiparty system is "less bad than a one-party system. In both systems the citizens and democracy are bounded." *NIN* 2030 (26 November 1989), pp. 16-17.

22. Ibid., pp. 10-11.

23. For a good overview of this trend see Miha Kovač, "The Slovene Spring," *New Left Review*, September-October 1988, pp. 115-28.

24. *FBIS-EEU-88-220*, 15 November 1988, p. 65.

25. *NIN* 2030, p. 14

26. *FBIS-EEU-89-118*, 21 June 1989, pp. 67-68.

27. *FBIS-EEU-89-117*, 20 June 1989, p. 70.

28. *FBIS-EEU-89-128*, 6 July 1989, p. 71.

29. *FBIS-EEU-89-131*, 11 July 1989, pp. 65-66.

30. Mario Nobilo, "Asimetrična federacija," *Danas*, 18 July 1989, pp. 30-31.

31. Olivera Vućić, "Lažna asimetrija federalne konfederacije," *NIN*, 11 June 1989, pp. 24-25.

32. *Danas* 8, no. 389 (1989), p. 12.

33. Ibid.

34. *FBIS-EEU-89-188*, 29 September 1989, pp. 58-59. Immediately prior to the decision by the Slovenian assembly, members of the federal-level party Central Committee voted 97-40 (with one undecided) that Slovenia should delay its vote on the constitutional amendments. Only the twenty Slovene representatives, sixteen members from Croatia (four were absent), and one or two members from other regions voted against the call for a postponement. The Serbian and Macedonian representatives voted unanimously for a postponement, as did almost the entire contingent from Bosnia, Montenegro, Vojvodina, and Kosovo. The amendments were later passed in the Slovene Assembly by a vote of 256 to 1. The single opposing vote was that of an army colonel who said that if he were an "ordinary delegate" he would have voted for the amendment. *Radio Free Europe Research, Situation Report, Yugoslavia*, 23 October 1989, p. 6.

35. Ibid., p. 11.

36. *FBIS-EEU-89-122*, 27 June 1989, p. 69.

37. *FBIS-EEU-89-105*, 2 June 1989, p. 67. During 1989 Milošević also angered the Slovenian leadership by insinuating that its enthusiasm to become more closely associated with the European economy reflected an attitude of cultural superiority vis-à-vis the rest of Yugoslavia, and also excessive deference to Western Europe. Slovene leaders called the Milošević accusation "insulting" and expressed pride in having "blazed Yugoslavia's trail to Europe." *FBIS-EEU-89-105*, 2 June 1989, pp. 69-70.

38. The party-like organizations now operating in Slovenia include the Slovene Social-Democratic Alliance, the Slovene Christian Social Movement, the Slovene Peasant Alliance, the "Greens" Union, the Slovene Democratic Alliance, and the Academic Anarchist Anti-Alliance Alliance.

39. *FBIS-EEU-89-117*, 20 June 20 1989, p. 69, and *FBIS-EEU-89-119*, 22 June 1989, p. 70.

40. Jovan Marjanović, "Reform SKJ i politički pluralizam," *Socijalizam* 32, no. 1 (1989); Milijana Belančić, "Pluralizam zahteva jedinstvo," *Komunist*, 26 May 1989, p. 6; and Najdan Pašić, "Gvozdeni zagrlaj birokratije," *Komunist*, 12 May 1989, p. 11. Dr. Janko Pleterski, who is a member of the Slovene League of Communists' Presidium, told his colleagues that political pluralism cannot be rejected because parties or alliances might form on a regional and not a federal basis. "Such 'arguments' ...resemble arguments for election laws in the prewar Yugoslav dictatorship, which permitted public activity only when it was state-wide." *FBIS-EEU-89-131*, 11 July 1989, p. 68. Slovene communist activist Lev Kreft has rejected the idea that ethnic parties destroyed interwar Yugoslavia. "Politicki pluralizam," *Socijalizam* 32, no. 1 (1989), pp. 84-87.

41. *FBIS-EEU-89-106*, 5 June 1989, p. 55. During late 1989, sources suggested that Tuperkovski and Milošević may have had a falling out over the latter leader's nationalist tactics.

42. *FBIS-EEU-89-124*, 29 June 1989, p. 65.

43. *Chicago Tribune*, 4 December 1989, p. 2.

44. *Associated Press Report*, 28 January 1989.

45. *FBIS-EEU-89-107*, 6 June 1989, pp. 44-45.

46. *FBIS-EEU-89-109*, 8 June 1989, p. 41.

47. Ibid., p. 44.

48. *FBIS-EEU-89-064*, 5 April 1989, p. 49.

49. *FBIS-EEU-89-073*, 18 April 1989, p. 59.

50. While Marković can serve up to five years as prime minister, under the current system of annual presidential rotation, Drnovšek will only be in his current post until May 1990. At that time he will be succeeded by the current vice-president, Serbia's Borisav Jović (a sixty-one-year-old economist with a doctorate in economics, experience as a commercial and financial director, and a former member of the Milošević Commission).

51. *FBIS-EEU-89-116*, 19 June 1989, p. 65.

52. For an overview of the unsuccessful reforms in the pre-Marković period, see Paul Shoup, "Crisis and Reform in Yugoslavia," *Telos* 29 (Spring 1989), pp. 129-47.

53. *FBIS-EEU-89-109*, 8 June 1989, p. 44.

54. *FBIS-EEU-89-118*, 21 June 1989, p. 60.

55. *FBIS-EEU-89-122*, 27 June 1989, p. 59.

56. Ibid.

57. *FBIS-EEU-89-145*, 31 July 1989, p. 53.

58. *FBIS-EEU-89-163*, 24 August 1989, p. 60.

59. *Associated Press Report*, 4 October 1989. Marković has generally avoided detailing a course of political reform, but when pressed on the issue during his United States visit he remarked that "the logic of pluralistic ownership, which demands a system of its own, will have to demand and open the society to a multi-party system." Ibid.

60. A public opinion survey conducted in Slovenia during early 1990 revealed that in a projected referendum 55.4 percent of the respondents would vote for separation from Yugoslavia, while 52.8 percent felt it would be impossible to reconcile the political conceptions of Serbia and Slovenia. *Danas*, 418 (20 February 1990), p. 18.

61. From January 24 to February 6, 1990, ethnic protests in Kosovo resulted in the deaths of twenty-eight Albanians (pushing the death toll for that group to approximately sixty over the past year), and the wounding of another ninety-four demonstrators. Some Serbian leaders continued to pour oil on the fire by advocating Slavic migration into Kosovo and even an armed Serbian uprising against the Albanians. Regime efforts to restore order included the imposition of a night-time curfew, restrictions on public gatherings, and action by the security forces assisted by tanks, armored vehicles, jets, and helicopters of the Yugoslav military. On February 6, 20,000 Albanians demonstrated in Pristina calling for the release of jailed Albanian activists and for free elections. The Democratic Alliance of Kosovo, a new independent Albanian group wishing to take part in coming elections, claimed more than 200,000 members, but that organization has not received official recognition.

62. Data from Croatia indicated that the League of Communists in the republic was rapidly losing membership while opposition parties were rapidly gaining in strength. In the Croatian city of Osijek, for example, research revealed that approximately 15 percent of the League's membership intended to vote for the nationalist and noncommunist Croatian Democratic Union in the April 1990 election. The hemorrhage of members from the League of Communists in Croatia was particularly heavy among ethnic Croats, who have traditionally constituted a significantly smaller proportion of communist membership in Croatia than their percentage of the republic's total population. *Danas*, 20 February 1990, p. 12.

63. *Associated Press Report*, 11 December 1989.

64. *Canadian Press Newstex*, 15 December 1989.

65. *Associated Press Report*, 24 December 1989.

66. *Danas*, 409 (19 December 1989), pp. 20-21. By 1990, Milošević's half-hearted commitment to pluralism began to engender increased criticism from emergent noncommunist democratic forces within Serbia. See Milan Andrejevič, "Growing Opposition to Milošević in Serbia," *Report on Eastern Europe*, 19 January 1990, pp. 26-29.

67. *Washington Post*, 4 February 1990, p. AO1.

68. *Associated Press Report*, 21 January 1990.

69. *Globe and Mail*, 16 December 1989, p. A2.

70. Aleksander Tijanić, "Promene u armiji," *NIN* 2022 (1 October 1989), p. 11.

71. Milovan Djilas has suggested that with the "arrival of Milošević, the unity between the Army and the Serbian leadership was destroyed. The Army does not support leaderships of individual republics. This also applies to Serbia." *FBIS-EEU-89-026*, 9 February 1989, p. 61. Djilas may be right. In April the deputy minister of defense, Simeon Bunčić, told a meeting of communists in the military that "nationalist passion" had reached almost a

point of "incandescence," caused by the "directed nationalism" of various republican leaders. Buncic balanced his critique of republican-based "confederal" schemes of multi-party reform with an attack on those advocating more centralized bureaucratic alternatives, and he stressed that "the army is firmly convinced that it is in the interests of stability and all our society that the federal organs be made capable of successfully implementing their social assignment of responsbility." *FBIS-EEU-89-073*, 18 April 1989, pp. 71-72. Bunćić delivered the same message to party leaders in July. *FBIS-EEU-89-145*, 31 July 1989, pp. 55-56.

The majority of the officer corps is Serbian, but planning for any military takeover must take into account the limited reliability of non-Serb conscripts and officers, the likelihood of popular resistance and civil war in areas such as Croatia, Slovenia, and Kosovo, and the problem that, even if successful in seizing and retaining power, a military regime would be devoid of legitimacy and ill equipped to resolve the economic crisis. See Marko Milivojević, "The Political Role of the Yugoslav People's Army in Contemporary Yugoslavia," in Marko Milivojević, John Allock, and Pierre Maurer, eds., *Yugoslavia's Security Dilemmas: Armed Forces, National Defense and Foreign Policy* (Oxford: Berg Publishers, 1988), pp. 15-59. Milan Andrejevich has suggested that a military solution to the Yugoslav crisis is unlikely given "the armed forces' penchant for barking and not biting." *Radio Free Europe Research, Situation Report, Yugoslavia*, 23 October 1989, p. 19.

72. Ironically, it is Slovene Vice-Admiral Stane Brovet who has expressed the military's strong feeling against party pluralism: "We are against multi-party pluralism for a number of reasons. First of all, the programatic reorientation of the majority of groups and movements who pretend to come into being as parties in our country, contain elements of nationalism, anti-socialism, confederalism, and also separatism. Secondly, it is a question of a struggle for power, but a struggle for power, in our opinion in these conditions cannot extricate us from the crisis, but in contrast can dangerously cause the crisis to deepen or even sharply threaten the integrity of our country." *NIN* 2026 (29 October 1989), p. 11.

73. In the second part of April 1990, noncommunist coalitions advocating greater autonomy, and possibly eventual independence for their regions, won impressive majorities in Slovanian and Croatian legislative elections. In a separate direct election for the presidency of Slovenia, reform communist official Milan Kučan campaigning under his party's new label — the Party of Democratic Renewal — won a substantial victory (approximately 59 percent of the vote), but both in Slovenia and neighboring Croatia, noncommunist political forces had become the decisive actors in regional affairs.

74. See the comments by Boris Piadyshev in "Perestroika: The 19th Party Conference and Foreign Policy," *International Affairs* 7 (July 1988), pp. 15-16.

75. Academician Oleg Bogomolov, in "The Market Teaches Lessons: Yugoslav Reforms — What We Draw From Them?" *Moscow News*, 21 (3373) (21 May 1989), p. 6. See also the discussion by the former *Pravda* correspondent in Belgrade, Timur Gaidar, "'Don't Repeat Our Mistakes' (Letter from Belgrade)," *Moscow News* 33 (3385) (13 August 1989), p. 6.

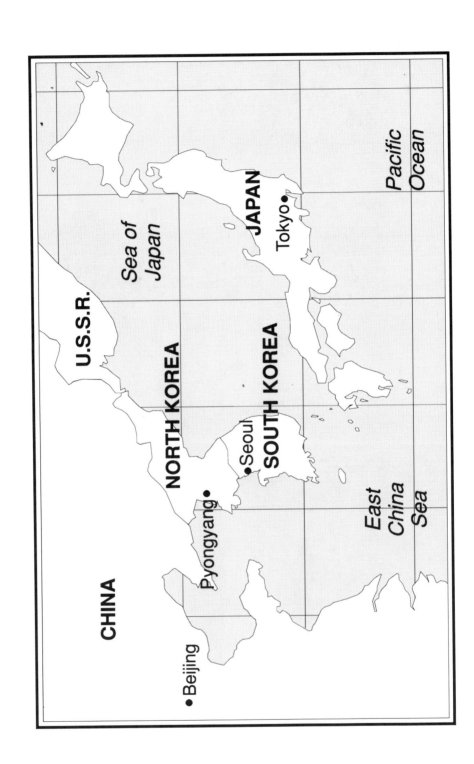

12. REFORM IN NORTH KOREA

Ilpyong J. Kim

Introduction

The Democratic People's Republic of Korea (DPRK) celebrated the fortieth anniversary of its founding on September 9, 1988, in Pyongyang and resolved to achieve "a complete victory of socialism" in North Korea during the period of the Third Seven-Year Economic Plan (Third SYEP) (1987-1993). There have been a series of debates and discussions among observers and analysts of communist systems in general and more specifically among Korean specialists on whether or not North Korea will follow the pattern of reforms that are in process in China, the Soviet Union, and the Eastern European countries. After forty-five years of rule, North Korean leader Kim Il Sung has not adopted a Chinese style "open door policy" or implemented the Soviet type of *glasnost/perestroika/demokratizatsiya* of the 1980s. In early 1984, the Kim Il Sung leadership briefly experimented with an open door policy, breaking away from a decade of isolation and "self-reliance," and moved cautiously to negotiate with South Korea and the United States by proposing a trilateral conference.

It is the proposition of this paper that despite North Korea's efforts to open its doors to the outside world and reform its economic and social system in the 1980s, it has not been successful in implementing a reform program largely because of the rigidity of its *Juche* ideology and its monolithic political system under the joint leadership of the elder Kim and his son, Kim Jong Il. Further, this paper will assess the attempts North Korea made in the 1980s to open its doors and to introduce changes into its economic and political structure.

The open door policy, which began in 1984, shifted to an ideologically oriented hardline policy five years later. It was reported in the Korean press that a centrally organized seminar for senior staff members of the Korean Workers' Party (KWP) on the "strategic line on building of socialism and communism" was convened in late August 1989, in Pyongyang. The policy established at this seminar called for the leadership cadres at various levels to sustain the "Three Revolutions" (ideological, cultural, and technological) and revitalize the *Chongsan-ri* method and the *Taean* work system, with special emphasis on shifting the priority to ideological revolution and class struggle. "These three lines of our party are the most correct ones with which to advance toward communism without the slightest *deviation* [perhaps meaning a reform] and twists and turns because they are based on the scientific principle in building socialism and communism with the *Juche* idea."[1] Thus, the purity of socialism without deviation was to be sustained, and the old Stalinist model of economic construction was upheld as correct.

Has there been a struggle for power and policy between the reformers who wanted to adopt a policy of reform, influenced by the Chinese and Soviet reforms, and the hardline conservatives who have persisted in the uninterrupted revolution? Why were the open door policy and the modest reform begun in early 1984 reversed? Was this change influenced by the events in China of June 1989 or the impact of the Thirteenth World Festival of Youth and Students which took place in July 1989? The shift in North Korea's policy line may be analyzed and understood in the context of the priority given to the Three Revolutions. In the heyday of "self-reliance" and the isolationist policy in the 1960s and 1970s, the North Korean leadership placed greater emphasis on ideological and cultural revolution, while in the later period of the open door policy and economic reform, from 1984 to 1989, priority was given to the technological revolution, i.e., more emphasis was placed on the development of science and technology.

I. From Self-Reliance to an Open Door Policy

After a decade (1973-1983) of isolation and a hardline policy, the North Korean leadership began to open its doors to the outside world and to reform its economic system. On January 26, 1984, the Supreme

People's Assembly (parliament) of North Korea adopted at its third session a resolution to establish international linkage with the capitalist countries, including the United States and Japan, and to promote foreign
trade. The resolution specifically called for the expansion of economic
exchanges with the capitalist countries, since the promotion of foreign
trade was essential for building the national economy and for improving
people's living standards.[2] The subsequent discussions and resolutions
adopted by the Korean Workers Party (KWP) Politburo seemed to indicate
that the need for an open door policy had been debated and the question
of whether or not to adopt the Soviet or Chinese model of reform was discussed. After a series of debates and consultations, the North Korean leadership adopted its own independent course of action.

As a part of the new open door policy, the DPRK government in
January 1984 proposed a trilateral conference among the United States,
China, and North Korea to discuss the ways in which a peace treaty could
be negotiated to replace the armistice agreement which had been in force
since July 1953, the end of the Korean War. This proposal expressed
North Korea's willingness to come to terms with the United States if and
when the United States was willing to negotiate with the North Koreans.
The open door policy included proposals by North Korea to convene a
North-South Korea economic conference, allow Red Cross talks to reunite
ten million family members separated after the Korean War, and conduct
preliminary talks to prepare for a North-South parliamentarians' conference and negotiations for joint sponsorship of the 1988 Summer Olympic
Games in Korea. Some negotiations such as the Red Cross talks and economic cooperation between the North and South proceeded rather well
and brought about substantial results in 1985 and 1986.

In order to overcome such economic problems as low productivity in
industrial plants, technological backwardness, absence of foreign currency, and lack of consumer goods, the causes of which were largely the failures of the self-reliance policy in the previous decade, the Kim Il Sung
leadership launched a new economic program. It was designed "to develop economic and technological exchanges and cooperation with the capitalist countries." This was the main thrust of the North Korean version of
the open door policy and economic reform.[3]

The Joint Venture Law formally proclaimed on September 8, 1984, by
the Supreme People's Assembly stipulated the liberalization of foreign
investment in such sectors as manufacturing, construction, transportation,
science and technology, and tourism. The joint ventures were to be conducted according to "principles of equality and mutual benefit." In the
process of formulating the Joint Venture Law, Prime Minister Kang Sung
San made an official trip to China August 5 to 10, 1984, during which he

reportedly praised China's economic reform and modernization programs. However, the ultimate decision to adopt the open door policy and economic reform was taken by the two top leaders, Kim Il Sung and his son, Kim Jong Il.

The factors that contributed to Kim's decision to shift his priorities to a technological revolution in the mid-1980s from the emphasis on ideological and cultural revolution in the 1970s were related to his two trips to the Soviet Union in May 1984 and October 1986.[4] It was reported in the North Korean press that the elder Kim believed scientific knowledge and modern technology were necessary in order to carry out a successful modernization of North Korea's economy. What North Korea needed at this juncture was a massive infusion of modern technology in its industries, most of which had been built with Soviet assistance in the 1950s, following the Korean War; they were in desperate need of refurbishing or overhauling with modern equipment and new technology.

In late 1986, the Soviet Union reported that over seventy of the major industrial plants of North Korea had been reconstructed or newly built with Soviet aid since the founding of the DPRK in 1948. According to Radio Moscow on November 11, 1986, the Soviet Union had agreed to construct nineteen additional industrial plants in North Korea during the Soviet Union's Twelfth Five-Year Economic Plan (1986-1985). Radio Moscow also stated that the Soviet Union's economic and technical aid to Pyongyang had enabled North Korea to build almost all of its industries, including those involving electricity, ferrous and nonferrous metals mining, metallurgy, chemicals, machinery, and commodity production and that these Soviet-built plants produced more than 28 percent of North Korea's steel, 29 percent of its ferrous metals, 50 percent of its petroleum products, and two-thirds of its electricity. The Soviet Union also agreed to assist North Korea in building a nuclear power plant, train North Korean nuclear engineers in the Soviet Union, and provide Soviet technicians to work on the plant in North Korea.

Earlier the same year, Radio Moscow reported that the Soviet Union had provided North Korea with more than 5,000 technicians and engineers, who had been dispatched to Pyongyang to construct industrial plants. At the same time, thousands of North Korean scientists and engineers were being trained in Soviet industrial plants. According to one such North Korean technician, in a conversation with this author in July 1988, the summit meeting between Soviet leader Mikhail Gorbachev and North Korean leader Kim Il Sung in Moscow in October 1986 had produced a framework within which North Korea could utilize Soviet assistance in introducing economic and technological reforms into its industrial sector.

The North Korean leaders' willingness to accept Soviet advice and technical assistance began with Kim Il Sung's visit to Moscow and to the Eastern European countries in May 1984. Debate in the KWP Central Committee and the Politburo about economic reform ensued. For example, Kim Hwan, a KWP Politburo member, delivered a lengthy report to the Eleventh Plenum of the KWP Central Committee in February 1986 in which he asserted that "the need to promote the *technological revolution* has now become our urgent task. A decisive turning point in the country's economic development should occur now." The plenum also addressed problems of the machine-building industry, the electronics industry, and other technological issues. It was stressed at the plenum that what the country needed most was to import *advanced technologies from abroad.* "The technological revolution means," a Politburo member asserted, "a machinery revolution," and emphasized the need for automation of the production system.[5] The tone of the speeches and the content of the debates seemed to indicate that there was some opposition to the shift in priority from the ideological revolution to the technological revolution.

Contrary to expectations, the Joint Venture Law which was adopted in early 1984 has not attracted a huge amount of foreign investment in North Korea or expanded the country's economic relations with the capitalist countries by expanding its foreign trade. Forty-four of the fifty joint venture projects established since 1984 have been undertaken by Japanese-Korean firms. One typical example of successful negotiations was the establishment of the Nakwon Department Store, a joint venture with Choil Company, Ltd, affiliated with the pro-Pyongyang General Association of Korean Residents in Japan. It opened its main store in Pyongyang on February 18, 1985, and subsequently set up branch stores in thirty-one cities throughout North Korea to market such consumer goods as clothing, food, and furniture. Another consumer-oriented venture was the Changgwang Coffee Shop, a joint venture of the General Association of Korean Residents in Japan and the External Service Bureau of Pyongyang, which opened on May 5, 1985.[6]

The Campenon Construction Company of France and the First Equipment Export-Import Company of North Korea signed an agreement on October 8, 1984, to construct the Yanggangdo International Hotel in Pyongyang. Under the agreement, each side would invest 50 percent of the capital needed for the construction of a 46-story hotel, with a total floor space of 87,000 square meters, to be completed in two years and seven months. But the construction of the hotel came to a standstill when negotiations between the North Korean government and the French firm became deadlocked in June 1986 over several problems, including the issue of the hotel's future management.

However, North Korea has continued to make an all-out effort to invite capital investment from Western countries, including the United States. Negotiations have been carried out with Scandinavian countries, as well as with Hong Kong, Singapore, and Thailand. North Korea has also negotiated about forty different joint projects with Japan in such fields as color television tube manufacturing, lead and zinc refining, synthetic rubber production, silicon and steel plate manufacturing, tomato juice processing, fish processing, and two hotels accommodating more than 1,000 guests. But not all of these negotiations have so far been completed. Some Korean-Americans on the West Coast of the United States have established firms to promote trade, joint ventures, and exchange of tourists with North Korea, but they have run up against State Department restrictions, so all these activities have been inconclusive.

Against the background of North Korean efforts to attract foreign capital and technology under the Joint Venture Law, the most significant development was the dramatic visit to Pyongyang of a top South Korean businessman, Chung Ju-yung, Chairman of the Hyundai Group, from January 23 to February 1, 1989, and the signing of a letter of protocol with the director of a North Korean bank for joint development of Mt. Kumkang (Diamond Mountain) into an international tourist resort. Chung's agreement with his North Korean counterparts also calls for the development of a shipyard and a rolling-stock plant in the Wonsan area; these projects will, if all goes well, amount to more than a billion dollars of South Korean investment in North Korea. Chung's letter of protocol included an agreement with the North Koreans for joint participation in Siberian development projects concerning salt, coke, and gas production. However, Chung's follow-up trip was stalled as the result of twists and turns in South Korean politics and South Korea's northern policy. [7]

Neither the Chinese nor the Soviet but the North Korean Model

Technological changes are usually accompanied by changes in institutions and value systems. In the process of modernizing a society, the Three Revolutions—ideological, cultural, and technological—that were launched in North Korea during the 1970s were aimed at the transformation of not only the economic and social structures but also the beliefs, values, and attitudes of the people, in the process of moving from a socialist-industrial society to a communist society. This was the primary objective of the North Korean leaders. Kim Il Sung believed that he had to transform not only the material basis but also the cultural and ideological foundations of North Korean society if he were to achieve the transition from socialism to communism.

As early as March 1963, Kim Il Sung stressed to a conference of scientists and technicians the need to raise the level of the scientific and technological sectors, including mechanical engineering, radio engineering, and electronics, all of which were essential to industrialization and the all-out technological revolution in North Korea. At that time, Kim linked the building of socialism with the transformation of a backward rural society, and he called for "the technical, cultural, and ideological revolution" to be "thoroughly carried out in the rural areas."[8] He defined the technical, cultural, and ideological revolutions as the central revolutionary tasks to be undertaken in the countryside, and he provided detailed guidelines by which the Three Revolutions were to be accomplished. The primary objective of Kim's rural policy was, of course, to close the widening gap between the urban industrial sector and the rural agricultural sector.

However, Kim's efforts to complete the stage of building socialism and make a rapid transition to communism in North Korea under the banner of the Three Revolutions encountered numerous difficulties in the 1960s, due largely to changes in the external environment, such as the intensification of the Sino-Soviet conflict, the escalation of the Vietnam War, and the increasing tension on the Korean peninsula. This forced the North Korean leadership to postpone the implementation of the Three Revolutions until the 1970s. In early 1973, Kim organized the "Three Revolution Team Movement," recruiting younger cadres to strengthen the KWP organization at various levels; this helped to avoid the mistakes of the Chinese Cultural Revolution. In a major speech, Kim switched his priority from the technical to the ideological revolution which was the objective of the Three Revolution Team Movement. He outlined his plan to dispatch the teams, their duties, the principles of their activities, and the norms of their life, as well as the tasks confronting them in executing the Three Revolutions.[9] In short, the primary objective of the Three Revolutions Team Movement was to replace the veteran cadres (who had been recruited in the 1940s and 1950s) with younger and more energetic cadres, similar to the Red Guards in China.

Some observers in South Korea and Japan also speculated that the Three Revolution Team Movement was directed by Kim Jong Il, who was being groomed to succeed his father as the leader of North Korea. Was Kim Jong Il successful in replacing the veteran cadres with his own generation of younger cadres? How effective was this Three Revolution Team Movement in the 1970s? Few answers are available to Western analysts. However, Kim Jong Il later expressed the frustration he encountered in dealing with the veteran cadres in the following words:

Now some officials do not implement the Party's decisions and instructions promptly. They dillydally over their implementation, complaining about bad conditions, and simply convey them to their subordinates without any methodology. Acting from self-centeredness and expediency, some other officials do not organize the work of implementing them with a due sense of responsibility and then shift the blame for their failure in their work onto their superiors or subordinates. Then there are some Party officials who, on the pretext of doing inner-Party work, neglect to carry out the Party's decisions and instructions with regard to administrative and economic affairs and feel no remorse even if they are not implemented as they should be.[10]

This is also an indication that the centrally formulated policy was not fully implemented at the local level. An initiative at the grassroot level of the cadres and managers was needed.

In a speech at the Consultative Meeting of Senior Officials of the Organizational Leadership Department and the Propaganda and Agitation Department of the KWP Central Committee on April 28, 1979, Kim Jong Il scolded the senior cadres by stressing that "failing to accept changes without reservation and paying no attention to or neglecting their implementation is not an approach to work that a revolutionary should adopt. People who behave like this are not fit to be party members."[11] What the younger Kim tried to achieve, according to this most succinct speech, was the replacement of the veteran cadres, one-third by the younger generation and one-third by the middle-aged group, since the old cadres were not able to execute policy directives because of complacency and secure positions within the KWP. As a result of this reform program, two-thirds of the veteran cadres were replaced by middle-aged and younger cadres. Thus, Kim Jong Il asserted:

Old cadres are rich in experience and know how to deal with things, whereas young cadres are energetic and vigorous, sensitive to the new and enterprising. It is only when the ranks of cadres are composed of a proper combination of old, middle-aged and young people that our Party will be able to continue to develop into an experienced and seasoned party, into a revolutionary party which fights, full of spirit and ardor, free from senility and stagnation.[12]

In the early 1980s, after a decade during which priority was given to the ideological and cultural revolution, the official emphasis shifted to the technological revolution, since the ideological revolution alone could not resolve the pressing economic problems by simply mobilizing the masses of the people. What was needed most was to provide material incentives to increase productivity as well as to reorder the priorities of the revolution from ideological and cultural to technological. North Korean leaders recognized that the Second Seven-Year Economic Plan (1978-1984) had not met the planned targets although they announced publicly that the plan had achieved its goal. The obsolescence of facilities in the industrial plants constructed in the 1950s with Soviet technical assistance contributed to the failure to meet the goals. What North Korea needed most was massive capital investment together with the decentralization of factory management. A huge amount of resources — more than a third of the national budget — was allocated to the defense buildup, thus creating an economic dilemma which could not be resolved by an ideological appeal or by mass mobilization. Thus the need for a Korean-style *perestroika* was acknowledged.

During the early 1980s, especially the years between the conclusion of the Second Seven-Year Economic Plan in 1984 and the beginning of the Third Seven-Year Economic Plan (1987-1993), a series of debates took place in policy-making circles in Pyongyang over whether or not to adopt the open door policy and economic reform. The conservatives seemed to be arguing that the country should continue to carry out its policy of self-reliance and persevere in the ideological, cultural, and technological revolutions without outside help, while the reformers argued that North Korea should learn more about the Chinese and the Soviet experiences with economic reform and should also open its door to the outside world.

As early as July 1984, Kim Jong Il stressed the need for technicians and specialists:

> This is the age of science and technology. Their rapid development urgently requires that the training of technicians and specialists be improved. Only when we improve this work in conformity with the trend of developments of modern science and technology can we rapidly advance our own, step up the technical revolution, and accelerate socialist economic construction at a high speed.[13]

However, the younger Kim continued to advocate the *Juche* ideology and stressed that "the younger generation are the people who are to carry forward the revolutionary cause of *Juche*. The victorious advance of our revolution and its future depend largely on how we educate them, the heirs to the revolution." Thus, Kim Jong Il placed himself in the middle of the debate between the conservatives and the reformers by putting a great deal of emphasis on the development of science and technology for the technological revolution but asserting at the same time that the education of the younger generation in the *Juche* ideology should be maintained.

Kim Il Sung emphasized the shift to technology in his 1986 "New Year's Message," declaring that the present task of economic construction in North Korea was to carry out a technological transformation and that the Third Seven-Year Economic Development Plan (1987-1993) incorporated the requirement of the technological revolution as an important task. The outcome of the 1984-86 policy debates, however, was a compromise in the sense that North Korea was to turn to the Soviet Union for economic and technical assistance to meet the requirements of technical transformation, replacing outdated machinery and equipment in industrial plants while maintaining *Chajusong* (independence) in carrying out the Three Revolutions. Thus, Kim Il Sung's trip to Moscow in October 1986 paved the way for the introduction of massive economic aid and technical assistance to re-equip the outmoded industrial plants in North Korea. A Soviet-North Korean agreement provided that more than 5,000 Soviet technicians would be dispatched to North Korea to construct or reconstruct industrial projects, and several thousand North Korean engineers and scientists would be sent to the Soviet Union for advanced training. Bilateral trade between Moscow and Pyongyang was to triple.

As a result of the internal North Korean policy disputes, the chairman of state planning was replaced in February 1986, and Premier Kang Sung San was removed in December of that year. The new premier, Li Gun Mo, is known to have studied mechanical engineering at the Leningrad Institute of Technology from 1949 to 1953. Upon his return from the Soviet Union in 1953, he started his party career as a section chief in the Organization and Guidance Department of the KWP Central Committee. He became a KWP Politburo member in September 1973, but he was known as a technocrat specializing in heavy industry. He played a leading role in the successful execution of the Six-Year Economic Development Plan (1971-1976). After serving three years in the late 1960s as minister of machine industry, Li was promoted to deputy premier of the Administrative Council (cabinet) in 1973. Li was considered a leading member of the group of reformers.

Because of illness, however, Premier Li was replaced in December 1988 by Yon Hyung Muk, another Soviet-trained technocrat and a reformer. Yon, born in Manchuria in 1925, attended the Urals Institute of Technology in the Soviet Union from 1950 to 1955. As had Li, he started his party career as a section chief of the Organization and Guidance Department of the KWP Central Committee, after returning from the Soviet Union in 1955. Yon was elected party secretary in charge of heavy industry and candidate member of the KWP Politburo in November 1970. In 1974 he was named by Kim Jong Il as the person in charge of the Central Guidance Department of the Three Revolution Team Movement. He has been a close follower of Kim Jong Il and a reformer.[14]

By 1986, the Kim Il Sung leadership recognized that North Korea needed more advanced technology, capital investment, and long-term credit — which China was unable to provide — if the country was to meet the requirements of the Third Seven-Year Plan (1987-93). Kim was reported to have said at a May 1987 KWP Politburo meeting, after his trip to China, that "the Korean and Chinese people should develop their own countries with due regard to their own situation." From Kim's point of view, China was less developed economically and technologically than North Korea; North Korea was already an advanced industrial state with a per capita income of more than $2,200.

Kim's solution to the development problem in North Korea was to formulate his own model of development. In a ninety-minute speech to a million people gathered on the occasion of the fortieth anniversary of the founding of the DPRK on September 9, 1988, Kim Il Sung emphasized the independent course North Korean development had taken for the past forty years as well as the country's economic and ideological achievements. "By displaying the revolutionary spirit of self-reliance and fortitude, however, our people courageously overcame the hardships standing in their way and successfully built a solid, independent national economy," Kim asserted. "They turned the country, once a colonial agricultural land far behind modern civilization, into a socialist industrial state with modern industry and developed agriculture."[15]

However, Kim was again shifting his priorities from the technological to the ideological revolution. In a response to questions raised by the bureau chief of Italian Radio and Television for the Far East the following month, Kim stressed that

> building a socialist and communist society requires the capture of the ideological and material fortresses of communism. The technical revolution must be carried out energetically in order to take the material fortress of communism, and *the ideological and cultural revolutions must be accelerated* in order to seize its ideological fortress. The ideological, technical, and cultural revolutions represent the fundamental way of taking these two fortresses together. In our efforts to conquer these fortresses we have firmly adhered to the principle of giving priority to the ideological fortress. Only in this way will we succeed in capturing the material fortress as well.[16]

During the Thirteenth World Festival of Youth and Students held in Pyongyang in July 1989, several prominent Western journalists were invited to report on the events. The picture emerging from the reports filed by these American journalists seems to indicate that North Korea has not adopted *glasnost* or *perestroika* and that the North Koreans believe that the open door policy and economic reform may be useful for the Chinese and the Soviets but are not useful for them. What they are proud of is having built socialism in their own way and formulated their own development strategies rather than following the Soviet or Chinese models. Therefore, their reform program, which included some decentralization of plant management, the adoption of an independent accounting system, and the increase of material incentives, was formulated on the basis of their unique conditions and, they insist, was not an emulation of either the Chinese or the Soviet model.

The open door policy of North Korea is fundamentally different from that of China, since China introduced such reforms as the responsibility system in agriculture and the self-management system in industrial plants in order to boost productivity after the adoption of its open door policy. North Korea adopted a policy of openness without introducing the market mechanism to regulate economic forces. At the local level, administrative control by the People's Committee (Executive Committee of the People's Assembly) and the Administrative Committee (the bureaucracy) of the province, city, and county were greatly strengthened in accord with Kim Il Sung's directives.[17]

Further, any attempt to analyze or understand the course and direction of changes in policy or the reform of the economic and social system should be made in the context of the monolithic ideology of *Juche* and its political system. The trinity of the father (Kim Il Sung), the son (Kim Jong Il) and the *Juche* ideology functions in a fashion somewhat similar to a version of the Christian trinity. The intensity of the cult of personality, centering not only on the senior Kim but including the younger Kim as heir-apparent, has been unprecedented in the world, and North Korean society is often characterized as a bleak and Orwellian land of regimented people who have been converted to faith in *Juche* ideology and to worship of their leader as a virtual deity.

Concluding Remarks

At the age of 79, Kim Il Sung has ruled North Korea for more than four decades, longer than any ruler in the communist world, including Mao and Stalin. He has systematically built up his cult of personality, introduced the "command and administrative system of management" in the party and government, and resolved the succession problem by designating his eldest son as his successor, something unknown in the lexicon of Marxism-Leninism. The political culture Kim has inculcated in North Koreans during the past four decades is somewhat similar to the Confucian political culture of the Yi Dynasty of Korea (1392-1910). The content of North Korea's political culture is based on the *Juche* ideology: independence in politics, self-reliance in economics, and self-defense in

national security affairs. In the aftermath of the Tiananmen Square incident of June 4, 1989, Kim Il Sung supported the Chinese military suppression of the pro-democracy movement, calling it a "rebellion."

In April 1989, Kang Mong Ho of the Council for External Relations
asserted that North Korea does not want either Soviet-style *glasnost* or the
Chinese model of "economic reform," and added that the current reform
policy of the communist nations has had no impact on North Korea whatsoever. "We are carrying out our own development, based on our own
method," Kang stressed. "We will sustain an independent development of
our own national economy which was created by President Kim Il Sung."
Kang implied that North Korea would not depend on foreign capital as a
basis for economic reform, and that economic development based on the
policy of self-reliance would continue in the future. [18]

What the Kim Il Sung leadership has attempted to do in the new era of
economic reform and political change in communist-ruled states is to
integrate slow and steady reforms into the economic structure. For example, a private plot of 100 square meters for each peasant household to
raise vegetables and cash crops is now permitted, as is the opening of
farmers' markets for free enterprise in the rural areas of the country.
Thus, some observers of the North Korean scene have speculated that if
and when Kim Il Sung relinquishes his position of power and the demise
of the monolithic political system occurs, Kim's successor will have to
introduce radical changes into the political system and drastic measures of
economic reform because of growing pressure from both intellectuals and
technocrats to resolve the contradiction between the monolithic political
system and the liberalization of economic structures. If he is to sustain his
leadership, Kim Jong Il will have to introduce a radical reform program
such as the one Deng Xiaoping adopted in post-Mao China or the *glasnost*
and *perestroika* Mikhail Gorbachev initiated in the Soviet Union after 1985.
It is quite obvious that the conservatives and reformers in the Politburo
and Central Committee of the KWP as well as in the hierarchy of the
bureaucracy are still in disagreement, and they are likely to conduct an
open debate in the post-Kim Il Sung era. Representing the new generation of North Korean elites who did not participate in the anti-Japanese
resistance movement or experience the harsh realities of the post-Korean
War society, Kim Jong Il's generation, unlike that of his father, is more sus-
ceptible to the policy arguments of the reformers. Moreover, there are
more than one and a half million scientists, technicians, and intellectuals,
including thousands of Soviet-trained technocrats, who may well push for
Gorbachev-style *glasnost* and *perestroika* in North Korea, unlike the Yeltsin
style of radical reform.

The Kim Jong Il leadership is more likely to give priority to scientific and technological development than to continue the emphasis on the ideological and cultural revolution in North Korea. However, the younger Kim also is committed to the Three Revolutions, "If we are to accelerate social progress we must give clear priority to the remolding of man in particular," Kim Jong Il has said, "although we have to carry on the transformation of all three simultaneously." This is because man transforms nature and society through the technological revolution, Kim stressed, and because the level of social progress is determined, in the final analysis, by "ideological consciousness and by [man's] cultural and technological standards....Without giving our principal attention to the remolding of man [through the ideological and cultural revolution], it would not be possible to promote the transformation of nature and society nor would it be possible to accelerate the revolution and [socialist] construction."[19]

In preparation for a gradual change in the political structure, the general election for the Supreme People's Assembly was held on April 22, 1990, six months earlier than the election date established by the constitution. At its first session, the Assembly elected Kim Il Sung president. In his inaugural address on May 24, 1990, Kim asserted:

> Our socialism is, in short, man-centered socialism, the embodiment of the *Juche* idea. The principal characteristic of our society is that it is a truly people-oriented society of which the popular masses are genuine masters and in which everything serves the masses.[20]

Thus, building socialism in North Korea has had, according to Kim, the characteristics of a mass line policy based on the *Juche* ideology (national identity) as well as the transformation of all the sectors of society in order to respond to popular demand. Kim stressed that

> transforming all the sectors of society creatively to meet the desire for independence of the popular masses, the subject of the revolution, is the basic direction in which to build man-centered socialism. Throughout the course of building socialism, our Party and the Government of our Republic have consistently maintained the independent and creative stands and implemented the line of independence, self-sufficiency and self-reliant defense. [21]

Against the background of *glasnost* and *perestroika* that have swept through the Soviet Union and the revolutions in the East European countries, Kim Il Sung apparently has begun to reconsider the role of government and the masses in it: "If the government of the Republic is to fulfill its honorable mission as people's state power, it must fully implement *socialist democracy* in state activity." The logic of Kim's argument is that the successful application of his *Juche* ideology would inevitably lead to the achievement of socialist democracy. Thus, Kim stressed that

socialist democracy in our country is politics of the people themselves which enables the people to hold the position of masters and fulfill their role as masters; it is the best of all democratic politics that makes it possible to combine the *Chajusong* [independence] of individuals closely with that of the collective and to realize both satisfactorily. In our country everyone exercises equal and independent rights as a genuine master of the state and society, and all the people develop their creative wisdom and talent helping and leading one another forward as comrades on the principle of "One for all and all for one."[22]

By introducing the concept of socialist democracy, Kim is trying to avoid a popular uprising, but the goal of socialist democracy is not yet accomplished, and he may have to recognize the need to introduce Soviet-style *perestroika* in order to achieve it. Thus, if and when Kim Jong Il succeeds his father in the 1990s as the leader of North Korea, he may be forced to adopt Gorbachev-style reform without a denunciation of the socialist system that his father created and sustained in the name of socialist democracy for a half-century. Nevertheless, change in the political system and reform in the economic structure are inevitable under the leadership of Kim Jong Il in the 1990s.

Notes

1. *Korea Daily News* (Published by Korea News Service in Tokyo), 25 August 1989, pp. 15-16.

2. For the Joint Venture Law, see Chin Kim, "North Korean Joint Venture Laws," *The California Western School of Law Journal* 19, no. 2, 1989.

3. Premier Kang Sung San's report to the Third Plenary Session of the seventh-term Supreme People's Assembly in July 1984.

4. For Kim Il Sung's visit to Moscow, see Ilpyong J. Kim, "Soviet-Chinese Rivalry over the Korean Peninsula," in Jane Shapiro Zacek, ed., *The Gorbachev Generation: Issues in Soviet Foreign Policy* (New York: Paragon House Publishers, 1988), pp. 273-95.

5. *Korea Daily News*, 8 February 1986.

6. *Vantage Point: Developments in North Korea* (Seoul: Naewoe Press, January 1988), p. 9.

7. See the press reports in *Dong-A Ilbo*, 1 February 1989.

8. See Kim Il Sung, *Theses on the Socialist Rural Question in Our Country* (Pyongyang: Foreign Language Publishing House, 1964).

9. Kim Il Sung, *Let Us Expedite the Ideological, Technical and Cultural Revolutions More Dynamically* (Pyongyang: Foreign Languages Publishing House, 1973).

10. Kim Jong Il, "On Thoroughly Establishing the System of Party Leadership," speech at a Consultative Meeting of Senior Officials of the Organizational Leadership Department and the Propaganda and Agitation Department of the Central Committee of the Workers' Party of Korea, April 28, 1979 (Pyongyang: Foreign Languages Publishing House, 1988), p. 2.

11. Ibid., p. 3.

12. Ibid., p. 14.

13. Kim Jong Il, "On Further Developing Educational Work," letter to the National Educational Activists, July 22, 1984 (Pyongyang: Foreign Language Press, 1984), p. 15.

14. For biographical information on Premier Yon, see *Vantage Point*, March 1989, pp. 24-25.

15. The text of Kim Il Sung's ninety-minute speech may be found in *Nodong Sinmun* (Workers' Daily News), 9 September, 1988.

16. Kim Il Sung, "Answers to Questions Raised by the Chief of the Bureau of the Italian Radio and Television for the Far East, on October 29, 1988" (Pyongyang: Foreign Languages Publishing House, 1989), p. 3.

17. Kim Il Sung, "On Enhancing the Role of the Officials of the People's Government Organs," speech delivered to the officials of People's Government Organs on April 20, 1978 (Pyongyang: Foreign Languages Publishing House, 1989).

18. Reported in *Dong-A Ilbo*, 2 April 1989, and *Chung-ang Ilbo*, 5 April 1989.

19. Kim Jong Il, "On Further Developing Educational Work," p. 4.

20. Kim Il Sung, "Let Us Bring the Advantages of Socialism in Our Country into Full Play," policy speech addressed to the First Session of the Ninth Supreme People's Assembly of the DPRK, on May 24, 1990, p. 2.

21. Ibid., p. 3.

22. Ibid., pp. 15-16.

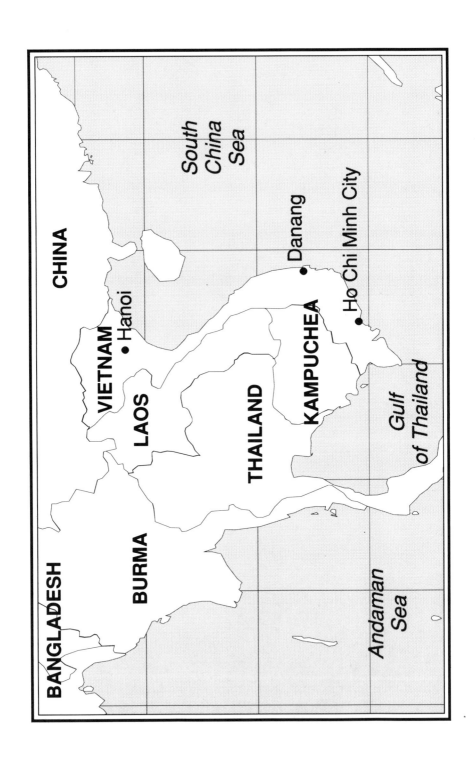

13. REFORM IN VIETNAM

Douglas Pike

Perhaps the most important security question now facing the United States, and the issue most central to its future in foreign policy terms, is whether the Leninist political systems of the world are currently undergoing fundamental, irreversible, systemic change, and if so, what this portends for us and the rest of the world.

It seems unarguable that the USSR presently is in the throes of some kind of significant change, which it labels *perestroika.* It can be asserted that we do not yet fully understand this phenomenon. Some argue that at best *perestroika* is only a transitory and largely superficial political development. Others assert it represents no breakthrough to a new political order and easily could be reversed in a reactionary backlash. I am convinced that the phenomenon of change in the USSR exists, that there can never be a going back to a Stalinist order, and probably no going back even to the Brezhnev era.

That same speculative judgment on change can be rendered on other Leninist systems, principally in East Europe. There is reduced clarity with respect to China. In some systems — for instance, North Korea — there has been no visible reform at all. In other, smaller systems — such as Vietnam, the country of our chief interest here — the degree of change appears to fall somewhere mid-range along the spectrum from Poland to North Korea.

Eventually this process of change (or non-change) will work itself out and all will become clear as to what exactly has transpired. In the meantime, however, ambiguity rules. Wisdom dictates that we constantly bear in mind that this change is a highly dynamic process. Only a foolish determinist would say the future is foreordained.

Examination of the reform process in Vietnam here is divided into five parts, following this brief introduction. First there is a scene-setter, an overview of contemporary Vietnamese history in terms of the reform process. Then comes a general discussion of the concept of reform as it applies to Vietnam — the ways it resembles the process elsewhere and how it differs. Third, there is an examination of the Hanoi style of politics, particularly as found at the highest or Politburo leadership level, and what this means for the reform effort. Fourth is a description of the several major impediments to reform. Finally, some conclusions are drawn.[1]

Postwar Vietnam

In order to understand the forces for reform (as well as the countervailing forces represented by the neoconservatives) in Vietnam it is necessary to review briefly the recent socioeconomic history of the country.

Contrary to the accounts of the short-stay visitors to Vietnam during the last two or three years, no renovation effort began in the late 1980s. The "news" commonly reported back by visitors was that Vietnam at long last had recognized the need for economic change and had embarked on a full-scale campaign to accomplish this, one that holds great promise for quick payoff and extensive benefits.

Actually a full-scale campaign of economic renovation was launched in September 1979 at the Vietnam Communist party's Sixth Plenum (Fourth Congress). The plenum assessed the economic scene, diagnosed economic ills, and set down a program later universally known as the Resolution Six Program. It was to end the decline that had begun in 1975 and was intended to lift Vietnam by its economic bootstraps. Directives were issued to loosen economic controls and to offer new economic incentives to farmers and food distributors, particularly in the southern private or non-collectivized sector of the economy. Centering Resolution Six reforms in the agricultural sector was logical, since Vietnam is essentially an agrarian society, with about 85 percent of its labor force assigned to food production, food distribution, and food processing activities.

The Resolution Six campaign succeeded in halting the precipitous decline of the Vietnamese economy, the postwar low point being the summer of 1979, when there were rice riots in some of the remote villages of northern Vietnam. Then the economic curve flattened out, neither worsening nor improving despite continuing effort by both state and party. There was no explanation for this at the time. Only later did it become evident that a major reason for the failure was extensive sabotage of Resolution Six programs by middle- and lower-ranking party cadres who saw the reforms shunting them aside at the grassroots level and thus presenting a direct threat to their careers.

During this period, which continued into the early 1980s (and in some ways continues today), an extraordinary pessimism settled on the Vietnamese people. It was a compound of disgruntlement and discontent on the part of party cadres and members; disillusionment and a sense of futility among the intellectuals; and a general sour mood among the public. The press labeled this "negativism." In the north the negativism was the worst because of the dashed expectations of northerners who had come to believe that postwar Vietnam would become "ten times more beautiful," an oft-repeated wartime pledge of Ho Chi Minh. The sense was that the country was being overwhelmed by economic and social problems beyond the capacity of its aging leadership. The party, which had enjoyed a wartime reputation for near infallibility, was seen as the central reason for this failure, hence it lost credibility among both its own members and the public. Antigovernment graffiti appeared on public buildings in Hanoi, something unknown a few years earlier. The mass media began a campaign of careful but explicit reporting of antiregime activity: food demonstrations, work-place strikes, systematic disobedience to governmental orders (particularly in the more remote provinces), economic sabotage, rising crime, social disturbances, rumor mongering, subversion, and counter-revolution.[2]

This basic dissatisfaction paved the way for the appearance of Nguyen Van Linh as party general secretary (in December 1986). He launched a campaign not of economic reform per se but of implementation of the economic reform program already on the drafting boards.

Basic reform policy had been set down a few months earlier, probably under Linh's guidance, at the Party's Eighth Plenum (Fifth Congress). The general objectives, as fixed by the Eighth Plenum resolution, and in its language, were:[3]

- To stimulate production, chiefly agricultural, within a rational structure by developing the potential found in the various economic sectors — that is, labor, land, trade, material-technological — always seeking higher quality, greater efficiency, and increased productivity.
- To stabilize (that is, to raise) the standard of living particularly for workers, farmers, civil servants, party members, and military personnel. (This requires better state party controls over production, distribution-circulation, the marketplace, prices, and state budget.)
- To generate new sources of state revenue to invest in the socialist

industrial system and to provide the necessary material-technical needs for true socialism.

• To spur transformation to a socialist economic system, with a strong state (owned) economy, collectivized agriculture, and full development of the household (cottage) industry sector.

• To ensure support for and the strengthening of the national defense and internal security systems, so as to combat enemy sabotage and struggle against negative phenomena in the society.

The conceptual framework of Resolution Eight, when stripped of its lugubrious terminology, was broad based and had a scope and breadth not found in earlier documents. It reflected Linh's influence in being a frank and honest acknowledgment of the fact that the Vietnamese economy is in serious trouble, and in admitting to past errors and shortcomings, whereas earlier plenum resolutions had tended to put blame for economic difficulties on external factors. The Linh approach is also radical in that it departs significantly from certain past orthodox economic positions. It represents a more sophisticated analysis, whereas earlier high-level economic pronouncements demonstrated little knowledge of economics, Marxist-Leninist or otherwise. Linh eschews many of the earlier, simplistic notions, recognizing the complexity and interrelatedness of the various elements of the economic sector. His policy guidelines do not represent anything new or never before said, but do convey willingness to break with past methods.[4]

Implementation of Linh's changes got underway in 1986 and began to pick up speed in 1987. Vietnam has now dismantled portions of its economic system that had been in place for decades. The primacy of agriculture has now been unequivocally established. Collectivization of southern agriculture has been firmly put on hold. The long-standing policy of economic development "balanced" between agriculture and industry has been replaced by a policy that assigns the food production sector almost automatic top priority. No more will there be Stalinist showplace steel mills simply to impress foreign visitors. Pragmatism in economic decision-making has cut into the monopoly once enjoyed by ideology, although this is a battle not yet irreversibly won. The program to decentralize authority in the economic sector, from the center in Hanoi to the inter-zone and provincial spheres, continues to be pressed. It is a virtual imperative, if there is to be increased productivity, to grant greater latitude to provincial party secretaries in key provinces (such as Haiphong Province) and to managers of major economic enterprises, particularly those generating exports. However, this also is a most delicate undertaking, since it strikes at the planning monopoly long enjoyed by the center and hence is pursued if at all in a hesitant and inconsistent manner. There is renewed emphasis on the importance of developing technical competence and scientific expertise, a task assigned to the legendary Gen. Vo Nguyen Giap. Eventually this may lead to the allocation of more resources to education, although there is no evidence that this has happened yet.

While the intent of the reform is to increase production and solve the more pressing trade and fiscal problems, to date most of the change has been limited to increasing plant investment and to capital accumulation. The promise of a rapid increase in the standard of living, with the exception of providing more food, still remains just that — a promise. A new salary scale has been introduced, geared realistically to prices and the cost of living; it includes wage differentials based on individual worker output and productivity. Inflation has been checked. A systematic effort has been launched to attract foreign economic investment and assistance. Joint venture legislation was passed by the National Assembly and began attracting investors, particularly from Southeast Asia.

Parameters of Reform

The "reform" process in Vietnam, which gradually unfolded during the mid- and late 1980s, when viewed from a broad philosophic perspective, both resembles and differs from the process in the other Leninist systems. That this should be the case — that there are both common patterns as well as distinct dissimilarities among these sister systems — is both understandable and to be expected. Commonality flows from their more or less identical social visions, which we call Marxism-Leninism, and which have been deliberately engineered. The differences that exist are the result of cultural factors and historical influences indigenous to the respective countries.

Scholars who are true cultural relativists argue that any parallel drawn between Vietnam and other systems is superficial, that attempts to compare them lead to conclusions that are meaningless, or worse, dangerously wrong. That may be too extreme a judgment, but we are well advised to be constantly aware of the pitfall of fallacious analogy.

The temptation to compare Vietnam's reform effort with that of the USSR has been encouraged by the semantic inventions of the Vietnamese themselves. Hanoi theoreticians describing the Soviet reform phenomenon employ a series of terms translated from the Russian. The four most important concepts they see at work are: *glasnost,* or openness; *perestroika,* or structuring of the system; *noveye myslenye,* or new thinking (that is, new ways of thinking); and *demokratizazia,* or democratization. *Glasnost* is seen as a political instrument that will bring into being the more important instrument, *perestroika*. Taken together the two represent "new thinking." The purpose of this effort, it is said in Hanoi, is to free the Soviet Union from stagnation and cause it to become a more prosperous and even more powerful nation.

There is no exact linguistic equivalent of *perestroika* in Vietnamese; two terms are employed meaning renovation: *doi moi* and *canh tan*. *Glasnost* is translated as *coi mo*, but its precise meaning is as vague in Vietnamese as it is in Russian (or in English, for that matter). *Novoye myslenye*, or new thinking, is translated into Vietnamese as *tu duy moi* but is little used except by party theoretical journals. The concept of "democratization" is studiously avoided. Ideology is something of an impediment here for the Vietnamese, since the idea of "restructuring" the perfect political system implies heresy. The press tends to substitute for *coi mo* the term *noi thang noi that* (speaking straight, speaking truth) and use it chiefly to mean the exposure of official malfeasance, which of course justifies the proposed reforms. For the general public the term connotes both punishment of corrupt officials and others responsible for the country's dire social and economic condition, and the aspiration for genuine social justice. For intellectuals *coi mo* connotes greater intellectual freedom, although within limits, and permits open criticism of individual leaders — in cafes and even in university seminar rooms, no longer only in whispers behind closed doors.

Not to be drawn into a linguistic bog, it must be noted that the difficulty in translating these Russian reform terms into Vietnamese and then into English, is that the concepts are alien to Vietnam unless put into the context of abstract Vietnamese political thought having to do with governance and leadership — with such ideas as *phu duc*, or virtue (also connoting merit/religious blessing), and *the* (literally "power" or "position of strength," though a term seldom used alone in Vietnamese, but usually as a modifier). The meaning is that there is no strict one-to-one conversion of these terms from Russian to Vietnamese. The system of equivalents that has been developed by Hanoi appears to have been not for semantic purposes so much as to impress Moscow, which of course is funding the economic reform.

For the past decade and a half the USSR has been involved in a serious and, one might say, comprehensive effort to help Vietnam lift itself by its economic bootstraps. Hundreds of joint economic programs have been launched, thousands of Soviet technicians have labored as advisers, large numbers of Vietnamese mid-level cadres and specialists have been given formal training in economics either in Vietnam or in the USSR. The joint effort has to a large extent gone on the rocks, accomplishing far less than either party had hoped or expected. The reason for this is not clear. In part it appears to be that some of the Soviet advice was bad or unworkable. In part it appears that the Vietnamese planners constantly rewrote their five-year plans, never allowing a plan to run its course long enough to be tested. In any event it is not that the two sides are in contention over what should be done so much as that both are puzzled as to why remedial measures do not work better than they do.[5]

Beginning in late 1988, when the reform movement throughout the Leninist world took on additional complexity, the Hanoi leaders sought to define the concept more sharply and to set down specific guidelines. To this end a wealth of official statements appeared in print — in the form of directives, speeches by Politburo figures, and National Assembly debate transcripts.[6]

For our purpose here, which is to suggest the parameters of the reform process, perhaps the most illustrative document was produced in December 1988 at an unusual Politburo meeting. Had it been held in the United States, it would have been considered a brainstorming session, that is, a free-wheeling, no-agenda discussion of what is right and wrong in Vietnam at the moment, and what needs to be done about it. The results were published as "Eight Conclusions" by *Nhan Dan* on December 8, 1988.[7]

Briefly, with some paraphrase and commentary, the eight points are:

1. The ultimate goal of the Vietnamese society remains "advancing to socialism," and all "widespread and distorted notions" to the contrary must be rectified. It is permissible to borrow science and technology from capitalist countries, but not institutions, ideas, or methods that counter orthodox Marxism-Leninism. The ideological reaffirmation was singled out and underscored in subsequent Hanoi press commentary on the eight points. In effect it fixes the outer limits of *coi mo* (openness).

2. Progress has been made in the *doi moi* effort to reform and overhaul the economy and parts of the society. However, most sectors remain "rife with numerous difficulties." This is a general assessment of the current scene by the Politburo, a judgment that there has been some commendable progress in agriculture, in economic decentralization, and in the various motivation and mobilization campaigns, but less success in raising productivity levels, either on the farm or in the factory.[8] The institutional revitalization of the Communist party has fallen short. And, most seriously, the "ideological task" of persuading both party members and the general public that Marxism-Leninism has the answers to Vietnam's various problems has made little progress.

3. The campaign against "negativism" (the catch-all term for what is wrong with the society) "has not, obviously, met expectations" and must

be pursued more vigorously. In addition to the party, the mass media, the mass organizations such as the Fatherland Front, and the National Assembly have this task. Essentially, the anti-negativism campaign is seen as a moral exhortation effort by all communications media, which are charged with exposing and denouncing "typical cases of negativism such as degenerate and deviate cadres, unhealthy lifestyles, the bad practices of hooligans, thugs and dishonest merchants" as well as the more abstract "obsolete mechanisms of management," all of which perpetuate negativism.

4 Still absent, and still badly needed, is some party-supplied comprehensive, unifying concept for organizing and administering the *doi moi,* or renovation, process. What is needed is some plausible and attractive ideological construct that will also prove to be workable. However, this is not a call for dogma or intellectual explanation but for a new generalized procedure to mobilize and motivate party members and energize the general public. Chiefly it involves the major existing institutions serving those purposes: the mass social organizations, the agit-prop cadre corps, the *khiem-thao* (criticism/self-criticism) mechanism, the mass media, the educational institutions, and the cultural sector. (It is to be noted that discussion of this point occupies some 40 percent of the entire statement.)

5. The responsibility for reform through *doi moi* must be more broadly assigned within the society; it does not rest simply with the party and high-level state leaders. This requirement appears directed chiefly at the National Assembly, and in fact a concerted effort currently is under way to allow the assembly greater authority if it will assume greater responsibility. Point five stresses the need for a "democratic atmosphere" in Vietnam in the search to "meet the people's legitimate demands." It also stresses the importance of officials "listening to the opinions of upright people in settling problems at the grassroots level in fair, reasonable, orderly and law-abiding ways." In point five the Politburo also makes a direct appeal to Vietnamese intellectuals, artists, and other creative influentials, to support renovation, offering as incentive greater artistic freedom or at least a reduction of coercive state and party controls.[9] (The statement calls on artists to limit their criticism through "self-imposed discipline.") Behind this forthright rhetoric, however, one hears a note of hesitancy, a sense of uncertainty that reflects the thinking of the still powerful neoconservatives on the Politburo as to exactly how far the people can be trusted in assuming authority over and responsibility for their own lives.

6. The party must remain central to all things in Vietnam. And to the extent that it has lost that position it must reclaim it. Essentially this

involves mobilization and motivation efforts within the party ranks. It also requires the ruthless weeding out of incompetent and corrupt cadres; more extensive training and retraining of party cadres, more agit-prop work, and a renewed search for a more persuasive ideological construct for the reform process.

7. The mass media must be expanded improved, and energized. More money must be spent on publishing, on agit-prop work, and on education. The next five-year plan must have a special fund for development of the press/information sector. Salaries of writers, reporters, editors, lecturers, and artists must be increased. Party schools must use their funds more rationally, "to improve teaching and not spend it on improving the living conditions of teachers and students."

8. Finally, a special committee is established to deal with all this (predictably, it would seem — the inevitable response of any government to a problem is to appoint a committee). It reports to the CPV Central Committee Secretariat and is charged with monitoring progress in renovation. It is also to evaluate systematically the "ideological status of both Party cadres and Party members," meaning that the party's semipurge, under way for several years, probably will continue unabated. And the committee is "systematically to evaluate the political mood of the people." This is indeed new and innovative, a serious effort to take Vietnam's political pulse.

The party's theoretical journal succinctly and candidly captured the problem Vietnam faces in statistical terms, as of the spring of 1989:

> The road to revolution is not paved just with glory. An "historical" irony has made itself felt. After 14 years of socialist construction nationwide and nearly 35 years for the North alone we are still groping our way about in the first stage of the transitional period. What is more, the national socioeconomic situation is fraught with prolonged, grave difficulties. With a population growth rate of 1 percent, an increase of 4 percent in national income is normally needed to ensure development; our population was up by 2.07 percent in 1987, but national income increased by only 2.1 percent. In the past almost 10 years, our national income incremental rate has dropped continuously — from 6.4 percent (1981–85) to 2.7 percent (1986–87). Labor productivity is very low and has, in recent years, remained at the rate of 6,700 dong per capita based on 1982 prices. Each dong of national income represents a profit of only 6 cents. Life is unstable, society is in turmoil, and ethics are on the decline.[10]

The difficulty with these reform measures is not that they are wrong or not needed. Rather, it is that they are largely marginal. They do not address the basic impediments to reform (discussed at length below). They are "band-aid" reforms, worthwhile perhaps, but not sufficient to meet the need.

Reform and Politburo Politics

The political environment in which the Hanoi leadership operates and which the political heritage has shaped over the centuries is both complex and interpenetrating. Its essence is ancient traditionalism encased in a martial spirit, shored up by modern ideology. As with all political cultures it is a product of heritage — in this case, Confucianism/Buddhism permeated by Marxism-Leninism — which has been hardened and reinforced for decades by the experiences and lessons-learned of its long-lived leadership. Its major characteristics, which can only be mentioned here, are geographic regionalism, the famed north-center-south (Tonkin, Annam, Cochin-China) division of the country that has come down as a political influence as important as caste is in India; lingering traditionalism characterized by Sinic factionalism, and within this factionalism, clandestinism in politics (the means by which the Vietnamese dealt with foreign occupiers, first the Chinese, then the French); the many religious and quasi-religious influences, primarily Confucianism, Buddhism, and Taoism; and the political fires of the twentieth century — anticolonialism, the drive for nation building, and the persuasive influence of Western thought, Marxism, Leninism, and Maoism.

More should be said about this political heritage: the long struggle between concentrated power and its dispersion, between the court and the village; the equally long-standing fluctuation between the forces of authoritarian government and those of controllable government, which ordinarily meant interpreting the emperor's behavior in light of his mandate from Heaven; the struggle between monism and pluralism; the new milieu created by the rise of the proletariat at the expense of the other classes and the subsequent emergence of a "new class" of the privileged party members; and finally the establishment of an extremely intrusive social system making continuous and intensive efforts to manipulate the beliefs and attitudes of the people. It must suffice here to note the existence of these conditioning factors, which influence policy makers and their policy decisions.[11]

The result of these influences has been a dark-edged, pessimistic philosophical view of the world as filled with the unreliable, and in which betrayal is the norm. As a result, the reform effort is marked by a kind of militant praetorian dogmatism, where reform is treated as a form of combat, as a strategic campaign best described as policymaking and problem solving through constant, never-ending, protracted struggle (or *dau tranh).* The concept is rooted in Marxism, primarily in the notion of historical determinism, but it is heavily influenced by both Confucian and Buddhist ideas having to do with time and change. *Dau tranh,* it is held, if applied in various forms and extended over time, will inevitably yield success, whether on the battlefield or in restructuring the economy.

The Hanoi leadership system that has emerged out of this heritage has a number of distinct characteristics: It is a system of competing factions held together by the principle of collective leadership. Power is truly shared by the fifteen men of the Politburo, and since the death of Ho Chi Minh there has not been even a preeminent figure, a "first among equals." Political infighting is over issues, as it is in every political system. Each of the Politburo members represents a sector of the political system, his "constituency," which both gives him political status and constrains his policy positions. Political power is highly concentrated, held almost without external challenge by the fourteen Politburo members, who face neither the institutional challenge found in the USSR nor the geographic challenge common to China. Political power is well integrated. It is forged of a constant forty-year association, Politburo members having shared the same experiences and the same social traumas. They hold a tightly shared consensus of what the society stands for, where it should go, what goals it should seek. There are sharp disagreements over how to achieve these goals and at what pace, but this is an agreement to disagree. Finally, it is a system ill equipped to recruit the kind of leadership now required — educated, technically competent individuals experienced in running a modern bureaucracy. Only two of the present Politburo members have the equivalent of a high school education. None of them has any significant knowledge of the science of economics. Those who are qualified are excluded from the Politburo-level decision-making process by the system — which puts value entirely on loyalty, ideological orthodoxy, and manipulative political skills.

To be successful the leadership of any country today must be able to cope with the challenge of the high-technology revolution. Politburo members in Hanoi are fully aware of the need to develop technologically. The Politburo's problem is how to convert desire into meaningful remedial programs. The problem is discussed in further detail below.

Impediments to Reform

Vietnam's abject postwar failure has been rendered even more graphic by the astounding success of its neighbors, the member countries of the Association of Southeast Asian Nations (ASEAN). It has been a double-helix phenomenon: a spiral downward by the three Indochinese states led by Vietnam, and beside this, an upward spiral by the seven ASEAN states. No one has been able to offer a fully satisfactory explanation for this. A common view, encountered in places like Singapore, is that it is a matter of *joss,* that is, fortuitous good luck.

A survey of the Vietnamese reform effort and of the many examples of the process failing to meet the need turns up a multitude of explanations, which can be grouped into several general clusters.

The first impediment to reform clearly is the failed Vietnamese leadership. It is difficult under the best of circumstances for a poor, underdeveloped country to achieve economic success — so great is the challenge, so numerous are the obstacles. But it is patently impossible without a leadership of firm if not ruthless determination. Leaders must be willing to make sacrifices in the name of reform, sacrifices in domestic social policy and in foreign policy.

The Hanoi leadership over the years has exhibited remarkable continuity and steadfastness. Probably no other ruling group in modern history has been more constant in purpose and more consistent in behavior. There is much to be said for such leadership characteristics. However, in the past decade Vietnam's leaders have proved themselves incapable of running a semi-modern economy, a fact that now seems widely acknowledged throughout Vietnam, including in the upper reaches of the party. The leaders are tough, implacable men whose wartime experience taught them that the way to solve any problem is through sustained application of maximum force — political, psychological, or, if necessary, physical force. They were exactly the kind of leaders needed for a long war against a formidable foe but the wrong kind for peacetime, when a softer, subtler, more flexible style of leadership is required.

The present leadership is old, calcified, rigid in mindset, possessed of a siege mentality. It has isolated itself from outside influence, even from the Central Committee level. What is needed is a leadership willing to put "economics in command," as the party slogan has it, a leadership with the will power to force subordination of those factors that impede the reform process. The present leadership will not do this because it cannot. The conclusion forced on us is that there cannot be true reform in Vietnam until the present old-guard leaders have passed from the scene. Even then, of course, there is no assurance that the new leaders, those produced by a generational transfer of political power, will prove to be equal to the needs of the system.

The second impediment to reform is the absence of a receptive social environment. In broadest terms this means there is no shared agreement by the leaders and the people as to the purpose and ultimate configuration of the reform process. Inevitably there will be disputation over detail, but beneath there must be consensus on both the nature and extent of reform. The social consensus to provide this flows from the leadership. It must propose or order goals (depending on whether the system is democratic or totalitarian), then persuade or compel acceptance of its vision. In Vietnam the leadership does not offer a clear vision of reform because it does not have one.

Despite its strong ethno-linguistic character the Vietnamese society has always been badly divided. In part this is a product of geographic regionalism, the famed north-center-south division that has been firmly entrenched over the centuries by competing sets of prejudices and self-perceptions. In part it is due to the curse of Chinese-style factionalism, which characterizes political behavior from the village to the Politburo. From this fragmentation flow differing world views on most matters, including the idea of reform.

The result is that Vietnam remains very much two (or in some ways, three) separate socio-psychological systems with competing views on reform. This makes the challenge of establishing social consensus even greater. In what was formerly North Vietnam, the regime's communication machine generally can persuade the population to accept limited reform efforts, providing they offer at least a few benefits. In what was South Vietnam the task is more formidable since the southerners have little faith either in the abilities of the Hanoi leadership or in the reform doctrine being advanced.

The impediment of an unreceptive social environment, while serious, is not quite as insurmountable as it appears on the surface, at least with respect to the reform process. While there is not — and is not likely to be — consensus on social organization, political participation, and external relations, there is tacit agreement on the need for an improved internal economic reform and generally a willingness to work for it. Differences over institutions and methods will remain, but almost everyone will support almost any reform program that gives promise of working.

The third general impediment to reform in Vietnam is weak governmental and economic administrative structure, usually described as infrastructure. It is a problem of institutionalization. Although Vietnam does have a bureaucracy — indeed, one of the world's densest bureaucracies — it lacks the institutional mechanisms for plan making, management development, economic coordination, and actual administration of production, both on the farm and in the factory. As Foreign Minister Nguyen Co Thach has observed, the rest of Southeast Asia runs on computers, but Vietnam is still in the bicycle age. Governmental institutions are both weak and inappropriate. There remains the persistent tendency by the

Politburo to monopolize decisionmaking, a necessary arrangement in wartime, when all authority must flow from the center. But the methods of conducting a war do not convert to the reform process. Now there must be latitude provided for local situations, greater allocation of responsibility, and premium placed on initiative rather than on blind obedience. The ponderous present arrangement — a *troika* of party, government, and mass organization — served well the administrative and psychic needs of war. But it is not a system designed to facilitate reform — that is, thinking through what needs to be done — nor does it permit development of the specialized and decentralized guidance so vital to the parallel advance of various sectors of the society.

Particularly, Vietnam suffers from an insufficient number of trained, technically competent individuals to work the system — engineers, scientists, economists, research and development personnel. Worse, it does not have adequate educational facilities, especially to teach technical subjects. Such education is largely done abroad, mostly in the USSR and East Europe, posing additional problems. Vietnam is aware that the success of the "tigers" of Asia — South Korea, Taiwan, Singapore — is the result of an early decision to invest massive amounts of money in technical education. Hanoi officials are aware of the need to emulate this example but have simply been unable to bring themselves to do so. They have not even been willing to halt the flow of technically trained graduates into the armed forces. If there is a single index to use in measuring actual commitment to reform in Vietnam it is investment in the educational sector.

The best source, indeed the only major present source, for technically trained personnel in Vietnam is the military. There are indications that Hanoi may cut its armed forces in half (from the present 1.2 million full-time and 1.7 million paramilitary), which will free skilled personnel for the reform effort. There is even the suggestion that troops be demobilized by unit, then transferred en masse to the civilian labor market. It is argued that such units represent a well-organized, disciplined labor force, possessed of collective skill (such as a construction battalion), which should be preserved, not scattered. There is precedent for this in several socialist countries. Both the Soviet armed forces and the People's Liberation Army in China operate their own factories, manufacturing not only military hardware but also clothing, tableware, construction materials, and other products for the civilian market. These systems have a reputation for higher quality control than their civilian counterparts. However, economists question whether, on the basis of economic rationality, a military unit can grow rice more productively or build a bridge more efficiently than can civilian organizations. Parallel institutions also represent duplication. From a strict cost-accounting standpoint it probably would be better to demobilize part of the Vietnamese army (PAVN) and transfer the individuals to the economic sector. However, it is probable that once the Cambodia war ends and the threat from China subsides, PAVN will be assigned an important, though as yet undefined, role in the reform effort.

The marketplace itself is perhaps Vietnam's weakest institution in terms of reform. It is a complex dual (or even triple) system that is widely disliked by the leadership, though for differing reasons. Probably the dual system will continue to exist for at least another decade simply because the state market will be dependent on the second economy to supply the system with its basic needs.[12]

Hanoi leaders have long been aware of these institutional weaknesses and have constantly railed against them. *Nhan Dan* and other newspapers are filled with Politburo speeches, critical editorials, and letters of complaint from readers. Party Secretary Nguyen Van Linh writes a column in *Nhan Dan* titled "What Is to Be Done," in which he cites examples of the system's failure: 360 tons of garlic buds destined for export were forgotten in a cold storage warehouse and rotted; aviation fuel arriving at Haiphong port must pass through eight government agencies, with all of the attendant paperwork, before reaching a plane's fuel tank; a Ministry of Agriculture official sold one of the ministry's tractors on the black market, an indiscretion conveniently overlooked by the ministry's internal affairs watchdog, his friend. Such criticism is ubiquitous. Even the once sacrosanct Central Committe-Politburo appears to be within range of reform's grasp although press references blaming the Politburo for lack of reform are most guarded.

It is evident from all this that the reform impulse is everywhere present in Vietnam. Absence of desire is not the problem; rather, it is a case of the spirit being willing and the flesh being weak. Indeed, there is something of a paradox: No one in Vietnam defends the status quo, no one asserts that the way it has been for the last fifteen years is the way it should be for the next fifteen. Yet change comes only at glacial speed and each reform is only grudgingly accepted.

The final major impediment to reform in Vietnam, simply put, is money — vast amounts of capital are needed, chiefly investment capital. Vietnam in effect is on the socialist world dole, receiving assistance estimated at $1.3 billion per year, mostly from the USSR (including commodity aid); Vietnam also has gotten about the same amount in military aid, although the military portion has been declining for several years and will probably continue to do so as Vietnam extricates itself from Cambodia.[13]

To launch true economic development, certainly the ultimate objective in the reform effort, Vietnam needs capital far in excess of what the USSR (or anyone) is prepared to offer. One example: UN economists estimate that it costs about $9,000 to transfer a worker from the agricultural to the industrial sector (that is, the expense of his training and the prorated cost of the new facility, infrastructure, etc.). Vietnam hopes to transfer three million of its agricultural labor force. The cost would therefore be about $9 billion. The question is, where will this money come from? Capital can be accumulated internally, that is, by "taking it out of the hides of the people," as Stalin expressed it. Or it can be borrowed from abroad, or received gratis. Vietnam has been obliged to take its funds from foreign sources. Although some investment capital can eventually be expected from capitalist countries, especially Japan, it is difficult to imagine that this will be enough.

Conclusions

It seems clear that the reform process in Vietnam is moving more slowly than in most other Leninist countries and that this is a condition that will exist at least as long as the present leadership remains in power. It also seems clear that many of the reform programs introduced to date are only marginal and that they avoid the more knotty fundamental reform requirements that sooner or later must be addressed.

It is equally clear that the slow pace of reform, as well as the more general lack of postwar economic development, is traceable primarily to failures of leadership. The individuals who serve in the Hanoi Politburo are bugs in amber, trapped by a wartime, bunker mentality, unable to break out of this mold, unable even to appreciate the fact that these are new times requiring new attitudes and new approaches. What once was virtue — implacableness — becomes a vice when flexibility is called for. Precisely those characteristics of leadership which enabled Hanoi to persevere to victory now inhibit it in its reform effort. The Politburo continues to operate on the assumption that spirit is what really counts. Material factors are discounted or ignored. Social and economic problems are addressed in moral or patriotic terms rather than in pragmatic or technical terms. The mindset is to make war on such problems. This is the Politburo's famous protracted-conflict mentality. It is the way to win a war but is singularly inappropriate in solving social and economic problems, which require flexibility and resourcefulness and in which bulldog determination often does more damage than good.

Outsiders seeking to push reform along in Vietnam should understand that they will have only a limited influence on such leadership behavior and policies. In particular, the effectiveness of economic goads, levers, or incentives will be slight. Vietnam's political culture disdains materialism and is reluctant to be ruled by economic considerations. Since Vietnamese communism, like other brands, is rooted in materialism, it is sometimes difficult to understand why money does not speak louder than it does in Hanoi, or why efforts to influence Vietnamese behavior through economic inducement are so often unsuccessful. In part the reason is that traditional Vietnamese scholar-gentry treated money, especially its acquisition, with contempt. In part, the reason is that external economic activity is associated with an unhealthy dependence on outsiders, which, exacerbated by latent xenophobia, is seen as a vague threat to national sovereignty. The result is an ambivalent attitude toward all external economic ties, even trade, and a determination never to be dictated to by outside economic influences.

All reform, particularly involving systemic change, requires taking calculated risks. All evidence suggests that the present leaders in Hanoi remain dominated by conservative sentiments, and while they are highly desirous of social change, they are unwilling to take any chances. They want risk-free reform, something that does not exist.

If it is true, as many economists argue, that political reform is a precondition for economic reform — and if it is true, as many political scientists argue, that political reform inevitably follows true economic reform — then, in the case of Vietnam it is unlikely that we will witness either kind of reform in the near future; it will occur at the earliest only after a generational transfer of political power in Hanoi.

In any event, it seems clear that reform in Vietnam turns on the question of leadership — present and future. It would be best for Vietnam if there were an abrupt, complete generational transfer of political power. But this is not likely. More probable is a gradual changeover, in which eventually the balance tips from the old guard to the younger, if not the young. Even then we cannot be certain that the next generation of leaders will be truly reform minded. In part this will depend on reform examples as they develop in other Leninist systems, particularly China. If the process in China proves to be a success it will have a profound influence on any future Hanoi leadership.

Notes

1. Surveying the literature on the Vietnam reform process in preparing this essay, I was struck by the paucity of analytical materials. While there is an enormous amount of original source materials — the Indochina Archive at the University of California contains perhaps 4,000 pages of documentation on the subject (chiefly from Hanoi) — refined source material was extremely rare. I found no full-scale studies, only a few journal articles and a number of perceptive accounts by journalists, academics, and government officials based chiefly on short visits to Vietnam. The most significant works I encountered are listed in the bibliography. Of the entries there, I particularly recommend those by

Tetsusaburo Kimura, Vo Nhan Tri, Geoffrey Gunn, Adam Fforde and David Marr; also the reportage of Giles Campion, Agence France Presse; Murray Hiebert, *Far Eastern Economic Review;* Barry Wain, *Asian Wall Street Journal;* and Alan Dawson, *Bangkok Post* columnist. See also such materials as are available from Vietnam's leading economist (one of the country's few fully trained economists), Nguyen Xuan Oanh (chiefly interviews by foreign journalists or transcripts of his lectures abroad).

2. For typical Hanoi press reportage of the time, see Radio Hanoi/*Nhan Dan,* 21 January 1980.

3. See the author's "Retreat in Vietnam: the Vietnamese Communist Party's Sixth Plenum Resolution on the Economy," Library of Congress, Congressional Research Service Brief, September 1980.

4. The divergence in viewpoint at the Politburo level, between the reformers and the neo-conservatives, is captured fully in *Vietnam in the Face of Today's Socio-Economic Problems* (Hanoi: Foreign Languages Publishing House, 1987). It contains two speeches which pit Party Secretary and reformer Nguyen Van Linh against chief ideologue and neoconservative Truong Chinh. The essence of their difference — since they agree on the need for reform — is how best to achieve it. Linh argues for material incentives, Truong Chinh for reform through moral exhortation.

5. The USSR-Vietnam economic relationship is explored in detail in the author's *Vietnam and the USSR: Anatomy of an Alliance,* (Boulder, CO: Westview Press, 1987), which also contains a list of the 450 or so major joint economic projects of the past thirty years.

6. The most authoritative being the CPV Sixth Plenum (Sixth Congress) Resolution (March 20–29, 1989) published by Vietnam News Agency, 26/27 April 1989, and available in FBIS-EAS-89-81 and FBIS-EAS-89-84, 28 April and 4 May 1989. *Nhan Dan's* column, "Seeking to Understand the Resolution of the Party Central Committee Sixth Penum," has a two-part series, "Uniformly Implement the Multi-Sectorial Economic Policy, Liberate All Production Forces," 12–13 May 1989, FBIS-EAS-89-113, 14 June 1989. See also "Readjust the Economic Structure" in *Nhan Dan,* 9–10 May, FBIS-EAS-89-110, 9 June 1989; and Radio Hanoi broadcast, 11 May, FBIS-EAS-89-93, 16 May 1989, on shifting from "the centralized mechanism based on state subsidies to the socialist cost-accounting economic management."

7. Radio Hanoi, "Political Bureau's 'Conclusions' Released," FBIS-EAS-88-237, 9 December 1988.

8. By way of detail, *Nhan Dan,* 11 December 1988, carried a year-end review describing the year 1988 as it was officially viewed: it was a year intended to be "pivotal" in terms of economic improvement but turned out to be "one of not tremendous but modest change." There were unexpected food shortages and hunger because of natural calamities (loss of 300,000 metric tons of rice); continued shortage of raw materials and investment capital; "chaos in prices and money supply"; inflation; growing foreign debt; "degradation of public order and safety, land disputes in Nam Bo [South] and outcries over heavy taxes and irrational tax policies... all having heavy impact on the public's thinking and its confidence" in the party and state. On the credit side were these year-end statistics: probably a 19 million metric tons grain harvest (1.5 million metric tons over 1987); industrial production up 7 percent; exports totaling 10 million rubles; and the start of 50 foreign investment projects with total capitalization of $300 million. Delicately but pointedly, the editorial made it clear that a major factor in the failure during the year was the continuing leadership disarray resulting from the still-unresolved factional political power struggle between the reformers and the conservatives. "Do we face continued deadlock or have we found a way out?" it asked rhetorically. The future was viewed pessimistically: "Looking squarely at the truth, examining all those things not yet done... we must

acknowledge that effecting a significant change is not easy, we must admit that great are the difficulties and many are the obstacles that lie ahead," *Nhan Dan,* 12 December 1988, FBIS-EAS-88-238.

9. For a fuller discussion of the intellectuals in Vietnam see the account of the famed October 1987 gathering in Hanoi when party chief Nguyen Van Linh faced several hundred critical Vietnamese intellectuals to debate the matter of freedom of cultural expression in Vietnam, in "Dissidences intellectuelles au Viet-Nam: L'Affaire Nhan Van-Giai Pham," (Intellectual dissidence in Vietnam: The Nhan Van-Giai Pham case) by Georges Boudarel in *Politique aujourd'hui en Europe,* January 1989 (Editions Michel de Maule).

10. *Tap Chi Cong San,* May 1989, p. 6, FBIS-EAS-89-134, 14 July 1989.

11. For full discussion, see the author's "Origins of Leadership Change in the Socialist Republic of Vietnam," in Raymond Taras, ed., *Leadership Change in Communist States* (London: Unwin Publishers, 1989).

12. David Wurfel, "Perestroika, Vietnamese Style: Problems and Prospects," in Richard Stubbs, ed., *Vietnam: Facing the 1990s,* Asia Papers No. 1, Joint Centre for Asia Pacific Studies, Toronto, 1989.

13. Suggested by General Secretary Nguyen Van Linh in an interview with *L'Humanite* correspondent Roland Leroy, published 28 October 1988 and reprinted in FBIS Daily Report, East Asia (FBIS-EAS 88–218).

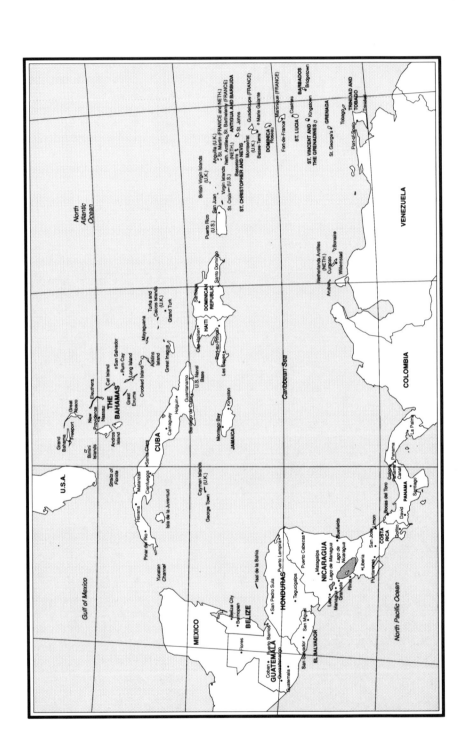

14. REFORM IN CUBA

Andrew Zimbalist
and
Wayne Smith

The perception in the United States often seems to be that Cuba is imper-meable to change, that its foreign policy and system of internal political controls remain locked in the patterns set during the sixties, and that Fidel Castro refuses to allow economic reforms of any kind. That is a mispercep-tion. Cuba experimented with Soviet-style economic reforms during the seventies, and while most institutions connected to these reforms have now been modified and *perestroika*'s institutions have not been accepted in their place, more appropriate economic policies and mechanisms are still being sought. New reforms are not ruled out. Cuba's foreign policy has also undergone a dramatic metamorphosis since the sixties: with one or two exceptions its support for guerrilla groups has ended and, instead, Cuba is now being reintegrated into the Latin American family of nations. There was even movement toward the relaxation of internal controls until the Bush administration's rejection of any thaw in United States–Cuban rela-tions removed a major incentive for continued improvement.

In this essay, we shall discuss the nature and contours of those changes in the Cuban economy and polity and try to anticipate future directions.

Economic Reforms

The inefficiencies of central planning have been apparent to scholars for some time. The 1980s witnessed a widespread recognition of this reality by the practitioners of central planning as well. The project of decentralizing reform, however, is economically complex and difficult, and politically it faces a formidable obstacle course set variously by politicians, planners, bureaucrats, and workers. The exigencies and the dynamic of economic reform have also set in motion a process of (or created pressures for) political reform.

Among the centrally planned economies (CPEs), Cuba seems to stand out not only for not declining to embrace the paths of *perestroika* and *glasnost*, but in fact for moving in the opposite direction. We hope to explicate the paradoxes of the Cuban reform process by considering both the dilemmas of economic reform in CPEs and the peculiarities of the Cuban case.

The Imperative for Reform

Nearly two million different goods circulate in the Cuban economy. It is simply impossible for central planners to plan the production and import levels as well as the allocation of all these goods. Consequently, planners take shortcuts: some goods are planned at decentralized levels, others are sold on "free" markets; enterprises use *jinetes* or pushers to obtain needed materials, or they make informal deals with each other as planning bureaucrats look the other way; many enterprises are simply told to produce at last year's level plus an increment, and so on. Even with these shortcuts, however, plans rarely work out, and imbalances at the microlevel are virtually ubiquitous. That is, enterprises regularly experience shortfalls of inputs or they receive improperly specified and, hence, unusable inputs; and citizens experience shortages of consumer goods. Both make adaptations, such as hoarding or dealing on gray or black markets, that only exacerbate the original shortages and make the plan's fulfillment more improbable. When some enterprises underfulfill their plan, linked enterprises do not receive their planned inputs, and a dangerous chain reaction can set in. Some workers, accustomed to input shortages and lack of consumer goods, reduce their work effort, and others leave work early to find uncongested public transportation, to locate goods in scarce supply, or to obtain a good place in the queue at the local grocery.

In the presence of these shortages, the plan has no efficient self-correction mechanism. Prices are set centrally (and infrequently[1]) and do not adjust when supply and demand are imbalanced. Rather than rectifying the imbalances, the logic of the plan ensures their permanence. Enterprises look not horizontally at the consumer but vertically at the planner/bureaucrat. It is the planner they must satisfy, because it is the planner who hands out the rewards. The verticality of the system implies that when goods do arrive they are often of poor quality or the wrong ones. Planners attempt to enlarge their bureaucratic domain by fostering an excess of investment projects, each generating ample demand for inputs already in short supply. More bottlenecks result.

To motivate greater economy in the use of resources, in 1965 the Soviet Union introduced a reform that, inter alia, told enterprises they would be rewarded according to their profitability as well as the fulfillment of the plan's output target. The Cubans introduced a similar reform in 1976 with the inauguration of their first five-year plan under their new planing system, the *Sistema de Dirección y Planificación de la Economía* (SDPE). This planning modification had little success in either country because profitability was not a significant construct so long as prices were set centrally, based on average cost, and adjusted at long, irregular intervals.[2]

In the presence of these and other obstacles, the conventional project of central planning grows more and more inefficient and untenable as an economy grows in size and complexity. The imperative for decentralization becomes increasingly apparent.

CUBAN PLANNING BEFORE THE LATE 1980S. Cuba did not have stable institutions of economic planning until the late 1970s. Indeed, Cuba's first five-year plan did not come until 1976–80. The gradual introduction of Cuba's new planning system, the SDPE, was begun in 1977.[3] It was basically modeled on the 1965 Soviet reforms and attempts to (1) put enterprises on a self-financing basis, (2) introduce a profitability criterion with its corresponding incentives, and (3) promote decentralization, organizational coherence, and efficiency.

As with the earlier Soviet reform, it has met with the obstacles, among others, of bureaucratic resistance, pervasive shortages, and an irrational price structure. Possibilities for decentralized decisionmaking in Cuba have also been constrained by an inadequate supply of skilled managerial and technical labor. Moreover, Cuba confronted additional difficulties in adapting the Soviet-style reform to Cuban political culture. The Cubans began tinkering with their new system almost from the outset.

A central theme of the SDPE was decentralization. Enterprises put on a self-financing regime and introducing profit sharing were supposed to be exercising increased autonomy from the center. This, in turn, was to promote efficiency. Nominal self-financing and profit sharing by themselves, however, did little, if anything, to enhance the scope of enterprise decisionmaking. Among other things, in the context of centrally fixed prices, centrally determined investments, and extensive input shortages these mechanisms did not alter the basic mode of operation of Cuban planning.

Prices centrally set only every five or more years were not a reliable, rational guide to production or allocation choices, nor could they systematically identify well-managed enterprises through a profitability index. With shortages commonplace, otherwise efficient enterprises were often thwarted in their production efforts because of non-delivery, untimely delivery, or delivery of improperly specified, poor-quality inputs. Bottlenecks and planning imperfections, in turn, necessitated amendments to the plan after the beginning of the year — often raising an enterprise's output target without increasing its supply of raw materials.

Enterprises, behaving rationally in this environment, hoarded inputs, thereby aggravating the shortage problem. Since the behavior of profits was fickle because of these and other factors, the planning authorities were compelled to limit, on equity grounds alone, the extent of profit retention and distribution, thus weakening the incentive effect. And since profits abounded in certain enterprises despite the absence of properly specified, high-quality production, the planners devised new administrative regulations to control this behavior. In the end, the profitability algorithm became hopelessly complicated and the incentive mechanism debilitated. Since the center determined what investment projects were to be undertaken, the fact that enterprises paid for increasing shares of investment costs out of their bank funds rather than state budget funds (the share of enterprise-financed investments in total investment financing in Cuba rose from 1 percent in 1981 to 30 percent in 1985[4]) did not imply a substantive decentralization of capital allocation.

To be sure, in at least one important respect the SDPE represented further centralization of the planning system. Prior to 1976, the system of material supplies was carried out by consolidated enterprises; subsequently, most material balances came to implemented by the central planning board (Juceplan) or the central state committee on technical-material supplies (CEATM).

The SDPE, then, like the 1965 Soviet economic reforms, failed to bring about a significant change in underlying centralization of decisionmaking in the economic mechanism. There were, however, peripheral changes that accompanied the SDPE, many introduced in an effort to adapt the Soviet centralized model to Cuban conditions, that did increase the flexibility of the system and allow for some decentralization of decisionmaking. Among these new policies was the post-1976 system of Popular Power that controlled the management of locally oriented service and production enterprises. In the mid-eighties, such enterprises amounted to 34 percent of all Cuban enterprises. The local budgets of the organs of Popular Power grew from 21 percent of the total state budget in 1978 to 26 percent in 1980, to 30 percent in 1982, and to 33 percent in 1984. The local budget share in the Soviet Union in 1980 was 17.1 percent.[5]

Another policy allowed for enterprises to make their own contracts for products that were not in the *nomenklatura* and were not centrally balanced. There has also been encouragement for the development of "secondary" (non-plan) production, once the plan is fulfilled. Further, the realization that there were growing stocks of unused inputs within enterprises led to the practice of "resource fairs" (first organized by the CEATM in 1979) where enterprises traded freely and directly with each other. The fairs of 1979 and 1980 witnessed the sale of 40 million pesos worth of inputs. Inventory sales of production inputs by enterprises have continued to grow. In October of 1982 the president of Juceplan reported that some 500 million pesos worth of such resources had already been identified.[6] In May 1985, at the conclusion of the Fourth Plenary on the SDPE, the judgment was reached that the CEATM was still allocating too many products and the number should be significantly reduced, allowing enterprises to contract directly with each other for these products.[7] In fact, the degree of centralization contemplated in the Soviet-designed system was never approached in Cuba, as it was resisted by sectoral and provincial planning bodies.

Other measures of decentralization were the strengthening of the Cuban Institute of Internal Demand, the introduction of free labor contracting in 1980,[8] and an increasing acceptance of private productive and service activity — most notably housing construction cooperatives and free farmers' markets. There was also some light manufacturing by artisans, and enterprises were permitted to use up to 30 percent of their profits to make input purchases from the private sector. Free farmers' markets were opened in 1980. Sales of fresh vegetables and fruits grew rapidly until the government crackdown on "abuses" (exorbitant prices, excessive middleman profits, resource diversion from the state sector, etc.) in February 1982. Sales began to grow again after the promulgation of new regulations (20 percent sales tax, progressive income tax on private farmer income from 5 to 20 percent, and the expansion of the state-controlled parallel market to compete with the farmers' markets) in May of 1983. However, new abuses, more serious diversion of resources from state uses, and reported incomes above 50,000 pesos for truckers, wholesalers, and some farmers led to the indefinite closing of these markets in May 1986. Although such free market sales of produce are permitted elsewhere in the Soviet bloc, private plots (except for Poland) tended to be no larger than one-quarter to one-half hectare. In Cuba, such plots typically range from 20 to over 60 hectares. Although private farmers are required to deliver a share of their output to the state, actual deliveries are often modest relative to output, leaving substantial produce to be consumed locally or marketed independently. For instance, Castro charged that some private farmers delivered no more than 10 percent of their output to the state.[9] Thus, the potential for economic and political disruption emerging from the private agricultural sector in Cuba was prima facie greater than elsewhere in the CMEA.

Nevertheless, these decentralizing measures taken together did not alter the key dynamic of Cuban planning. Prior to the beginning of the rectification campaign in April 1986,[10] it was apparent from various government documents and speeches that the need for further decentralization and greater worker participation was clearly perceived. In particular, the documents of the Fourth Plenary evaluating the SDPE, held in May 1985, laid out a series of decentralizing measures that the Cubans intended to carry out. With the severe difficulties concerning foreign exchange earnings that Cuba began to experience around that time, along with the growing excess of uncompleted investment projects, however, resources became too scarce to sustain the momentum toward decentralization; and the state tightened its grip on the economy in order to economize on the use of foreign exchange as well as to bring existing investment projects to successful completion.

Unintended or profligate use of resources in both the private and public spheres came under increasing scrutiny, as did the lack of coordination among sectoral ministries of the economy and among state planning institutions (for example, the State Committee on Finances, the State Price Committee, the National Bank, Juceplan). Together with the difficulties of increasing labor indiscipline (exacerbated by shortages of inputs and consumer goods), enterprise overstaffing, and corruption among officials, these problems brought on the rectification campaign in early 1986. Market-oriented decentralization was put on hold, although some efforts at administrative decentralization have continued.

CHARACTERIZING THE PRESENT PERIOD. There is no question but that the rectification campaign brought a halt to the previous trend toward liberalization and increased emphasis on material incentives. Many prominent interpreters of Cuban reality, however, have exaggerated the nature and meaning of this shift, either by misapprehending the substance of the SDPE or by misconstruing the new policies. Both Jorge Pérez-López and Jorge Domínguez, for instance, claimed that the SDPE itself represented market socialism, and the trimestral publication of Radio Martí declared the dissolution of the SDPE with the rectification campaign.[11] Pérez-López also charged that Cuba had suspended worker productivity bonuses.[12]

Carmelo Mesa-Lago wrote that most urban private-sector activity had b
eliminated.[13] Pérez-López, Dominguez, Mesa-Lago, and others have c
pared the rectification campaign period to the late 1960s, a time w
there were no individual bonuses, no overtime pay, no unified cer
plan, no cost accounting, no national budget, and little record keepin;

The reality is different. As we have noted, the SDPE did not appro
market socialism, and its basic structure is still intact. Worker produc
bonuses were never as prominent in Cuba as elsewhere in the CMEA
they are still very much in evidence. Urban private-sector activity has c
under increasing regulation, but it is still permitted. None of the sa
characteristics of the late 1960s economy are present in the rectific;
campaign, although one can readily observe the strong hand of]
Castro in both.

In our view, the best way to interpret the initiation of the rectific
campaign is as a moratorium/retrenchment in the CPE reform (
Periods of liberalization in CPEs inevitably generate economic, poli
and social tensions as well as outcomes that are antithetical to the s
goals of socialist society. It is natural, if not inevitable, that liberaliz
policies provoke periods of reassessment and retrenchment, as e>
enced in Hungary and China. Of course, the nature, timing, and int
of the cycle depends on factors peculiar to each country and to the
national political and economic climate.

The Policies of Rectification

BALANCING MATERIAL AND MORAL INCENTIVES. Material incentives are
lematic in centrally planned, shortage-type economies. Not only are
ideological concerns with inequality and attitude, but there are lin
motivating workers and managers with more money if there are no
able goods available for purchase. These limits, of course, become
severe for CPEs with lower levels of economic development, esp
during times of severe foreign exchange constraints. Another dif
with material incentives at the workplace affects market and pl;
economies alike: measuring individual contribution to the quanti
quality of output is never straightforward. Each of these problems w
tinent to the Cuban situation in the mid-eighties.

Three types of material incentives for workers are used in Cuba: *r*
or piece-rates; *primas*, or bonuses; and *premios*, or profit-sharin;
details of their operation are peripheral to our main concern.[15] It i:
ever, relevant to note the following: *Normas* were applied to 1.2 r
workers (37.2 percent of the labor force) at the end of 1985. Three
ters of the normas were "elementary," that is, not determined by a time

and-motion study. Income paid for overfulfillment of *normas* grew from 121.7 million pesos, or 3.9 percent of worker income on average in 1980, to 274.5 million pesos, or 6.0 percent of worker income in 1985. *Primas* were introduced experimentally in 1979 and then gradually applied throughout the economy in 1980. Varieties of *primas* abound in Cuba, but most involve giving a bonus to a group of workers for increasing exports, saving on raw materials or energy, overfulfilling quality or quantity targets, or developing new products. The value of *primas* paid out grew steadily from 14 million pesos in 1980 to 90.7 million in 1985, the latter figure still representing only 1.9 percent of the basic wage. *Premios* were introduced experimentally in 1979. By 1985 total *premio* payments amounted to 71.1 million pesos or 1.6 percent of the basic wage. Among other things, the extension of *premios* was frustrated by Cuba's system of administered prices, making the meaning of profit or any financial indicator dubious. Taken together, the three material incentives grew rapidly during the early eighties but still accounted for only 10.6 percent on average of the basic wage in 1985, considerably below that of other CMEA members.[16]

In addition to the problems mentioned above, it was discovered that often the three incentives overlapped; the worker was paid twice or thrice for the same work. For example, sugar mill workers were paid for exceeding their *norma*, for working overtime, and for increasing exports. Hence, to avoid this duplication many *primas*, especially those related to export production, have been curtailed. In other cases, incentives were applied that had little justification, such as mechanics being paid five times for repairing the same piece of machinery, or radio announcers working on piece-rates. In yet other cases, elementary *normas*, set with the participation of the affected workers, were too low. In 1986, more than one-third of all workers with *normas* produced over 130 percent of their rate.[17] In these instances, the design of certain incentives and output goals were reevaluated. Overall, rectification brought a streamlining of the three incentive systems, but each scheme was maintained.

At the same time, recognizing the limitations of material incentives in fostering productivity increases, Castro sought to reemphasize moral incentives and voluntary labor. Voluntary labor does indeed seem to have been reinvigorated, but the efficacy of moral incentives at the workplace is more difficult to evaluate. In our view, political exhortations and moral incentives will not successfully motivate workers over a sustained period, especially in the absence of more democratic decision-making practices.

In sum, although rectification has signified an effort to rebalance the importance of moral versus material incentives, the basic incentive structure of the SDPE has been retained. Hence, comparisons between rectification and the economy of the late 1960s are overblown.

REDUCING THE SCOPE OF PRIVATE SECTOR ACTIVITY. The most important policy of rectification regarding private activity was the abolition in May of
1986 of the free peasant markets. As noted above, the leadership perceived a plethora of threats from these markets. Private farmers were
enriching themselves, among other things dispiriting the membership on
the newly formed cooperative farms. Castro gave examples of a farmer
who made 50,000 pesos from planting a hectare of garlic and of another
who hired four workers and owned two trucks and earned 150,000 pesos.
Castro claimed that it was virtually impossible to effectively collect taxes on
these high peasant incomes. Urban workers and consumers were supposedly not only demoralized by the easy money made by private farmers but
also indignant at the astronomical prices they were obliged to pay for
fresh produce on these markets. More significantly, the operation of these
markets entailed a substantial diversion of resources (use of trucks, shirk-
ing at work or leaving early, pilfering of gasoline, insecticides, etc.) away
from the state plan and toward the private sector. They also prompted
farmers to reduce deliveries to the state of exportable produce in order to
sell it at better prices on the free markets. With rectification, the state has
attempted to replace these markets, which accounted for less than 5 percent of food sales, according to official figures, by expanding the state-run
parallel markets. Also, a new distribution enterprise, Frutas Selectas, has
been set up, and farmers have been offered higher prices for sales to the
state. To say the least, this new arrangement has created considerable
inconvenience for large numbers of consumers who have been forced to
locate new sources of supply for many food items.

Another significant change was regulating the sale of private housing.
The 1984 housing law provided for making all tenants into owners of their
homes (it was already the case that over 60 percent of dwellers owned
their homes) within twenty years. The state had already sanctioned private
home construction and greatly eased private access to building materials.
The result was twofold: a construction boom with private construction
accounting for one-third of new houses in the 1980s and a speculation
boom with skyrocketing prices for real estate. To curb the latter and its
beneficiaries, the state decreed that all housing sales would have to pass
through a state agency that would regulate prices. The 1984 housing law
itself was left intact.

Other private-sector activity has come under tighter state regulation,
and the scope of some activities has been reduced. The principal new
restriction is that private service workers (plumbers, electricians, mechanics, and the like), artisans, street vendors, taxi drivers, and so on must be
licensed and must receive all materials through a state-issued certificate.
That is, the state still recognizes that many services can be provided more

iciently by the private sector, but it does not want the success of this sec-
_or at the expense of diverted resources and pilfered materials. In the
spring of 1989, the private advertising section in the popular magazine
Opina, which had been curtailed, was reopened. The number of private-
wage workers and workers for their own account fell from 52.1 thousand
in 1985 to 43.2 thousand in 1987 as private non-farm income fell from
102.5 million pesos to 67.8 million pesos. Private non-farm income began
to recover in 1988, rising to 80.7 million pesos.[18] Thus, urban private-sector activity has been reduced, but it has hardly been obliterated.

Despite the abolition of the peasant markets, private farm income has
actually increased from 495.6 million pesos in 1985 to 528.9 million pesos
in 1988. In the private agricultural sector, incomes of workers in producer
cooperatives fell from 161.8 million pesos in 1985 to 152.5 million in
1988, while the incomes of individual private farmers expanded from
333.8 million pesos to 376.4 million.[19]

EFFORTS AT ADMINISTRATIVE DECENTRALIZATION. Although market-oriented
decentralization has for the moment been eschewed, the Cuban government has actively pursued policies aimed at administrative decentralization. Even though the main architect of the 1975-85 liberalization policies,
Humberto Perez, was replaced in early 1985 as head of the central planning board, the perception of a torpid, overcentralized system remained
and was widespread among government economic functionaries and managers. The momentum toward decentralization, though slowed and redi-
rected, has not been broken.

Several ongoing efforts, such as the formation of production brigades
in agricultural and industrial enterprises, as well as the formation of and
transfer of planning functions to *uniones de empresas* (industrial associations), have continued. Other initiatives are new. In early 1988, following
the recommendations of a special commission to study the SDPE, several
new procedures were adopted in the planning process.[20] The number of
commodities and commodity groups subject to central planning was to be
drastically reduced, from 2,300 to 800.[21] The number of directive indicators to the enterprise was to be cut from an average of 28 to 18.[22] The system of material balances was to be decentralized by "extending direct ties
in order to eliminate intermediaries in the process of elaborating and executing the plan of material and technical supplies."[23] Concretely, the number of material balances performed by the central state supplies committee, CEATM, was to be diminished by 382, or 31 percent, and passed down
to the level of the industrial association or the enterprise.[24] Further,
according to a February 1989 report of the Comisión Nacional del

Sistema de Dirección de la Economía,[25] direct supplies contracting was established between enterprises for 518 different products during 1988.

Separately, experiments are being carried out in a variety of sectors that are also intended to promote greater flexibility, enhanced worker participation and more local autonomy. Some initial success has been reported, particularly in the case of "continuous planning" at the enterprise level. This enables the enterprise to draw up a production and input plan based on the previous year's levels and its expectations for the coming year prior to receiving the plan control figures from the national ministry. Previously, control figures often arrived at the enterprise too late for serious discussion or for any meaningful amendments to the plan. Not only does "continuous planning" avoid the last-minute rush syndrome, but it allows for some initiative at the enterprise level. It does this, of course, at the expense of a possible loss of coordination, but given the failure of the planning authorities to produce a realistic, balanced, comprehensive plan in the past, it is not clear what if anything is lost by the new method.[26]

Whether these changes lead to improved efficiency is an interesting question to which we do not have the answer. We remain skeptical that the reforms will alter the behavior of the system in an appreciable way. Nonetheless, we do believe it is significant that the efforts at reform are being made because they denote an awareness of the imperative for substantive decentralization. This awareness, in turn, suggests the eventual return to a course of liberalization. The timing and extent of such liberalization, of course, will depend upon political and economic circumstances in Cuba, not the least of which will be the policy preferences and the permanence of Fidel Castro.

Why is Cuba Different?

Why is Castro moving Cuba in the opposite direction of the changes taking place elsewhere in the CMEA? At one level the answer to this question is obvious. There is little reason a priori for Cuba to be at the same cyclical juncture as the other countries. To be sure, not all the CMEA economies are moving at the same pace of reform, nor did they begin with equal degrees of centralization.[27] With the exception of Yugoslavia, Cuba stands out among its trading partners in Eastern Europe as having the only home-grown revolution. Further, Cuba is among the least developed and smallest of the CMEA economies. Central planning offers many potential advantages in terms of positively gathering and channeling resources for development. The smaller and less complex an economy, the more it lends itself to central planning and the less likely that central planning will

encumber the growth process. Cuba, after all, did not experience the sec-
ular growth slowdown of the Soviet Union. On the contrary, the early
eighties were a period of rapid growth for Cuba, and since 1970 the
Cuban annual rate of real growth has been 4.1 percent versus 1.2 percent
for the rest of Latin America.[28]

What was true about Cuba's macroeconomy prior to the onset of the
rectification campaign was that Cuba, as a very trade-dependent country,
began to face an increasingly severe foreign debt and foreign exchange
crisis. Cuba's hard-currency current account began to deteriorate rapidly
in 1984, going from surpluses of 297.1 million pesos in 1982 and 262.7
million in 1983 to deficits of 211.6 million pesos in 1984 and 505.8 million
in 1985. Accordingly, Cuba's hard-currency debt, which had fallen from
$4.5 billion in 1980 to $3.2 billion in 1983, rose to $3.9 billion by the end
of 1985 and to $4.7 billion by the end of 1986.

In 1986, low sugar prices, plummeting petroleum prices (Cuba's reex-
port of Soviet petroleum provided roughly 40 percent of its hard-currency
earnings during 1983-85), devastation from Hurricane Kate, several con-
secutive years of intensifying drought, drastic dollar devaluation, the tightening of the United States blockade and growing protectionism in
Western markets all combined to reduce Cuba's hard-currency earnings
by $337.1 million, or 27.1 percent. Cuba responded with (a) a program to
promote nontraditional exports and import substitution, (b) tighter controls on foreign trade, (c) suspension of interest service on the debt, (d)
an austerity program to save on foreign exchange, and (e) the rectification campaign. On the one hand, the campaign would enable the state to
prevent (or, at least, diminish) the diversion of exportable produce to the
farmers' markets and of imported materials to the private sector. On the
other hand, the campaign signalled a recognition that it would be increasingly difficult to use material incentives to stimulate work effort. The
scarcity of hard currency denoted greater shortages of consumer goods
and, hence, the absence of a material counterpart to higher peso
incomes. Such imbalances are always a problem in shortage-ridden CPEs,
but in Cuba during 1986–88 they became particularly acute.

It should also be noted that Castro has not hesitated in the past to be a
nonconformist in either economic or political policy. In the late 1960s, for
instance, as the Soviet Union was implementing its Liberman reform,
Cuba was abolishing cost accounting and material incentives. In the mid-
and late 1970s, as Cuba was introducing the Soviet-style SDPE, the model
came under continual criticism in Cuba for being too centralized. At the
time, Cuba pioneered in establishing its system of Popular Power with contested local elections and in turning over the management of local enterprises to the newly elected municipal bodies. Miguel Figueras, vice-presi-

dent of Juceplan at the time, commented to one of the authors that between 1977 and 1981 the Cubans were decentralizing 15 percent of the Soviet-style planning institutions each year.[29] Thus, it was not surprising in early 1986 when Cuban Vice-President Carlos Rafael Rodriguez commented favorably upon the early stages of *perestroika* at a CMEA meeting in Bucharest, drawing "specific attention to what he called the mood of imaginativeness and flexibility now abroad among the Moscow allies, with which he associated the Cuban process."[30] Castro has also gone against the Soviet grain repeatedly in his political policies.

The rectification campaign, of course, was also motivated by ideological factors. Standard concerns about "bourgeois" mentality, growing corruption, and inequality were joined by the leadership's preoccupation with Cuban youth. Cubans entering the labor force for the first time in the mid-1980s were born after the revolutionary struggle against Batista, after the literacy campaign, after the Bay of Pigs, and after the Cuban missile crisis. To many it seemed that they did not have the same emotional commitment to the revolution and its socialist values. Their formative years occurred during a time of ascendancy of material incentives, from 1970 to 1986. The rectification campaign has sought to rebalance material and moral incentives, to transform the incipient materialist ethos, and to reeducate Cuban youth. Nonetheless, it is difficult to imagine Castro's exhortations substituting for the historical events listed above or for more democratic institutions.

To argue that the rectification campaign was initially motivated by certain internal economic and ideological problems is not to say that the campaign is sustained solely or chiefly by these same problems. Indeed, it appears that Castro's commitment to his course has rigidified in the last two years as the world has witnessed the tremendous social and political turmoil unleashed by the reform programs in Poland, the Soviet Union, Hungary, and China. Castro no doubt has also observed that the path of market-oriented reform of CPEs offers no guarantees. The record of economic performance over the last decade in Hungary and China is at best mixed, while the 1989-90 economic reforms in Eastern Europe and the Soviet Union are still more problematic. The dilemma is that piecemeal and partial measures of reform do not unlock the logic of central planning. On the contrary, by generating contradictory signals and administrative conflict they may do more harm than good. Hence, early measures engender the necessity of subsequent, more fundamental reform. Enterprise autonomy and cost accounting, for instance, make little sense without scarcity prices. In short, economic reform via market decentralization threatens economic stability and political power.

In the face of repeated American efforts to assassinate Castro, destabilize Cuba's economy, and overthrow the regime, Castro — authoritarian by nature anyway — drew the lesson early on that he needed complete control over the political apparatus to withstand outside aggression. Nothing has happened to change Castro's mind or reduce his paranoia about destabilization from abroad. With this perspective, Castro's renewed intransigence and socialist dogmatism are better understood. Hence, barring a major political change,[31] neither a significant political opening nor a return to market-oriented reform is likely in the near future. In the meantime, tinkering with the planning system and ongoing efforts at administrative decentralization will continue. Eventually, market-type decentralization will come. The best way to accelerate that process would be to promote normalization in political and economic relations between the United States and Cuba.

Reforms of a Political Nature

Internally, there has been more change in tone and style than in the structure of Cuba's political system. The organization of the party, the system of Popular Power, and the various ministries of government have been altered little since their institution in the 1960s and 1970s. But there has been some relaxation in style. For the first decade, when the leaders of the revolution were intent on consolidating their power and felt threatened by internal opponents, the government ruled with an iron hand. Virtually no dissent was permitted, and any deviation from the line laid down by the party was severely punished. Conditions in Cuban prisons were abominable; and as of the mid-1960s, there were as many as 60,000 political prisoners.

Going into the 1970s, as the revolution became more securely entrenched and as the siege mentality dissipated somewhat, this deplorable situation began to change — a change seen most clearly, perhaps, in the implementation of a penal reform law initiated in the mid-1970s. Conditions in the prisons improved dramatically. Some of the oldest and most unpleasant prisons — several dating back to the seventeenth century — were closed; modern, better-ventilated structures were built to replace them. The number of prisoners in all categories was reduced. Treatment also became far more humane. Meaningful work was provided, and the prisoners were paid as though they were on the outside, thus enabling them to support their families. Conjugal visits and a system of furloughs encouraged the continuity of family life. The reform program eventually converted the Cuban penal system from one of the worst to one of the best in the world — setting aside the question of political prisoners, who continued to receive harsher treatment until well into the 1980s. The number of political prisoners, however, also began to decline in the 1970s; and by 1977, there were only an estimated 7,000 to 8,000 left. A mass release program encouraged by the Carter administration returned some 5,000 of these to their families, and hundreds of others have been freed since then. As of 1989, then, the number of political prisoners is down from the 60,000 or so in the mid-sixties to only some 200 to 300, and the remaining handful — hopefully to be released soon — are held under generally satisfactory conditions.

Penal reform and the release of political prisoners were accompanied by a growing disposition on the part of the Cuban government to permit outside — and even internal — scrutiny of the human rights situation in Cuba. During 1987 and 1988, members of Americas Watch, the International Red Cross, and the United States-based Human Rights Project were all permitted to inspect Cuban prisons and meet with the remaining political prisoners. In January of 1989, a delegation of the United Nations Human Rights Commission was welcomed to Cuba and prepared a report on conditions there — a report that drew no conclusions but in essence said that things were improving but still had a long way to go.

In addition to the visits of foreign human rights delegations, Castro grudgingly tolerated the establishment of a Cuban Commission for Human Rights and National Reconciliation. This group, led by Elizardo Sanchez, highlighted human rights violations in Cuba and called for the release of all political prisoners. At the same time, it emphasized that it did not advocate the overthrow of the Cuban revolutionary government; it simply wished that the government respect the rights of its citizens as established by the UN Charter.

Another aspect of the inchoate internal relaxation was a rapprochement between church and state that began in the late 1970s. Catholics and other practicing believers were no longer persecuted for their faith — though, to be sure, it remained difficult for them to prosper in a system that advanced atheism as its official creed. A dialogue was initiated between church leaders and government representatives, which it was hoped would produce solutions to some of their differences, such as how many priests there would be in the country, to what extent the publication and distribution of religious literature could be expanded, and so on.

As of this writing, movement toward greater internal relaxation is in doubt. Shortly after taking office in January of 1989, the Bush administration announced in Washington that there would be no thaw in United States–Cuba relations. This removed a major incentive for continued progress in the human rights field. Not surprisingly, an internal crackdown soon followed in Cuba — a crackdown that included the arrest of Elizardo Sànchez and other human rights leaders. Even from his jail cell, however, Sànchez continues to call for an easing of tensions between the United States and Cuba as the best way of encouraging the further relaxation of internal controls in Cuba. He understands better than anyone that so long as the Cuban government feels threatened by the United States, so long as it retains its siege mentality, it is likely to demand internal discipline and orthodoxy. It would be interesting to see how much the Cuban government would be willing to relax if an opening to a normal relationship with the United States should ever become an active possibility. Castro rejects *glasnost,* yes, and is authoritarian by nature, but he has shown that he is capable of moving in a more liberal direction if that implies a clear gain for Cuba. Further, a variety of popular pressures are pushing Cuba in the direction of greater political openness. As of the moment, however, the Bush administration has ruled out any such equation.

Cuba's foreign policy has undergone far greater positive change than has the penal system. During the 1960s, Castro aimed at the overthrow of virtually all the other governments of the hemisphere (with the exception of Mexico). In the Second Declaration of Havana in 1962, he virtually declared war on them. He vowed to turn the Andes into the Sierra Maestra of South America and said that in the process he would give assistance to guerrilla groups anywhere and everywhere.

The problem was that his tactics did not work. Nowhere did guerrilla movements gain power. Thus, by the end of the 1960s, with his own tactics a failure and under steady pressure from Moscow, which had all along disagreed with those tactics, as well as from the United States, Castro began to moderate his stance. By the early 1970s, he had drastically reduced his support to guerrilla movements in Latin America and shifted instead to efforts to re-establish normal diplomatic and trade relations with the other governments of the hemisphere. As of 1989, Cuba's position little resembles what it was in the 1960s. Today, Cuba says that while armed struggle remains a valid revolutionary tactic *provided* the proper conditions exist, the fact is that in all of Latin America, those conditions only exist in one country, El Salvador — and even there, Cuba and the Soviet Union would prefer a negotiated settlement.

Not only has no evidence been presented of significant material Cuban assistance since 1981 to subversive groups in Latin American countries other than El Salvador, but Cuba's official position is that that would be a contradiction in terms. The conditions for revolution do not exist in those countries, nor do the conditions for socialism or socialist construction. Senior Cuban officials now say openly that the Cuban revolution is most unlikely to be replicated anywhere in the hemisphere.

Nor is it correct to say, as spokespeople for the Bush administration do, that Fidel Castro will never give up his "right" to export revolution. In fact, Castro claims no such right. He will always see himself as a revolutionary, to be sure, and Cuba's constitution does indeed require that the government always express solidarity with national liberation movements. But whether or not that should be offensive to anyone depends upon *how* he expresses his revolutionary proclivities and how the Cuban government demonstrates its solidarity with liberation movements. If analyzed in that context, Cuba's position is seen to be little different from that of the other member nations of the non-aligned movement, all of whom are required by their by-laws to demonstrate such solidarity. As a senior member of the Cuban Foreign Ministry put it in 1987:

> How Cuba indicates its solidarity will depend upon case-by-case analysis and often will take the form of statements expressing moral support, or of votes for solidarity resolutions in the United Nations. These do not in any way violate international norms. Indeed, however Cuba elects to articulate its solidarity with national liberation movements, it will always act in accordance with the United Nations Charter and the norms of international law.[32]

It is not a matter of simply accepting the word of Cuban officials as to what Cuba's position is. Those statements, together with the dearth of evidence of Havana's support for revolution and the fact that the majority of other governments of the hemisphere now feel sufficiently convinced of Cuba's metamorphosis to have reestablished diplomatic and economic relations, suggest that real change has taken place.[33]

Conclusions

In sum, Cuba is not immune to change. Significant reform and modifications have been registered in its economy and in its foreign policy, and even in the degree of internal political controls. Movement in the direction of liberalization has been stilled for the moment, in part because of the absence of any causal relationship between that change on the one hand and a positive United States response on the other. The doors to further reforms, nonetheless, are by no means locked. They could most easily be opened by some thaw in United States–Cuban relations — a thaw that in any event is long overdue.

Notes

1. Cuba's last general price reform was in 1981; the next is scheduled for 1991. Price adjustments for individual goods are made more frequently.

2. For a discussion of this point and its application to Cuba, see A. Zimbalist and C. Brundenius, *The Cuban Economy: Measurement and Analysis of Socialist Performance* (Baltimore: Johns Hopkins University Press, 1989), ch. 8.

3. The adoption of the SDPE occurred in 1976, but the first year was designated as a year of study and preparation. The gradual implementation of the system began in 1977. Since mid-1986, it is more commonly referred to as simply the SDE.

4. Banco Nacional de Cuba, *Informe Económico*, March 1986, p. 6.

5. Nelson Mata, "Los gastos de presupuesto de los Organos Locales de Poder Popular," *Finanzas y Crédito*, no. 5 (1986), p. 56.

6. *Granma*, 5 October 1982, p. 2. Additional data through 1984 and analysis is provided in Oscar U-Echevarria et al., "Consideraciones metodologicas para el calculo de la demanda de piezas de respuesto," *Cuba: Economía Planificada* 1, no. 2 (1986), pp. 110–39.

7. Juceplan, *Dictámenes de la IV Plenaria* (1985), p. 25.

8. This system was actually begun on an experimental basis in 1979 in the province of Pinar del Rio and was not implemented until 1986 in Havana. The Soviet Union, of course, has had this system for many years.

9. Carmelo Mesa-Lago, "The Cuban Economy in the 1980s," in Sergio Roca, ed., *Socialist Cuba: Past Interpretations and Future Challenges* (Boulder, CO: Westview Press, 1988).

10. The "rectification campaign" is the name given to the current period of reevaluating the balance of material and moral incentives, redressing the perceived excesses connected to materials incentives and private-sector activity, and addressing other problems of economic and political management.

11. Staff of Radio José Martí *Cuba Quarterly Situation Report*, 1986, vol. 3, no. 3, sec. 3, p. 13. Jorge Pérez-López, "Cuban Economy in the 1980s," *Problems of Communism* (September–October 1986), p. 34. Jorge Domínguez, "Blaming Itself, Not Himself: Cuba's Political Regime after the Third Party Congress," in Roca, *Socialist Cuba*. Also see the essay by Rhoda Rabkin, "Cuba: The Aging of a Revolution," in Roca, who asserts that there was "managerial autonomy" prior to the rectification campaign (p. 35).

12. Pérez-López, "Cuban Economy in the 1980s," p. 16.

13. Mesa-lago "Cuban Economy in the 1980s," pp 74-80.

14. See sources in earlier notes; also see, inter alia, Jorge Dominguez, "Cuba: Charismatic Communism," *Problems of Communism* (September–October 1985); Joseph Treaster, "Castro Recoils at a Hint of Wealth," *New York Times*, 8 February 1987, p. III-1.

15. For a full discussion of these incentives and their evolution over time, see A. Zimbalist, "Incentives and Planning in Cuba," *Latin American Research Review* 24, 1 (January 1989).

16. In the mid-1970s, for instance, the variable part of the basic wage ranged from 15.2 percent in Hungary to 55.2 percent in the German Democratic Republic, with Bulgaria at 39.8 percent, Poland at 31.7 percent, the USSR at 36.4 percent, and Czechoslovakia at 43.8 percent. José Acosta, *Teoría y práctica de los mecanismos de dirección de la economía* (Havana: Editorial de Ciencias Sociales, 1982), p. 291.

17. *Granma*, 14 January 1987, p. 5.

18. Indications are that it continued to increase in the first half of 1989 when total private sector incomes increased 4.7 percent. *Anuario estadístico de Cuba*, 1987, p. 193; Comite Estatal de Estadísticas, *Balance de ingresos y egresos monetarios de la población*, July 1989, p. 21, and August 1989, p. 3.

19. Ibid., July 1989, p. 21.

20. The new planning procedures are published in two volumes, entitled *Decisiones adoptadas sobre algunos elementos del sistema de dirección de la economía* (Havana: Juceplan, March 1988). An abridged version is published in *Cuba: Economía Planificada* (the journal of Juceplan), vol. 3, no. 3 (1988), and vol. 4, no. 1 (1989).

21. Ibid., vol. 1, p. 8.

22. Ibid., p. 9.
23. Our translation, ibid., p. 7.
24. Ibid., p. 35.
25. *Balance de las tareas para el perfeccionamiento del sistema de dirección de la economía*, p. 10.
26. Since September 1988 the Grupo Central has been replaced by a smaller body, the Executive Committee of the Council of Ministers, as the primary state organ responsible for orienting the economic plan. It is not apparent what, if any, influence this has had on the degree of centralization or decentralization in the planning process. The Executive Committee reports meeting bi-weekly to discuss a broad range of sectoral and administrative issues, usually with representatives from enterprises or administrative bodies in the affected areas. *Granma*, 25 September 1989, pp. 2–5.
27. China, of course, is not in the CMEA and has taken, since June 1989, a rather sharp, if not brutal, turn against reform.
28. The Cuban growth estimate is from Zimbalist and Brundenius, *The Cuban Economy*, ch. 5. The figure for Latin America is from the Inter-American Development Bank, *Economic and Social Progress in Latin America*, Washington, D.C., 1988, p. 20.
29. Conversation with Zimbalist, Havana, Cuba, January 1985.
30. The Economist Intelligence Unit, *Country Report: Analysis of Economic and Political Trends for Cuba, Dominican Republic, Haiti, Puerto Rico*, no. 4 (1986), p. 10.
31. For instance, Castro's exit or a reopening of relations with the United States. As improbable as these may seem, regarding the latter, the Cubans face the prospect of a gradual diminution of economic aid and trade from the Soviet Union and the CMEA and are likely to find a rapprochement with the United States more and more compelling from an economic point of view. Of course, such a development will also require a new, more rational attitude on the part of the United States. Regarding the former, it is well to remember that Castro has just turned sixty-three and rumors of his ill health have been circulating for a few years.
32. Statement of Vice-Minister of Foreign Relations Jose R. Viera in 1987.
33. It should be added that on October 18, 1989, Cuba was elected to represent Latin America on the United Nations Security Council with 146 out of a possible 156 votes, the largest majority ever garnered by a country elected to the council. A week earlier, the presidents of Argentina, Brazil, Colombia, Mexico, Peru, Uruguay, and Venezuela (the so-called Group of Eight, minus Panama) signed a declaration calling for the reintegration of Cuba into the Organization of American States.

15. CONCLUSIONS AND PROSPECTS

Jane Shapiro Zacek

The essays in this volume have examined various aspects of change, reform, and, in some cases, transformation of elements in the existing system and structure within communist-ruled states. In many instances, particularly in Eastern Europe, events have moved so swiftly that the observer needs to step back and assess clusters of change in order to try to determine their real impact. Do they constitute genuine reforms? At what point can the reforms be properly called transformational? A return to the definitions we suggested in the introduction would be useful.

We have used the term *change* when new policies or procedures have been introduced, adopted, and implemented, aimed at producing specific desired results or outcomes. These changes are generally limited in scope, depth, intensity, and duration. They connote efforts to establish improved methods of managing identified problems and typically do not involve structural alterations or, if they do, only in minor ways that may be readily restrained or reversed if sufficient opposition builds to sway policy direction, or circumstances arise that render these changes incompatible with newly determined needs. An example of *change* is the adoption of material incentive payments in Cuba. These payments may have enhanced worker productivity in some measure but did not impact on the basic structure or operation of the economy in any substantial or extensive way.

Reform implies an ongoing process. It encompasses movement from one mode of operation to another. It is composed of a variety and number of substantial change elements and includes policies and practices designed to bring about very different consequences than if reforms had not been adopted and implemented. Procedurally, the development, adoption, and implementation of reforms necessitate a broader base of support among policy makers and implementors (or, in the absence of support, sufficient coercion, or a mixture of coercion, pressure, suasion, and incentives to reach sufficient consensus on what is to be done and how it is to be achieved). Reform as used here implies substantial structural changes adopted to implement new procedures or processes. While the scope and intensity of these structural changes may be difficult to measure or quantify, they must be consequential enough to make a real and sustained difference in outcome and not be readily reversible. An example of reform is the establishment and consolidation of family farming on a broad scale in China, coupled with incentives that directly link effort with reward. Although reversible, perhaps, the scale and depth of the reform suggest that the political leadership would have difficulty in doing so. Still, it can certainly be the case that what is perceived as real reform turns out later not to have made much difference in outcome.

While reform presumes structural changes, the pre-reform structures are still quite in evidence. *Transformation* implies much greater movement from what has existed to what is being created, so that the previous condition is scarcely recognizable in the new one. It involves a much more drastic movement from the old to the new than does reform. Because of its encompassing nature, transformation is much more difficult to put in place and sustain, and a longer observation period is needed than for reform in order to determine its durability and the extent to which it has achieved the goals established for it. Transformation may involve overturning some basic tenets in communist-ruled states. When private ownership replaces state ownership or state control of property and the new owners can determine how much to produce without limitation on sales, this clearly is far beyond mere reform in ownership. When party-directed censorship of publications and the mass media is ended and self-censorship is lifted, this changes the very character of communications and information available to the public as well as the behavior of those involved in its preparation.

In each case, but clearly in reform, and especially in transformation, there are unintended and unanticipated outcomes along the way of implementation, and continual policy intervention is likely. Nonetheless, and even at this interim stage of describing, analyzing, and trying to assess the nature and extent of change, reform, and transformation in communist-ruled states, it is possible to differentiate among the three terms we are utilizing.

Why have the 1980s been a period of such important and extensive reform in so many communist-ruled states? Indeed, as Communist parties (CPs) relinquish their monopoly on political power, it will very soon be incorrect to refer to these states as "communist-ruled." Reform was undertaken largely as a consequence of CP leaders' recognition that centrally planned economies do not adapt sufficiently to modern technology and are not capable of producing efficiently enough to satisfy not only what the political leadership has determined is necessary but what popular demands and expectations insist upon as well. In many cases (particularly in the Soviet Union and the People's Republic of China), political leadership changes were required before sustained attention to reform of the economy could be undertaken. In some instances, such as in Hungary, long-term changes and some reforms failed to bring about the desired results. In other instances, such as in Poland, the party leadership ultimately proved incapable of introducing and managing economic reform satisfactorily. Thus, at least an initial condition for economic reform was a political leadership that believed itself capable of planning reform strategies, harnessing sufficient support within the system and among the polity to start the reform process moving, and continuing to build support to keep the process going, attempting all the while to shape it both proactively and reactively as necessity and political realities demanded.

Structural reforms in Eastern Europe could not have succeeded (or even been seriously contemplated) without the Soviet decision to refrain from intervention both formally and informally. Indeed, without the Soviet willingness to create a climate conducive to change both domestically and in Eastern Europe, it is unlikely that events would have unfolded as they have and at such a rapid pace. Important changes in party leadership in Eastern Europe have had the support of the Soviets, and it is likely that many leaders who are currently in office will be replaced as the reform process takes root.

Reform-minded policy makers have generally recognized that economic reforms cannot be successfully implemented without concurrent and accompanying administrative reforms. The central planning system and process cannot be decentralized meaningfully without also decentralizing the administrative structure and facilitating decentralized economic policy determination and implementation. Deliberately limiting the authority of the central institutions necessarily assigns greater responsibility and accountability to regional and local officials. Administrative decentralization usually includes greater accountability not only to meet established production criteria but also in some measure to the relevant constituencies as well.

While decentralization is generally viewed as essential to economic and political reform, it is not easily introduced, established, or maintained. It necessarily reduces the authority if not the size of the central bureaucracies and those who run them. Those directly involved can be expected to oppose such policies even while supporting the general principles of reform. Broader political reforms, such as the call for democratization in the USSR, carry with them the potential for mass social unrest, such as sustained strikes and work stoppages in essential industries. What mechanisms can the political leadership put in place to respond to and manage these events? What is the range and scale of response by the political leadership at all levels of governing? If local authorities cannot or are unwilling to curb worker unrest, at what point and on what basis do central authorities step in? And what happens to the idea of devolution of economic and administrative authority when this occurs?

The ramifications of devolution of administrative power are many and varied. Typically, even the most reform-minded of those at the center favor limits on decentralization. Recent debate in the USSR Supreme Soviet about the amount of autonomy in economic authority to be granted to the republics suggests that the latter are anxious to take the lead in promoting decentralization to help alleviate the economic crisis that the country faces. A leadership proposal was roundly rejected by the deputies as not being substantial enough to make a difference to republics seeking greater control over economic decisionmaking for the benefit of their own regions.[1] Less than a week later, much more sweeping autonomy was formally granted.[2] But, if ultimate authority does not rest at the center, how will the system hold together? It is more than the sum of its constituent parts, as the Yugoslav experience has demonstrated. Moreover, the center may prove more reform-oriented than the regional and local levels of authority. While the latter often press for greater autonomy, they may not necessarily promote reform primarily to achieve greater economic performance, productivity, and efficiency. Although it clearly is in the interests of the central authorities seeking to augment available revenues to reduce state subsidies to the production process, for example, it may not be of similar interest to those being subsidized, unless they too are reform-minded. State subsidies deliberately fail to take into proper account the real costs of production. Economic realities are superseded by perceived political necessities. We will return to the important issues of administrative and political devolution of power and decisionmaking below, as well as to their associated reforms.

What were some of the economic conditions that the reform process was designed to address and ameliorate? Not all states experienced these difficulties to the same extent, of course. In most states, economic growth rates had declined and showed little sign of recovery. Productivity was low, costs of production high, and workers typically had little incentive to perform better. Operating inefficiencies were enhanced by supply difficulties, by too many workers to do the work efficiently (adding to production costs that of excess, under-utilized labor) because of the ideological insistence on "full employment," and by too many requirements established externally (through the central planning mechanisms). Enterprises did not have access to credit unless it was built into the plan, and managers did not have the authority to determine when and how to expand plant production. Often, expansion was determined centrally rather than at the plant level when efficiency clearly dictated otherwise. In some cases, when plants operated profitably, there were taxes imposed on the profits in order to reduce state budget deficits. Such a policy discouraged efforts at greater profitability. Moreover, with state-established prices for industrial goods, profits often did not reflect reality, as prices usually did not. Changes in the pricing structure were frequently adopted: prices for essential consumer goods were held artificially low, inducing scarcities, while prices for many other consumer goods were permitted to respond to market forces and engendered inflationary pressures and popular dissatisfaction. Still other goods were priced artificially high to absorb some excess consumer savings and yield a substantial return to the state budget.

Another important element has been the quality of goods produced: not only has the domestic consumer (wholesale and retail) become more difficult to satisfy, but international sales and the imperative to generate revenues through international markets have been quite severely restricted because of poor-quality goods, which often have had to be priced below output costs in order to sell competitively. A related and increasingly important issue has been how to acquire and incorporate up-to-date technologies into production. And with the continuing computer revolution worldwide, how to keep current with the technologies, maintain an adequately trained workforce, and have the resources necessary for technological investment within established limits on profits are all continually nagging problems. Indeed, adopting and adapting to the technologies are critical problems that have not yet been resolved. Lacking the appropriate technology, contemporary production methods become outmoded rapidly and noncompetitive internationally. Moreover, technology without the necessary accompanying infrastructure is especially unsatisfactory. All of these and a variety of other related economic difficulties have been amply described in the literature.[3] What reform measures could be devised and put into place to best manage these enormous and growing difficulties?

Implementing economic reform is expensive. Some states have accumulated huge international debts on which they can scarcely meet interest payments, and they still have not experienced the kinds of reform results they were seeking. International credits have typically been used to finance imports, including consumer goods, rather than to assist directly in the economic reform process. When debt repayment or financing schedules cannot be met, states have found that additional borrowing is an easy "solution," however temporary. Some states have been reluctant to permit direct foreign investment and control of industrial plants within their borders (encouraged, for example, in the Chinese foreign economic zones system), for fear of limiting state authority over economic development. Short of massive borrowing, how can budgetary reserves be built up to assist in the reform process? Other than through vastly improving productivity (which, had it been possible under current conditions, would have rendered reform unnecessary) or through heavily taxing profits (which, as noted above, severely limits entrepreneurial incentive), the options seem quite limited. Economic reform planners have argued that economic necessity must override other considerations, political as well as ideological. Take the example of Soviet alcoholic beverage production and sale, which were severely limited in the early years of the Gorbachev regime. The leadership discovered that substantial losses in tax revenues resulted from this policy. So production has been increased, as have legalized sales (with the attendant problems of increased alcoholism on the job, reduced worker productivity, higher incidence of industrial accidents, additional state-subsidized medical costs, etc.) in order to increase revenues for the state budget. In any event, illegal production and distribution of alcoholic beverages flourished during the years of more restricted legal sales so that total consumption was not reduced significantly.

In a number of cases (China and Hungary are examples), real political reforms did not accompany efforts at economic reform. One major issue was the redistribution of political power between the Communist party and other organized parties and political groupings. Until 1989, with the consequences of the Polish parliamentary elections, no CP permitted (or failed to prevent) the establishment of a non-CP-led and -dominated government. Until 1989, the issue was considered wholly in party-state terms: Has the party been willing to reduce its direct role in and direct control over economic decisionmaking, thereby permitting state institutions to assume greater responsibility? Given the fact that the party tradition includes control over state institutions (despite social science research and writings about bureaucratic rivalries among various institutional sectors in communist-ruled states), the issue was not one of curbing party control in favor of non-party authority, but rather direct or indirect party control in the context of the party's continuing monopoly on political power.

The rules of the game are changing rapidly in many states. Controlled elections for national parliaments are being replaced by a system that provides voters a choice among competing candidates and one in which noncommunist parties or groups offer candidates who are electable and able to defeat communist-backed opponents. (The issue of parliamentary authority is crucial, and one we shall turn to in a moment.) Once Communist parties agree to run candidates in elections where there are no restrictions on the number of seats to be filled competitively, and to accept the consequences, they have agreed to relinquish their monopoly and share power. From current events unfolding in Eastern Europe, it seems clear that once CPs have agreed to multiparty elections, they are destined to play only a dwindling political role in a very short period of time. Indeed, even in the instance of the Polish parliamentary elections, where the number of seats for which Solidarity candidates could compete was restricted, the ultimate result was that the Polish Communist party could not form a government that the parliament would support. By early 1990, all of the Communist parties in Eastern Europe had undergone major reorganizations, including name changes, in order to enhance their appeal to the electorate before national parliamentary elections were held. Thus far, no CP has fared well at the polls. At best they have captured only a small percentage of parliamentary seats. Although a number of East European states permitted noncommunist parties to exist in the post-communist consolidation period, the latter were deprived of any political authority. In the USSR, Gorbachev was quoted in November 1989 as saying that "competition of parties is not an automatic solution" in developing greater democratization. But, he added, the future may eliminate current "anxieties" about this issue.[1] Three months later, the Soviet Communist party officially renounced its monopoly on political power. In republic-level parliamentary elections held in 1990, noncommunist parties and groups offered candidates who were elected to office, defeating their Communist opponents.

At the very time that many states are wrestling with the issues of multipartyism, parliaments and the cabinets constructed out of them or approved by them are demanding, or have already gained, greater authority than at any time since CPs came to power.

As has been pointed out frequently, such authority needs to be institutionalized in order to provide some permanence. Here again, the East European states, especially Hungary and Poland, are trail-blazing. While Poland was the first state to establish a noncommunist-led government in mid-1989, it was agreed that the Polish CP would retain control of the important defense and internal security portfolios. The March 1990 Hungarian parliamentary elections resulted in the Hungarian Socialist (formerly Communist) party and the reconstituted Communist party seat-ing fewer members than other parties and political groups. Neither is likely to be granted any special privilege with respect to securing any particular ministry. In fact, neither is likely to participate in the governing parliamentary coalition. The proliferation of new political groupings in addition to actual parties (some may be turned into parties, offering candidates and platforms, while others remain less formally organized) in a number of states suggests that the transformation from one-party to multiparty rule will be neither direct nor simple. Too many small groups clamoring for representation may result in governmental chaos and a failure to adequately strengthen parliament.

A second element of reform has been the opening up of free expression, especially through publications and the rapid diminution of censorship leading to its virtual elimination. *Glasnost,* commonly translated as "openness," has been a password for the Gorbachev reform efforts. Again, several East European states have moved faster and farther than the Soviets in this regard, permitting virtually anything to be published or aired, and barely limiting the availability of Western materials (books, journals, newspapers) to the local population. Permitting foreign journalists to broadcast events of historic significance ("CBS Evening News" from Beijing before and during the Tiananmen events of June 1989; "NBC Nightly News" reporting directly from East Berlin in November 1989, as the Berlin Wall was opened to permit free passage between East and West) casts a new light on openness, one that was quite inconceivable as little as a year ago. It is difficult to measure the impact that Western journalists may have on local populations and on their political leaders. The government repression of the Beijing student demonstrations may have been delayed but was not stopped by international public opinion. Publicity accorded both the Chinese and East German events probably encouraged the local populations to act more boldly. In the Chinese case, that backfired; in the East German one, it may have persuaded the leadership that opening up travel would not necessarily swell the exodus from the country to the West. Still, the population's underlying and continuing lack of trust in the political leadership profoundly affects the regime's capacity to introduce and implement controlled change. If reforms are to be ultimately successful, the process will take time to set in place and produce wanted results. Popular suspicion or outright hostility severely limits the time available to the leadership in instituting reform and any hope of rendering it productive. In those countries where Communist party leadership has been routed, systemic reform has, at least for the time being, given way to transformation.

A consistent feature of the political reform process has been the effort to reduce and limit the role of the CP and party personnel in positions of authority *(nomenklatura)* within the policy-making and policy-implementation process. As mentioned above, the move toward political pluralism by definition drastically reduces the party's role. It also reduces the party's control over decisionmaking. Within the party itself, further restrictions have been imposed in many instances by mandatory limitations on the permissible terms of officeholding and associated personnel turnover. The rapid changes of leadership at high levels within the party that occurred during 1989 in Eastern Europe, for example, resulted in part from an effort by the top leaders to bolster their positions at a time of increasing political and social unrest. Within months, these CPs were thoroughly discredited at the polls. In the Soviet Union, the Gorbachev leadership continues to seek to replace opponents of "restructuring" or those who do not appear capable of managing it effectively. Critics of the reform process inside the party are more openly expressing their views now than in the past. Open criticism of the leadership, duly publicized, has become routine. Whether these critics will be able to garner enough support to capitalize on growing popular discontent by seeming to represent a more stable alternative has by no means been resolved in the Soviet Union.

A number of states are engaged in formalizing the reform process, or elements of it, by constitutional amendment or even by rewriting the document altogether. But the important issue is whether the constitution will be regarded in a different light than in the past, when it served not to limit the regime's political activities but rather to justify them as needed. There is new attention to the rule of law and to strengthening the legal system as part of the drive to end the party's monopoly on rule. Indeed, as laws and their impartial implementation and interpretation come to be widely considered applicable also to everyone, including the political power holders, the more likely constitutions will be to take on new meaning and authority. These processes take time to accept both for those whose authority they limit and for the polity as a whole, whose civil rights are or will be taking on a new importance.

Attention to civil rights includes demands for greater freedom of expression, (such as in demonstrations, strikes, and publications critical of current official policies); freedom of travel and emigration; and reduced scope of internal security organs' authority, particularly against critics of official policies and their creators and implementors. Changes in official policy in these areas have occurred in part in response to popular pressures that the regimes determined it would ultimately be unwise to resist. Presumably, these changes will be incorporated into the context of political reform. In some cases (Yugoslavia, for instance), these basic reforms had developed earlier than elsewhere, although with many detours. In other cases (North Korea, Vietnam, Cuba), such reforms have yet to be adopted and widely implemented.

Marxist-Leninist ideology has taken a back seat to much of the reform process. Referred to much less frequently in those states where Communist parties are looking to bolster their declining popularity, ideology seems to be more of a hindrance than a help to the party as it seeks to maintain a dominant position in the reform process. In the Soviet Union, for example, Gorbachev's emphasis on "new thinking," despite his earlier deliberate efforts to tie the new strategies to Leninist policies of the 1920s, especially economic policies, now seems less concerned with the need to do so (and less able in fact to accomplish it anyway). Ideological considerations seem more useful in justifying control of the reform process, especially if it appears to have gathered too much momentum on its own. Again, one points to the Chinese events. There are other examples as well. Perhaps, as a leading American analyst of communist affairs has argued, Marxism-Leninism has outlived its usefulness — or, more precisely, its relevance — as the twentieth century draws to a close.[5] It has, especially within the European context, lost its intellectual appeal as a way of restructuring society, and it clearly does not provide an acceptable model for socialist economic development. While Communist party rule as we know it may have been useful as a means for moving societies rapidly into industrialization, it clearly cannot maintain itself without force after industrialization has been established and consolidated. Soviet-type economies cannot sustain economic growth within a competitive, increasingly interdependent international economy.

In the non-European context, in those communist-ruled states where industrialization was only barely established, Marxism-Leninism was less relevant from the start, although central planning and traditional communist emphasis on heavy industrialization hastened the industrialization process. As these states modernize, however, and the first generation leadership gives way to less ideologically oriented successors, ideology, even in an updated "contemporary version," is less likely to serve as a useful guide or rationale for action. Indeed, ideology is likely to be utilized as a restraint on the reform process, not as its beacon.

Implications for United States Policy

What do rapid change, efforts to establish and institute reform, and movement toward real transformation within some communist-ruled states mean for the United States? What are the policies most appropriate for the United States to adopt toward these states?

Perhaps most important, we need to bear in mind that the situation, especially in the Soviet Union and Eastern Europe, but in fact almost universally within the communist-ruled "world," is very much in flux.

Dramatic developments seem to be the order of the day. Leadership changes have come quickly and sometimes quite unexpectedly. It is likely that many further changes are in store and that the recently installed leaders will be only interim ones. Even those leaders who are selected after parliamentary elections have been held may not hold office long. What seems to matter in the current context is the extent to which these leaders are able to institute the kinds of reform that mass demonstrations are demanding, and to do so in a way that is not too destabilizing. Indeed, the real danger is that popular demands for reform coupled with the collapse of Communist party rule and the rapid creation of numerous political parties and groups will create great instability, threatening the relative stability of neighboring states. It is clearly to our advantage that the transfer of political power in communist-ruled states does not result in domestic turmoil. If it does, we will have a very limited ability to influence events short of direct involvement.

Indeed, this is a critical point. The amount of influence that we can bring to bear on internal events in any of these states is quite limited. We can vigorously publicize our support for any regime striving to move toward establishing democratic principles and practices, but we are not likely to encourage such movement in the absence of sustained internal pressures for reform in this direction. We can provide useful assistance in helping to build a democratic infrastructure once a state has determined that it will create democratic institutions. The United States Agency for International Development, for example, in 1990 provided initial funding to assist Hungary in developing a research, bill drafting, tracking, and retrieval capability for its national legislature. Other funding from the same source will assist one of Hungary's major universities to develop an institute of public affairs to provide practical training for legislators and legislative staffers. Similar initiatives are under way in Poland.

So far as the Soviet Union and Eastern Europe are concerned, there are a number of areas in which we could constructively assist what appear to be the first stages of a revised post-World War II European order. We should assist in developing a framework for greater dialogue and "constructive engagement" between the two parts of Europe. Negotiating the end of the cold war (if indeed that turns out to be feasible) will not happen overnight or without spurts and false starts. But the appropriate framework may be something quite different from bilateral or multilateral negotiations in arms reductions or more favorable trade arrangements. We have an important role to play here, and we should not underestimate it.

The changes we are witnessing offer real possibilities for a reduction of international tensions and building a measure of cooperation between former adversaries. A reduction of tensions, especially within the European context, carries with it real advantages for both sides, and we should continually stress the mutuality factor in bilateral and multilateral contacts and negotiations. We need to proceed cautiously, however, in promoting improvements in East-West relations and not rush headlong into dismantling long-standing military alliances. We should, in fact, promote communication and peaceful engagement between the alliances (the North Atlantic Treaty Organization [NATO] on the one side, and the Warsaw Treaty Organization [WTO] on the other).

We should continue to press for meaningful and substantial arms reductions, both nuclear and conventional. Recognizing that the Soviets continue to be greatly concerned with the size of their defense budget, especially in the context of focusing on economic reform with its attendant costs, we should continuously stress the advantages of reducing military expenditures. While negotiating for arms reductions, we need to keep a proper perspective and negotiate what is to mutual advantage, with meaningful safeguards and precautions.

Within this context, we should firmly encourage Soviet troop withdrawals from Eastern Europe. While the Soviets will press for United States troop withdrawals from the NATO alliance, we should seek a measure of disengagement but stop far short of complete withdrawal from Europe. It is unlikely that the Soviets will withdraw completely from all Warsaw Pact nations' territories soon. Even if they did pull back into Soviet territory, geographical realities permit rapid redeployment if deemed necessary.

We should strongly encourage political reforms in those states that are beginning to pay sustained attention to democratic tenets and protection of human rights. It is surely in our interests to advance the cause of human rights everywhere, and to encourage the movement from autocracy to democratization — the direction that the reform process currently seems headed — to the extent that it has taken hold in these states.

If we choose to offer direct economic support, we should try to link it directly to economic reform efforts that focus on enhanced productivity and efficiency. We can provide technical assistance to those states that are actively seeking to move from a centrally controlled to a market economy. Indeed, a number of such efforts by governmental agencies, private foundations, and private institutions have started to do so in Poland and Hungary, and perhaps elsewhere as well. More favorable trade arrangements should also be connected to economic reform that improves economic performance, but we should not assess a state's every policy choice in determining whether to continue or modify our own economic policies toward it. In general, we should support what appear to be longer-term trends toward greater productivity despite probable temporary detours. We should be very careful not to rush headlong into dismantling limitations on trade with communist-ruled states because of military implications; should events change, such a system might prove needed. We may want to reexamine those limitations in light of technological advances. Indeed, caution is well advised, and careful, considered response to important developments is in order.

Insofar as we provide economic assistance through credits or other financing for major industrial projects, we should collaborate with Western Europe and Japan. We should be selective in what we support economically because we can longer afford to be the world's banker, nor should we strive to be. Moreover, it is particularly important that we work collaboratively with our allies on economic issues as well as on diplomatic, political, and military ones with respect to the communist-ruled states.

Much of this discussion has focused on Eastern Europe and the Soviet Union. The spirit of the reform, indeed transformation, process has caught on particularly in Eastern Europe and has spread quickly throughout the area. In the Soviet Union, the need to attend to internal reforms that will bring about enhanced economic performance has dictated a willingness on the part of the political leadership to negotiate on important foreign policy issues, especially those related to arms control and troop reductions. In general, though, the United States should not permit the current and likely future attention focused on the Soviet Union and Eastern Europe to obscure the need to attend to relations with the Asian communist-ruled states as well.

Our economic policies toward the People's Republic of China since "normalization" of political and diplomatic relations a decade ago have been more conciliatory than those with respect to the Soviet Union. Indeed, we developed United States–China relations not unmindful of our policies toward the USSR. Now that United States–Soviet relations have improved substantially and are likely to continue to do so, at least in the short term, we may be inclined to downplay relations with China. We need to encourage Chinese leaders to attend to their internal political reform process, especially in light of the recent repression. But, as elsewhere, we need to recognize that we have very limited possibilities for real impact.

Our economic relations with China should be geared directly toward economic reform, much as with Eastern Europe. China is a strong regional power and a growing trade partner with both the United States and Japan, as well as with other Pacific and East Asian states. While China is much less prone to use economic credits for consumer goods purchase than a number of other communist-ruled states, its encouragement of foreign economic investment has been substantial. Providing capital for such investments ought to be linked directly to reform.

Improved United States relations with North Korea and Vietnam are likely to develop slowly. With respect to North Korea, the post-Kim Il Sung leadership is likely to be much more open to international economic and trade negotiations and agreements as well as internal reforms. Improved relations between the two Koreas may develop and may be influenced by continuing international discussions and negotiations around the issue of future German reunification.

Because of the Vietnam War, the havoc it wreaked on American society, and its aftermath for Vietnam veterans, economic and political relations between the United States and that country are likely to improve very slowly. If it manages to introduce and implement an economic reform process that will gather steam and consolidate, Vietnam could become an important power in Southeast Asia because of its population, size, and geographical location. As the Soviets become less and less interested in continuing to subsidize the Vietnamese economy and fears of the PRC's domination persist, Vietnam will surely be looking for other benefactors, especially distant ones. Japan and the ASEAN states may provide sufficient assistance, if they are willing to do so. In any event, the United States needs to assess Vietnam's potential importance and how that will affect us before we consider embarking on investment and assistance policies.

Altogether, for students of comparative communism, these are exciting times. Not since Communist parties consolidated their control in most of the states considered in this volume have events moved so quickly. In less than a year, Communist parties have been toppled from power in Eastern Europe and have done very poorly in freely held national elections. In the USSR, there has been a substantial shift of power from party to state organs and this trend is likely to continue. Internal political reform currently has not gained momentum in the Asian communist-ruled states (except in Mongolia, where demands for democratization have already resulted in important changes). Reform could accelerate at any time, however. Consequently, a book of this kind runs far more than the usual risks of being dated quickly. Still, it can provide a very useful basis for analyzing many of the important issues related to change, reform, and transformation in these states.

Notes

1. *New York Times*, 21 November 1989.
2. Ibid., 26 November 1989.

3. See, for example, Paul Marer, "Hungary's Reform and Performance in the Kádár Era (1956–88)," in U.S. Congress, Joint Economic Committee, *Pressure for Reform in the Eastern European Economies* (Washington, D.C: Government Printing Office, 1989); Jan Adam, "The Hungarian Economic Reform of the 1980s," *Soviet Studies* 39, no. 4 (October 1987); Heath B. Chamberlain, "Party-Management Relations in Communist Industries: Some Political Dimensions of Economic Reform," *China Quarterly,* no. 112 (December 1987).
4. See the discussion in Stuart R. Schram, "China after the 13th Congress," *China Quarterly,* no. 114 (June 1988).
5. *New York Times,* 17 November 1989.
6. Zbigniew Brzezinski, *The Grand Failure* (New York: Scribner's, 1989).

About the Contributors

Thomas P. Bernstein is Professor of Political Science at Columbia University. He has written widely on Soviet and Chinese politics and rural affairs, including *Up to the Mountains and Down to the Villages* (1977) and *China's Rural Reforms* (forthcoming), as well as numerous journal articles.

Parris H. Chang is Professor of Political Science and Director of East Asian Studies at Pennsylvania State University. He is the author of several books, including *Power and Policy in China* (2d ed., 1978) and *Elite Conflict in the Post-Mao China* (1983), as well as numerous articles and chapters in edited volumes.

Lenard J. Cohen is Associate Professor of Political Science, Simon Fraser University, British Columbia. He is the author of *The Socialist Pyramid: Elite and Power in Yugoslavia* (1989) and co-author of *Political Cohesion in a Fragile Mosaic* (1983).

Joseph Fewsmith is an analyst on Chinese affairs at the U.S. Foreign Broadcast Information Service. He was formerly on the political science faculty at Kent State University. He is the author of *Party, State and Local Elites in Republican China* (1985) and numerous articles on political and economic reform in contemporary China.

Roger E. Kanet is Associate Vice Chancellor of Academic Affairs, Director of International Programs and Studies, and Professor of Political Science at the University of Illinois at Urbana-Champaign. His most recent books are *The Limits of Soviet Power in the Developing World* (1989) and *The Cold War as Cooperation* (forthcoming), both co-edited with E.A. Kolodziej.

Ilpyong J. Kim is Professor of Political Science at the University of Connecticut. His publications include *The Politics of Chinese Communism: Kiangsi under the Soviets* (1973), *Communist Politics in North Korea* (1975), and he is editor of and contributor to a multi-volume series on contemporary Chinese politics, economics, society, and foreign affairs (1988-90).

Andrzej Korbonski is Professor of Political Science at the University of California, Los Angeles, and Director of the UCLA Center for Russian and East European Studies. He has published numerous articles and book chapters on various aspects of Soviet and East European politics and economics.

Susan J. Linz is Associate Professor of Economics at Michigan State University. She is the editor or co-editor of *The Impact of World War II on the Soviet Union* (1985) and *Reorganization and Reform in the Soviet Economy* (1988).

Paul Marer is Professor of International Business at Indiana University, Bloomington. He is the author or editor of *East European Integration and East-West Trade* (with J.M. Montias, 1980), *East-West Technology Transfer* (1985), and *Creditworthiness and Reform in Poland* (1988), as well as numerous articles and book chapters on centrally planned economies.

Alexander C. Pacek is Assistant Professor of Political Science at Texas A & M University. He has published several articles on East European politics and is completing his doctoral dissertation, "Changing Political Processes in European Communist Systems," at the University of Illinois at Urbana-Champaign.

Douglas Pike is Director of the Indochina Studies Project at the University of California, Berkeley, and editor of *Indochina Chronology*. He is a retired U.S. Foreign Service officer who served in Saigon, Hong Kong, Tokyo, and Taipei. He has published a number of books on Vietnam as well as dozens of monographs and articles on Indochina and Southeast Asia.

Wayne S. Smith is Adjunct Professor of Latin American Studies and Director of Cuban Studies at the Johns Hopkins School of Advanced International Studies. He is a retired U.S. Foreign Service officer who served in the USSR, Argentina, and Brazil. His last position was as chief of mission at the U.S. Interests Section in Havana. His publications include *Closest of Enemies* (1987) and *Castro's Cuba* (1984).

Rolf H. W. Theen is Professor of Political Science at Purdue University. He is the author of *Lenin* (1973), co-author of *Comparative Politics: An Introduction* (1987), and has published widely on Soviet domestic and foreign affairs.

Don A. Van Atta is Assistant Professor of Government at Hamilton

College. He has published a number of articles on Soviet agricultural policies.

Jane Shapiro Zacek is Senior Project Director at the Rockefeller Institute of Government, State University of New York. She has edited a number of volumes on Soviet and East European politics, including *Politics and Participation under Communist Rule,* (co-edited, 1983) *The Gorbachev Generation: Issues in Soviet Foreign Policy* (1988), and *The Gorbachev Generation: Issues in Soviet Domestic Policies* (1989).

Andrew Zimbalist is Professor of Economics at Smith College and the Five College Graduate Faculty. Among his recent publications are: *Comparing Economic Systems* (1987) and *The Cuban Economy* (1989), both co-authored. He has published widely on comparative economic systems and economic development.

Selected Bibliography

Aganbegyan, Abel, *The Economic Challenge of Perestroyka* (Bloomington: Indiana University Press, 1988).

Ash, Timothy Garton, "Eastern Europe: The Year of Truth," *New York Review of Books* (February 15, 1990).

Batt, Judy, *Economic Reform and Political Change in Eastern Europe: A Comparison of the Czechoslovak and Hungarian Experiences* (London: Macmillan Press, 1986).

Bialer, Seweryn, *Politics, Society and Nationality Inside Gorbachev's Russia* (Boulder: Westview Publishers, 1989).

Bialer, Seweryn and Joan Afferica, "The Genesis of Gorbachev's World," *Foreign Affairs*, 64, 3 (1986).

Bialer, Seweryn and Michael Mandelbaum, eds., *Gorbachev's Russia and American Foreign Policy* (Boulder: Westview Press, 1988).

Brzezinski, Zbigniew, *The Grand Failure: The Birth and Death of Communism in the Twentieth Century* (New York: Scribner's Publishers, 1989).

Brzezinski, Zbigniew K., *The Soviet Bloc*, rev. ed. (Cambridge: Harvard University Press, 1967).

Bukowski, Charles and Mark A. Cichocki, eds., *Prospects for Change in Socialist Systems: Challenges and Responses* (New York: Praeger Publishers, 1987).

Chang, Parris H., *Power and Policy in China*, 3d ed. (University Park: Pennsylvania State University Press, 1978).

Colton, Timothy J., *The Dilemma of Reform in the Soviet Union*, rev. ed. (New York: Council on Foreign Relations, 1986).

Connor, Walter D., *Socialism's Dilemmas: State and Society in the Soviet Bloc* (New York: Columbia University Press, 1988).

Davies, R.W., *Soviet History in the Gorbachev Revolution* (Bloomington: Indiana University Press, 1989).

Dawisha, Karen, *Eastern Europe, Gorbachev and Reform: The Great Challenge* (Cambridge: Cambridge University Press, 1988).

Gorbachev, Mikhail S., *Perestroyka: New Thinking for Our Country and the World* (New York: Harper & Row Publishers, 1987).

Gunn, Geoffrey, "The Prospects for Reform in Indochina," *Pacific Review* 1, 4 (1988).

Gurtov, Mel, ed., *The Transformation of Socialism: Perestroyka and Reform in the Soviet Union and China* (Boulder: Westview Press, forthcoming).

Harding, Harry, *China's Second Revolution: Reform after Mao* (Washington, D.C.: The Brookings Institution, 1987).

Hewett, Ed A., *Reforming the Soviet Economy: Equality versus Efficiency* (Washington, D.C.: The Brookings Institution, 1988).

Johnson, Chalmers, ed., *Change in Communist Systems* (Stanford: Stanford University Press, 1970).

Kaplan, Cynthia S., *The Party and Agricultural Crisis Management in the USSR* (Ithaca: Cornell University Press, 1987).

Kittrie, Nicholas W. and Ivan Volgyes, eds., *The Uncertain Future: Gorbachev's Eastern Europe* (New York: Paragon House publishers, 1988).

Korbonski, Andrzej, "The Politics of Economic Reforms in Eastern Europe: The Last Thirty Years," *Soviet Studies* 41, 1 (January 1989).

Liebowitz, Ronald D., ed., *Gorbachev's New Thinking* (Cambridge: Ballinger Books, 1988).

Linz, Susan J. and William Moskoff, eds., *Reorganization and Reform in the Soviet Economy* (Armonk: M.E. Sharpe, 1988).

McCauley, Martin, ed., *The Soviet Union Under Gorbachev* (New York: St. Martin's Press, 1987).

Medvedev, Zhores A., *Gorbachev* (New York: W.W. Norton, 1986).

Nove, Alec, *Glasnost in Action* (Boston: Unwin Hyman Publishers, 1989).

O'Donnell, Guillermo and Philippe C. Schmitter, *Transitions from Authoritarian Rule* (Baltimore: The Johns Hopkins University Press, 1986).

O'Donnell, Guillermo, Philippe C. Schmitter, and Laurence Whitehead, eds., *Transitions from Authoritarian Rule: Comparative Perspectives* (Baltimore: the Johns Hopkins University Press, 1986).

Pike, Douglas, "Origins of Leadership Change in the Socialist Republic of Vietnam," in Raymond Taras, ed., *Leadership Change in Communist States* (London: Unwin Publishers, 1989)

Pye, Lucian W., *The Dynamics of Factions and Consensus in Chinese Politics: A Model and Some Propositions* (Santa Monica: The RAND Corporation, 1980).

Raina, Peter, *Independent Social Movements in Poland* (London: Orbis Books, 1989).

Roca, Sergio, ed., *Socialist Cuba: Past Interpretations and Future Challenges* (Boulder: Westview Press, 1988).

Sik, Ota, *The Communist Power System* (New York: Praeger Publishers, 1984).

Smolar, A. and P. Kende, *The Role of Opposition: The Role of Opposition Groups on the Eve of Democratization in Poland and Hungary, 1987-1988* (Munich: "Project," 1989).

Stubbs, Richard, ed., *Vietnam: Facing the 1990s* (Toronto: University of Toronto Joint Centre for Asia Pacific Studies, 1989).

Sutter, Robert, *Vietnam in Transition: Implications for U.S. Policy* (Washington, D.C.: Congressional Research Service, 1989).

Tan, Canh, "Perestroyka or Disastroyka: Hanoi's Renovation Program," *Vietnam Commentary* (Singapore), (March 1988).

Wadekin, Karl-Eugen, ed., *Communist Agriculture: Farming in the Soviet Union and Eastern Europe* (London: Routledge, 1990).

Zaslavskaya, Tatyana I., *A Voice of Reform* (Armonk: M.E. Sharpe Publishers, 1989).

Zimbalist, A. and C. Brundenius, *The Cuban Economy: Measurement and Analysis of Socialist Performance* (Baltimore: The Johns Hopkins University Press, 1989).

Zimbalist, A., "Incentives and Planning in Cuba," *Latin American Research Review* 24, 1 (January 1989).

Index